The Rise of
Free Trade Imperialism

The Rise of
Free Trade Imperialism

Classical Political Economy
the Empire of Free Trade
and Imperialism
1750–1850

BERNARD SEMMEL

*Professor of History, State University of
New York at Stony Brook*

CAMBRIDGE
AT THE UNIVERSITY PRESS
1970

Published by the Syndics of the Cambridge University Press
Bentley House, 200 Euston Road, London N.W.1
American Branch: 32 East 57th Street, New York, N.Y.10022

Library of Congress Catalogue Card Number: 71–112473
Standard Book Number: 521 07725 7

Made and printed in Great Britain by
Spottiswoode, Ballantyne & Co. Ltd.,
London and Colchester

In memory of my father

Contents

Preface

This study of the rise of free trade imperialism grew out of two previous studies of later periods in the history of England, in which, as in this effort, the themes of empire-building and the threat of revolution come together. In this work, I have attempted to uncover certain of the intellectual origins of the 'imperialism'—indeed, of the two 'imperialisms'—of the 'classic period', with which I have dealt in my first book, as well as the sources from which later theories of imperialism were constructed; I also wished to consider from a different perspective the character of the 'ideology' which underlay the dismantling of the old colonial system, and the construction of the Victorian Pax Britannica, which formed the background of my second book. The present study discusses the development and diffusion of a number of the central arguments of the 'science' of political economy—from the standpoint of a historian rather than an economist—which were crucial not only to the construction of theories of capitalist imperialism, but also served as a spur both to the efforts at colonization, and to those of establishing a British Workshop of the World, during the period considered in this study and afterward.

This book has been a long time in the making, and I should like to acknowledge the help of a number of people who read drafts, in whole or in part, in various stages, or with whom I spoke about its ideas. They include Professor Lord Robbins and Professor D. V. Glass of the London School of Economics; Professor Bert F. Hoselitz of the University of Chicago; Professor R. K. Webb of Columbia University; Professors Robert Lekachman, David Trask and John Williams, colleagues at the State University of New York at Stony Brook; and Morris Pearl. Of course, none of these persons found themselves concurring in all of my views.

For a number of summers, I enjoyed the support of the Research Foundation of the State University of New York, and during the academic year, 1964–5, I was able to spend a year in England, as a Fellow of the American Council of Learned Societies. I am most appreciative of this aid. I am also grateful for the secretarial help of my wife, and of my assistant, Sonia Sbarge, who also checked the accuracy of the citations. The librarians of the British Museum, the New York Public Library, the Public Record Office, the University College Library, and the Prior's Kitchen, The College, Durham, were most helpful in making the books and the manuscript collections under their care available to me. Parts of the book have appeared in the *Journal of Economic History*, the *Economic History Review*, and the *Economic Journal*, as well as in a chapter, 'On the Economics of "Imperialism"', included in Bert F. Hoselitz, ed., *Economics and the Idea of Mankind* (New York: Columbia University Press, 1965). I am grateful for permission to reprint, in altered form, this material.

As in the past, I should like to make special mention of the help and support I have always received from my wife Maxine, and from my mother; recently, I have enjoyed the sympathetic understanding of my son Stuart, who would have preferred, I suspect, that I spend less of my time in my study. The book is dedicated to the memory of my father, after whom Stuart was named.

Stony Brook, L.I., March, 1969   Bernard Semmel

CHAPTER 1

Introduction

We went over the whole of Mill's articles in the Encyclopedia, over the more popular works of Bentham, and thence we plunged into the recesses of political economy. I know not why this study has been termed uninteresting. No sooner had I entered about its consideration, than I could scarcely tear myself from it. Never from that moment to this have I ceased to pay it the most constant attention . . . [A chief aim of its study is to demonstrate] how inseparably allied is the great science of public policy with that of private morality.

> Lord Lytton, *Pelham, or the Adventures of a Gentleman*, 1828

This yearning after the distant and the unseen is a common propensity of our nature; and how much is the force of that 'secret impulse' cherished and strengthened in the minds of us Englishmen, by all the associations in the midst of which we are educated! Masters of every sea, and colonists of every shore, there is scarcely a nook which our industry has not rendered accessible, scarcely a region to which the eye can wander in the map, in which we have not some object of national interest—some factory for our trade, some settlement of our citizens. It is a sort of instinctive feeling to us all, that the destiny of our name and nation is not here, in the narrow island which we occupy; that the spirit of England is volatile, not fixed; that it lives in our language, our commerce, our industry, in all those channels of inter-communication by which we embrace and connect the vast multitude of states, both civilised and uncivilised, throughout the world.

> Merivale, *Lectures on Colonization and Colonies*, 1861

OVER twenty years ago, the late Professor R. L. Schuyler published his *Fall of the Old Colonial System*,[1] which discussed the same general questions which form the core of this work. Schuyler's theme was the dismantling of the system of mercantilist colonialism, a process completed by the repeal of the corn laws in 1846, and of the Navigation Acts in 1849, and the inauguration of a new cosmopolitan system of trade, established upon the principle of an international division of labor. The leading figures in this process, and in Schuyler's study, were Tucker, Brougham, Huskisson, Cobden, Joseph Hume, and the chief 'Colonial Reformers',

---

[1] R. L. Schuyler, *The Fall of the Old Colonial System; A Study in British Free Trade, 1770–1870* (New York: Oxford University Press, 1945), *passim*.

particularly Durham, Buller, and Molesworth. These men were viewed by Schuyler as the spokesmen for the 'anti-imperialism' stemming from the outlook of Adam Smith's *Wealth of Nations* and the climate of opinion which followed the independence of the American colonies, which, in the long accepted fashion, was regarded as having dominated the early and middle decades of the nineteenth century. This happy time when the sentiments of cosmopolitanism, internationalism, humanitarianism, and pacifism (all that a later generation was to call 'Cobdenism') held sway, sentiments rooted in and confirmed by England's system of free trade, was, generally, depicted as an interlude between the mercantilist imperialism of the eighteenth century, and the new imperialism, of which Hobson and Lenin were to write, which was to come upon the stage in the last quarter of the nineteenth century.

Some fifteen years ago, our view of this period was considerably modified when we were told by Gallagher and Robinson of 'the Imperialism of Free Trade', of the efforts that were made in this 'anti-imperialist' mid-century to make trade secure, efforts which might be peaceful enough in Latin America, for example, but which had culminated in wars and annexations elsewhere, as along the Indian frontier. There was, we were persuaded, continuous imperial expansion during this period, which led quite naturally into the neo-mercantilist imperialism of the end of the century, when other nations challenged the 'cosmopolitan' imperialism which had marked the era of British predominance.[1] But, still, such examples of imperialist expansion, flying in the face, it seemed, of an anti-imperialist ideology which saw even a protectionist Disraeli, in 1852, speaking of 'these wretched colonies' as 'a millstone round our necks',[2] might be explained as aberrations: England's role in India (as also in Ireland) was, admittedly, atypical,[3] and special explanations might be discovered to explain, for example, the wars with the New Zealand Maori. Colonial armies and settlers might be seen as making almost reflex responses, very much out of line with the prevailing sentiments and policy of the 'anti-imperialism' which Schuyler had scrupulously recorded; diplomatic and strategic considerations might be judged to have overwhelmed, in specific instances, the reasoned anti-imperialism which was the fruit of the 'science' of political economy.

[1] J. Gallagher and R. Robinson, 'The Imperialism of Free Trade', *Economic History Review* VI, no. 1 (1953), 1–15; see also R. Robinson, J. Gallagher, A. Denny, *Africa and the Victorians* (London: Macmillan, 1962), pp. 1–6.

[2] Quoted in Earl of Malmesbury, *Memoirs of an Ex-Minister* (London: Longmans, Green, 1884), I, 343–4.

[3] India and Ireland are omitted from this study not only because they are atypical, but also because excellent studies of the subjects already exist. See R. D. Collison Black, *Economic Thought and the Irish Question, 1817–1870* (Cambridge: Cambridge University Press, 1960); E. Stokes, *The English Utilitarians and India* (London: Oxford University Press, 1959).

Imperialism, indeed, is a term of which students of empire have become, understandably, cautious. It has become identified with the neo-Marxist formulation which has seen modern empire-building as rooted in the development of capitalism, as, indeed, a necessary and inescapable result of that system. Especially in its Leninist form, this view has become the accepted dogma not only of the Communist world, but of large sections of the 'uncommitted' third world which has emerged from the dissolution of the great colonial empires. It has no doubt been in good part in reaction to this widespread acceptance of the theory of 'capitalist imperialism', that a number of scholars have, most ably, sought to demonstrate that such a theory can hardly be regarded as depicting the sole, or even the overwhelming, motivation for the empire-building in which the European powers participated so enthusiastically in the generation which preceded the War of 1914.[1] Western Marxists and third-world intellectuals have rushed to the defense of the theory which, it must be remembered, had succeeded in convincing all sections of opinion in Europe and America, at least of its plausibility, in the period between the two world wars; indeed, for a generation, it had been accepted virtually as a 'law' of economic development.

The attack upon the neo-Marxist theory began in 1919, with Schumpeter's essay on imperialism, whose argument, stressing the essential irrationality of modern imperialism, was based, in good part, on the predominance of an ideology of anti-imperialism in the mid-Victorian heyday of British capitalism.[2] There is no question but that such an anti-imperialist ideology, one which helped to precipitate 'the fall of the old colonial system', existed. But what is not so well understood is that, with one or two exceptions, the same men whom Schuyler, Schumpeter, and Hobson, as well as others, have regarded as the spokesmen of this anti-imperialism,[3] because they were the leaders of those groups who wished to dismantle the old colonial system of mercantilism, were also the spokesmen and, in some cases, the theorists of a new free trade imperialism which, they held, would prove

---

[1] See, for example, W. K. Hancock, 'Agenda for the Study of British Imperial Economy, 1850–1950', *Journal of Economic History* XIII (1953), 257; D. K. Fieldhouse, '"Imperialism": An Historiographical Revision', *Economic History Review*, 2nd Series, XIV, no. 2 (December 1961), 187–209; D. Landes, 'Some Thoughts on the Nature of Economic Imperialism', *Journal of Economic History* XXI, no. 4 (December 1961), 496–512; Robinson, Gallagher, Denny, *Africa and the Victorians*.

[2] See J. A. Schumpeter, *Imperialism and Social Classes* (New York: Meridian Books, 1966), pp. 64–98, and *passim*.

[3] Schumpeter saw the 'Philosophical radicals'—of which group Sir William Molesworth was the only one specifically named—as the spokesmen of this free trade, anti-imperialistic capitalism. (See Schumpeter, *Imperialism*, p. 70.) Hobson, similarly, placed both Molesworth and Edward Gibbon Wakefield in his category of anti-imperialistic, 'liberal-minded politicians'. (See J. A. Hobson, *Imperialism: A Study* (London: George Allen & Unwin, 1938), p. 118.)

more effective and profitable, given England's altered economic position. Basing their views upon the doctrines of the classical economists, who, of course, had condemned mercantilism, they constructed theories of capitalist imperialism which held that empire-building was a necessity if the new industrialism were to survive, and advocated policies, both in and out of parliament, which later theorists of imperialism, in its 'classic' period, would have been obliged to recognize as almost classically imperialist.

From the standpoint of ideology, then, from the perspective of theory and policy no less than from that of activities, it is possible to see continuity, rather than an interlude of anti-imperialism. Indeed, the period of the fall of the old colonial system may be viewed as one of the rise of a free trade imperialism.

To speak of theories or policies of a 'free trade imperialism' is, apparently, to go in the face of almost all previous theory. Hobson, in 1900, was among the first to insist that an imperialist in so far as he was logical must become a protectionist.[1] The imperialism depicted by Bauer and Hilferding,[2] in the first decade of our century, of monopoly capitalism, the final stage of capitalism, in which high finance presided over gigantic industrial cartels, was dependent upon high tariff walls, which had made such cartelization possible, and Lenin's view of imperialism[3] in 1917 was based on similar assumptions. Schumpeter, writing two years later, was equally convinced that free trade, by its very nature, was anti-imperialistic, and observed that it was the revival of an atavistic protectionism which had helped to persuade selfish entrepreneurs to ally themselves with the pre-capitalist aristocratic and military classes, motivated by similarly atavistic tribal impulses, in mounting the new imperialism.[4] Both Hobson and Schumpeter were convinced, then, that the principles of free trade economics, which underlay capitalism, left no room for imperialism, that in a world where free trade prevailed, all trade would be regulated by impartial economic law; both saw the English free traders as having sought, in conformance with the doctrines of international trade formulated by classical economics, to extirpate the old aggressive passions, or at least to subject them to the appeal to reason exerted by economic law. A scholar has argued recently that to speak of 'the imperialism of free trade' makes as little sense as to speak of 'the imperialism of *laissez-faire*'.[5]

[1] See Hobson, *Imperialism*, p. 67; see also pp. 64–70.
[2] See O. Bauer, *Die Nationalitätenfräge und die Sozial Demokratie* (Vienna, 1907); and R. Hilferding, *Das Finanzkapital, Eine Studie über die jüngste Entwicklung des Kapitalismus* (Vienna, 1910).
[3] See N. Lenin, *Imperialism; the Highest Stage of Capitalism* (New York: International Publishers, 1939)—originally published in 1917.
[4] See Schumpeter, *Imperialism*, pp. 11, 76, 84, 89, 91, 94, 96, and *passim*.
[5] D. C. M. Platt, 'The Imperialism of Free Trade: Some Reservations', *Economic History Review*, 2nd Series, XXI, no. 2 (August 1968), 305 f.n.

Yet it must be remembered that the British 'imperialism' of the generation before 1914, which Hobson, Lenin, and Schumpeter analyzed, was, strictly speaking, a later stage of free trade imperialism, for Britain did not embark on a system of protection and imperial preference until 1931. We hope to show that the essentially mercantilist assumptions and objectives embodied in the 'classic' pre-1914 imperialism were far from absent in the thinking of the economists and politicians who erected the system of free trade in the last half of the eighteenth and in the first half of the nineteenth centuries.

Another characteristic shared by the classical economists and the early twentieth-century theorists of capitalist imperialism is a mood of helplessness in the face of inexorable economic law. It was this mood which dominated the early decades of nineteenth-century English industrial society—which lay behind and was furthered by the Malthusian 'law' of population, the Ricardian 'iron law' of wages, and the various analyses which prophesied the inevitable decline of the rate of profit. This was why political economy was called the 'dismal science' by Carlyle. It depicted society in such pessimistic tones that its blackness could only be relieved by the Marxian apocalyptic revolution, to which an industrial society was said to be approaching by equally inexorable 'law', or, more hopefully, it might be relieved by the expansion of foreign trade and colonization. The mood of Augustinian and Calvinistic 'fatality' which the Council of Trent had endeavored to banish from Catholicism, and which Arminius in Holland and Wesley in England had driven from Protestant theology, reappeared in the necessitarian economics of the classical economists, itself nurtured in the 'laws' of historical sociology of the Scottish enlightenment. This climate of social despair had not yet begun to lift in the early years of the century, when the 'law' of capitalist imperialism was again invoked as an all-embracing, 'scientific' explanation of contemporary events.

Since recent scholars have suggested that the classic concept of 'imperialism' existed almost exclusively on the level of ideas,[1] it seems especially useful to pursue the problem on this plane. In this volume, we hope to examine the development of the theories and policies of this free trade imperialism. To accomplish this, it will be necessary to make a rather considerable journey into the history of economic thought from, roughly, 1750 to 1850, to discover how the theory of imperialism emerged from the encounter, frequently hostile, of mercantilist, physiocratic, and properly classical doctrines and 'systems', and to relate this clash of doctrines to England's economic, political, and imperial development. It will also be

[1] See D. K. Fieldhouse, '"Imperia lism": An Historiographical Revision', pp. 187–8, and *passim*.

5

necessary to search through the contemporary newspapers, periodicals, and pamphlets, as well as the debates of parliament and the minutes of parliamentary committees, and caches of private papers, to understand the development of the policies of free trade empire-building, and the motivations and perceptions of the empire-builders, and to view the complex interrelationships which existed between these perceptions and policies and the developing 'science' of political economy.

The French historian Michelet has suggested that France was a 'person', Germany a people, and England an empire. Certainly, an insular and maritime England, from the sixteenth century to the present day, has turned its energies not to the European mainland, which has remained the principal focus of other powers, but outward, across the seas to lesser-known continents. England's colonies were not mere plumage with which to flatter the vanity of monarchs, nor mining sites to be exploited and then abandoned; her colonial trade was not regarded an appendage, but a vital part of the national strength. Consequently, the loss of her American colonies in 1783 produced forebodings of disaster. At about the time of this loss, however, Great Britain was entering upon a new period in her national development. It had been in the middle decades of the eighteenth century, probably in the 1760s, that London surpassed Amsterdam as the premier financial and commercial mart of Europe. To such an ascendancy, imposing as it was, was added the industrial lead which was to become a virtual monopoly as a result of conditions during the wars with the France of the Revolution and of Napoleon. England was not only to succeed to the position of commercial predominance which had previously been occupied by Holland; she was to become what Holland had never been, the leading manufacturer of goods, and a manufacturer, moreover, benefiting from the increased productivity of the new steam-driven machinery. De Pradt, an archbishop and *philosophe* of Napoleon's empire, was able to write, as early as the second decade of the nineteenth century, of 'the power of England, and the force of the double lever with which she moves the world, her capital and her industry'. 'As England has adopted the most ingenious mechanical improvements', de Pradt observed, she possessed a 'superiority in all the markets of Europe', and indeed, the archbishop continued, 'almost all of the world' had been transformed by her industrial predominance, had been 'changed into empire, the more powerful too, the more it is voluntary'.[1]

Could such a predominance be preserved? Venice, Antwerp, and Holland

[1] Dominique Dufour de Pradt, *The Colonies, and the Present American Revolutions* (London, 1817), p. 121.

6

had enjoyed similar positions, and had lost them; must England, too, yield to a superior power? Even were this unavoidable, how might England prolong its enjoyment of the fruits of its superiority? To help answer such questions, Englishmen turned to the new 'science' of political economy: it might even be said that the English statesman of the nineteenth century was obliged to become an amateur economist in order to understand and to maintain the kind of empire of which de Pradt wrote. Of course, a thriving foreign and colonial commerce had already, as early as the seventeenth century, given rise to subtle speculation concerning economic affairs in the writings of Mun, Child, and Petty, but when England was able to add the experiences afforded by her industrial pioneering, her economists had ready at hand a stock of information not elsewhere available in such stimulating and persuasive quantities. Britain became the chief seat of political economy, the home of Adam Smith, of Malthus, of Ricardo, and of the Mills. Just as the political speakers and writers of the seventeenth century had relied upon Biblical quotations, and the parliamentarians of the eighteenth had studded their orations with passages from the Greek and Latin classics, so did the adherents of the economists employ their writings as the sum of all social wisdom, possessing an almost scriptural force.

What gave political economy a special political significance in the first half of the nineteenth century was that, as Élie Halévy wrote, 'Ricardo's abstract formulae' were 'but the faithful expression of the spectacle presented by the history of his own time': 'a duel was being fought out under his eyes between two societies', Halévy observed, between the English middle classes, the men of a dynamic capitalism who wished to complete the transformation of Great Britain from an agricultural to an industrial country, and the upholders of the traditional agrarian order.[1] It was the industrial classes who made political economy—with its message of *laissez-faire* and free trade—into a kind of secular scripture, possessing both moral and scientific authority, and who called upon the legislature—an English parliament composed of country gentlemen, who prided themselves upon common sense, upon doing things as they had been done before—to adopt an abstract, rational system, which bore all the marks of the 'pernicious' French enlightenment, and to make legislation conform to its dictates.

Richard Pares observed some thirty years ago that as England became industrialized, 'a very different way of thinking' about empire became prevalent. Historians had concerned themselves 'with its negative side—the

---

[1] Élie Halévy, *The Growth of Philosophical Radicalism* (New York: A. M. Kelley, 1949), pp. 336, 342.

rejection of mercantilism'; it had also 'a positive side', and 'this positive theory of empire', Pares concluded, 'is the better worth discussing because the free trade era was the great age of colonization and colonial trade'.[1] Since Pares wrote, a number of excellent works have appeared upon aspects of this positive theory of empire.[2] A principal subject of our concern, how-ever, is one which has been examined only peripherally: it is that of the theoretical origins and development of the two leading conceptions of empire-building, the two chief forms of Britain's Empire of Free Trade, during the nineteenth century. The first saw England wielding an 'informal' dominion by virtue of her industrial monopoly, her position as the Workshop of the World. The second stressed Britain's activities in colonization, in developing her 'formal' empire. Both conceptions were elaborated in terms of political economy and substantially moulded by struggles over economic principle; they both originated in the mercantilist analysis of the pre-classical period, were passed on, in altered form, to the time which saw the fall of the old colonial system, were extended, in the age of 'imperialism', into rival party programs, and, indeed, with further alterations, are with us today.

Halévy described Ricardo as the theorist of 'the great English manufactur-ers, who dreamt of making the economic conquest of the world'. The weapon which the would-be conquerors intended to employ was an international free trade, justified by the doctrine of comparative advantage; the form of this projected economic dominance was to be a trading system established upon England's leading position in industrial production. One Whig, speaking before the House of Commons during the Corn Law debate of 1846, described free trade as the beneficent 'principle' by which 'foreign nations would become valuable Colonies to us, without imposing on us the responsibility of governing them'.[3] It was a vision which saw Great Britain as the Workshop of the World, exchanging, on advantageous terms, its manufactured products, its textiles, and hardware, for the food and raw materials of the less developed, agricultural nations of the world; it was a vision which prompted protectionists like List and Carey to rebel against

---

[1] Richard Pares, 'The Economic Factors in the History of Empire', *Economic History Review* VII, no. 2 (May 1937), 130. See also W. H. B. Court, 'The Communist Doctrines of Empire', in Sir Keith Hancock, *Survey of British Commonwealth Affairs* (London: Oxford University Press, 1964), vol. II, part I, pp. 293–305.

[2] See K. E. Knorr, *British Colonial Theories, 1570–1850* (Toronto: University of Toronto Press, 1944); D. Winch, *Classical Political Economy and Colonies* (Cambridge, Mass.: Harvard University Press, 1965); D. K. Fieldhouse, *The Theory of Capitalist Imperialism* (New York: Barnes & Noble, 1967).

[3] *Parliamentary Debates*, 3rd Series, LXXXIII (23 February 1846), 1399–1400. [Hereafter, the *Parliamentary Debates* will be referred to as *P.D.*]

English political economy, which, they maintained, was designed to perpetuate England's lead, and which would consign less-advanced countries to a permanent colonial status.

The view that a freer trade would facilitate the perpetuation of England's industrial predominance was foreshadowed, in a mid-eighteenth-century debate, by Josiah Tucker, a mercantilist, who had become convinced that free trade was in the British national interest. Tucker's arguments studded the parliamentary speeches in the discussions of Pitt's trade proposals in the eighties. We can follow the development of these ideas in the writings of James Mill, Robert Torrens (whose vision of trade-empire in 1815 was virtually an 'ideal-type' of free-trade mercantilism), David Ricardo, and Edward Gibbon Wakefield, among others. That this substantially mercantilist goal of making England the Workshop of the World, a goal largely set by the economists, was widely accepted, is apparent in surveying the parliamentary debates which led to the abolition of the corn laws, in the course of which Joseph Hume and, finally, Sir Robert Peel made themselves its leading spokesmen; outside of parliament, though less directly, the great campaign to abolish the corn laws pressed the same theme.

Even though, when Tucker advocated a freer trade and when Pitt and later Peel followed in the course of his argument, he and they were largely moved by the essentially mercantilist hope of achieving a virtual industrial monopoly for Great Britain, the new, liberal economics seemed to eschew the aggressive spirit of the past, and attempted, on the whole, to see commerce in less invidious terms. Mercantilist economists, as well as anti-mercantilist physiocratic economists, in the eighteenth century, had agreed that while a growing agricultural production, by its very nature, would call forth a population to consume an increasing supply, this was not the case with industrial production. The latter was characterized by a surplus which had to be disposed of by foreign trade;[1] even Adam Smith saw colonies and foreign trade, in the mercantilist manner, as a necessary vent for surplus industrial production. In the first decade of the nineteenth century, J. B. Say and James Mill extended the happy agricultural principle to industry: Say's Law of Markets, stating that an increase of industrial production was also necessarily accompanied by a corresponding increase in consumption, was the most optimistic part of the orthodox classical political economy. Unlike the mercantilists, therefore, the classical economists thought foreign trade unnecessary, though, undeniably, useful. This law of markets, however, was rejected by Malthus and others who persisted in regarding glut—

[1] J. A. Schumpeter has noted the similarities between physiocratic and mercantilist analyses of trade in his *History of Economic Analysis* (London: Allen & Unwin, 1955), p. 235 f.n.

overproduction of goods or a surplus of capital—as among the inevitable characteristics of a commercial system. Malthus, whose sympathies were with the traditional, agrarian order, mounted, largely on the basis of the physiocratic attack on the Colbertism of the *ancien régime*, a damning critique of the new industrial system, denying its viability because of such inner contradictions.

Yet, despite the adherence to Say's Law by Ricardo, the Mills, and McCulloch, among others, many writers on political economy, in other respects entirely orthodox, appeared not to have faith in the capacity of the home market to consume increasing amounts of industrial production. They turned to the world market as the sphere to which Say's Law might properly be said to apply, and saw an industrial England, much as had the mercantilists, as dependent on foreign trade. This, for example, was the view of much of the free trade literature of the anti-corn-law campaign of the forties. Even the Ricardians who more faithfully adhered to Say's Law had other grounds for doubting England's future self-sufficiency. Ricardo himself argued the necessity of an increasing dependence on foreign trade because it would provide a means of overcoming the declining rate of profit, the effects of the law of diminishing returns in agriculture, a clear flaw, though, in his view, not an immediately pressing one, in a rapidly industrializing England with an increasing population.

The second of the imperial conceptions of which we have spoken is largely identified with the ideas of Edward Gibbon Wakefield. Wakefield—anticipated, in part, by his later disciple, Robert Torrens—while accepting the orthodox goal of an industrial England, and orthodox means, such as free trade in corn, of assuring its growth and prosperity, also accepted the heterodox Malthusian critique. Wakefield and his 'school' of followers saw the trading system to be erected upon the repeal of the corn laws and of commercial restrictions as a means of providing some relief from glut, and of helping to assure a rapid rate of advance to industrialism. Still, in adapting the Malthusian analysis to suit Ricardian goals, Wakefield also insisted that an industrial system could not be made viable by free trade alone; England might grow and prosper, without crises or social unrest, only if she also turned to colonization. The Radicals who associated themselves with a more orthodox outlook tended, on the other hand, to be hostile to colonization, and sometimes even to emigration, and to insist that the end of the corn laws would solve all Britain's difficulties. For the Wakefield school, colonies would become the sites for the investment of England's overflowing capital, and would provide the markets for Britain's surplus manufactures. Indeed, such empire-building, they believed, could provide an answer—the answer—to virtually all the most pessimistic prophecies of the practitioners of the dismal science. 'Multiply and replenish the earth' might be substituted for 'moral restraint'; new fertile lands over the seas would delay the progress onto increasingly inferior acres at home, and the law of diminishing returns in agriculture might be bypassed; class conflict, with its threat of revolution, could be alleviated. Wakefield, in fact, fully anticipated the later neo-Marxist analysis of the necessity of 'imperialism' to a capitalist system.

While the Malthusians, in calling for the end to the growth of industry, prophesied doom for those who had departed from the old and godly tillage, the Promethean Ricardians had dared to snatch the firebrand from the heavens, sustained as they were by Say's Law, which comforted them for the present, and by the dream of an international free-trading community, which would counter, for a time, declining returns from agriculture, in the future. The school of Wakefield saw in the Empire of Free Trade— in both an 'informal' trading community and in colonization—the talisman against all the punishments which the gods might precipitately invoke, almost as the means of transforming a 'dismal science' into one of optimism, of providing the mechanism of genuine salvation for a commercial and industrial society.

We hope not only to describe the origins and development of these two imperial conceptions, but also to discuss the uses to which they were put in the shaping of colonial and trade policy. The discussion of colonization will center upon Wakefield's theory of 'systematic colonization', the heart of the practical program of the Colonial Reformers for a middle-class empire to replace the old colonial system; that on trade policy will stress the parliamentary struggle to repeal the corn laws, as a means of strengthening England's position as the Workshop of the World, a conflict marked by the growing acceptance of economic 'science' by both sides. We will describe two principal Radical groups, one led first by Hume and then by Cobden, who were partisans of a species of trade empire on a roughly orthodox basis, and unfriendly to colonization; and the other, a group of Colonial Reformers, who insisted upon the need both for such a trading system and for colonization, on the basis of the analysis set down by the agrarian economists and extended by Wakefield. While both groups of Radicals were antagonistic to the old colonial system—leading to the view of the period when they gained their victories as one of anti-colonialism—neither, before Cobden set his seal on Radicalism, was free of an interest in empire-building. In the penultimate chapter, we will describe certain confirmations of many of the accusations of the national economists which appeared in the writings of the leading political economists, and we will see in Robert Torrens' writings a demonstration of the disadvantages of a unilateral free trade, at least so far as the free importation of foreign manufactures was concerned, a reversion to mercantilist ideas, a foreshadowing of the neo-mercantile 'imperialism' of the decade before the War of 1914.

We hope to show, indeed, that the persistence of characteristically mercantilist attitudes and assumptions in the thinking of the mainstream of classical political economy, assumptions extended and distorted by the even more crudely expressed mercantilism of leading Radicals—in Parliament and among the propagandists of the Anti-Corn Law League—underlay the effort to repeal the corn laws, and other restrictions upon trade. We hope to show, further, that the persistence of assumptions of traditional agrarian economics concerning the instability of a commercial and industrial system underlay the theory of capitalist imperialism developed primarily by Edward Gibbon Wakefield, a theory which was employed widely and in high places, as a justification for a program of both trade empire and colonization. These intellectual and psychological survivals of the pre-industrial age were frequently superimposed upon the more characteristically 'orthodox' principles of the new political economy, providing them with a mood and a direction rather different from the one with which a subsequent generation, further removed from the time of relative economic stasis and scarcity, were to endow them. Both the 'Cobdenites' and the neo-mercantile imperialists of Joseph Chamberlain's generation were to see the heyday of free trade through the roseate spectacles of a victorious Cobdenism, and were, consequently, to see an era in which the foundations of a new 'imperialism'—by almost any of the later standards—were being laid, as simply one of the decline of the old colonial empire.

The background of this work, then, is, roughly, the century between 1750 and 1850, from the free-trade mercantilism of Tucker, which anticipated the new political economy, to Adam Smith and his followers, Malthus, Ricardo, Mill, and their disciples, who dominated economic science until the 'marginal revolution' of the 1870s. These are the years which saw the destruction of the old colonial system and the erection of an Empire of Free Trade, years which saw a middle class brought to a position of considerable wealth through the revolutionary processes of the new industrialism, determined to translate their control of the new productive powers of the factories into greater political power within their country, and then, if possible, to extend their influence throughout the world. From the theoretical disputations of the founders of political economy, there were formed conceptions of empire-building which were both a spur and a weapon, and were to serve as an accepted justification of an Empire of Free Trade at whose core was the dream that England would be the Workshop of the World, the center of a cosmopolitan international economy which would constitute the basis of a Pax Britannica.

The beginnings of this British predominance—at first, financial and commercial, and later, industrial—are to be found in the eighteenth century. It was in the second half of this century that a first generation of free-trade economists were to see colonies, regarded as a necessity by the mercantilists, as useless, and to see the advantages of a freer foreign trade to Great Britain if she were to maintain and extend her position. It was at that time, also, that these political economists made their first conversions among British statesmen; by the 1780s the converts were seeking to put the new principles into practical effect.[1]

---

[1] Professor Harlow demonstrated the crucial role played by Shelburne and Pitt, following the example of earlier officials, in laying the economic and administrative foundations for an empire based on trade not power. See V. T. Harlow, *The Founding of the Second British Empire, 1763–1793* (London: Longmans, Green, 1952 and 1964), 2 vols. See also Peter Marshall, 'The First and Second British Empire: A Question of Demarcation', *History* XLIX (February 1964), 13–23; G. C. Bolton, 'The Founding of the Second British Empire', *Economic History Review*, 2nd Series, XIX, no. 1 (April 1966), 195–200.

CHAPTER 2

Theory and politics of Free Trade Empire in the eighteenth century

To understand Mr Pitt, one must understand one of the suppressed characters of English history, and that is Lord Shelburne . . . [who adopted] a plan of commercial freedom, the germ of which may be found in the long-maligned negotiations of Utrecht, but which were soon in time matured by all the economic science of Europe, in which he was a proficient . . . for the first time since the Revolution, [Pitt and Shelburne] introduced into modern debate the legitimate principles on which commerce should be conducted . . . The commercial treaties of '87 were struck in the same mint, and are notable as the first effort made by the English government to emancipate the country from the restrictive policy which had been introduced by the 'glorious revolution' . . . In ordinary times the pupil of Shelburne [Pitt] would have raised this country to a state of great material prosperity, and removed or avoided many of the anomalies which now perplex us; but he was not destined for ordinary times; and, though his capacity was vast and his spirit lofty, he had not that passionate and creative genius required by an age of revolution.

Benjamin Disraeli, *Sybil* (1845)

Tucker (vs. Hume) on Free Trade Empire

IN 1752, the philosopher, historian, and economist, David Hume, the pride of the Scottish Enlightenment, had argued in one of his tracts that, under conditions of free trade, wealth would be transferred from a richer to a poorer state until the riches of both states were equal. Hume may have had in mind the example of Spain whose American treasure had been drained through trade with the other European states in the sixteenth and seventeenth centuries. Perhaps, also, he was attempting to account for the improving conditions of his native Scotland—he was born at Edinburgh in 1711—during the decades following the Act of Union with England in 1707, or, perhaps, in loyal fashion, he wished only to assure himself that Scotland would, inevitably, continue to make economic progress. The theory of the automatic mechanism, which Hume himself had set forth earlier as an attack upon mercantilist trade theory, had asserted that the precious metals distributed themselves in accordance with the requirements of trade, and

14

that, therefore, restrictions upon the movement of gold and silver were unavailing. Consequently, if the amount of the precious metals in England were to be halved overnight, the low wages and low prices which would result, in accordance with the quantity theory of money, would so promote English exports that the influx of precious metals paid by foreigners for these exports would replace the gold and silver lost, as well as restore former wage and price levels. Arguing less carefully, Hume proceeded to suggest that as a consequence of its low wage and price levels a poor country might, in similar fashion, drain a richer country of its precious metals.

Hume's analysis provoked Josiah Tucker, the Dean of Gloucester, to present so effective a counter-argument that Tucker appears to have been justified in his assertion, some years later, that though he could not boast of having made Hume 'a *declared* Convert', yet in what Hume had written subsequently, Hume acted 'as if he was a *Convert*'.[1] In this instance, Hume, the religious skeptic and the critic of pure reason, found his economic syllogisms undermined by the arguments of an empirically-minded clergyman. Tucker, the son of a farmer, was educated at St John's College, Oxford, and, in 1758, was appointed to the deanery of Gloucester. The remainder of his life was devoted to superintending, rather well, the estates of the See of Gloucester, and to his writings upon questions of trade, some of which were translated by Turgot into French. As an economist, he has proved difficult to classify; some authorities, remembering his views on the balance of trade, on population, and on the evils of forestalling, have called him a mercantilist, and others, thinking of his opinion on colonies and on trade policy, have set him down as a liberal.[2] In his argument with Hume, we shall see him as both free trader and economic nationalist, a prophetic combination.

Tucker's starting-point in this argument, however, stemmed from an enlightened theology. Tucker had been disturbed by Hume's implied conclusion that 'every poor Country is the natural and unavoidable Enemy of a rich one', and that the rich one, in its own interest, would be obliged 'to make War upon the poor one, and to endeavour to extirpate all its Inhabitants'. Such an order of things was inconsistent with 'the fundamental Principle of universal Benevolence' established by 'Divine Providence'.[3] Taking England and Scotland as independent nations, Tucker

---

[1] Josiah Tucker, *Four Tracts Together With Two Sermons, On Political and Commercial Subjects* (Gloucester, 1774), p. v.

[2] For a view of Tucker as a mercantilist, see W. E. Clark, *Josiah Tucker, Economist* (New York, n.p., 1903), pp. 174–6 and *passim*; R. L. Schuyler accepted this view in his *Josiah Tucker: A Selection from His Economic and Political Writings* (New York: Columbia University Press, 1931), pp. 13–14; in his *Fall of the Old Colonial System*, however, he sees Tucker rather differently (p. 42).

[3] Tucker, *Four Tracts*, pp. 11–12.

suggested that if England were suddenly to become immensely richer than Scotland because of the discovery of rich mines or because of privateering, then Hume's conclusions would undoubtedly be correct. However, they would just as surely be false if this increase of wealth were acquired 'in the Way of *general Industry*'.[1]

Tucker regarded the question as ultimately this: 'Which of these two Nations can afford to raise Provisions, and sell their Manufactures on the cheapest Terms?' Tucker insisted that the richer country had all the advantages. First of all, 'as the richer Country hath acquired its superior Wealth by a general Application, and long Habits of Industry, it is therefore in actual Possession of an established Trade and Credit . . . a great Variety of the best Tools and Implements in the various kinds of Manufactures . . . good Roads, Canals, and other artificial Communications; good Pilots, and trained Sailors . . . Whereas the poor Country has, for the most Part, all these Things to seek after and procure.' The richer country had 'superior Skill and Knowledge'; it had the capital to make experiments, to embark upon 'expensive and long-winded Undertakings'; it had a prosperous home market. In the richer country, because of the intensive division of labor, each person became an expert artisan: 'Is it not much cheaper', he inquired, 'to give 2s. 6d. a Day in the rich Country to the nimble and adroit Artist, than it is to give only 6d. in the poor one, to the tedious, awkward Bungler?' In the richer country, goods were cheaper as a result of the competition of rival tradesmen. Finally, 'in the richer Country, the Superiority of the Capital, and the low Interest of Money, will ensure the Vending of all Goods on the cheapest Terms', and would make possible the granting of longer credits.[2]

Tucker proposed a 'law', which was to gain considerable support, in altered form, among the later economists: 'That *operose*, or *complicated Manufactures* are cheapest in rich Countries;—and *raw Materials* in poor ones: And therefore in Proportion as any Commodity approaches to one, or other of these *Extremes*, in that Proportion it will be found to be cheaper, or dearer in a rich, or a poor Country.'[3] Timber was always cheapest in a poor country, but not cabinetry.[4] Although Tucker was able to recognize the enormous advantages which rich nations possessed over poorer ones, he was not so illiberal as to wish to keep backward nations from progressing. Since no nation could 'ever be ruined but by itself', Tucker urged that the English, because of 'the very Largeness of their Capitals, and their Vicinity to *Scotland*', might help the Scots by loans and technical assistance. The increasing prosperity of neighboring nations would make them better

---

[1] Tucker, *Four Tracts*, p. 20. [2] *Ibid.* pp. 21–7. [3] *Ibid.* p. 28. [4] *Ibid.* pp. 30–3.

customers.[1] In this fashion, liberal trade principles would serve the national interest.

David Hume replied to Tucker's argument in a letter, dated 4 March 1758, addressed to Lord Kames, a Scottish friend of both Tucker and Hume. Hume was willing to admit all the advantages favoring the richer nation which had been noted by Tucker, but insisted that there would come a limit, a '*ne plus ultra*', at which point the rich nation would check itself 'by begetting disadvantages, which at first retard, and at last finally stop their progress'. Among these were 'the dear price of provisions and labour, which enables the poorer country to rival them, first in the coarser manufactures, and then in those which are more elaborate'. Arguing upon a basis as tenuous as the belief in Divine Providence of his clerical rival, Hume suggested that 'were it otherwise, commerce, if not dissipated by violent conquests, would go on perpetually increasing, and one spot of the globe would engross the art and industry of the whole'. This would be unthinkable: 'It was never surely the intention of Providence, that any one nation should be a monopolizer of wealth: and the growth of all bodies, artificial as well as natural, is stopped by internal causes, derived from their enormous size and greatness.' Hume spoke on behalf of his native Scotland: 'I still indulge myself in the hopes that we in Scotland possess also some advantages, which may enable us to share with them [the English] in wealth and industry ... and tho a rich country, by its other advantages, may long maintain its ground against a poorer, which makes attempts towards commerce, it will not be able entirely to annihilate or oppress it.'[2]

Tucker made two rebuttals, one publicly, in 1774, and another in a private letter, in 1758. In his public reply, Tucker denied that he had suggested that progress would be '*ad infinitum*', since he was 'not Metaphysician enough to comprehend what INFINITY really means', but stated that such progress could be carried on so far that 'no Man can positively define, *when*, or *where* it must *necessarily* stop'. The 'richer manufacturing Nation will maintain its Superiority over the poorer one, notwithstanding this latter may be likewise advancing towards Perfection'. To Hume's argument that one nation, engrossing the trade of the world, would 'beggar all the rest', Tucker replied that 'every Nation, poor as well as rich, may improve their Condition if they please'. Although the poorer nation could not compete with the manufactures of the richer nation in the international market, there were yet '*local*' advantages of climate or soil or situation or even 'the natural Turn and peculiar Genius' of a nation which the poorer country

---

[1] *Ibid.* pp. 34–6.
[2] J. Y. T. Greig, ed., *The Letters of David Hume* (Oxford, 1932), I, 271–2.

was 'at Liberty to cultivate'. Indeed by being able to borrow from the richer country, 'at a low Interest', which 'is no small Benefit', and because 'a rich Neighbour is more likely to become a good Customer than a poor one', the advanced country could be of direct service to the less highly developed one. Moreover, the 'very same Country may be relatively both richer and poorer than another at the very same Time, if considered in different Points of View'. For example, Scotland and Ireland, though poorer in most branches of production than England, had the head-start, and were richer, in respect to linen manufacture. Tucker cautioned Hume lest, in his analytical description of the advance of a poorer country from simpler to more complex manufactures, he neglect to take into consideration that prices, wages, etc. would be rising along with this progress, thus depriving the poorer country of many former advantages.[1]

In this public rebuttal, Tucker anticipated, at many points, the nineteenth-century view of the international free trade economy and presented the arguments which, in one form or another, the English industrial classes were to employ against their domestic opponents, the landed and the old mercantile and financial aristocracy, who were to suggest that those who wished to make England the manufactory to the world were the dupes of a false pride and would be undone by the transitoriness of fortune. In his private rebuttal in a letter to Lord Kames on 6 July 1758, Tucker anticipated the program which was to be put forward by economists of less-developed countries who sought to challenge British industrial predominance, men such as Hamilton, List, and Carey. Tucker wrote: 'It is true likewise, that all of them [the poor countries] have it in their power to load the manufactures of the rich country upon entering their territories, with such high duties as shall turn the scale in favour of their own manufactures, or of the manufactures of some other nation, whose progress in trade they have less cause to fear or envy.' And, again like List and Carey, Tucker concluded, that 'thus it is, in my poor apprehension, that the rich may be prevented from swallowing up the poor;

---

[1] Tucker, *Four Tracts*, pp. 41–7. James Oswald of Dunniker, a friend of Hume's, also took issue with him upon this matter. In a letter to Hume, 10 October 1749, Oswald described the advantages of a rich country:

A countrey in this situation would, in some measure, be the capital of the world, while all neighbour countreys would, in respect of its advantages, tho' not of their own, be as its provinces. Neighbour countreys could not throw in such obstructions in its way . . . as to prevent it from having all the necessarys of life, materials of manufacture, labourers, and, consequently, labour, as cheap as with them, together with a balance of treasure arising in its favour; and, notwithstanding this last circumstance, it would soon appear, that . . . it could make up manufactures cheaper than in any other part of the world.

See Eugene Rotwein, ed., *David Hume: Writings on Economics* (Edinburgh, 1955), pp. 194–5. For Hume's reply to Oswald, see Greig, ed., *Letters of David Hume*, I, 143–4.

at the same time, and by the same methods, that the poor are stimulated and excited to emulate the rich'.[1]

Tucker (vs. Burke) on the colonial system

Paradoxically, Tucker's mercantilist objectives led to his denunciation of the colonial system of mercantilism. According to mercantilist canon, colonies were prized because their possession made more practicable the autarchic ideal of a self-sufficient empire, with colonies supplying needed imports rather than the competing foreigner, thereby bringing profits to one's own countrymen, helping to conserve the necessary hoard of the precious metals, and even, possibly, through re-export of staples, helping to increase that hoard. The colonial would serve as a customer of metropolitan manufactures—industries which might compete with those of the mother country were prohibited in the colonies—and as a supplier of tropical products, for the colonialism of the eighteenth century, resting upon sea-power, was based upon the trade in the staples, like tobacco, sugar, coffee, tea, spices, raised mostly by slave labor in the New World or in East Asia. The mercantilist regarded commerce and manufacturing as superior occupations—we have observed Dean Tucker's views on this matter—as essentially more profitable than the raising of raw materials, which embodied less labor and supported fewer inhabitants; Tucker would also have accepted the mercantilist contention that through manufactures a numerous and vigorous population, so necessary to national defense, might be maintained at home. The metropolis carefully regulated colonial commerce: by a series of acts, in the seventeenth and eighteenth centuries, for instance, the parliament provided that certain enumerated articles—such as naval stores, rice, tobacco, sugar, and cotton—could be shipped only to England; preferential treatment was extended to some colonial products in the English market, and even bounties were sometimes granted, as compensation for restrictions upon colonial trade which heavily favored English products; by certain provisions of a series of Navigation Acts, to cite a final example, only English-owned ships, manned by English sailors, were permitted to bring American, Asian, or African goods into England or her colonies— foreign ships might only bring goods of their own production to English ports.[2] Despite his mercantilist ideals and preconceptions, Josiah Tucker,

[1] Letter included in A. F. Tytler, *Memoirs of the Life and Writings of the Honourable Henry Home of Kames* (Edinburgh, 1814), III, 160.

[2] Our material has been drawn from Eli F. Heckscher, *Mercantilism* (London: Allen & Unwin, 1935), 2 vols.; Knorr, *British Colonial Theories*; G. L. Beer, *The Old Colonial System, 1660–1754* (New York: Macmillan, 1912), 2 vols.

in the middle decades of the eighteenth century, declared that colonies were absolutely useless to Great Britain, and that the various restrictions of the old colonial system, so long regarded as of great advantage, were positively injurious to British commerce.

Tucker had been consulted in the sixties by Earl Shelburne, then president of the board of trade, who had wished his advice concerning the best system of regulations for islands acquired from the French after the Seven Years War. Tucker's view, at that time, was that 'these Islands, or any other Acquisitions, at so great a Distance from the Mother Country', were not worth 'the Costs both of Men and Money, which had been, and would be, bestowed on them'.[1] His opinions concerning colonies seemed extreme even to the anti-colonial physiocrat, the Abbé Morellet, who wrote, in 1774, of Tucker's view that the American colonies ought to be granted their independence, that Tucker seemed to him like 'un homme à qui son valet a cassé une pièce de porcelaine et qui, de dépit, jette tout le reste par la fenêtre'.[2] Writing in 1783, after the loss of the thirteen mainland colonies, Tucker employed, possibly for the first time, the metaphor which was to be associated with the Cobdenite view of colonial possessions in the first half of the nineteenth century: '*America*, I have proved beyond the Possibility of a Confutation, ever was a Milstone hanging about the Neck of this Country, to weigh it down: And as we ourselves had not the Wisdom to cut the Rope, and to let the Burthen fall off, the *Americans* have kindly done it for us.'[3]

Tucker, a supporter of Lord North, has been regarded as an enemy to the colonies, and Edmund Burke as their defender, but the circumstances surrounding the effort, during the sixties and seventies, to secure a substantial colonial contribution to imperial defense, and a more effective enforcement of colonial trade regulations, saw Burke in a less clear-cut position, as we shall see. A Stamp Act passed in 1765 provoked a boycott of British goods in the colonies, on grounds that the Act constituted taxation without representation; the Rockingham ministry, whose spokesman Burke

[1] Josiah Tucker, *Four Letters on Important National Subjects Addressed to the Right Honourable The Earl of Shelburne* (Gloucester, 1783), pp. 2–3.

[2] Lord Fitzmaurice, ed., *Lettres de l'Abbé Morellet à Lord Shelburne* (Paris: Plon, 1898), p. 58; Turgot wrote to Tucker in 1770: 'Je vois avec joye, comme citoyen du monde, s'approcher un événement, qui, plus que tous les livres des philosophes, dissipera le phantome de la jalousie du commerce. Je parle de la séparation de vos colonies d'avec la métropole . . .' Turgot also confessed 'd'être étonné, que dans une nation qui jouit de la liberté de la presse, vous soyez presque le seul auteur qui ait connu et senti les avantages de la liberté du commerce.' Quoted in Josiah Tucker, *Cui Bono? Or, An Inquiry, What Benefits Can Arise Either to the English or the Americans, the French, Spaniards, or Dutch from the Greatest Victories, or Successes in the Present War* (London, 1782), pp. xi–xii.

[3] Tucker, *Four Letters to Shelburne*, pp. 7–8.

was, repealed the Stamp Act in 1766. After Rockingham himself was succeeded by the elder Pitt in that same year, Charles Townshend, the minister in charge of colonial questions, heeding the quibble that the colonists objected only to revenue taxes, not those imposed for the regulation of trade, secured the enaction of new 'trade' duties on goods entering the colonies. Once again there was American resistance, and troops had to be dispatched. Wishing an end of these difficulties, in 1770, the government repealed all duties except the one upon tea. After the Boston Tea Party of 1773, the Tory Lord North unleashed a policy of repression which led to a colonial struggle for independence. The American colonies claimed to be fighting not to undo the commercial regulations of the old colonial system, but because they rejected the claim that they might be taxed by a parliament in which they were not directly represented. A number of British statesmen, among them Edmund Burke, supported them in this contention.

In later years, Burke was to be known as a disciple of Adam Smith.[1] He was to glory in the name of 'economist', he told the House in 1796,[2] and his *Thoughts on Scarcity*, published the previous year, was a tract of the new liberal economics.[3] But, in the seventies and eighties, Burke had not freed himself from the fundamental presuppositions of the old commercial system, nor, at a time when interest counted for much, did he find himself neglecting the demands of faction. Burke, indeed, did urge the cause which the colonists had emblazoned upon their revolutionary standards: 'Leave the Americans as they antiently stood,' he told the House of Commons in April 1774; 'do not burthen them by taxes; you were not used to do so from the beginning.' However, joined to his view that Americans ought to be free of parliamentary taxation was a conviction that the restrictions of the old colonial system had to be retained. In the same address, he asked the parliament to 'be content to bind America by laws of trade; you have always done it', adding that at a time when the American colonists 'bear the burthens of unlimited monopoly', it would be most unwise to try to impose 'the burthens of unlimited revenue too'.[4] Representing the enlightened opinion of the merchants of Bristol in the House of Commons, and no city

---

[1] See C. R. Fay, *Burke and Adam Smith* (Belfast, 1956), pp. 11–20, and *passim*. See also D. Wecter, 'Adam Smith and Burke', *Notes and Queries* CLXXIV (30 April 1938), 310–11; W. C. Dunnes, 'Adam Smith and Edmund Burke: Complementary Contemporaries', *Southern Economic Journal* VII (January 1941), 330–46; and Donald Barrington, 'Edmund Burke as An Economist', *Economica*, N.S., XXI, no. 83 (August 1954), 252–8.
[2] Edmund Burke, *A Letter to a Noble Lord on the Attacks Made Upon Him and His Pension by the Duke of Bedford and the Earl of Lauderdale* (London, 1796), pp. 27–8.
[3] Edmund Burke, *Thoughts and Details on Scarcity* (London, 1800), especially pp. 1, 12, 25, 29. Originally published in 1795.
[4] Edmund Burke, *Speech on American Taxation*, 19 April 1774 (London, 1775), pp. 89–90, 96.

in the kingdom was more heavily committed to the American trade, Burke, in a speech in that city immediately before he was re-elected as one of Bristol's M.P.s in 1775, reassured those electors who had become concerned lest their member had become an advocate of colonial separation. 'I have held, and ever shall maintain, to the best of my power,' he told them, 'unimpaired and undiminished, the just, wise, and necessary constitutional superiority of Great Britain.' 'This great city, a main pillar in the commercial interest of Great Britain, must totter on its base by the slightest mistake with regard to our American measures,' he concluded.[1]

The parliamentary representative of Bristol could not regard with equanimity the view that the American colonies were useless. During the seventies, Burke directed his special venom at the Dean of Gloucester. Tucker, unlike Burke, who was a good Whig, was contemptuous of the *political* principles of the American colonies, principles with which Burke sympathized: in a letter in 1781 Tucker called it 'Mob-ocracy' begot of 'a Spirit of Insanity';[2] the Americans were 'Mr Locke's Disciples', he declared, and their views 'would necessarily unhinge, and destroy every Government upon Earth'.[3] Burke was especially sensitive to Tucker's charge that Whig opposition to the Stamp Act in the sixties had 'encouraged the Americans to their resistance'. Tucker's views on this matter, of course, and on others, had been welcomed by the Tory government of Lord North, which caused Burke to sneer that 'this Dr Tucker is already a dean, and his earnest labours in this vineyard will, I suppose, raise him to a bishoprick'.[4] In 1775, Tucker defended himself against Burke's 'Abuse and Scurrility',[5] and disparaged Burke's notion of a sentimental tie between England and America. 'Trade is not carried on for the Sake of Friendship,' Tucker informed Burke in a tract written in 1776, 'but of Interest,' and the American colonies, even after independence, could not afford to suspend their trade with Great Britain.[6]

Reverting to arguments he had employed in his debate with Hume, Tucker declared that the American trade rested upon 'the Superiority of the *British* Capitals over those of every other Country in the Universe', as was evidenced in the ability of the British exporter to grant long-term

[1] Edmund Burke, *Speeches At His Arrival At Bristol, and At the Conclusion of the Poll* (London, 1775), p. 13.
[2] Letter to a Lady, 3 February 1781, Miscellaneous Papers, New York Public Library.
[3] Josiah Tucker, *A Letter to Edmund Burke* (Gloucester, 1775), pp. 11, 2–29, 43, 56.
[4] Burke, *Speech on American Taxation*, p. 71.
[5] Tucker, *Letter to Burke*, p. 5. See also Josiah Tucker, *A Series of Answers to Certain Popular Objections Against Separating from the Rebellious Colonies* (Gloucester, 1776), *passim*.
[6] *Ibid.* p. 28.

credit. Indeed, the trade of the world was carried on, 'in a great Measure', by '*British* Capitals' and while this 'superiority shall last, it is morally impossible that the Trade of the *British* Nation can suffer any very great or alarming Diminution'. Let the Americans go where they pleased, and 'try all the Nations on the Globe. When they have done, they will suppliantly return to *Great Britain*, and entreat to be admitted into the Number of our Customers, not for ours, but for their own Sakes.' Nor, in the event of separation, need England fear that the Americans would set up their own manufactures. British industrial superiority had already enabled her to export manufactures to many European countries which had attempted to rival her, and America, moreover, 'naturally labours under many capital Defects respecting Manufactures', particularly 'their small capitals, and want of credit'.[1] Writing in 1782, he proclaimed that the best system for England would have been 'to have thrown up all foreign Dominions at once; and to have trusted solely to the Goodness and Cheapness of our Manufactures, and to the long Credit we can give, for procuring them a Vent', and to have relied on 'the Strength of our great Capitals' to command the goods of the world.[2]

On the other hand, Tucker proclaimed, the system of colonial trade restriction did England great immediate and direct injury: 'Do we wish to encourage some advantageous Trade with a foreign Country; a Country, which abounds with raw Materials, but is destitute of Manufactures?— We must not do it; if such a Trade should be supposed to interfere with the Trade of the Colonies.' England ought to be free to purchase her raw materials at the best market, yet, instead, the colonial system compelled her to offer the Colonies 'great Bounties for raising such Commodities, as might be imported from other Countries much better in *Quality*, much greater in *Quantity*, and without any *Bounties* at all;—nay, tho' these Countries should agree to take our own *English* Manufactures in Return'. In this, the English had for long been victims of 'the GREATEST INFATUATION'.[3] By ending trade restrictions, Britain could better avail herself of more profitable European markets, and still not lose her American trade. 'When all Parties shall be left at full Liberty to do as they please, our *North-American* Trade will rather be increased, than diminished,' he asserted,

---

[1] *Ibid.* pp. 30–1, 41–5.
[2] Tucker, *Cui Bono?*, pp. 5, 16–19, 36, 129. Morellet, writing to Shelburne in 1783, was convinced that similarities of language, religion, and customs, and the strength of old connections would also help to restore England's former commerce with America, and would, indeed, increase it as the Americans continued to prosper. Fitzmaurice, ed. *Lettres de l'Abbé Morellet*, pp. 201–2, 213–14.
[3] Josiah Tucker, *The Respective Pleas and Arguments of the Mother Country, and of the Colonies, Distinctly Set Forth* (Gloucester, 1776), pp. 59–60.

'because it is Freedom, and not Confinement, or Monopoly, which increases Trade.'[1]

Dean Tucker's arguments failed to convince Edmund Burke of the futility of the restraints upon colonial trade, although they appeared to have, at least partially, convinced Lord North, without at the same time diminishing his intention of bringing the colonies back to obedience. Burke, in a speech to the House of Commons in 1775, chided North for holding the colonial trade system as 'of no advantage to us, and of no burthen to those on whom they are imposed; that the trade to America is not secured by the acts of navigation, but by the natural and irresistible advantage of a colonial preference'. 'I cannot agree with the Noble Lord,' Burke declared, 'nor with the pamphlet from whence he seems to have borrowed these ideas, concerning the inutility of the trade-laws'—a reference to one of Tucker's tracts. 'For without idolizing them,' i.e. the trade laws, 'I am sure they are still, in many ways, of great use to us; and in former times, they have been of the greatest.' 'They do confine,' Burke concluded, 'they do greatly narrow the market for the Americans.' Burke, unlike Tucker who understood that the Americans were really interested in doing away with the entire system of trade restrictions, insisted that if only the colonials were satisfied in the matter of taxes, 'previous commercial relations could be resumed'.[2]

Smith's attack upon the old colonial system

In 1776, the political economist whom Burke was later to regard as his master published the *Wealth of Nations*, the first reasoned British critique of the mercantilist system, and the cornerstone of nineteenth-century political economy. While Tucker had hacked at mercantilist colonial policy with instruments of largely mercantilist making, Smith used many of the tools of the French physiocrats, who had disavowed the commercial system root and branch, found trade wholly unproductive and the profits of foreign trade procured by a species of thievery. The influence of the physiocrats upon the *Wealth of Nations* was unmistakable. Smith's chapter upon 'the different employments of capitals', for example, gave the favored place to agriculture. The capital employed in trade was least advantageously situated, Smith insisted, and the capital in the carrying trade, striking at another bulwark of the commercial system, was 'altogether withdrawn from support-

---

[1] Josiah Tucker, *An Humble and Earnest Appeal* (London, 1776), p. 61; see also Tucker, *A Series of Answers*, pp. 49, 86, 77.

[2] Edmund Burke, *Speech on Moving His Resolution for Conciliation with the Colonies*, 22 March 1775 (London, 1778), pp. 53–5; see Tucker, *Letter to Burke*, pp. 35–6.

ing the productive labour' of a particular country, to supporting that of foreign countries. Of the kinds of wholesale trade, Smith found that the home trade supported the greatest amount of labor; the foreign trade of consumption gave only 'one-half the encouragement to the industry or productive labour of the country'; the distances involved in the colonial trade resulted in less frequent turn-overs of the capital employed, besides making it 'more irregular, and more uncertain too'. Under such circumstances, Smith could only regret that 'private persons frequently find it more for their advantage to employ their capitals in the most distant carrying trades of Asia and America, than in the improvement and cultivation of the most fertile fields in their own neighbourhood'.[1]

The publication of Smith's great work in 1776, the year of the American Declaration of Independence, dramatized his conclusion, like Tucker's, that English commerce would be benefited if the restrictions which clogged the colonial trade were eliminated, a view he also offered the government, at its request, in a private memorandum on the colonial question.[2] England might purchase its tobacco more cheaply than could France, he noted, as a result of trade restrictions, but not more cheaply than would be possible under an entirely free trade. At every point, the mercantile system sacrificed the interest of the consumer of goods to that of the producer and the merchant;[3] indeed, 'the home-consumers have been burdened with the whole expence of maintaining' the empire.[4] Moreover, since the passage of the Navigation Acts, Smith declared, the colonial trade had been 'continually increasing', while other branches of foreign trade, particularly the European trade had been 'continually decaying'. This increase did not so much constitute an addition to British trade, as a 'total change in its direction': the monopoly had forced capital into the carrying trade where it necessarily maintained a smaller quantity of 'productive labour'; it had depressed the wage level in the mother country; by raising the rate of mercantile profit, it had discouraged the improvement of the land and depressed rents.[5] The artificially heightened profits of the colonial monopoly had, furthermore, maintained the general rate of profit in all trades at a level higher than would otherwise be the case, a circumstance which caused Britain injury in all trades in which

---

[1] Adam Smith, *An Inquiry into the Nature and Causes of the Wealth of Nations* (London, 1930 (Cannan edition), I, 340, 343–54, 459–60; II, 101–4.

[2] See G. H. Guttridge, 'Adam Smith on the American Revolution: An Unpublished Memorial', in *American Historical Review* XXXVIII, no. 4 (July 1933), 714–20. The Memorial was dated February 1778.

[3] Smith, *Wealth of Nations* (Cannan edition), II, 95–6.

[4] *Ibid.* II, 160.

[5] *Ibid.* II, 97–109.

she had not a monopoly;[1] indeed, a reduction of the general rate of profit would give Great Britain 'a superiority over other countries still greater than what she at present enjoys'. In sum, the colonial monopoly had 'broken altogether that natural balance' among the different branches of the British economy.[2]

Smith, on the other hand, although he joined the physiocrats in subordinating both the foreign and the colonial trade, was too much a Briton to deny their many advantages. Despite physiocratic prejudices, and even while regretting that colonial discoveries had helped 'to raise the mercantile system'—with its harmful consequences—to 'a degree of splendour and glory', Smith nonetheless delighted in the stimulating effects that the discoveries of new continents had had upon the European economy. 'Two new worlds' had been opened to European industry, each 'greater and more extensive than the old one'. 'Instead of being the manufacturers and carriers for but a very small part of the world,' the commercial towns of Europe had 'become the manufacturers for the numerous and thriving cultivators of America, and the carriers, and in some respects the manufacturers too, for almost all the different nations of Asia, Africa, and America'. America had provided 'a new and inexhaustible market' for 'that surplus part of the produce of their land and labour' for which there was no demand, and had, in consequence, given occasion to 'new divisions of labour' which would otherwise not have taken place. As a result, the 'productive powers of labour', and with them the 'real revenue and wealth' of all Europe, had increased immeasurably.[3]

The benefits of this trade, Smith readily conceded, greatly outweighed the disadvantages of the colonial monopoly: the 'new produce and the new capital' created by the colonial trade, maintained in Great Britain a 'greater quantity of productive labour' than could have been 'thrown out of employ-

[1] Smith, *Wealth of Nations*, II, 96–7, 99–100. Smith's views upon this issue were the focus for much subsequent controversy. McCulloch spoke for the Ricardian school: 'Dr Smith supposed that the monopoly increased the field for the employment of capital; and as he supposed that the rate of profit depended on the extent of the demand for capital, compared with its amount, he naturally concluded that it increased the rate of profit ... The rate of profit is not, as has been already seen, in the slightest degree dependent on the magnitude of the field for the employment of capital; but is determined entirely by the productiveness of industry at the time.' McCulloch also denied that the colonial monopoly raised the general rate of profit, again standing with Ricardo, adding, however, that the import of corn could raise profits by lowering wages. J. R. McCulloch, ed., Smith, *Wealth of Nations* (Edinburgh, 1828), IV, 406–9. See also 'Colonial Policy—Value of Colonial Possessions', *Edinburgh Review* XLII, no. LXXXIV (August 1825), assigned to McCulloch by Fetter: 'The truth is that *the RATE of profit is not in the slightest degree dependant on the magnitude of the field for the employment of capital; but that it is determined entirely by the productiveness of industry at the time.*' (p. 287).
[2] Smith, *Wealth of Nations* (Cannan edition) II, 104–5, 108, 111–13, 115–16.
[3] *Ibid.* II, 125–6; I, 413–14.

ment by the revulsion of capital from other trades of which the returns are more frequent'.[1] But, Smith noted, there had been a *general* advantage for all of Europe, not an advantage enjoyed by the imperial nations alone: 'no country has yet been able to engross to itself any thing but the expence' of the colonies.[2] Although the abandonment of the colonial monopoly would be 'contrary to the private interest of the governing part' of the nation, which would lose 'many places of trust and profit', Smith observed in conclusion, it would be a great advantage to all other Englishmen, if Britain were to grant her colonies independence and to establish a system of free trade.[3]

Adam Smith: physiocrat, mercantilist, or classical economist?

Henry Brougham was, in 1803, to speak of 'political sects' with 'very opposite opinions with respect to the general advantages of colonial establishments'. The 'disciples of the Mercantile system', by 'imposing such restraints as might render the industry of the inhabitants subservient to the wealth of the mother country, and by opening for her produce, a market of growing extent, in which positive regulations might secure an exclusive preference, or fix a high price', have 'viewed such establishments with a decided partiality'. On the other hand, 'the Oeconomists', the French physiocrats, 'have viewed, with more than common jealousy, those distant settlements, which are peopled and cultivated at the mother country's expence, and which hold out the temptations of foreign trade, to allure capital and industry from the great source of national riches—the improvement of the productive powers of the land'. 'Such settlements', moreover, 'were never likely to be made, without views of monopoly and restriction', which were 'utterly inconsistent with the very liberal and enlightened views of the Oeconomical system'. 'Between these two opinions,' Brougham was to conclude, 'Dr Smith has adopted a middle course'.[4]

Adam Smith was, in the years to come, to be seen both as a harbinger of Cobdenite anti-colonialism, and as a mercantilist. A number of historians have suggested that Smith, like Tucker, was guided by thoroughly nationalist and even 'imperialist' objectives; both men, certainly, defended the policy of ending colonial restrictions as being in Britain's immediate, national interest. One economist saw Smith as having anticipated the views of the imperialist Joseph Chamberlain, as having exploded the old colonial system

---

[1] *Ibid.* II, 108–9.
[2] *Ibid.* II, 127; see also p. 120.
[3] *Ibid.* II, 116–17.
[4] Henry Brougham, *Inquiry into the Colonial Policy of the European Powers* (Edinburgh, 1803), I, 5–7.

in order to replace it with a new conception of empire, one rooted in England's new commercial predominance;[1] Smith had, indeed, depicted a British commonwealth, with an imperial parliament, of quasi-independent countries, modelled upon the empire of ancient Athens.[2] The colonizers of the thirties and forties, as we shall see, were to seize upon Smith's writings on the utility of colonies as markets for surplus production, a view which a proper Ricardian such as McCulloch would denounce as mercantilist heresy.[3] There were other grounds for McCulloch's suspicions that Smith was not free of mercantilist assumptions. Smith had, for example, much to McCulloch's displeasure, defended the Navigation Acts. 'Defence', Smith had declared, 'is of much more importance than opulence', and he added that 'if any particular manufacture was necessary, indeed, for the defence of the society, it might not always be prudent to depend upon our neighbours for the supply; and if such manufacture could not otherwise be supported at home, it might not be unreasonable that all the other branches of industry should be taxed in order to support it'.[4] Moreover, although Smith had declared that 'nothing' could 'be more absurd than this whole doctrine of the balance of trade', he frequently came close to the mercantilist notion of the balance of employments.[5]

What, then, can we call Adam Smith? Was he a physiocrat, a mercantilist, or a classical economist? In subsequent chapters, we will argue that the views of Malthus and Chalmers came very close to an ideal-type of physio-

---

[1] See J. S. Nicholson, *A Project of Empire: A Critical Study of the Economics of Imperialism, With Special Reference to the Ideas of Adam Smith* (London: Macmillan, 1909).

[2] See D. A. E. Veal, 'Adam Smith on Imperial Union', *Empire Review* XXIX, no. 180 (January 1916), pp. 537–40; E. A. Benians, 'Adam Smith's Project of Empire', *Cambridge Historical Journal* I (1925), no. 3, pp. 249–83.

[3] J. R. McCulloch, ed., Smith, *Wealth of Nations* (1828), IV, 385, 396–7.

[4] Smith, *Wealth of Nations* (Cannan edition), I, 427–9; II, 23.

[5] *Ibid.* I, 453–4. Compare, for example, with Edward Misselden, *The Circle of Commerce* (London, 1623), p. 35; Gerrard de Malynes, *A Treatise of the Canker of England's Common Wealth*, 1601, in R. H. Tawney and E. Power, *Tudor Economic Documents* (London, 1951), III, 399; Charles Davenant, 'An Essay on the East-India Trade', in *The Political and Commercial Works* (London, 1771), I, 87. An especially good example in Nicholas Barbon, *A Discourse of Trade* (London, 1690), pp. 40, 75–6. Josiah Tucker, very much a mercantilist on this question, wrote:

when two countries are exchanging their produce or manufactures with each other, that nation which has the greatest number employed in this *reciprocal* trade, is said to receive a balance from the other. If there are only *ten thousand* persons employed in *England* in making goods or raising some kind of produce for the market of *France*; and *forty thousand* in *France* for the market of *England*, then we must pay these additional 30,000 *Frenchmen* in gold and silver; that is, be at the charge of maintaining them . . . The general principle, that labour (not money) is the riches of a people, will always prove, that the advantage is on the side of that nation, which has most hands employed in labour.

(In *A Brief Essay on the Advantages and Disadvantages Which Respectively Attend France and Great Britain With Regard to Trade* (London, 1787), pp. iii–iv. Reprint of 3rd edition of 1753.)

cracy, while Torrens' ideas of trade-empire came similarly close to an ideal-type of mercantilism; almost by definition, Ricardo, McCulloch and, to a lesser extent, James Mill embodied classical political economy, which was soon to be represented in the political arena, though not without dilution and distortion, as we shall see, by Richard Cobden. Smith was to be claimed by Malthus and Chalmers, as well as by Ricardo, Torrens, and Cobden. It is clear from our discussion of Smith's eclectic analysis that it would be impossible to declare wholly in favor of any of the contenders for his remains.

A more subtle distinction is that between mercantilism and the promotion of the national interest, and here, too, Smith poses a problem. Mercantilism is frequently distinguished from the outlook of classical political economy by its emphasis upon power rather than profit. Smith's dictum in favor of the Navigation Acts, that 'defence is of much more importance than opulence', and his willingness to protect 'particular' manufactures necessary 'for the defence of the society' by tariffs are undeniably mercantilist in tone, though when set in the context of Smith's free-trade system and outlook, it can readily be argued that Smith was primarily a spokesman of the national interest. A system of free trade, however, we have suggested in our discussion of Tucker, can be mercantilist, as in the context of Tucker's view, to be shared by Pitt, that a freer trade would be the mechanism for establishing an almost unlimited commercial and industrial predominance. But such a goal was not foremost in Adam Smith's system, as it was to be, we shall argue later, in that of Peel and the Radicals of the forties who dreamed of extending Britain's position as the Workshop of the World.

In the early eighties, other contemporaries of Smith and Tucker set down opinions similar to theirs. James Anderson, for example, followed Smith in denouncing the colonial monopoly for having raised the prices of English manufactures, concluding that the loss of that monopoly would enable England to undersell all her competitors.[1] Thomas Tod was similarly convinced that 'an open and independent market, rather than a boundless sovereignty' was to the 'interest and advantage of a mercantile, active, and manufacturing nation'; because of 'the superiority of British manufacture', he declared, America must continue to buy English goods. Tod, hoping that among the consequences of the American war would be the exploding of 'prejudice and wrong ideas' which 'ignorantly shut up commerce', looked forward to the opening of the South American market to English

---

[1] James Anderson, *The Interest of Great Britain With Regard to Her Colonies Considered* (London, 1782), pp. 24–34, 36, 60, 72–5, 100–1, 105, 110–11.

manufactures.[1] Even a supporter of the mercantile system, the Earl of Sheffield, in a tract protesting at the younger Pitt's attempt to relax the Navigation Acts, did not doubt that England would retain the American market after independence through her ability to grant long credits, and to sell cheap manufactures.[2] It was not long before these ideas made an appearance in political debate, through the efforts of three statesmen—Shelburne, Pitt, and William Eden—all disciples of Tucker and Smith, who, in the eighties, seemed on the point of bringing Great Britain over to a freer trade—indeed, to a system of minimal trade restrictions such as Huskisson was to achieve in the 1820s. These statesmen were attracted to free trade not because of impartial scientific considerations or because of cosmopolitan inclinations, although it would be wrong to suggest that such matters did not play some role, but because—following Smith and Tucker—they believed such a policy would rebound to Britain's great economic benefit. Their efforts were opposed by Burke and his party, still in the grip of the more traditional economic thinking.

Pitt's trade policy

In 1783, by the Treaty of Paris, the independence of the United States was recognized by the British government, no doubt hopeful that Tucker's and Smith's optimism would be justified, but nonetheless experiencing some anxieties. The eighteenth century witnessed a great and fairly steady expansion of British overseas trade—the value of British exports, calculated at constant prices, was to quintuple by the end of the century. There had been a great spurt forward in the 1740s; and much to the relief of English statesmen, there was another in the 1780s. The commercial consequences of American independence were all the more anticipated with some concern since the eighteenth century also saw a shift in the destinations of British exports: while only 10 per cent of English domestic exports found markets in America and the West Indies in 1700–1, in 1772–3, just before the Revolution, these markets took 37 per cent of British exports; by the end of the century, in 1797–8, fully substantiating the arguments of Tucker and Smith, the figure had risen to 57 per cent. But, during the eighties, there continued to be some doubts as to whether the expansion of English industry, seemingly so closely tied to the enormous expansion of the overseas, predominantly colonial trade, could continue. It was against the background

[1] A Merchant [Thomas Tod], *Consolatory Thoughts on American Independence; Showing the Great Advantages that Will Arise From It* (Edinburgh, 1782), pp. 2–3, 13, 16–20, 25, 32, 54–5, 66.
[2] John Baker Holroyd, Earl of Sheffield, *Observations on the Commerce of the American States With Europe and the West Indies* (London, 1783), pp. 1, 4–5, 45–50, 63, 65, 71.

of this uncertainty that Pitt, and before him, Shelburne, were to attempt to convince Britain of the beneficial effects of a freer trade.[1]

It was the Earl of Shelburne who, first in the Rockingham government, and then in his own, was, perhaps, most responsible for the generous terms which the United States obtained in the Treaty of Paris, in 1783. Shelburne's role in the negotiations led an anonymous critic to accuse him of standing 'superior and alone, amid the ruins of the Commonwealth, like Marius among the remains of the Carthaginian grandeur', and to proclaim that from Shelburne's ministry 'historians yet unborn, will date the downfall of the British Empire'.[2] The Earl of Shelburne, a great-grandson of the famous seventeenth-century economist, William Petty, was the friend, and some-times patron, of the great men of the British and French Enlightenment— Hume, Smith, the young Bentham, all belonged to his circle. The French economist Morellet, who, Shelburne was to say, had 'liberalized' his ideas,[3] credited the Earl with having been responsible for the new spirit of liberalism in the eighties: 'M. Smith, et quelquefois le doyen Tucker chez vous,' Morellet observed, 'les ont bien saisies, ces vérités, mais ils n'ont fait que les mettre dans les livres et vous les avez mises dans le monde.'[4] But Shelburne was too soon put out of office to realize his objectives—to cite just one of them, a liberal treaty with France for which a provision of the Treaty of Paris, at his insistence, had called. Perhaps the Earl's most signal service on behalf of liberal policy was his recommendation, upon his own resignation, that the King grant a commission to William Pitt, the second son of the Earl of Chatham, who, in December 1783, when not yet twenty-five years old, assumed office as first lord of the treasury.

Pitt may have been converted to free trade by Shelburne; certainly he was confirmed in free-trade opinions by his mentor. He came to office deter-mined to press for parliamentary and administrative reform, and in conform-ity with advanced economic thinking, he set afoot a large-scale reform of the customs, with a substantial reduction of duties, and worked to rationalize the collection of revenues and the payment of the debt. Pitt's lowering of the customs duties helped to stimulate demand for imports—helped to spur, for example, the expansion of Jamaican coffee plantations—and thus extended the purchasing power of Britain's overseas customers, who, of course, could

[1] Unless otherwise noted, I have used the statistics provided by P. Deane, and W. A. Cole, *British Economic Growth 1688–1959* (Cambridge: Cambridge University Press, 1967.)

[2] Portius, pseud., *A Letter to the Earl of Shelburne on the Peace* (London, 1783), pp. 38, 39–40.

[3] John Morley called Shelburne the 'one practical statesman whom the historian of political opinion in England may justly treat as a precursor of Cobden's school'. John Morley, *Life of Richard Cobden* (London: J. Fisher Unwin, 1920), p. 110. On the influence of Morellet, see Lord Fitzmaurice, *Life of William Earl of Shelburne* (London: Macmillan, 1912), II, 430.

[4] Fitzmaurice, ed. *Lettres de l'Abbé Morellet à Lord Shelburne*, p. 209.

only buy British manufactures to the extent to which they were able to sell their own produce. In 1783, to overcome distress in the islands, Pitt introduced a bill to secure a relaxation of the Navigation Acts and to permit the admission of American-owned vessels, carrying American goods, to the British West Indies, and, further, to permit the shipment of all West Indian goods to the United States. This would have made possible the continuance of the long-established channels of trade between New England and the West Indies, upon which the West Indian planters were dependent. In these efforts, he was supported by Shelburne and Adam Smith.[1] The shipping interest, led by Lord Sheffield, succeeded in blocking this bill until 1788 when it was passed with some amendments. In all this, the influence of Adam Smith, along with that of Shelburne, has been held to have been paramount, and, no doubt, properly.[2] On the other hand, the rather considerable influence of Dean Tucker upon Pitt's trade policy has been entirely overlooked.

Pitt's first large effort to reform the commercial system, to secure the liberalization of trade between Great Britain and Ireland, owed very much to Tucker, as well as to Smith. Tucker, writing about the benefits which a wealthy country might derive from trade with a poorer country, had, following Hume, discussed England and Scotland. But while England and Scotland had been one economic unit since 1707, Ireland, with her own parliament under the British crown, was the target of highly restrictive British trade legislation. If Tucker's arguments were correct, where could the principle of freer trade more readily be applied than in Great Britain's relations with her sister kingdom across the Irish Sea? In 1779, soon after the relaxation of certain Irish trade restrictions had been proposed, Adam Smith had been asked his view of free trade with Ireland, and had replied that he could not believe that British manufactures 'can for a century to come suffer much from the rivalship of those of Ireland, even though the Irish should be indulged in a free trade'. Writing in terms which Tucker had made familiar, Smith declared that Ireland had 'neither the skill, nor the stock which could enable Her to rival England, and tho' both may be acquired in time, to acquire them compleatly will require the operation of little less than a Century'.[3] Spurred by a similar confidence in Britain's

---

[1] See Harlow, *Founding of the Second British Empire*, *passim*; also letter of Adam Smith to William Eden, 15 December 1783, in Bishop of Bath and Wells, *The Journal and Correspondence of William, Lord Auckland* (London, 1861), I, 65.

[2] See J. Holland Rose, *Life of William Pitt* (London: G. Bell, 1923), I, 183-4, 241, and *passim*; Earl Stanhope, *Life of William Pitt* (London: John Murray, 1867), II, 141; IV, 402-3.

[3] Quoted in Oscar Browning, 'Adam Smith and Free Trade for Ireland', in *English Historical Review* I, no. 2 (April 1886), 309.

industrial lead, William Pitt, in 1785, proposed to the British and Irish parliaments that the many restrictions which hampered the economic intercourse of the two kingdoms be substantially modified. In that same year, Tucker, in support of Pitt's proposals, declared that his earlier analysis affected Ireland 'in a much stronger degree' than Scotland.[1] These Irish proposals set on foot a parliamentary debate between those who saw expanding British opportunities in the light cast by Tucker, and those who, less optimistically, followed the arguments of the old commercial system, or those of Hume.

1. The Irish proposals

The first debate upon the subject of Irish trade took place in February 1785, in the British House of Commons, and discussions continued for some months afterwards. The prime minister, Pitt, in presenting his proposals, denounced earlier imperial policy 'of debarring Ireland from the enjoyment and use of her own resources' in order 'to make the kingdom completely subservient to the interests and opulence of this country', noting that, fortunately, 'this system of cruel and abominable restraint' had been 'exploded'. For, 'however necessary it might be to the partial benefit of districts in Britain, it promoted not the real prosperity and strength of the empire'. The restrictions upon Irish trade and industry had subjected Ireland to a 'state of thraldom'. What Pitt proposed was a system based upon 'a community of benefits' which, 'without tending to aggrandize the one or depress the other, should seek the aggregate interests of the empire'. Using the arguments, and sometimes the very phrases, which Tucker had employed in support of his more general, theoretical case, Pitt pronounced British manufacture 'so superior' that 'there would be no danger in admitting the Irish articles to our markets'. There was nothing to fear for 'there were great obstacles to the planting of any manufactures' in Ireland, for 'it would require time for arts and capital' to be accumulated there, while 'in an established manufacture improvement was so rapid as to bid defiance to rivalship'. Although the price of Irish labor was lower than that of English, 'as their manufactures and commerce increased, this advantage would be incessantly growing less', Pitt urged. Indeed, there was a need of

---

[1] Josiah Tucker, *Reflections on the Present Matters in Dispute Between Great Britain and Ireland* (London, 1785), p. vi. See also Josiah Tucker, *Union or Separation* (London, 1799). Indeed, as early as 1750, Tucker had protested 'our ill judged Policy, and unnatural Jealousy in cramping the Commerce and Manufactures of Ireland'; this was 'a most unaccountable *Infatuation*', since 'if *Ireland* gets rich ... England will be rich too'. At this time, Tucker even advocated a union with Ireland. See [Josiah Tucker] *A Brief Essay on the Advantages and Disadvantages Which Respectively attend France and Great Britain With Regard to Trade* (London, 1750), pp. 43, 58–62.

'a habit of industry and ingenuity' in manufacturing, which the Irish did
not possess; 'a man's wages might be extremely low, and yet the price of
his labour very dear, provided that he did but a small quantity of work',
so that, in reality, wages in Ireland were higher than English wages, and
there could be no thought of underselling. It might be that there were
'some branches in which Ireland might rival, and perhaps beat England',
but Englishmen ought to 'calculate from general and not partial views'.
'It required not philosophy to reconcile us to a competition which would
give us a rich customer instead of a poor one.' Ireland's 'prosperity would
be a fresh spring to our trade'. If certain English manufacturers were beat
by the Irish, why then, Pitt declared in liberal fashion, they could 'turn
their thoughts to some other line of business'. Pitt 'most earnestly entreated
the House not to suffer themselves to be carried away with the idea that a
poor country, merely because she enjoyed some comparative exemption from taxes, was therefore able to cope with a rich and powerful
country'. Indeed, the prime minister concluded, 'for if one country ex-
ceeded another in wealth, population, and established commerce, in a
proportion of two to one, he was nearly convinced that that country would
be able to bear near ten times the burthens that the other would be
equal to'.[1]

Pitt received the support, in the House of Lords, of Shelburne, now,
since 1784, the Marquis of Lansdowne, who, in a debate in June, employed
the same arguments. By this time, however, English manufacturers had
made known their opposition to Pitt's proposals, and Lansdowne felt
obliged to warn them that the nation would not long 'bear the burthen of the
manufacturers'. 'A country without a capital could not be a rival,' Lansdowne declared, and consequently it would be a very long time indeed
before Ireland could catch up with England; nor would England 'neglect
all her own advantages, and stand still to wait for Ireland'.[2] Lord Camden,
an old adherent of Chatham, also defending Pitt's proposal, insisted that
Irish cheapness 'must only continue during the rudeness of art'. 'Greatness
of capital' divided 'manufactures into so many branches', he continued,
'that though the price to each artist distinctly might be high, the facility
and perfection which they attained by being confined to a single branch,
was productive of great benefits; and those benefits this country now had,
and would preserve.' Camden pointed to the example of Holland which had
prospered despite all apparent disadvantages. 'The English were active,

---

[1] *The Parliamentary History of England, from the Earliest Period to the Year 1803* (London, 1815)
xxv, 316–27 (22 February 1785), and 584–6 (12 May 1785).
[2] *Ibid.* pp. 856–60 (8 July 1785).

sober, and industrious'; the Irish 'were the contrary'. Under the circumstances, what had England to fear?[1]

The opposition, led by Charles James Fox, took up the cause of the old commercial system. In opposing Pitt, moreover, the opposition was acting as the spokesman for commercial and industrial interests, since a General Chamber of Manufacturers had been formed, with Wedgwood, the pottery manufacturer, as chairman, to oppose the bill; other prominent industrialists, such as Boulton and Watt, had taken a similar position. Members of the House were warned by Pitt's opponents that Irish grain imports would ruin Scottish landlords, and among the many petitions opposing the treaty was one, signed by 80,000 manufacturers of Lancashire, prophesying the destruction of the English cotton industry by the admission of Irish fustians and cotton.[2] Fox denounced Pitt's bill as 'a perversion of an established maxim of commercial policy', and hoped that Britain would not 'purchase her tranquility at the expense of her trade, her commerce, and her navigation'.[3] Upon a subsequent occasion, Fox objected to Pitt's argument that 'great capital would in all cases overbalance cheapness of labour', adding that 'I know this to be the fashionable position of the present times, and of the present government: but general positions of all kinds ought to be very cautiously admitted.' He warned that Ireland 'cannot make a single acquisition but to the proportionate loss of England'.[4] At a still later sitting, Fox accused Pitt of having 'indulged the benevolence of his own mind, and the luxuriance of his fancy, with a picture of a liberal system of commerce without any restraint whatever', and suggested that Pitt give up 'hunting for systems, which, however beautiful in theory, were perfectly incapable of being reduced to practice'[5].

Both Edmund Burke and William Eden supported Fox. Party loyalty no doubt played a role in Burke's position at this time, for Burke had earlier displayed a loyalty both to principle and to his native Ireland when he supported a freer trade with that country in 1778, despite a weighty opposition to this latter measure in his Bristol constituency.[6] Party loyalty was no doubt also an important consideration in 'determining the position of William Eden, who regarded himself as a disciple of Adam Smith, about

---

[1] *Ibid.* pp. 842–5 (8 July 1785).
[2] See *ibid.* pp. 339 (22 February 1785); 347–8 (3 March 1785); 354, 357 (11 March 1785); 409–14 (7 April 1785); see also *A Letter From a Manchester Manufacturer to the Right Honourable Charles James Fox, On His Political Opposition to the Commercial Treaty with France* (Manchester, 1787), p. 9.
[3] *Parliamentary History*, xxv, 333, 335 (22 February 1785).
[4] *Ibid.* pp. 613, 615, 620 (12 May 1785).
[5] *Ibid.* pp. 968–9 (25 July 1785).
[6] *Ibid.* pp. 648–9 (19 May 1785).

whom he had written, in 1778, that 'our friend Mr Adam Smith, whom political science may reckon a great benefactor, has discussed this subject so fully, that it is hardly possible to say any thing new with regard to it',[1] and who, that same year, had decried 'the monopolizing spirit' of the English which had made of the Irish 'mere hewers of wood, and drawers of water, to their neighbours'. Eden, in 1778, had sneered at the old principle 'that whoever is the cause of another's advancement, contributes to his own diminution', declaring it 'now well understood that the flourishing of neighbouring nations in their trade is to our advantage'. At that time, he had been convinced that there was no danger that Ireland would soon rival England in manufacturing: Ireland, he observed, had little coal, was 'ill provided with wood', and 'without inland navigations', noting most particularly, that 'the constitution and establishment of a flourishing community imply a well-regulated order through the nation, a steady and effective police, habits of docility and industry, skill in manufactures, and large capitals in trade'—in all of which Ireland was notoriously deficient.[2] In 1785, however, Eden's position, like Burke's, was to be entirely different. 'The plan proposed', Eden told the House at that time, 'was a total and sudden voluntary revolution in the whole system of commerce,' and, if adopted, would result in 'the sinking of British rents, and the destruction of the funds and of public credit'.[3] Although admitting the truth of the principle upon which Pitt had based his proposal, a principle 'replete with philanthropy and liberality', he declared that 'it would, indeed, be little consolation to the suffering bodies of men in this country, to be told in the words of the Address, "That the subjects of each Kingdom will be taught to apply themselves to those branches which they can exercise with most advantage"'. 'Such phrases were suitable enough in theoretical essays,' Eden concluded, 'but calamitous when made applicable to the complicated state of this great kingdom.'[4]

In the upper house, Lord North expressed the fear that, were Pitt's proposals carried, Ireland would supply England with foreign sugar, to the disadvantage of the West India interest. 'Among the enemies to monopoly in general, he would class a very respectable man, and a very able writer, who had long laboured for the public good; he meant the dean of Gloucester: but still, notwithstanding this great authority, he would not consent that the monopoly of our market, enjoyed by the West India planters, should be

[1] William Eden, *Four Letters to the Earl of Carlisle* (London, 1779), p. 88.
[2] *Ibid.* pp. 127, 130-1, 136, 139, 142, 144.
[3] *Parliamentary History*, xxv, 338-9 (22 February 1785).
[4] *Ibid.* pp. 962, 964-5 (25 July 1785).

destroyed.' Despite what had been said about 'the benefits arising from the cheapness of labour and provisions in Ireland' being 'sufficiently balanced by the superior skill and capitals of the English manufacturers', North continued, manufactures had already been established in Ireland which rivalled their English counterparts. What if, he asked, 'the opulent manufacturers of England emigrate to Ireland, and carry with them their skill, their workmen, and their capitals'?[1] Lord Loughborough decried 'these modern doctrines, or rather old and exploded doctrines revived', since similar attempts to abolish monopolies had been made in the reign of Charles II, and had greatly injured Britain. The proponents of Pitt seemed to wish 'that his system of commercial freedom, like that of the Dean of Gloucester's, should throw open all the ports of Britain to the manufactures of all the world'.[2] Lord Beauchamp opposed Pitt's 'innovation' which had been 'introduced in such dark and oracular theorisms of trade, that even members of this House were so puzzled with them, as to declare that they supported the system, not because they understood it, but because they placed an unbounded confidence in the minister who proposed it'.[3]

Pitt's Irish Trade Bill was defeated, it finally developed, not by the opposition of Fox, Burke, and Eden, but when the Irish parliament refused to accept it.

It might be useful to ask why it was that—although the opposition made allusions to the influence of the Dean of Gloucester in the debates—neither Pitt nor Shelburne made any acknowledgement to Tucker. Pitt was to say kind words about Smith, and Shelburne spoke readily of the influence upon his views of both Smith and the physiocrat Morellet. Why was not a similar generosity displayed toward Tucker? The question is complex, and we can only offer suggestions. The Earl of Shelburne was a patron of men of letters, as we have observed, a man accustomed to be courted by the great thinkers of the day; the young Bentham, for example, had schemed, and successfully, to obtain entrance into Shelburne's circle. In the early sixties, Shelburne had volunteered his much sought-after protection to the Dean of Gloucester, but Tucker, a difficult and proud man, had refused to be patronized.[4] Such presumption was compounded in the seventies, during the troubles with the American colonies: Shelburne sympathized with the political principles of the rebels but desired their continued connection with the empire, and, as noted earlier, Tucker's view was opposite in both particulars. Shelburne, Pitt and the other Whigs were especially sensitive

---

[1] *Ibid.* pp. 634–5, 639 (19 May 1785).   [2] *Ibid.* pp. 865–6 (7 June 1785).
[3] *Ibid.* p. 945 (25 July 1785).
[4] See Tucker, *Four Letters to Shelburne*, pp. 2–3.

to Tucker's charge that Whig opposition to the Stamp Act in the sixties had encouraged American resistance, a view welcomed by Lord North, who, as noted, thought Tucker 'very respectable' and 'very able'. If only because Tucker was a favorite of the opposition, neither Shelburne nor Pitt could present themselves as Tucker's disciples. But they *were* his disciples, as the record of the debates on the Irish bill makes abundantly clear.

2. The French treaty

The debate in both houses of parliament in 1787 on the Pitt ministry's proposed treaty of trade with France—the consummation of Shelburne's intention, as noted in the Treaty of Paris in 1783—revealed no substantial opposition, probably because no considerable economic interest felt it would be adversely affected. A chief actor in the events of 1787 was William Eden, who served as the chief British negotiator of the French trade treaty. We have noted that in 1785, although he had taken a more liberal stand on a similar matter in 1778, Eden adopted a position hostile to Pitt's Irish proposals, and had defended the old commercial system. In still another debate in that same year, Eden opposed Pitt's effort to make certain concessions to the United States in the supplying of Newfoundland, declaring at that time that 'the present system of our trade and navigation laws, however inapplicable to abstracted theories of free commerce, has become essential to this country from her peculiar circumstances; and that it was this system alone which could enable an island like Great Britain to maintain a flourishing trade and landed opulence, together with public credit and naval strength, under the pressure of accumulated taxes'.[1] In December 1785, Eden was offered a government office by Pitt; he accepted and, without apparent hesitation, reverted to his earlier espousal of liberal trade principles—a confirmation, in all probability, of what we have been told of the primary motivation of late eighteenth-century British politicians. It was Eden who negotiated the treaty on behalf of England, while the physiocrat Dupont de Nemours was among Eden's French opposites.[2]

In the Commons, Pitt took the lead in defending the treaty. He readily admitted that free-trade principles had not always been to England's advantage—that, indeed, the Whigs had most probably been correct when they caused the rejection of the trade provisions of the Treaty of Utrecht, in 1713, on grounds that a more liberal commerce with France would make

[1] *Parliamentary History*, xxv, 274 (7 February 1785).
[2] See W. O. Henderson, 'The Anglo-French Commercial Treaty of 1786', in *Economic History Review*, 2nd Series, x (1957), no. 1, 104–12. Also J. P. W. Ehrman, *The British Government and Commercial Negotiations With Europe, 1783–1793* (New York: Cambridge University Press, 1962).

England entirely dependent upon that country for her manufactured goods. But conditions had changed decisively. Indeed, the manufacturers who had always fought to maintain trade restrictions—who, indeed, had done so as recently as 1785 when the Irish bill had been debated—did not object to his French proposals. By the eighties, we now know, to a considerable extent spurred by her overseas trade, the industrial revolution which Britain was undergoing was beginning to take hold and become effective. It seems likely that the increasing awareness of the accelerating expansion of British industry, which was placing Great Britain in a position in which she had little to fear from a freer trade, and possibly much to gain, was responsible for the change of attitude on the part of the manufacturers in 1788.

Although, so far as natural produce was concerned—e.g. wines, brandies, oils—France had the advantage of the trade, Pitt told the House of Commons, in certain important branches of manufacturing, which Britain had made 'exclusively her own', and in others, in which 'she had so completely the advantage of her neighbour as to put competition at defiance', the gains were all on England's side. 'Having each its own and distinct staple—having each that which the other wanted; and not clashing in the great and leading lines of their respective riches', France and England had the possibility of a great and mutually beneficial commerce. There could be a great increase in the exports of 'our woolens', 'our earthen ware', and our 'sadlery'. 'A market of so many millions of people—a market so near and prompt—a market of expeditious and certain return—of necessary and extensive consumption, thus added to the manufactures and commerce of Britain, was an object which we ought to look up to with eager and satisfied ambition.' If Adam Smith dominated the first part of Pitt's argument, the latter part was to have a distinctly mercantilist quality. So far as the division of the benefits of trade were concerned, Pitt continued, 'the excellence of our manufactures was unrivalled, and in the operation must give the balance to England'. If the treaty was advantageous, as it was, to France, 'it would be more so to us': France 'procured a market of eight millions of people, we a market of twenty-four millions'; France gained this market, 'for produce, which employed in preparation but few hands, gave little encouragement to its navigation, and produced but little to the state', while England 'gained this market for our manufactures, which employed many hundreds of thousands, and which, in collecting the materials from every corner of the world, advanced our maritime strength, and which, in all its combinations, and in every article and stage of its progress, contributed large to the state'. Furthermore, the prime minister declared, 'it was in the nature and essence of an agreement between a manufacturing country and a country blessed with peculiar productions, that the advantages must terminate in favour of the former'. Nor was it proposed, Pitt assured the Commons, that 'the tools and manufacturers' of England be exported to France.[1]

Supporting Pitt, in phrases reminiscent of Tucker, Lord Mornington asserted that 'the industry and ingenuity of our manufacturers, the opulence which these had diffused through various channels, the substantial foundation of capital on which they had placed our trade,—a capital, which had that night been well described, as predominant and tyrant over the trade of the whole world—all these as they had been our best consolation in defeat, were the most promising sources of future victory; and that to cultivate, to strengthen, and to augment these could not be inconsistent with the glory of the kingdom'.[2] William Wyndham Grenville, later Lord Grenville, also boasted of the extent of British capital, which would keep England above French competition: 'Such was our capital', he declared, that 'we should possess every advantage from the Treaty, without France being able to enter into competition with us in any of our markets.'[3] William Wilberforce, who before he undertook his crusade against slavery was widely regarded as a 'coming man' within Tory ranks, supported his friend Pitt; the Eden treaty would not only promote peace, but by its means, he declared, England 'took away much of the spur to French industry, by supplying them with our articles in a more perfect and finished state than they could hope at first to produce by their own efforts'.[4] In the House of Lords, the Marquis of Buckingham, defending the treaty, admitted that France would have the advantage in certain products, such as large plate glass, products which could be classed as luxuries for the rich minority of Englishmen. English manufactures of cotton, pottery, and hardware—'most of them necessaries' —would, however, supply all Frenchmen, 'from the prince to the peasant'; 'our buttons would be worn in the sleeves of the lower order of people, and the labourer in France would purchase an English knife to cut his dinner with'.[5]

Fox and the Whigs fought the treaty largely upon political grounds. No such trade treaty ought to be made with the 'enemy'; the Whigs stood by the Methuen treaty with Portugal, and refused to toast the new era in claret.[6] Fox damned what he professed to regard as an attack on Portugal, 'our old ally'.[7] Charles Grey, later Earl Grey, made his maiden speech in

---

[1] *Parliamentary History*, XXVI, 384–9, 392–5 (12 February 1787).
[2] *Ibid*. pp. 492–3 (21 February 1787).
[3] *Ibid*. p. 498 (21 February 1787).
[4] *Ibid*. p. 440 (15 February 1787).
[5] *Ibid*. pp. 537–8 (1 March 1787).
[6] *Ibid*. pp. 346–9 (5 February 1787); p. 398 (12 February 1787).
[7] *Ibid*. p. 361 (9 February 1787).

opposition to the treaty, declaring '*Timeo Danaos et dona ferentes.*'[1] Fox protested at this 'new system, in which not only the established doctrines of our forefathers were departed from, but by which the great and most essential principles in our commerce, principles which, whether wise or erroneous, had made us opulent, were to be completely changed'.[2] Philip France attributed English prosperity 'to that long established, wise, and successful system of commerce, which the present Treaty with France professes to alter materially, if not totally to subvert'.[3]

To this amalgam of prejudice, Henry Flood, who had made his reputation in Irish politics, added economic argument from a familiar source, David Hume. After dilating upon the uncertainty of foreign markets as opposed to a home market, Flood declared that in any trade treaty, 'that nation would have the advantage which was the poorest and the most abstemious'. 'Would not France,' therefore, 'with her wines, brandies, and olives, draw from us our specie in proportion to her wants and our own superiority in wealth?' 'As it was a fact', he continued, 'that the poorer nation would always drain from the richest in all commercial intercourses, France must ultimately diminish our specie and increase her own.' Spain, 'by neglecting protecting duties, had lost her trade, and ruined her finances', Flood warned. Furthermore, he added, 'two bordering countries can seldom supply each other with advantage'.[4] Another Whig, Powys, was also concerned lest 'a great part of the British capital' be 'transferred over to France'.[5] No one raised the question as to why Portugal had not drained Britain of specie after so many years of trading.

Edmund Burke's contribution to the argument did not revert to Hume's exploded view, as did Flood and Powys; Burke, rather, accepted Tucker's rebuttal to Hume—upon the general reasoning of which Pitt had based both his Irish and French proposals—and turned it down a surprising channel. 'Our capital gave us a superiority which enabled us to set all the efforts of France to rival our manufactures at defiance,' he declared; 'the powers of capital were irresistible in trade; it domineered, it ruled, it even tyrannized in the market; it enticed the strong, and controlled the weak'. This being so, Burke granted that England would gain the advantage from Pitt's treaty with France. However, England was being led down the garden path by Gallic subtlety; properly understood, 'we had reason to admire the depths of the designs of France'. Such a treaty would bring France to share these British resources of capital, and, indeed, 'an alliance in commercial

---

[1] *Ibid.* p. 473 (21 February 1787).   [2] *Ibid.* pp. 346–7 (5 February 1787).
[3] *Ibid.* p. 415 (12 February 1787).   [4] *Ibid.* pp. 430–4 (15 February 1787).
[5] *Ibid.* p. 445 (15 February 1787).

undertakings would soon blend the property of the two kingdoms'. France, consequently, 'was ready to put up with a temporary loss in trade', because of 'the superiority of our manufactures', in exchange 'for a permanent, future advantage in commerce'. The example of Holland demonstrated that 'commerce is more than a compensation for manufacture', and Germany provided an example that 'with manufactures a state may be plunged into the abyss of poverty'. This, then, was France's cunning scheme: 'through her rivers and canals she intended to pour the commodities of England into other countries'. France had 'already, by her politics, contrived to wrest our share of the Levant trade from us'. By the treaty of 1787, Burke concluded, France stood to gain 'political, naval, and commercial' advantages—'ours will consist only in the sale of manufactures'.[1]

Burke's exaltation of commerce over manufacturing set forth the conventional point of view of eighteenth-century Whiggery. Economic conditions were regarded as, relatively, static by most eighteenth-century economic theorists, who devoted themselves to describing exchanges of wealth, rather than, as was later to be the case, its production. Closely allied to this notion was that which saw commerce—that is, the role of the middle-man who profited by facilitating the exchange of the produce, whether agricultural or manufacturing, of one part of the world for that of another—as decidedly more remunerative than that of the actual production of goods. A commercial and maritime Holland had triumphed over the provinces of the Southern Netherlands, which had busied themselves with manufacturing, and the lesson had not been lost upon the formulators of economic policy.[2] In these early days of the Industrial Revolution, many Whigs, Burke among them—we must remember his arguments on colonial trade in 1774—were unable to understand the productive potentialities of the new steam-driven machinery which was making manufacturing *qualitatively* different from what it had previously been. The Whigs, generally, seemed prisoners of the position they had adopted in 1713. They represented the old commercial interests; the manufacturers were turning to the Tories.

No longer could Fox and Burke regard themselves, as they had in 1785, as spokesmen for a united manufacturing interest. Wedgwood, the leader of the agitation against the Irish bill, gave his full support to the Eden treaty. A tract by an anonymous 'Manchester manufacturer', addressed to Fox, outlined the difference which the events of recent years had made in England's position. 'Our manufactures are reared to maturity,' he wrote,

[1] *Parliamentary History*, XXVI, 487–9 (21 February 1787).
[2] See [J. R. McCulloch] 'Rise, Progress, and Decline of Commerce in Holland', *Edinburgh Review* LI, no. CII (July 1830), 418–43.

'and brought to a degree of perfection, that dreads no competition.' The Manchester manufacturer objected to Fox's concern 'for *the political, rather than the commercial consequence*' of the treaty. 'The Irish propositions, we conceived, had a tendency injurious to our trade'; the Whigs had opposed them, 'and gained the thanks of a grateful people'. But, the anonymous manufacturer concluded, 'the present Treaty is replete with advantages to us and to the nation at large'.[1] It should be noted that the rapidly expanding cotton industry of Lancashire which had consumed an average of about 2.81 million pounds of raw cotton annually in the 1750s, was in the 1780s to consume an annual average of about 15.51 million pounds; the average annual consumption of the decade 1795–1804 was to stand at 42.92 million pounds.

The most forceful attack upon the treaty in the House of Lords was made by the Whig Bishop of Llandaff, Dr Watson, who urged the peers not to abandon 'a commercial system, by which we had risen to our present height in the scale of nations'.[2] On a subsequent occasion, the Bishop asserted that 'it was by our machines, presses, dies, and tools, that the British manufacturers were enabled to baffle all competition with foreign markets, notwithstanding every disadvantage of high price of labour, high taxes', and so on. Now, despite all attempts to prevent the export of tools, France was copying them; furthermore, coal was likely to be found in France in plentiful quantities, once French forests gave out and a search was instituted. The French iron industry was already a competitor. The Eden treaty, the Bishop warned, 'incited the French nation to become a manufacturing nation', and were this to occur, given France's greater population, 'our ruin will be inevitable'.[3] Viscount Stormont, in support of Llandaff, raised the traditional cry against the treaty, and urged the government to look toward 'power' not 'profit'.[4] The answer to Stormont and Llandaff was given by Shelburne, now Marquis of Lansdowne, in a paean in behalf of free trade: 'A great minister in Holland first opened the eyes of modern Europe upon commercial subjects,' Lansdowne observed; 'men of letters in different countries contributed their aid to develop and extend the principles of free trade'. 'The old calculation, so much dwelt upon by the right reverend prelate, gradually became exploded; and the idea of estimating the balance of each trade was given up.' 'It was a proud thing,' Lansdowne concluded,

[1] *A Letter from a Manchester Manufacturer*, pp. 7–9, 14–15; one parliamentarian, William Young, argued that the treaty would extend French indebtedness to English finance, and would undermine France's commerce and navy. *Parliamentary History*, XXVI, 504 (21 February 1787).
[2] *Ibid.* p. 523 (23 February 1787).
[3] *Ibid.* pp. 544–6, 549–50 (1 March 1787).
[4] *Ibid.* p. 551 (1 March 1787).

'and gave a most immense idea of the trade and wealth of Britain, to see the manufacturers of this country agree to risk the home market—that ready-money market which they so much dwelt upon about the Irish propositions.'[1]

Lansdowne's adherence to the principle of free trade was maintained to the last. In the midst of the wars with Napoleon, in 1802, he wrote his friend Morellet that 'I have not changed an atom of the principles I first imbibed from you and Adam Smith. They make a woeful slow progress, but I cannot look upon them as extinct; on the contrary they must prevail in the end like the sea. What they lose in one place they gain in another.'[2] The revolution in France, and the wars which followed between a revolutionary France and England, had put an end to the plans of Pitt and of Lansdowne, Pitt's mentor, to liberalize English trade, as well as to many of Pitt's other schemes for reform. Only the objectives of Pitt's Irish proposals of 1785 were to be realized during his lifetime when, by the Act of Union of 1801, Ireland was joined with Great Britain to form the United Kingdom. But the faith of the adherents of the new liberal principles, although repressed by political circumstances, was passed on to a new generation of Pittites, who proved as hostile to the colonial system, and as perceptive of the immense possibilities, for England, of a trade empire erected upon England's industrial lead and a free trade, as Tucker and Pitt had been.

Henry Brougham

We cannot fail, at this point, to take into account a political economist, on his way to becoming a leading Liberal politician, who was to describe himself, in the years ahead, as the 'Apostle of Free Trade', Henry Brougham. Brougham, like Tucker and Smith, wished Great Britain to abolish certain commercial restrictions which he believed were highly disadvantageous to her trade; he regarded Adam Smith as his master, and, throughout his career, urged a freer trade policy. Born at Edinburgh, in 1778, he had studied for the bar at the University there; in 1802, he became a founder of the *Edinburgh Review*, writing many articles which—as in his noted review of a book by Lauderdale—gloried in exposing the 'exploded' doctrines of 'agrarian' economists in favor of a policy which saw Britain's greatness as dependent on an expanding commerce. Brougham was to make his parliamentary reputation as an opponent of the restrictive Orders-in-Council, during the Napoleonic Wars, and he was to serve as the counsel for the

---

[1] *Parliamentary History*, XXVI, 555 (1 March 1787).
[2] Quoted in Fitzmaurice, *Life of Shelburne*, II, 430–1; see also I, 18–19.

merchants petitioning against commercial restrictions in 1820.[1] However, if, as we have noted, some later free-trade economists were to be critical of Adam Smith because he had not more forcefully condemned mercantilist doctrines, Brougham, in his early and only book on political economy—the *Colonial Policy of European Nations*, published in 1803—inveighed, rather, against what he regarded as Smith's failure to appreciate fully the advantages of the colonial trade and of the colonial monopoly. In so doing, he anticipated the view—very different from that of Tucker and Smith—that the new developments in the British economy had made colonies a necessity for England, thus constituting, in his advocacy both of a Free Trade Empire and of colonies, a link between mercantilism and the later followers of Wakefield.

Brougham was especially critical of Smith's view that the colonial trade was less profitable than other trades because the great distances involved occasioned fewer turnovers of capital; although 'another trade might give quicker returns and employ more British labour', he observed, it did not follow that, by giving up the Baltic trade, for example, England would find 'another source, from whence the same commodities might be obtained, or another market to take off her surplus produce'. The 'metropolis' was 'always a creditor to the country', Brougham declared, and 'a rich to a poor trading nation, in the same manner as the mother country is to the colonies'. The world was hardly so full of commercial opportunities, he argued, that the colonial trade should be yielded upon academic grounds. Indeed, 'long credits' and 'slow returns' were 'the necessary consequences of great national wealth'.[2] 'The richer stockholders naturally resort to the colony trade, of which they possess a kind of monopoly,' and they did not object to the lessened turnover when it was accompanied by commensurably larger profits.[3] Holland had already experienced the 'effects of an overflowing capital'; 'the wealth of Great Britain appears, from several symptoms, to be arriving at the same state of overgrown magnificence; and, of course, to require more and more the outlet of new colonies'. In proof, Brougham cited the huge British investments in Dutch colonies during the brief period 'of the late war that they remained in our power'. Why then should such capitals be even partially devoted 'to enrich foreign nations'?[4]

Brougham anticipated almost all of the arguments which subsequent theorists and advocates of colonization would put forward. The colonies, he noted, provided the type of market which a rapidly expanding British

[1] See C. W. New, *The Life of Henry Brougham to 1830* (Oxford: Clarendon Press, 1961), *passim*.
[2] Brougham, *Inquiry into Colonial Policy*, I, 168–73; see also pp. 201–3, 209–10.
[3] *Ibid.* pp. 194–8.   [4] *Ibid.* p. 214–15.

industry required, a market which 'continually and rapidly increases', a market in a 'progressive state'. Colonies provided opportunities for laborers from the mother country—the 'overflowing, or rotten part of the state's population' had 'found a vent in the distant parts of the empire'—and for members of the middle classes who had found it difficult to maintain their status in the older, less fluid society at home.[1] (It was 'so very absurd a prejudice', Brougham declared, to think that colonies were a 'drain' upon the population of the mother country, when there existed so considerable an excess of persons in Britain.)[2] This benefit of colonies had been enormously supplemented by their usefulness for the investment of 'superabundant' capital. There was a new and pressing need to increase 'the lines of employment for stock', i.e. capital, to keep pace with the constantly increasing stock, or 'profits are diminished'. 'The settlement of a new country opens new sources of profit,' he observed, 'creates an issue for capital which was ill employed.' Colonies provided 'greater safety' for investments than did foreign lands.[3] Without colonies, 'overflowing' Englishmen and 'superabundant' capital would simply emigrate to foreign countries or foreign colonies, though hardly as advantageously. The ancient world had seen many colonies established from 'overflowing' populations, Brougham observed; the modern world alone had reached 'such a pitch of wealth, as to give rise to an overflowing capital' as well.[4]

Brougham opposed bounties and exclusive privileges for individuals or companies and declared that the 'monopoly is prejudicial' to the mother country, but, he insisted, 'much less so than has generally been imagined'.[5] Brougham felt that discouragements to manufacturing in the colonies, for example, were rather 'superfluous' since agriculture was a more profitable colonial pursuit,[6] and the ever-expanding needs of the colonies for capital would keep the rate of profit on colonial stock higher than at home. It was therefore not the monopolies and restrictions of the old colonial system, as Smith had alleged, which had determined the flow of capital to colonial areas: as proof of this contention, he noted that after American independence, 'in spite of free trade', more British capital was poured into the American trade.[7] 'After an entire freedom of trade,' Brougham concluded, 'the larger capitals, then, of any country, will generally find their way to the colonies in preference to the home market, or the nearer foreign markets, and to the colonies of that country in preference to the foreign colonies.'[8]

[1] Brougham, *Inquiry into Colonial Policy*, I, 159–60, 213; see also pp. 148–50.
[2] *Ibid.* p. 167.   [3] *Ibid.* pp. 217–18, 159–62.
[4] *Ibid.* pp. 217–18, 222.   [5] *Ibid.* pp. 224, 249–50, 239; see also pp. 233, 236.
[6] *Ibid.* p. 240.   [7] *Ibid.* p. 263; see also pp. 259, 256.
[8] *Ibid.* p. 260.

Brougham listed the qualities which made for imperial power—'capital, industry, and marine'.[1] If there were no trade restrictions, Brougham believed that there was a 'connexion between the whole three, which renders it certain that a nation will obtain the superiority in all'. Indeed, he was convinced that Great Britain had already secured 'a general superiority in all three circumstances'.[2] Britain possessed, moreover, more of those capitals which were especially 'fitted for the colony trade'—that is, large capitals in the hands of a few, rather than a wider distribution of smaller capitals. British commodities were 'better and cheaper', as a result of 'the greater extent of manufacturing capital, and the superior skill or industry of its workmen'. Britain, finally, possessed 'the greatest number of good dock-yards, and ships-carpenters, and the largest body of skilful seamen', which would thereby 'be able to afford carrying on the trade of supplying the colonies at a smaller expence of freight, and somewhat smaller charge of insurance, than any other nation'. Brougham, like Smith, favored the navigation laws.[3]

If, like Tucker and Smith, Brougham saw England as having arrived at that stage of economic development where a free trade was the most useful policy, and was even to retain—because of his acceptance of the view of glut (Brougham's 'overflowing capital') common to both mercantilist and physiocratic economics—a favorable view of colonies, there were to be others who would reject such an outlook, root and branch. These economists, like Hume, Flood, Burke, and the Bishop of Llandaff, saw inevitable foreign competition making Tucker's dream impossible. However, these scoffers were not Whigs maintaining the traditional outlook and prejudices of the merchant class, but were, rather, economists devoted to the agricultural system. They were the agrarian opponents of mercantilism who saw an economy based upon a growing dependence on commerce and industry as one possessing inner contradictions of an almost insuperable character, and, consequently, making necessary a return, unprofitable in the long run, to the mercantilistic imperialism of the seventeenth and eighteenth centuries. Denouncing the growing devotion to commercial pursuits, they urged England to return to the land as the true source of all riches.

[1] *Ibid.* p. 271.   [2] *Ibid.* pp. 270–1.   [3] *Ibid.* pp. 266–8.

CHAPTER 3

The agrarian critique and the emergence of orthodoxy

'A T present I feel a very great difficulty, for I confess I do not very clearly perceive what Mr Malthus' system is,' wrote Ricardo to McCulloch in May 1820, shortly after the publication of Malthus' *Principles of Political Economy*, in the course of discussing Malthus' special view 'on the benefits resulting from foreign trade'. Earlier in this letter, Ricardo observed that 'I am surprised that rent should be still spoken of as a surplus produce, differing in that respect from the produce of manufactures.' Ricardo was also unhappy about Malthus' views on the subject of value, and was especially disturbed by Malthus' opinions 'on the bad effects from too great accumulation of capital and the consequent want of demand for the goods produced';[1] in a later letter, this time to Malthus himself, Ricardo declared that 'the great and leading point in which I think you fundamentally wrong is that which Say has attacked in his letters',[2] i.e., Malthus' rejection of Say's Law asserting the impossibility of general glut. These grounds of difference between Malthus and Ricardo during the early years of the founding of classical political economy are well known. What has been largely forgotten is the answer to Ricardo's initial question. We must try to complete the rediscovery of what was understood by a number of Malthus' contemporaries, especially in France, the 'system' upon which most of the doctrines which separated Malthus from classical orthodoxy—his suspicions of foreign trade, his denial of the efficacy of Say's Law, his special view of value and of rent—were based.

More important for our purposes, we will show how Malthus erected a full-scale critique of the commercial and industrial order upon this 'system'. Malthus hoped, by displaying what his analysis revealed as the inner contradictions of such an order, to demonstrate that a trade empire based upon an industrial predominance was not viable, and thus to slow down industrial growth, and to prevent the destruction of British agriculture. Malthus'

[1] Piero Sraffa, ed., *The Works and Correspondence of David Ricardo* (Cambridge, 1952), VIII, 181–3.
[2] *Ibid.* p. 229.

opponents—supporters of industrial growth like Ricardo and James Mill—were to construct the foundations of what was to become the orthodox school of political economy in conscious opposition to the 'system' espoused by Malthus and other agrarian economists. In the process, the new economic orthodoxy was to elaborate upon the arguments of Tucker and Pitt, so as to fit them for the new conditions in which England found herself in the first two decades of the nineteenth century, and to extend the grounds upon which the theorists of the earlier generation had seen trade empire as useful to Great Britain.

The last decades of the eighteenth century and the first decades of the nineteenth were a time of transition, a time when the chief 'schools' of political economy were testing their leading—frequently, conflicting—doctrines against each other. Most economists, in eclectic fashion, borrowed concepts from more than one of the 'schools' in the formulation of their individual systems. Although Smith's debt to physiocracy has many times been commented upon, it has been forgotten just how influential the opinions of the school of Quesnay were during this period, for there were economists who refrained from making formal acknowledgements to Quesnay or to his disciples—sometimes specifically disowning the 'exploded' doctrine of the physiocrats which was associated with the excesses of the French Revolution—but whose ideas were almost precisely the same as those of the French economists. Some, indeed, had not even read the Economists, as the physiocrats were then called, in any depth, while others had built their systems primarily upon earlier English thought; they had all, however, come to strikingly similar conclusions because they shared a common lodestar—the concern for the prosperity of the agricultural classes. Among these economists of an agrarian bent were William Spence, the only one to acknowledge himself a disciple of the physiocrats, Thomas Chalmers, Dugald Stewart, and, of course, Malthus. None can be described as rigidly doctrinaire, but all owed a great deal to physiocracy not only in such matters as the theory of value, for example, or the single tax, but more particularly in their attitude toward colonies and foreign trade, and toward the commercial system, generally. They all shared the gravest doubts as to whether an England which sought to base its economy not upon the land but upon commerce, and, more significantly, upon foreign commerce, could survive disaster.

Malthus' early critique of the commercial system

Thomas Robert Malthus was born near Guildford, Surrey, in 1766, the son of Daniel Malthus, a correspondent of Voltaire, a literary executor of

Rousseau, whom he had befriended in the course of the latter's visit to England, and an admirer of the systems elaborated by the *philosophes* of contemporary France. Daniel Malthus undertook the early education of his son, in the fashion of *Émile*, but the boy soon enjoyed more conventional training at the hands of the noted Gilbert Wakefield, and at Jesus College, Cambridge. In 1798, he took orders as a clergyman of the Church of England, and in that same year he published his *Essay on Population* which secured for him, in 1805, the first English chair in political economy, that of the East India Company's College at Haileybury. In his *Essay*, as is well known, the young curate, conscious of the doom of original sin, reacted against the optimistic views of human perfectibility so stoutly defended by his father, who had followed the main line of eighteenth-century French thought climaxed by Condorcet in France and by Godwin in England; but in rejecting one school of *philosophes*, he was to embrace another.

Malthus can perhaps best be described as an agrarian economist, not a doctrinaire physiocrat. But since the physiocrats had worked out virtually all the theoretical implications of an economic system based upon the land, an able agrarian economist could not help but be heavily in their debt. The evidence for Malthus' early adherence to a quasi-physiocracy lies largely in the first two editions of the *Essay on Population*, those of 1798 and 1803, in chapters which were to be substantially altered in subsequent editions; consequently, what was clear to contemporaries was to be largely forgotten. One contemporary, William Spence, an avowed physiocrat who had frequent recourse to quotations from Malthus in defense of his own opinions, was to declare, indeed, 'that nearly all the main tenets of the Economists have been embraced and defended by Mr Malthus',[1] and this judgment was not wide of the mark. The close ties between Malthus and physiocracy were noted in the last century, by the editors of French translations of his two major works,[2]

---

[1] William Spence, *Agriculture The Source of the Wealth of Britain* (London, 1808), pp. 24–5, 27, 36–40, 59–60, 108.

[2] See T. R. Malthus, *Essai sur le principe de population* (Paris, 1845); the original translation, with extensive notes, was made by P. and G. Prévost in 1809, and this translation and these notes were reproduced in the 1845 edition brought out by P. Rossi and Charles Comte. See vol. 1, p. 644: 'Des différents systèmes qui ont été soutenus relativement au fondements de la richesse nationale, il y en a peu qui s'accorde mieux avec la théorie du principe de population, que celui des philosophes connus en France sous le nom d'*économistes* . . . comme ils excitaient à sacrifier tout à la culture, à se mettre en état d'exporter les aliments, en particulier le blé . . .' Malthus was depicted as the superior of the Economists in having added to their theory the principle of population: 'Il était donc bien nécessaire d'ajouter, comme l'a fait M. Malthus, cette grande maxime à toutes celles des économistes: ABSTENEZ-VOUS DE MULTIPLIER AU-DELÀ DE VOS MOYENS DE SUBSISTANCE.' (p. 646). See also T. R. Malthus, *Principes d'économie politique considérés sous le rapport de leur application practique* (Paris, 1846); edited with notes by Maurice Monjean. Monjean, in his preface, p. 2 f.n., wrote that 'Malthus avait fait une étude approfondie des doctrines' of the physiocrats, adding, on p. 33 f.n., that 'le système que soutient Malthus a plus

by his biographer, Bonar,[1] and by more recent students.[2] Curiously, Malthus was not aware, in 1798, that the Economists had anticipated him in the view that the means of subsistence limited population; by the time he was ready with a much expanded second edition in 1803, he had learned of physiocratic theories of population,[3] but in 1798 he had already accepted other aspects of physiocracy, and not unnaturally, since these were quite harmonious with his theory of population, and, logically, a part of the same system. The physiocratic bent of the second edition of the *Essay* was even more pronounced.

While it would have been difficult for an Englishman, whose country was advancing in commerce and manufacturing, to enter into the view that such pursuits were entirely unproductive—in this matter Malthus preferred the position of Adam Smith—on many important questions he upheld the physiocrats against Smith. For example, Malthus, in contrasting Smith's concept of wealth as material goods with the physiocrats' view of wealth as exclusively derived from the land, maintained that the condition of the laboring poor might not at all be materially improved by the increase of 'wealth' in Smith's sense of the term, although it most certainly would be if that 'wealth' conformed to the meaning of the French Economists. If one nation 'applied itself chiefly to agriculture, and the other chiefly to commerce, the funds for the maintenance of labour, and consequently the effect of the increase of wealth in each nation, would be extremely different': in the agricultural nation, 'the poor would live in great plenty', while in the commercial nation, 'the poor would be comparatively but little benefited'.[4] 'The French Oeconomists', Malthus continued, 'consider all labour

d'un rapport avec celui des Économistes du XVIIIe siècle...' See also p. 526 f.n. [In the translation of Malthus' Definitions attached to the volume of the *Principes*, Monjean added that Malthus 'est de tous les économistes anglais, si l'on en excepte Adam Smith, celui qui a le mieux connu les Physiocrates, auxquels il se rattache étroitement par ses doctrines sur la nature de richesse, le travail productif et la production territoriale' (p. 416 f.n.). Yet Monjean did perceive that there were important differences between the doctrines of Malthus and those of physiocracy (p. 526 f.n.).

[1] James Bonar, *Malthus and His Work* (New York: Macmillan, 1924), pp. 247–8; see also Sir Leslie Stephen, *The English Utilitarians* (London: Duckworth, 1900), II, 181–2, 244.

[2] See Ronald L. Meek, 'Physiocracy and the Early Theories of Under-Consumption', in *Economica* XVIII, no. 71 (August 1951), 229–69. Meek asserted that 'Book Three of the second edition of the *Essay on Population* contained, indeed, some of the most Physiocratic passages which had appeared in British economic writing since Cantillon' (pp. 250–51). See also Mark Blaug, *Ricardian Economics, A Historical Study* (New Haven: Yale University Press, 1958), pp. 94–7. (Meek's article also appears in R. L. Meek, *The Economics of Physiocracy* (London: Allen & Unwin, 1962).)

[3] T. R. Malthus, *An Essay on the Principle of Population* (London, 1803—Second Edition), pp. iii–iv.

[4] T. R. Malthus, *An Essay on the Principle of Population* (London, 1798—First Edition), pp. 325–6; see also pp. 323, 329, 335.

employed in manufactures as unproductive. Comparing it with the labour employed upon land, I should be perfectly disposed to agree with them.'[1] But while the Economists had argued that the land alone provided a surplus above wages of labor and profits on capital, Malthus believed that manufactures could also provide such a surplus. However, though 'a capital employed upon land, may be unproductive to the individual that employs it', it might 'yet be highly productive to society'. It was for this reason that Malthus regarded 'manufacturing labour unproductive, in comparison of that which is employed in agriculture'. The manufacturer could promote his own interest and profit, without adding 'to any essential part of the riches of the state'. An agricultural laborer working under conditions in which the returns for his labor 'so far from affording a rent to a third person, would but half replace the provisions used in obtaining the produce', would still be more productive than an artisan who worked to 'gratify the vanity of a few rich people'.[2] In all this, Malthus revealed himself more fundamentally agrarian in bias than the physiocrats—who would certainly not have accepted his argument concerning farming at a loss.

The second edition of Malthus' *Essay* was more consciously physiocratic than the first. Land, declared Malthus in this new edition, was 'incontrovertibly the sole source of all riches'; 'the great position of the Economists will always remain true, that the surplus produce of the cultivators is the great fund which ultimately pays all those who are not employed upon the land'.[3] The English were 'so blinded by the shewiness of commerce and manufactures, as to believe that they are almost the sole cause of the wealth, power, and prosperity' of their country, while in reality they were simply the consequences of England's superior agriculture.[4] Manufactures were 'no new production, no new creation', but a 'modification of an old one, and when sold must be paid for out of a revenue already in existence, and consequently the gain of the seller is the loss of the buyer. A revenue is transferred, but not created.' Because of monopolies and 'superior machinery', manufactures were generally sold at a price above 'their real worth'.[5]

Upon this physiocratic groundwork, Malthus proceeded to mount a critique of the direction in which the British economy was being urged by

---

[1] Malthus, *Essay on Population* (1798 edition), p. 329.
[2] *Ibid.* pp. 331–3; see also pp. 334, 336.
[3] Malthus, *Essay on Population* (1803 edition), pp. 434–6. For a similar statement, see T. R. Malthus, *An Inquiry into the Nature and Progress of Rent, and the Principles by which It is Regulated* (London, 1815), pp. 16–17.
[4] Malthus, *Essay on Population* (1803 edition), pp. 437–8.
[5] *Ibid.* pp. 433–4.

the commercial and industrial classes. A passage in the 1798 edition of the *Essay* contrasted the differing views of foreign trade of the Economists and of Adam Smith, and favored the former.[1] For Malthus, as for the physiocrats, in so far as foreign trade brought benefits, they were largely exploitative in character, and, moreover, Malthus found such benefits perilously ephemeral. A commercial and industrial society was built upon quicksand because 'monopolies are always subject to be broken; and even the advantage of capital and machinery, which may yield extraordinary profits for a time, is liable to be greatly lessened by the competition of other nations', Malthus observed. The turning of capital away from agriculture would raise the price of corn, and consequently of labor, to a 'prodigious' extent, and this would 'ultimately check all our dealings with foreign powers', and give a 'fatal blow to our commerce and manufactures'. In what seemed a curious repetition and elaboration of Hume's rebuttal of half a century earlier, Malthus admitted that 'the effect of capital, skill, machinery, and establishments, in their full vigour, is great; so great, indeed, that it is difficult to guess at its limit; but still it is not infinite, and without doubt has this limit'. The war with revolutionary France had given British trade a temporary trade monopoly, and, consequently, high profits 'in spite of the high price of labour'. However, he warned, 'when the other nations of Europe shall have had time to recover themselves, and gradually to become our competitors, it would be rash to affirm, that, with the prices of provisions and of labour still going on increasing, from what they are at present, we shall be able to stand the competition'. 'Have we not some reason to fear', he added, that England's commercial prosperity was not only temporary, but 'belongs a little to that worst feature of the commercial system, the rising by the depression of others'.[2]

The 'commercial system' was to be shunned not only because of its immoral and parasitic character, but also because it sapped the vitals of national well-being. High commercial profits had a most unfavourable effect upon 'the increase of that more essential and permanent source of wealth, the improvement of the land'. The national debt, by providing a ready market for redundant capital, and thereby keeping up the rate of interest, had 'prevented this capital from overflowing upon the soil'; moreover, through the means of the debt, a mortgage had been established upon the lands, the interest of which was 'drawn from the payment of productive labour and dedicated to the support of idle consumers'. Commerce, Malthus insisted, had not done much for agriculture, but agriculture

---

[1] Malthus, *Essay on Population* (1798 edition), p. 336.
[2] Malthus, *Essay on Population* (1803 edition), pp. 443–5, 437.

had done 'a great deal' for commerce, for it had been the improved cultivation of the land, despite great discouragements, which had created the necessary 'surplus produce' which enabled the nation 'to support so vast a body of people engaged in pursuits unconnected with the land'.[1]

'About the middle of the last century,' Malthus wrote, 'we were genuinely, and in the strict sense of the Economists, an agricultural nation.' Commerce and manufactures were 'then in a very respectable and thriving state; and if they had continued to bear the same relative proportion to our agriculture, they would evidently have gone on increasing considerably, with the improving cultivation of the country'. This would have been a wholly desirable progress: 'There is no discoverable germ of decay' in such a system. Now, however, England had entered a state in which 'the commercial system clearly predominates', and as a result there was 'but too much reason to fear' that this imperilled even commerce and manufacturing.[2] It was a 'very great error to suppose that their [the physiocratic] system is really unfavourable' to commerce and manufacturing, he declared. 'On the contrary, I am disposed to believe that it is the only system' by which these pursuits 'can prevail to a very great extent, without bringing with them, at the same time, the seeds of their own ruin'.[3] Malthus' apocalyptic vision of the fate of the 'commercial system' resembled Marx's vision of the destiny of capitalist development, but whereas Marx saw the Last Judgment and the proletarian meek inheriting the earth, Malthus fixed his gaze upon the Four Horsemen.

Dugald Stewart

Dugald Stewart, born at Edinburgh, in 1753, the successor of Adam Ferguson to the chair of moral philosophy at the University of Edinburgh, may be regarded as one of Malthus' earliest disciples, and, of course, one of the disciples of the physiocrats as well. For some years, beginning in 1800, he gave a special course of lectures in political economy, lectures which greatly influenced the views of such subsequent advocates of agricultural protection as the Earl of Lauderdale and the historian Archibald Alison, who were among Stewart's students and, indeed, disciples, as were both Jeffrey and Horner, who were to establish the *Edinburgh Review*.[4]

Dugald Stewart had been Adam Smith's friend and biographer, yet his economics, like Malthus', as Stewart's admiring biographer observed,

---

[1] Malthus, *Essay on Population* (1803 edition), pp. 438–42.   [2] *Ibid.* pp. 443–5.   [3] *Ibid.* p. 437.
[4] John Veitch, *Memoir of Dugald Stewart*, in Sir William Hamilton, ed., *The Collected Works of Dugald Stewart* (Edinburgh, 1855), x, li–lv.

displayed 'a leaning, in more than one instance, to the views of the Economists, when these do not precisely coincide with the opinions of Smith'.[1] Stewart was also a vigorous advocate of Malthusian population theory, and he understood that the principles of population, based as they were upon the primacy of agriculture,[2] 'coincide, in most essential respects, with the system of the Economists and of Quesnai'.[3] Stewart repeatedly urged the study of the writings of Quesnay, Turgot, and Mirabeau, declaring their theory much superior to that of Smith.[4] In physiocratic—and Malthusian—manner (his debt to Malthus is everywhere evident), Stewart called into question a 'system of policy which has considered manufactures and commerce as *ultimate* objects, instead of regarding them in their due *subserviency* to agricultural improvement', criticizing, in the process, in virtual paraphrase of Malthus, Smith's view of national wealth in favor of 'that of the French economists, who measure it by *rude produce*';[5] on the issue of whether manufacturing and commerce were 'unproductive', he asserted that 'I must confess, the advantage seems to me to be on the side of the Economists';[6] in opposition to Adam Smith, Stewart defended the primacy of the landowner in the process of the circulation of wealth, along the lines of Turgot and Quesnay, and consequently maintained what were to become heterodox views on questions such as expenditure and glut;[7] finally, in opposition to Smith, he urged that the exportation of grain be encouraged by a bounty, which, he noted, 'is highly extolled by the French Economists'.

Adam Smith had argued too much 'on abstract principles', Stewart declared, and Malthus, in his *Essay on Population*, 'has clearly pointed out more than one vulnerable part of Mr Smith's argument'. Stewart, like Malthus, was convinced that the example of Holland, a purely commercial country, could not be followed by Great Britain. 'I agree with the general doctrines of this sect [the physiocrats] so far', he observed, 'as to feel it incumbent on me to remark, that in a great agricultural country such as ours', we must 'advance to the utmost possible extent our independent agricultural resources'. Like Malthus, as well, as we shall see, Stewart urged the imposition of a tariff on corn imports to encourage British agriculture.[8]

---

[1] *Ibid.* x, xlix, li–lv.
[2] *Works of Stewart*, VIII, 11, 201.
[3] *Ibid.* VIII, 208; see 59–252, *passim*.
[4] *Ibid.* VIII, 289, 306.
[5] *Ibid.* VIII, 252.
[6] *Ibid.* VIII, 273; see also pp. 277, 283.
[7] *Ibid.* VIII, 255–7.
[8] *Ibid.* IX, 114–15, 118–20; VIII, 284.

The Spence–Mill debate of 1808

William Spence, a young man who was subsequently to make his mark as an entomologist, became the central figure in a noteworthy controversy when, in 1808, he published his *Britain Independent of Commerce*, a tract which presented the views of the French physiocrats on a variety of questions, particularly on trade. Spence's theme was that England was not dependent upon foreign trade for prosperity—that a nation's real wealth consisted in the cultivation of its own soil. The tract proved enormously popular with Englishmen whose trade was then hampered by Napoleon's continental system; it went through four editions in the year of its publication. The tract was highly praised by *Cobbett's Register*, to the cry of 'Perish Commerce',[1] and denounced by the *Edinburgh Review*.[2] McCulloch, in discussing the pamphlet in later years, scored the public's readiness 'to lend a willing ear to the wildest paradoxes'—i.e., the 'exaggeration of the exploded errors of the Economists'.[3] During the months immediately following the publication of *Britain, Independent of Commerce*, nearly three dozen books and pamphlets poured from the presses, either supporting the Spence thesis or opposing it. Among them were fledgling efforts of James Mill, Thomas Chalmers, and Robert Torrens, with Mill's essay being the most thorough-going critique.

Spence founded his economic system upon a curious *mélange* of views, but he spoke of himself, and was generally regarded, as a disciple of the French 'Economists'. As such he denounced what he believed to be the absurd opinions concerning trade held by his fellow countrymen. 'Though

---

[1] See M. L. Pearl, *William Cobbett* (Oxford: Oxford University Press, 1953), pp. 84–5.

[2] 'Spence on Commerce', *Edinburgh Review* XI, no. XXII (January 1808), 429–48. F. W. Fetter in his 'The Authorship of Economic Articles in the Edinburgh Review, 1802–47', in *Journal of Political Economy* LXI, no. 3 (June 1953), 246, attributes this to 'T. R. Malthus (probably)', basing his opinion upon a reference in a letter from Horner to Jeffrey, which, however, Fetter grants might well refer to a Malthus article of July 1808. It seems to be more probable that Malthus did not write the article on Spence. Many of Spence's views were too congenial to Malthus to have received such a drubbing from him; indeed, in Spence's reply to the *Review*'s article, Spence quoted at length from Malthus' writings for support against the *Review*. See Spence, *Agriculture the Source, passim*. Who, then, again 'probably', wrote the article? A subsequent article on Spence was the work of Jeffrey, and, of course, he emerges as a possibility. However, this second article does not reveal the economic sophistication of the first, and Jeffrey, although he tried his hand at economic articles, was rather a novice in such matters. The January 1808 article is probably the work of Brougham, who reviewed frequently for the *Edinburgh* during this period, and had previously been employed in the writing of polemical reviews—as in the case of his article on Lauderdale in 1804. ('Lord Lauderdale on Public Wealth', *Edinburgh Review* IV, no. VIII, 343–77.) It was written in Brougham's style—the style of the Lauderdale review; certain forms of thought and terminology—on such questions as colonies, the 'middle doctrine' of Smith, and so on—resemble Brougham not Malthus. See Bernard Semmel, ed., *Occasional Papers of T. R. Malthus* (New York: Burt Franklin, 1963), pp. 14–15.

[3] J. R. McCulloch, *The Literature of Political Economy* (London, 1845), p. 56.

Europe and America, Asia and Africa, were to resolve never more to use an article of British manufacture,' Spence declared, 'still this favoured isle has the means within herself, not merely of retaining the high rank which she possesses, but of progressively going on in her career of prosperity and of power.'[1] This was a good thing, for although, at the moment, Britain had, 'from the amount of our capital, and the excellence of our machinery', the 'power of underselling all competitors in the foreign market', she could not long 'retain this superiority'. Britain's advantages were 'already counterbalanced by the high wages of labour';[2] furthermore, 'it is impossible that we should be able to keep secret the construction of any large machine'. France and Germany, consequently, would soon manufacture for themselves.[3] But, Spence concluded, 'the diminution of our commerce' was 'a matter of perfect indifference to us';[4] equally unimportant to Britain would be the loss of her colonies. Spence, in the manner of the Economists, looked to home commerce not foreign commerce as the true source of riches,[5] and set forth an autarchic goal, concluding that 'though Britain . . . were surrounded with a wall of brass, ten thousand cubits in height, still she would as far excel the rest of the nations of the globe in riches, as she now does'.[6]

Running through Spence's tract was a second argument, also derived from the physiocrats. Not only would high wages and the impossibility of maintaining a monopoly of machinery undermine the effort, so well regarded by many Englishmen, to create a wide trading system based upon British industrial predominance, there was a more pressing flaw: glut of goods and glut of capital. British superiority in capital resources would be rapidly diminished, Spence warned, for 'when capital is at all acquired, it rapidly accumulates'. Indeed, if British capital increased at the same rate as that of her rivals, the fact of this accumulation would reduce the profits of stock 'so low' that 'we should be willing to lend it, as the Dutch did, to any other nations, which, in consequence of the cheapness of labour, could afford to give more for it'.[7] Malthus had noted this flaw in passing, but was not to address himself fully to the subject until after 1815. Spence praised the national debt as a useful method of draining off surplus capital.[8]

---

[1] William Spence, *Britain Independent of Commerce* (London, 1808), p. 4; see also pp. 1–2.
[2] *Ibid.* p. 69.   [3] *Ibid.* p. 75.   [4] *Ibid.* pp. 76, 78–80.
[5] *Ibid.* pp. 56–7, 66. Malthus' view concerning the comparative lack of importance of foreign trade was, of course, like Spence's. See, in addition, T. R. Malthus, *The Grounds of an Opinion on the Policy of Restricting the Importation of Foreign Corn* (London, 1815), pp. 29, 32–3, and passim.
[6] Spence, *Britain Independent of Commerce*, p. 85.
[7] *Ibid.* p. 75.   [8] *Ibid.* pp. 27–32.

In his reply to Spence, in 1808, James Mill, a Scotsman educated for the ministry, who was at work upon a *History of India*, not only denied the inevitability of glut, he also refuted the physiocratic view of the uselessness of foreign commerce. Mill's *Commerce Defended*, indeed, was to become one of the essential tracts of the emerging orthodoxy. Following Jean-Baptiste Say's statement of the law of markets in 1803, Mill observed that 'every country will infallibly consume to the full amount of its production',[1] adding that 'the production of commodities creates, and is the one and universal cause which creates a market for the commodities produced'.[2] The Say–Mill law, a proclamation of confidence in the harmonious, virtually automatic operation of the new industrial order, was to become a stronghold of classical economics. Mill's restatement, in this tract, of the Turgot–Smith view that unproductive expenditure was unmitigated evil, and his urging that expenditure for the sake of further production was the only means by which the accumulation of capital, upon which the welfare of society depended, might be effectively promoted was to become another doctrinal pillar of orthodoxy. Mill, on these grounds, opposed Spence's support of a national debt,[3] asserting the impossibility of having too much capital: 'the augmentation of capital', he declared, was of 'extraordinary importance to every community', and 'our humanity as well as our patriotism, will become deeply interested in the doctrine of parsimony'.[4]

Mill also criticized Spence's definition of wealth, and, of course, his view of foreign trade.[5] He bemoaned 'the propensity of mankind to run from one extreme to another', from a mercantilism which believed wealth obtainable only from foreign trade to a physiocracy which, denying this, established exclusive wealth-creating powers in the land; he wished 'to rest in the wise and salutary middle'.[6] Spence, like the French Economists, had held, Mill wrote, that 'nothing is useful or valuable to man but the bare necessaries of life, or rather the raw produce of the soil'. It was to the manufacturers, however, Mill argued, to 'that division of labour which set them apart as a distinct class', that the 'augmentation of riches' so apparent to all Englishmen was 'entirely owing'.[7] Faithful to Say's Law, Mill observed that foreign commerce was 'in all cases a matter of expediency rather than of necessity'—it was not necessary 'to furnish a vent for the produce of the industry of the country, because that industry always furnished a vent for

---

[1] James Mill, *Commerce Defended* (London, 1808), p. 79.
[2] *Ibid.* p. 81; see pp. 81–4.   [3] *Ibid.* p. 90.
[4] *Ibid.* p. 86–7.   [5] *Ibid.* pp. 17–24.
[6] *Ibid.* p. 14.   [7] *Ibid.* pp. 28–9.

itself'.[1] But, for Mill, foreign commerce made possible the cheap and liberal supply of commodities, without which the British standard of living would be significantly depressed.[2] Mill agreed that British commerce had not been endangered by the Napoleonic blockade, but only because England could still turn to the United States, to the West Indies, to South America, to Africa, and to India: 'While Britain is mistress of the sea,' he wrote, 'she might have scope for a boundless commerce, though the whole continent of Europe were swallowed up by an earthquake.'[3] (It might be useful to recall that although about four-fifths of English exports had had a European destination in 1700, while only one-fifth went to other parts of the world, by 1800, largely because of the steadily growing protection of continental markets, the proportions were reversed.)

In this tract, Mill presented a theory of the territorial division of labor, which hinted at the principle of comparative cost. To Spence's suggestion that the commerce of import was simply an exchange of equal values, Mill replied that what made the country rich was not the sale of the goods at home, but their purchase abroad 'with a quantity of British goods of less value'.[4] Speaking in more general terms, Mill declared that when other nations were 'so situated that certain articles which England affords bear in them a very high price, while many other articles in them which England wants bear a very low price, it suits England to manufacture a great deal for foreign markets, because, with a small quantity of what she produces, she can supply herself with a great quantity of what they produce'.[5] Mill did agree with Spence that commerce was not worth the wars waged on its behalf, and that it was strictly subordinate to agriculture and to manufacturing for the home trade.[6]

In replying to his critics, Spence was to single out Mill, since he had found him 'more versed in Political Economy than the majority', as his principal antagonist.[7] Spence could not, of course, accept Mill's optimism concerning British commercial opportunities in America, Africa, and Asia. The East India Company, Spence reminded Mill, had had to use specie in its trading since the Indians did not wish to purchase British products; and the wages of Indian labor were so low that the Indians could 'undersell us in every one of our staple manufactures'. Unless England were determined to destroy the handicrafts of the Orient, Spence inquired prophetically, how could she 'send earthen ware to the Chinese; or manufactured cotton and

---

[1] *Ibid.* p. 86. [2] *Ibid.* pp. 107–8, 115–16.
[3] *Ibid.* p. 9. [4] *Ibid.* pp. 35–9; 33.
[5] *Ibid.* p. 116. [6] *Ibid.* pp. 107–8, 115–16.
[7] Spence, *Agriculture The Source*, p. 4.

muslins to the Hindoos'?[1] In concluding, Spence noted that, given Mill's view of the 'falsity of the mercantile system, and of the inferiority of commerce when compared with agriculture', a reader might see no reason for him 'to controvert the arguments of a work in whose conclusions he so nearly acquiesced'.[2]

In truth, of course, despite its repeated denunciations of mercantile principles and practice, the emergent orthodoxy *was* less hostile to the objectives and to the methods of the old commercial system than was physiocracy, as another of Spence's opponents at this time, Robert Torrens, was to display forcefully.

Robert Torrens' vision of Trade-Empire: 1808 and 1815

Robert Torrens was on duty as a captain of marines when, in 1808, he wrote *The Economists Refuted*[3] in reply to Spence's pamphlet. Although there was a hint of the new dispensation in Torrens' view that 'when our surplus labour and capital are employed to supply, indirectly, [through trade] the articles adapted to the soil and climate of other countries, we obtain such articles in greater abundance than if our labour and capital were employed to supply them directly', the remainder of Torrens' 1808 tract was decidedly mercantilist in tone. While he took care, for example, to deny the special value attached by mercantilism to bullion, and to criticize mercantilist ideas of the balance of trade, he could still insist, following traditional economic thinking, that when England exchanged hardware for Spanish fruit, she was exchanging a 'durable' for a perishable commodity, and the trade consequently benefited Spain.[4]

With respect to colonies, Torrens even more clearly revealed that his objectives, and even his methods were no different from those of the old

---

[1] Spence, *Agriculture The Source*, pp. 19–20.   [2] *Ibid.* pp. 16–17.

[3] Robert Torrens, *The Economists Refuted; Or, An Inquiry into the Nature and Extent of the Advantages Derived From Trade* (London, 1808); reprinted as appendix to *The Principles and Practical Operation of Sir Robert Peel's Act of 1844* (London, 1858). There was a dispute concerning whether, in this pamphlet, Torrens had anticipated the Ricardian theory of comparative advantage. Mill appears to have accepted Torrens' claim of anticipation. See J. S. Mill, *Principles of Political Economy* (London: Longmans, Green, 1909) (Ashley edition), p. 576 f.n. (1862). Torrens' claim was further supported by Edwin R. A. Seligman, 'On Some Neglected British Economists', *Economic Journal* XIII (September 1903) pp. 335–63, and December 1903 (pp. 511–35). Hollander took issue with Seligman's position, and ably disposed of the Torrens claim; see Edwin R. A. Seligman and Jacob H. Hollander, 'Ricardo and Torrens', in *Economic Journal* XXI (September 1911), 448–68. See also Jacob Viner, *Studies in the Theory of International Trade* (London: Allen & Unwin, 1955), pp. 441–4. Lionel Robbins, in his *Robert Torrens and the Evolution of Classical Economics* (London: Macmillan, 1958), pp. 31–5, argues that Torrens' claim was in reality more modest and probably legitimate.

[4] Torrens, *Economists Refuted*, pp. 48–53.

colonial system.[1] While opposing the grants of exclusive trading privileges to particular companies or ports, Torrens favored 'restrictions on the colonial trade which have for their object to render the mother country the mart, or *entrepôt*, for conducting the commercial intercourse between the colonies and foreign countries',[2] in order to preserve the commissions, and profits upon 'that portion of mercantile capital which consisted of docks, wharfs, and warehouses'.[3] He also favored 'those restrictions which have for their object to secure to the productions of the mother country a monopoly in the colonial market', though they likewise 'have the effect of enriching the mother country at the expense of the colonies'. While not objecting to restrictions drawn up in the interest of the mother country, Torrens strongly condemned countervailing ones which eighteenth-century mercantilism had erected to 'secure to colonial productions an exclusive privilege in the home market'. When inferior Canadian timber was given preference over Norwegian timber, 'the interests of England were blindly sacrificed to those of Canada'; and England 'renders herself tributary to her own colonies'. 'We cannot conceive', he concluded, 'that it is ever the real object of legislators to enrich a colony by impoverishing the parent state; because this would be to counteract the only end for which colonial possessions are maintained.'[4]

If, in 1808, in conformance with an autarchic ideal, and despite his brief for foreign trade, Torrens had still, like Spence and Malthus, urged that England grow sufficient food to feed herself in years of average harvest, by 1815 he had changed his mind. By this time, England's industrial lead, confirmed and widened as a consequence of the wars with Napoleon, appeared almost unchallengeable. In his *Essay Upon the External Corn Trade*, published in that year, Torrens called for a free trade in corn, as the basis of a trading system which would bring Great Britain to unexampled heights of power and prosperity, thus going well beyond both Mill's and his own positions of 1808, and placing Tucker's conceptions in terms of the new conditions in which England found herself in 1815. Torrens had become persuaded that if Britain were to have a market for its hardware and cloth, it must import its corn from those who would buy English manufactures; and he had come to believe that only through foreign trade, through the export of hardware and cloth, could England obtain the food needed for an increasing population.

'To those who have embraced the opinions of the French economists,' he observed, addressing his argument to the agrarian economists, 'it may,

---

[1] *Ibid.* pp. 33–5. [2] *Ibid.* pp. 37 ff.
[3] *Ibid.* p. 39. [4] *Ibid.* pp. 40–3.

perhaps, appear somewhat paradoxical to say, that a measure [the corn laws] which should extend agriculture, and increase the value of land, would be injurious to prosperity, and diminish wealth.'[1] But this was the case, for even agriculture, in a manufactures-exporting country, would benefit by a free trade in corn—a trade which would effect the greatest possible accumulation of capital, and its ultimate overflowing onto the land.[2] To Malthus' and Spence's warnings of the dangers of famine, Torrens replied that England, like Holland 'in the days of her commercial prosperity', would become 'the granary of Europe', the entrepôt, 'the great store-house of the nations',[3] the 'emporium of the world', the metropolis of a great trade empire. Moreover, like Holland in the seventeenth century, Britain would obtain a predominant position in the carrying trade: 'the flourishing state of our internal industry,' Torrens declared, 'promoted by a cheap and steady supply of subsistence, would powerfully co-operate with a free external trade, in enabling us to avail ourselves of the advantages of our position, and to become the carriers of the world'.[4]

It was most important, Torrens observed, to avoid 'an increase in the natural price of subsistence' which would diminish 'the productive powers of all branches of industry';[5] for 'every reduction in the money price of corn, reduces the money price of labour',[6] and every rise in the price of corn 'raises the price of labour; and, through labour, the price of the other necessaries of life',[7] even the price of goods imported from foreign countries.[8] In this *Essay*, Torrens, anticipating Ricardo, set forth the law of comparative advantage. If, because of British manufacturing skill, 'any given portion of our labour and capital can, by working up cloth, obtain from Poland a thousand quarters of wheat, while it could raise, from our own soil, only nine hundred; then, even on the agricultural theory, we must increase our wealth by being, to this extent, a manufacturing, rather than an agricultural people'. Our manufactures would, in this fashion, have increased the wealth of England, and have given England 'a species of property in the soil of Poland'[9]; 'our accurate divisions of employment, and the wonderful perfection of our machinery for abridging labour, have increased, to such an astonishing extent, the productive powers of our manufacturing industry, that a given portion of our capital, when directed to supplying the foreign demand for wrought goods, can obtain, in return, a larger quan-

---

[1] Robert Torrens, *Essay Upon the External Corn Trade* (London, 1815), p. 221.
[2] *Ibid.* pp. 51–2.
[3] *Ibid.* pp. 275–8.
[4] *Ibid.* pp. 301, 303.
[5] *Ibid.* p. 72.
[6] *Ibid.* p. 76.
[7] *Ibid.* pp. 83–4.
[8] *Ibid.* p. 86.
[9] *Ibid.* pp. 221–2; see Robbins, *Robert Torrens*, p. 32.

tity of corn, than it could raise by cultivating wastes of the greatest fertility'.[1]

A people whose industry limited itself to the 'supplying of the home market', Torrens continued, a people without a foreign trade, deprived themselves of the benefits of foreign divisions of employment, and, therefore, could 'never make any very considerable advances in wealth and power'. Such a country had 'limits' set to both its population and its wealth: 'every step in the progress of prosperity is, to a merely agricultural state, more tardy and more operose than that which preceded it'; such a state would be 'stationary' in character, 'slow in recovering from the effects of deficient seasons, or from the waste of war', and terribly exposed to the raids of neighboring states. On the other hand, 'no limit could be assigned' to the increase of the resources of a state with foreign trade. Its prosperity would advance 'with an accelerated pace', until she came to the stage of importing her food. From this point onwards, her wealth would accumulate at an even greater rate, until the excess capital flowed over upon the land and made even her agriculture flourish. At this state of her development, 'prosperity would encounter no check'; every addition to the quantity of food imported would give employment to a greater number of workmen, since it would 'create, in the foreign market, an additional demand for the equivalents which purchased it', he observed, in an extension of Say's Law which was to become common among later free trade advocates. 'The limits of commercial prosperity cannot be assigned,' Torrens declared, claiming for commercial states all the virtues which Malthus had reserved for agricultural ones.

Torrens, like the mercantilists of the preceding century, saw trade as the means to power, and to empire. He urged the examples of Sidon and Tyre, of Athens, Carthage, Venice, Genoa, and Pisa, of the Hanse Towns, and, most particularly, of Holland, which had acquired by their industry and commerce 'an opulence, of which there is no example amongst nations', and a 'degree of political power and consideration, to which, had they been limited to the resources of their own territories, they could never have ventured to aspire'. Speaking of Holland and Venice, he proclaimed: 'What fleets and armies they put forth;—what kingdoms, what confederations they resisted;—and what a leading,—what a preponderating part they acted in the affairs of Europe!' The question was not whether 'extended commerce, or extended territory' was 'the most stable foundation upon which national greatness can rest'. It was whether a country with a given territory 'should, by the prosecution of external trade, establish a species

[1] *Ibid.* pp. 265-6.

of property in the territory of her neighbours, and acquire accessions of population, wealth, and power, which would be unattainable if she confined herself to her internal resources'. For England, the question was whether, being inferior to France or Austria or Russia in territory and population, she 'should avail herself of the artificial, and even, perhaps, less permanent, advantages, placed within her reach, and by the wonders of her commerce, create the means for taking an ascendancy in Europe'.[1] The agrarian economists had urged that England again become an exporter of corn; a corn-exporting England, Torrens warned, would be 'bankrupt and depopulated, sunk from her place in Europe, and, perhaps, deprived of her existence as an independent nation'.[2]

Torrens' final answer to the arguments of the agrarian economists was that 'as long as the abandonment of commerce cannot create additional lands, so long must we cherish that compensation, that substitute for extended territory, which a flourishing external trade confers'. 'Without extended commerce, there can be no naval preponderance' without which 'an insular state must, in all her foreign relations, be perfectly insignificant'.[3] The alternative to this—the maintenance of the corn laws—would be 'tantamount to laying a tax upon bread, for the purpose of pensioning off the landed aristocracy'; it would be 'legalized robbery, taking the money out of the pockets of the poor and industrious, in order to lavish it on the idle and the rich';[4] 'if the industrious classes are compelled to purchase their corn at an artificially elevated price, we must speedily cease to be a manufacturing and commercial people'.[5] The ultimate result of restrictions would be 'impoverishment and depopulation';[6] 'the foreigner, gradually acquiring capital and skill, will certainly be enabled to undersell us'. England which had 'become the greatest manufacturing country that ever yet existed', might face social revolution: 'What, then, is to become of our unemployed manufacturing population,' he expostulated, 'and how are we prepared to meet the tremendous vengeance they would take for the infliction of artificial famine?'[7]

The corn laws and Malthus' later critique

When the corn laws became a political issue in 1814–15, Malthus, inevitably, opposed the arguments of the free traders against agricultural protection, and denounced their efforts to lower food costs in order to expand England's

[1] Robert Torrens, *Essay Upon the External Corn Trade*, pp. 321–35.
[2] *Ibid.* p. 256.   [3] See *Ibid.* pp. 333–5.
[4] *Ibid.* p. 317.   [5] *Ibid.* p. 237.
[6] *Ibid.* p. 256.   [7] *Ibid.* pp. 226–7.

foreign trade. His arguments had already been set forth. Adam Smith had disputed the physiocrats' belief in the *bon prix*, the high price which would accompany agricultural abundance, and had set forth what was to become the orthodox view that the combination of abundance and low price was most desirable. In the *Essay*, Malthus had attacked Smith's view that dear corn benefited no one, and opted in favor of the physiocrats' *bon prix*, referring the reader to the argument in 'the Physiocratie, by Dupont de Nemours'.[1] He found the 'high price of corn and of rude produce in general', under free competition, 'a very great advantage', and 'the best possible encouragement to agriculture', and had no sympathy with the suggestion that corn be imported in order to lower wages. This would 'probably aggravate the evil tenfold', and be 'the ruin of our agriculture'; pasture would triumph over plow land, and England would be perilously dependent upon the foreigner. 'How dreadfully precarious would our commerce and manufactures, and even our very existence be, under such circumstances!'

If other countries turned to manufacturing as well, and began to import food, it would be impossible for the agricultural nations, with their rising populations, to feed them: the price of wheat would rise so high that 'the poor manufacturers would be totally unable to pay it, and want and famine would convince them too late of the precarious and subordinate nature of their wealth'. If the principal nations of Europe turned to manufacturing and became dependent upon Russia and America for their food, they would see 'the growing prosperity' of the agricultural nations as the 'signal' of their own 'approaching ruin'. 'A system,' Malthus concluded, 'which, like the present commercial system of England, throws a country into this state, without any physical necessity for it, cannot be founded on the genuine principles of the wealth of nations.'[2]

When the corn laws became the leading political issue, Malthus repeated all these arguments, adding, in 1815, the very physiocratic one that the entire community would suffer if the income of the landed classes declined, since agriculture, being the most productive of occupations, produced the surplus product which, when expended by the landed interests, was the necessary beginning of the circulation of wealth through the community— as in Quesnay's *tableau économique*.[3] Spence presented the same arguments at this time, in justifying his own support for the corn laws.[4]

[1] Malthus, *Essay on Population* (1803 edition), p. 458 f.n.
[2] *Ibid.* pp. 445–7.
[3] Malthus, *The Grounds of an Opinion, passim*, especially pp. 33–7.
[4] William Spence, *The Objections Against the Corn Bill Refuted* (London, 1815), 4th edition, pp. 11–13, 18–25, 34, 38–41.

Was not Malthus, in supporting agricultural protection, violating a crucial physiocratic principle? But the free trade policy of the French agrarian economists of the *ancien régime* would not have suited the circumstances of English agriculture. It is frequently forgotten that behind the free trade program of physiocracy lay the desire to end mercantilistic restrictions against the *export* of wheat, thus encouraging the combination of abundant wheat production and high wheat prices, a *summum bonum* of the French Economists. What the physiocrats proposed for the French wheat grower— the freedom to export—the British wheat grower already enjoyed. Since for Malthus, as for the physiocrats, the most desirable economic condition in which a nation could find itself was to be an exporter of corn, Malthus had proposed, in the second edition of the *Essay*, that England return to the system of encouraging such exports by bounty. This view, therefore, like his later support of the corn laws, was only on the surface antagonistic to physiocratic policy; properly understood, both export bounties and protection were necessary if Great Britain were to achieve the physiocratic ideal of the good society.[1]

In 1817, intensifying his attack on the commercial system, Malthus again warned advocates of trade empire of the inevitability of foreign competition; he added, significantly, that, if that should be far off, 'domestic competition produces almost unavoidably the same effects', i.e., overproduction, and falling prices and profits. From this time onward, Malthus emphasized *glut*—of capital and of goods—as the grand flaw in the operation of the commercial system,[2] the argument which Spence had stressed in 1808. He once more cautioned those who hoped to see Britain emerge as the workshop and common carrier of the world that 'it is generally an accidental and temporary, not a natural and permanent, division of labour, which constitutes one state the manufacturer and the carrier of others'. As long as agricultural profits continued high in landed nations, these nations might continue to rely on others for manufacturing and transport services, but

[1] Dugald Stewart saw the physiocrats in a similar light in his *Works*, x, 91. The opposite position has been maintained, most forcefully, by Karl Marx, who suggested that the Physiocrat William Spence had become a 'mere caricature' of physiocracy because of Spence's defense, in the course of which he 'employed Physiocratic doctrines', in 1814–15, of the corn laws, despite the fact that Physiocracy, 'above all else, preached free trade'. See Karl Marx, *A History of Economic Theories From the Physiocrats to Adam Smith* (New York: Langland Press, 1952), p. 49. Malthus' support of the corn laws similarly brought a volley of invective. Malthus, wrote Marx, was a '*bought advocate*' of the landed aristocracy, and an opponent of 'historical development': Malthus 'wants bourgeois production in so far as it is not revolutionary, in so far as it is not a historical force, but merely creates a broader and more convenient material basis for the "old" society'. Quoted in Ronald L. Meek, ed., *Marx and Engels on Malthus* (London, 1953), pp. 122–3, 157.
[2] T. R. Malthus, *Additions to the Fourth and Former Editions of An Essay on the Principle of Population* (London, 1817), p. 109.

when the profits on land fell, the accumulating capital would turn toward commerce and manufactures. This would be 'the signal of decay and destruction', for not only would they cease to be customers, they would withdraw their food in order to feed their own manufacturers and merchants. This was the lesson to be drawn from the history of Venice, Bruges, Antwerp, and Holland; this was the fatal flaw in the temporarily profitable commercial state.[1] Furthermore, Malthus argued, with some perception, without an increasing economic progress abroad, the manufacturing country might be obliged, 'as its skill and capital increased', to give 'a larger quantity of manufactured produce for the raw produce which it received in return', but even with such lower prices it might not be able to sell its goods.[2]

Malthus continued to stress the need for a balanced development of agriculture and commerce, and the superiority of the home to the foreign market. 'In the wildness of speculation it has been suggested,' Malthus observed, '(of course more in jest than in earnest), that Europe ought to grow its corn in America, and devote itself solely to manufactures and commerce, as the best sort of division of the labour of the globe';[3] however, he insisted, 'it is the union of the agricultural and commercial systems, and not either of them taken separately, that is calculated to produce the greatest national prosperity'.[4] A country which devoted considerable capitals both to land, and to commerce and manufactures, with 'neither preponderating greatly over the other', possessed 'the advantages of both systems', while remaining 'free from the peculiar evils which belong to each, taken separately'.[5] Such a country would have at its fullest and most profitable development 'the great and most important of all trades, the domestic trade carried on between the towns and the country'. 'When its manufacturing capital becomes redundant', it would be transferred 'to its own land' to 'raise fresh products', and vice versa, until 'the level between the profits of agriculture and manufactures' was restored. Such a country, Malthus continued, 'might evidently go on increasing in riches and strength, although surrounded by Bishop Berkeley's wall of brass', without being susceptible to injury by the 'natural progress' of other states. Only by a system of bounties upon the export, and restrictions upon the import of corn could an economy in which agriculture and manufactures were 'nearly balanced' be maintained.[6]

In 1817, David Ricardo's *Elements of Political Economy*, which was to become, as we know, the core work of classical 'orthodoxy', made its appearance;

---

[1] *Ibid.* pp. 117–24. [2] *Ibid.* pp. 114–15. [3] *Ibid.* p. 187.
[4] *Ibid.* p. 146; see also p. 133. [5] *Ibid.* pp. 125–6. [6] *Ibid.* pp. 131–3, 128.

Malthus' *Principles of Political Economy*, published in 1820, was designed as a reply to Ricardo's *Elements*. In this work, Malthus extended the physiocratic basis of his system considerably. Rent, for example, was no longer described in terms of the law which he himself had set down, and Ricardo had developed, but, rather, its rise and fall was made to coincide with the rise and fall of the surplus product. This 'surplus', furthermore, was depicted as 'a bountiful gift of Providence',[1] which, as Ricardo was to remark, was an unusual description for a book of political economy.[2] Malthus, moreover, revealingly depicted agricultural production *alone* as possessing 'the peculiar quality' of giving 'a value to this surplus by raising up a population to demand it', a point, he noted, which had been 'strongly insisted upon by the Economists'.[3] 'Where are the under-stocked employments, which, according to this theory ought to be numerous, and fully capable of absorbing all the redundant capital, which is confessedly glutting the markets of Europe in so many different branches of trade?' he asked the adherents of Say's Law.[4] Malthus also mounted an attack upon Smithian frugality—'the principle of saving', he wrote, 'pushed to excess, would destroy the motive to production'—and pressed his view that undue parsimony would result in gluts of production and of capital which would impede the growth of national wealth.[5] Much to Ricardo's subsequent horror,[6] Malthus called for 'the maintenance of unproductive consumers', praised the economic effects of the national debt, and of taxation, and recommended an increase of government establishments and of government expenditures, as in public works, as useful means of overcoming glut.[7] In the *Principles*, Malthus, unveiling the full scope of the agrarian position defended the economic advantages of primogeniture, with its accompanying larger landholdings—the physiocrats' *grande culture*—as well as its political advantages; an aristocracy was an essential element in the British constitution, he argued, and its demise—and this would be the effect of the abolition of primogeniture and of more equitable landholding—would be the prelude to a military despotism.[8]

The sum of Malthus' message in 1820, as earlier, was that a trade empire simply would not work. While free trade, as he had granted in 1817, would

[1] T. R. Malthus, *Principles of Political Economy Considered With a View to Their Practical Application* (London: John Murray, 1820), pp. 226–9.
[2] Straffa, ed., *Works of Ricardo*, II ('Notes on Malthus'), 210.
[3] Malthus, *Principles of Political Economy*, p. 144.
[4] *Ibid.* p. 499.
[5] *Ibid.* p. 8.
[6] Straffa, ed., *Works of Ricardo*, II, 240.
[7] Malthus, *Principles of Political Economy*, pp. 498–500, 511.
[8] *Ibid.* pp. 433–9.

certainly promote the wealth of the world, there was little reason to expect individual states to 'consent to sacrifice the wealth within their own confines' to general world welfare.[1] The clergyman-economist bemoaned the worship of riches of commerce and manufacturing, the products of Mammon, and the neglect of the incomparably greater, and ultimately more significant, riches of the soil, produced under the beneficent eye of God. The unproductive parasitism of the commercial system sapped the strength of the state, and injured, beyond compensation, the interests of the great bulk of the people and their posterity, even though it did, no doubt, profit a few manufacturers and merchants. Malthus praised the happy state of a landed nation with 'a fertile soil', for 'states so endowed are not obliged to pay much attention to that most distressing and disheartening of all cries to every man of humanity—the cry of the master manufacturers and merchants for low wages, to enable them to find a market for their exports'. 'If a country can only be rich by running a successful race for low wages,' he declared, 'I should be disposed to say at once, perish such riches!' 'But,' Malthus concluded, 'though a nation which purchases the main part of its food from foreigners, is condemned to this hard alternative, it is not so with the possessors of fertile land.'[2]

It was hardly surprising that agrarian economists who wished to cast some doubts concerning the optimistic picture of a harmonious, virtually automatic operation of a commercial and industrial system, as depicted by Say, Mill, and Ricardo, should have had recourse to the more pessimistic view of a commercial system, and of the difficulties it must inevitably encounter, which Quesnay and his disciples had formulated to challenge the Colbertist mercantilism of the *ancien régime*. Dupont de Nemours, the last of Quesnay's disciples, in a tome addressed to Say, asked justice for the physiocratic position; he denounced the system 'née de la cohabitation de *Smith* avec je ne sais quelle demoiselle de la maison de Colbert', and mocked the goal of 'cette éphémère prospérité' of England, much vaunted in France by 'les Colbertistes et les Anglomanes'.[3] Dupont, on the other hand, was full of praise for Malthus whom he found 'encore plus profond et plus tenace que Smith'.[4] After Dupont's death, his widow, in a letter to Sismondi, who also had doubts concerning Say's Law, congratulated the French economist for having defended, in an essay, the possibility of general

[1] Malthus, *Additions* (1817), p. 211.
[2] Malthus, *Principles of Political Economy*, pp. 235–6.
[3] P. S. Dupont de Nemours, *Examen du Livre de M. Malthus Sur Le Principe de Population; Auquel on a joint la traduction de quatre chapitres de ce livre supprimés dans l'édition française; et une lettre à M. Say* (Philadelphie: Lafourcade, 1817), pp. 123, 138, 158, 20.
[4] *Ibid.* p. 30.

overproduction as upheld by 'notre bon Malthus' against the specious arguments of 'ce Ricardo'.[1] Both M. and Mme Dupont, it would appear, saw 'notre bon Malthus' as challenging a rebirth of Colbertism in Ricardian guise.

Ricardo and diminishing returns

Whereas Torrens had doubts about the soundness of Say's Law, and had called for the erection of a trade empire because of such doubts, David Ricardo, a wealthy stockbroker who had been persuaded by James Mill to use his leisure time to set down the principles of political economy, had every confidence in that logically unexceptionable proposition. Yet, as is well known, Ricardo's view of the future of the industrial system was hardly a naïvely optimistic one. Mill, we recall, in 1808, had seen foreign commerce as not essential to an industrial England, given Say's Law, although he granted that it would certainly enlarge her opportunities. Torrens, on the other hand, in calling for a trade empire, had written of 'that substitute for extended territory, which a flourishing external commerce confers', and had foretold dire consequences for England if she did not avail herself of this remedy. Ricardo was to provide a more thoroughgoing theoretical groundwork for Torrens' suggestion.

While the agrarians had spoken of declining profits arising from too great an accumulation of capital, and a lack of effective demand, Ricardo believed that such a decline would occur only when society arrived 'at the end of its resources',[2] which he defined in the Malthusian terms of the inability of the land to support an increasing population. Until, as he wrote Malthus, in 1820, 'a country has arrived to the end of its resources from the diminished powers of the land to afford a further increase', it was 'impossible that there should [be, at the] same time, a redundancy of capital, and of [population]'. 'Profits may be for a time very l[ow] because capital is abundant compared with [labour but] they cannot both I think be abundant at one [and the same time.]'[3] In a pamphlet upon the 'Funding System', in 1818, Ricardo dealt more fully with the issue. The chief problem, he wrote, was to supply 'food and necessaries for the increasing population, which a continually augmenting capital would employ'. With 'every increased difficulty' of producing such raw materials, the price of corn would rise, and,

[1] Quoted in Sraffa, ed., *Works of Ricardo*, VIII, 224 f.n. For further discussion of Malthus and Say's Law, see B. Corry, *Money, Saving, and Investment in English Economics, 1800–1850* (London: Macmillan, 1962).
[2] Sraffa, *Works of Ricardo*, VIII, 181.
[3] *Ibid.* VIII, 185.

of course, wages would rise as well. A 'real rise of wages' was 'necessarily followed by a real fall of profits', and when 'the land of a country is brought to the highest state of cultivation, when more labour employed upon it will not yield in return more food than what is necessary to support the labourer so employed, that country is come to the limit of its increase both of capital and population'. Society would be brought to this stage of crisis, then, by the operation of the law of diminishing returns in agriculture.

What was to be done under such circumstances? Though Ricardo's approach was somewhat different, his remedy was substantially the same as that of Torrens. Although insisting that England was 'far distant' from such a dilemma, Ricardo noted that the solution was at hand: if food and other raw produce could be 'supplied from abroad in exchange for manufactured goods', he observed, it was 'difficult to say where the limit is at which you would cease to accumulate wealth and to derive profit from its employment'.[1] In an address in 1822, Ricardo set forth more clearly a vision of an increasingly industrialized England. He noted lamentations in some quarters that England was becoming 'too much of a manufacturing country'. Such people might 'as well complain of a man's growing old as of such a change in our national condition'. 'Nations grow old as well as individuals', Ricardo continued, and 'in proportion' as England grew 'old, populous, and wealthy', must Englishmen become manufacturers and England become 'a great manufacturing country'. Indeed, that England would need to import a greater proportion of her food was 'a proof of prosperity'; 'there would always be a limit to our greatness, while we were growing our own supply of food: but we should always be increasing in wealth and power, whilst we obtained part of it from foreign countries, and devoted our manufactures to the payment of it'.[2] In 1822, we see, Ricardo, joining Torrens, answered the objections of the agrarian economists, and set for England the objective of becoming a Workshop to the World.

The reviews, the new orthodoxy, and Malthus after 1815

From its founding in 1802, the *Edinburgh Review* conveyed, most sympathetically, the ideas of the economists to the British public;[3] indeed, two economists—Francis Horner and Henry Brougham—were among the founders of the *Review*. Before 1815, the *Edinburgh* had welcomed articles from Malthus, the practical implications of whose views—an un-Smithian support of protection for agriculture, for example—were yet to be sharply

[1] *Ibid.* IV, 179. [2] *Ibid.* V, 180.
[3] See John Clive, *Scotch Reviewers* (Cambridge, Mass.: Harvard University Press, 1957), *passim*.

drawn.[1] The time of decision for the *Edinburgh Review* came with the publication of Malthus' defense of the corn laws in 1815. Jeffrey, the chief editor of the *Edinburgh*, and Horner were divided on the corn laws. In a letter in May 1814, Jeffrey, who had learned his economics from Dugald Stewart, declared that Malthus was 'very much of my way of thinking on the subject', but that 'Horner is much more Smithish'.[2] In a letter to Murray, in January 1815, Horner observed, with some annoyance, that 'the most important convert'—though this was hardly the right term—'the landholders have got, is Malthus', adding that 'there is not a better or more informed judgment, and it is the single authority which staggers me'. Horner's opinions were not always so; for Horner, like Jeffrey, had been a disciple of Dugald Stewart, and an admirer of Morellet and Turgot, and, indeed, had been so impressed by Turgot's 'admirable views' on all subjects, particularly upon the corn trade, that he had planned to translate all of Turgot's works.[3] Only a few years previously, he had commented upon 'a new speculation' of Malthus' 'about the importance of the people being fed dear', which 'has the look of a paradox', but, he added, 'I have not yet detected the fallacy, if there is one'; and even in 1815, Horner felt obliged to write Malthus to 'treat me still as one of whose conversion from heresy some hopes may be entertained'. However, such hopes were indeed slight as party and class controversy increasingly shaped the direction of economic argument, and Horner, clearly sympathetic to the outlook of the commercial classes, added, in this letter to Malthus, a denunciation of the 'audacious and presumptuous spirit of regulating, by the wisdom of country squires'.[4] The *Edinburgh*, in 1815, published an article critical of Malthus' views on the corn laws in just this spirit—it did 'not think that the great mass of the community should be taxed for the benefit or relief of the landed proprietors'[5] —as Jeffrey, relying upon Horner's superior judgment in economic matters, set aside his own preferences. The *Edinburgh* was feeling its way toward what was becoming the new orthodoxy.

In 1817, Ricardo's *Elements*, a keystone of that 'orthodoxy', appeared;

---

[1] For the favourable view of Malthus of the *Edinburgh*'s editors, see Jeffrey's letter to Malthus, 21 April 1809, in Lord Cockburn, *Life of Lord Jeffrey* (Philadelphia, 1852), II, 104; also Leonard Horner, ed., *Memoirs and Correspondence of Francis Horner, M.P.* (Boston: Little Brown, 1853), I, 446, 464–5.

[2] Cockburn, *Jeffrey*, II, 120.

[3] See Horner, *Francis Horner*, II, 221–2; see also I, 101, 119, 129, 160, 204–5.

[4] *Ibid.* I, 434; II, 226–7, 22.

[5] 'Malthus on Corn Laws', *Edinburgh Review* XXIV, no. XLVIII (February 1815), Article XIII, 491–505; see also Semmel, ed., *Occasional Papers of T. R. Malthus*, pp. 7–14; and Morton Paglin, *Malthus and Lauderdale: The Anti-Ricardian Tradition* (New York: Augustus Kelley, 1961), *passim*.

in 1818, in a eulogistic review, in the *Edinburgh Review*, J. R. McCulloch acknowledged the English stockbroker as his master, and employed the rest of his life to advancing Ricardian principles and stamping out the embers of opposition. McCulloch, who was to be its leading economic reviewer between 1817 and 1837, converted the *Review* into an organ of Ricardian orthodoxy. Indeed, what helped to make Ricardianism 'orthodox' was the dominance of McCulloch over the pages of the highly influential *Edinburgh*, and over the content of the economic articles in the *Encyclopædia Britannica*, in the early twenties.[1] McCulloch denounced 'the poisonous nostrums' of Malthus, and declared his 'reputation as an Economist to be very much overrated'. Malthus, for his part, recognized McCulloch's enmity, and was to note that the *Edinburgh* had 'so entirely adopted' Ricardo's system that he, Malthus, could no longer obtain a hearing for his views in that journal.[2] In the twenties, Malthus was to turn to the *Quarterly Review* for his audience.

The *Quarterly* saw Malthus in an increasingly friendly light during the twenties. In contrast to the *Edinburgh*, the *Quarterly*, founded by a group of Tories in 1809, at first paid little attention to economic questions, and was never to have that overriding faith in the new science which the *Edinburgh* had evidenced from its earliest issues. Still, certain of the founders of the *Quarterly* were sufficiently perceptive to recognize that T. R. Malthus' economic opinions, grounded upon a favorable view of the landed interests, were most suitable for a Tory review, and as early as 1808, Scott and Murray had been anxious to secure Malthus as a regular reviewer.[3] Malthus, it would appear, declined. When Malthus, in 1815, came out upon the side of the landowners on the corn law issue, the possible usefulness of political economy dawned upon many Tories, but prejudice against 'abstract theory'—and sentiment against the 'hard-hearted' theory of population[4]— was still too great. The gap between Toryism and Malthusian economics was partially bridged during the years following 1815 by two *Quarterly* articles which spoke rather favorably of the principle of population,[5] and Malthus

---

[1] See Blaug, *Ricardian Economics*, pp. 38–46.

[2] These letters are to be found in Sraffa, *Works of Ricardo*, VIII, 366, 139, 167, 376.

[3] See letter of Scott to Gifford, 25 October 1808, in H. J. C. Grierson, ed., *The Letters of Sir Walter Scott* (London: Constable, 1932), II, 108.

[4] See, for example, Southey's 'Inquiry into the Poor Laws, &c.' *Quarterly Review* VIII, no. XVI (December 1812), Article IV, 319–56; 'The Poor', *Quarterly Review* XV, no. XXIX (April 1816), Article VIII, 183–235.

[5] See 'Malthus on Population', *Quarterly Review* XVII, no. XXXIV (July 1817), Article IV, 369–403; also 'Godwin and Malthus on Population', *Quarterly Review* XXVI, no. LI (October 1821), Article VII, 148–68. On p. 168 of the 1821 article—written, Fetter has told us, by George Taylor, who was to be, for a time in 1832, Secretary to the Commission of Inquiry into the Poor Laws, we see an attempt to compromise between full acceptance of Malthus' law and Southey's hostility

was again asked to contribute. At this time, Malthus was finding it difficult to obtain a hearing for his views from the *Edinburgh*, and the overtures of the Tory organ must have been rather welcome.

In 1823 and in 1824, Malthus contributed two important articles to the *Quarterly*, in both of which he set forth the leading points of difference, that had become so pressing since 1815, between himself and the 'new school' of Ricardianism. In these articles, written anonymously, Malthus, taking up the cudgels on behalf of the school of 'Adam Smith and Mr Malthus', criticized the Ricardians' reliance on abstract deduction, the labor theory of value, and Say's Law,[1] and described 'the specific error of the new school in England' as 'the having taken so confined a view of *value* as not to include the results of demand and supply, and of the relative abundance and competition of capital'. 'The competition of capital acting on a slack demand, foreign and domestic' would 'necessarily' produce 'a general fall of profits accompanied by all the appearances of a general glut', Malthus insisted. In opposition to the Ricardian school, Malthus further declared that 'the relative abundance and competition of capital'—as Smith had maintained, and as, in Malthus' view, the events of the preceding thirty years had amply demonstrated—was of greatest importance as a regulator of profits. It was not the absolute amount of capital that was at issue, Malthus contended, but the 'relative difficulty of finding *profitable* employment for it'; 'the continued increase of capital, in a limited territory, must unavoidably terminate in a fall of profits'.[2]

Malthus' reference to 'limited territory' gains meaning when we observe some of his earlier speculations concerning empire-building. Briefly and impressionistically, in 1817, Malthus had written of colonies as a means of relieving the metropolis of gluts emanating from the commercial system. A largely commercial country 'engaged principally in manufactures' would soon experience a declining rate of profit as a result of 'an increase of capital'; but 'this country,' Malthus had observed, 'from the extent of its lands, and its rich colonial possessions, has a large *arena* for the employment

---

to it: 'The important truth of those [Malthus'] principles must not be suppressed,' Taylor wrote, 'because the unfeeling and the vicious may occasionally pervert them to disguise from others, and perhaps from themselves, the selfishness of their hearts.'

[1] [T. R. Malthus], 'Tooke—On High and Low Prices', *Quarterly Review* XXIX, no. LVII (April 1823), Article VIII, 214–39; on the question of value, it is interesting to observe that as early as 1803, Malthus had argued that 'the ultimate value of every thing, according to the general reasoning of the Economists, consists in being *propre à la jouissance*'. See Malthus, *Essay on Population* (1803), p. 434.

[2] [T. R. Malthus], 'Political Economy', *Quarterly Review* XXX, no. LX (January 1824), Article I, 297–334; John Stuart Mill wrote an excoriating criticism of this article in the *Westminster Review* III, no. V (January 1825), Article IX, 213–32.

of an increasing capital'.[1] Malthus had also noted that while it would be unwise to depend upon a foreign country for food, because of differing political interests, it would be otherwise in the case of 'the interest of a province with regard to the empire to which it belongs'. The accumulation of capital and its employment in manufactures which would result in 'the withdrawing of the exports of corn in the one case, would leave them perfectly undisturbed in the other'.[2] Later, the hint was amplified: 'the British empire', Malthus had declared, 'might unquestionably be able, not only to support from its own agricultural resources its present population, but double, and in time, perhaps, even treble the number'.[3] Yet despite such flights of imperial fancy, Malthus, in his main argument, still maintained the semi-autarchic, largely physiocratic position we have described.

This imperial line of thought, however, was to be taken up during the following decades by Edward Gibbon Wakefield, a political economist who gave almost all of his attention to problems of empire, and whose views can be said to have had their prime source in the leading Malthusian heresies. In his 1824 article for the *Quarterly Review*, Malthus had described 'three systems' of political economy—that of the physiocrats, that of the Ricardians, and that of a 'third school', which he described as that of Smith and Malthus.[4] Quite deliberately and self-consciously, Wakefield was to develop the doctrines of this 'third school', and to apply them to England's condition in the second quarter of the nineteenth century. Wakefield was to employ the Malthusian critique of a commercial society to prove that England required both an extensive trading system and, following Malthus' hints, colonies of settlement, to overcome problems caused by the competition of capital—overproduction and a falling rate of profit.

[1] Malthus, *Additions* (1817), pp. 111–12; see Sraffa, ed., *Works of Ricardo*, VI, 103–4.
[2] Malthus, *Additions* (1817), p. 119.
[3] *Ibid.* p. 199.
[4] Malthus, 'Political Economy', *passim*. The *Quarterly Review*, in the years following, very nearly became the organ of heresy, or at least of the heresy of this third school, rather than that of simple, if intermittent, opposition to the very subject of political economy. Although Malthus wrote but two articles for it, many of the same views upon demand and related subjects were upheld by G. Poulett Scrope, who, in the early thirties, appeared to be on his way toward becoming the *Quarterly*'s McCulloch—he wrote about ten articles between 1831 and 1833. However, proper Toryism reasserted itself with John Wilson Croker who, after 1832, became the leading influence upon the *Review*'s politics. Croker was unhappy about Scrope's support for free trade, and Scrope was dropped. The *Quarterly* never did resolve its ambivalence concerning political economy.

CHAPTER 4

The third school: Wakefield and the Radical economists

THE chief theorist of empire-building during the first half of the nineteenth century was the projector of 'systematic colonization', Edward Gibbon Wakefield, a political economist of uncommon abilities. During the thirties and forties, he became the virtual 'head', and his writings the center of focus for the 'third school' of political economy, the school of Malthus and Smith, of which the former had written. Availing himself of both Malthus' and Ricardo's analyses, he constructed a picture of an industrial society which, though beset by flaws, might be made viable by a program of empire-building. He embraced the goal of making England the Workshop of the World, as it had been sketched by Torrens and Ricardo, and saw its realization, in association with a program of systematic colonization, as the means of overcoming the internal contradictions of a commercial and industrial system, as described by Malthus—most particularly, stultifying glut, of goods, of capital, and of men. Since Wakefield was 'sound' on trade questions, that is opposed to the corn laws, and since his theory of systematic colonization had been erected upon impeccably Ricardian foundations, and his personal connections with middle-class Radicalism were substantial, his 'heresies' stirred less opposition. His writings and a forceful and engaging personality, in fact, secured for his leading ideas a remarkable degree of acceptance. Indeed, he appears, as we shall see, to have won over such stalwarts of the Ricardian school as Bentham and both the Mills, to many of his views, although there were glimmerings of heterodoxy in the writings of these Radicals even before Wakefield had made his appearance. Herman Merivale was a more unambiguous convert, among political economists, to the Wakefield school.

Anticipations: Torrens and Chalmers

There had been a number of anticipations, by earlier theorists, of many parts of Wakefield's system. In 1803, for example, as we have seen, Henry Brougham had praised colonies for their peculiar capacity to relieve the metropolis from the pernicious 'effects of an overflowing capital';[1] there were similar foreshadowings in the curious mixture of quasi-physiocracy and mercantilism to be found in the writings of the Earl of Lauderdale, both of which economic tendencies made him one of the foremost supporters of the corn laws.[2] William Playfair, in a book published in 1805, anticipated much of Wakefield's later analysis of the difficulties with which an advanced industrial system would be confronted, as well as substantial portions of Wakefield's remedy.[3] John Barton, a disciple of Malthus, and a proponent of the corn laws, developed what might be called a 'monetary theory' of colonization which bore a marked resemblance to Wakefield's later concepts.[4] William Ellis, as his friend J. S. Mill later noted, anticipated, though in somewhat uncertain fashion, some of Wakefield's ideas in a *Westminster Review* article in 1824.[5] Wakefield himself acknowledged two predecessors: 'Quite recently, indeed,' Wakefield noted, 'a sort of heresy in political economy has thrown light on many points which had been left in total darkness by those who imagine that the science was perfected by Ricardo'; the 'most distinguished preachers' of the heresy which demonstrated 'that

---

[1] See Chapter 2, above.

[2] See Earl of Lauderdale, *An Inquiry into the Nature and Origin of Public Wealth* (Edinburgh, 1819), 2nd edition, pp. 141–2, 243–4, 248, and *passim*; Earl of Lauderdale, *A Letter on the Corn Laws* (London, 1814), pp. 18–19, 56, 60–7, 76–80; and Lauderdale's *Sketch of An Address to His Majesty* (n.p., 1821), *passim*. See also *P.D.*, N.S., XIX (13 June 1828), 1336–42. In May 1827, Huskisson, exasperated by Lauderdale's protectionist diatribes, declared that 'I have been an attentive observer of his [Lauderdale's] public career for the last five-and-thirty years. I have done more. I have read all the multifarious works which he has published during that period, whether on general politics, political economy, or political philosophy—all the theoretical lucubrations with which he has enlightened the world . . . I have read them all; and, in saying this, I am aware that I have executed a task, of which very few men besides myself can boast. The conclusion to which I have come . . . is that, among the many mercies which have been vouchsafed to this country, since the breaking out of the revolutionary war in 1792, there are few for which she ought to be more thankful, than for those fortunate occurrences which . . . have disappointed the aspiring ambition of that individual . . . [and] have hitherto prevented his being placed in any station of power, in which he might have been enabled to inflict the application of his own extravagant theories—and theories more extravagant were certainly never conceived by man—either upon the people of this country or upon that far more numerous, but more helpless, population, which is placed under our protection in another quarter of the world.' *P.D.*, N.S., XVII (7 May 1827), 621–2.

[3] See H. Grossman, 'W. Playfair, the Earliest Theorist of Capitalist Development', *Economic History Review* XVIII (1948), nos. 1 and 2, 65–83.

[4] John Barton, *Observations on the Circumstances Which Influence the Condition of the Labouring Classes of Society* (London, 1817), pp. 29–30, 70–1; also John Barton, *An Inquiry into the Expediency of the Existing Restrictions on the Importation of Foreign Corn* (London, 1833), pp. 43–5, 63, 67–8, 72–5, 82–94, 98 and *passim*. See also G. Sotiroff, 'John Barton (1789–1852)', in *Economic Journal* LXII, no. 245 (March 1952), 87–102.

[5] [W. Ellis], 'Employment of Machinery', *Westminster Review* V, no. IX (January 1826), 101–30; see J. S. Mill, *Principles of Political Economy* (London: Longmans, 1909) (Ashley edition), p. 728. In later works, Ellis emerged, rather, as a disciple of Wakefield on matters of colonization: see, for example, W. Ellis, *Lessons on the Phenomena of Industrial Life* (London, 1854), pp. 180–7.

great evils arise from *superabundance of capital*, are Colonel Torrens and Dr Chalmers'.[1]

Torrens found himself in the unusual position of being an apparently orthodox economist who, though he might argue against the agrarian opposition to foreign commerce, colonies, and the corn laws, nonetheless could not subscribe to Say's Law. His doubts concerning Say's Law were apparent in his *Economists Refuted*, in 1808, where he agreed with Spence's analysis of the circulation of wealth, and, consequently, with Spence's views on the questions of unproductive expenditure, public works, and gluts;[2] following Smith, he had observed, at that time, that 'when trade is left free and capital very abundant, competition will lower the profits of stock'.[3] There appeared to be a substantial modification of Torrens' views on glut after 1815, and in 1819, when Torrens wrote an article for the *Edinburgh*, Malthus had mistakenly attributed it to McCulloch, because of its acceptance of Say's Law; when Ricardo informed Malthus of the true state of affairs, Malthus, as Ricardo wrote McCulloch, 'could hardly believe that Col. Torrens agreed so completely with the doctrines which both you and I have advocated'.[4] Yet, Torrens' 'conversion' to Say's Law was by no means firm, and Ricardo continued to regard Torrens, as he did Malthus, as among those who might 'assist in disseminating many sound principles', but who adhered 'too firmly to their old associations' to make 'a very decided progress'.[5]

Indeed, in his *Essay on the Production of Wealth*, which appeared in 1821, Torrens returned to his opposition to Say's Law,[6] and drew particular attention to the colonial trade as a means of relieving glut.[7] In this tract, repeating the mercantilist analysis of his 1808 pamphlet, Torrens stressed, as Wakefield would a decade later, the 'reciprocal benefits' of a free trade between England and America,[8] an example of 'the most beneficial of all branches of commerce, namely, that which is carried on between old and new countries'. While agreeing with the agrarian economists that as a new country progressed in its development, such a trade would become less profitable, Torrens argued that there was no sense in refusing to enjoy a

---

[1] E. G. Wakefield, ed., *An Inquiry into the Nature and Causes of the Wealth of Nations* (London, 1835), I, p. xiii f.n. (Hereafter referred to as *Notes upon Wealth of Nations*.)
[2] Torrens, *Economists Refuted*, pp. 57–60, 61, 18–19; see also pp. 36–7.
[3] *Ibid.* p. 23.
[4] From J. H. Hollander, ed., *Letters of David Ricardo to John Ramsay McCulloch, 1816–1823*, in Publications of the American Economic Association, x, no. 5–6, 52/686.
[5] From *ibid.* pp. 25/659.
[6] Robert Torrens, *Essay on the Production of Wealth* (London, 1821), p. ix.
[7] *Ibid.* pp. 148–289.   [8] *Ibid.* pp. 267–70, and *passim*.

present advantage because in time it must be lost; he concluded, in the manner of his earlier panegyric of trade empire, that 'when we consider the situation of the countries bordering on the Baltic and the Euxine,—when we look to Southern Africa and to the vast continents of North and South America, we shall be convinced that centuries must roll away before the full peopling of the world interposes difficulties in the way of England's exchanging her cheap manufactured goods for the cheap agricultural produce of less advanced countries'.[1]

The most direct link between Malthus and Wakefield was Thomas Chalmers. Wakefield was to regard himself as Chalmers' disciple in political economy in much the same way as Chalmers thought himself the disciple of Malthus. Chalmers is best known as the leader of those reformers who seceded from the established Church of Scotland in 1843,[2] and he believed, with some justice, that his careers as clergyman and economist were inextricably intertwined. Chalmers' central thesis, like Malthus', was that an increasing population constituted the necessary limit to prosperity—and that the only sure remedy for this increasing population was 'the Christian education of the people'; indeed, his *Principles of Political Economy*, although it constituted a complete system of political economy, was organized to prove 'the inefficacy of all schemes', other than Christian education, to improve the condition of the people.[3]

Like Malthus, Chalmers had been much influenced by the physiocrats. In 1808, in his *Enquiry into the Extent and Stability of National Resources*, the young clergyman had set forth views on foreign trade and manufactures—the non-essential activities of a 'disposable' population—which were much the same as Spence's. Trade, he had written at this time, was 'a bugbear framed by mercantile policy, and conjured up to mislead the eye of the country from its true interests', the cultivation of the land.[4] His later writings were in the same mould. In McCulloch's phrase, Chalmers' political economy was 'mostly borrowed from the Economists and Mr Malthus',[5] and, in his *Political Economy*, Chalmers himself distinguished

---

[1] Torrens, *Essay on the Production of Wealth*, pp. 288–9.
[2] In this connection, *The Economist* v (5 June 1847), 641–2, was to call him 'the most influential Scotchman', excepting only Sir Walter Scott, 'of the age'.
[3] Thomas Chalmers, *Political Economy in Connexion With the Moral State and Prospects of Society* (London, 1832) in *Select Works* (Edinburgh, 1856), edited by Rev. William Hanna, IX, 29 and *passim*.
[4] Thomas Chalmers, *Enquiry into the Extent and Stability of Natural Resources* (Edinburgh: Oliphant & Brown, 1808), pp. 7, 137, 123; for other evidences of physiocratic influence, see pp. 20–2, 29, 56, 64, 81–3, 115, 123, 137, 185, 226, 251, 364.
[5] See McCulloch, *Literature of Political Economy*, p. 19; see also [McCulloch], 'Dr Chalmers on Political Economy', *Edinburgh Review* LVI, no. CXI (October 1832), 71–2.

between his teachings, based upon 'the doctrines of Smith and Malthus', and 'the notions of Mill and Ricardo'.[1] Chalmers' political economy must be seen in the context of his wholehearted dedication to the landlords' cause: he condemned an electoral system which gave so large a voice to the classes of a 'subordinate and subservient' character;[2] he asserted that landed wealth ought, by right, to have 'the ascendancy in Parliament'.[3] Like Malthus, he approved of primogeniture because it contributed to the maintenance of a powerful landed aristocracy.[4] Unlike the physiocrats, Chalmers declined to call the clergy 'unproductive', preferring to emphasize their economic role, like that of the landed classes, as one of spending and thereby providing 'an impulse to trade'.[5]

Most particularly, Chalmers pressed the Malthusian view that an over-accumulation of capital was the great flaw in an industrial society,[6] since it drove down the rate of profit. He urged not only the landlord, but also the capitalist to *spend* if the rate of profit was to be maintained at a good level.[7] Great Britain, in Chalmers' view, was capital-saturated: 'perhaps there is no first-rate nation so near, in this respect, to its extreme limit as Britain', where 'a low interest, a high-wrought agriculture, the distress both of a redundant population among the labourers, and of a redundant capital among the mercantile classes go hand in hand'.[8] In the older countries, where the pressure of the population upon food was the keenest, gluts were 'most frequent' and most severe,[9] but gluts of production were possible even in new, underpopulated countries, as a result of overinvestment and underspending.[10] The amount of capital which any country could accumulate was dependent on its agriculture—'when the agriculture itself extends, everything else extends along with it'.[11] A 'new' country, Chalmers continued, might have high profits because upon its 'unbroken tracts which yet lie open for cultivation', as in the United States of America, the 'exuberance of capital may overflow, and find profitable investments for generations to come'.[12]

Chalmers opposed 'progress', as the Radicals and Ricardians understood the term, and urged caution in 'advance' lest industrial growth should

---

[1] Chalmers, *Political Economy*, p. 7.
[2] *Ibid.* pp. 187–8; he noted the danger of 'an assembly of mercantile legislators' anxious to protect their private interests, 'whether by tariff or by war'. *Ibid.* p. 317; see also Thomas Chalmers, *Supreme Importance of a Right Moral to a Right Economical State of the Community* (1832), in *Select Works*, IX, 406.
[3] Chalmers, *Political Economy*, pp. 187–8.
[4] *Ibid.* pp. 218–33; see also pp. 228–9.
[5] *Ibid.* p. 216.
[6] *Ibid.* pp. 57–8.
[7] *Ibid.* pp. 61–9; also pp. 80–1, 90–113.
[8] *Ibid.* pp. 87–8.
[9] *Ibid.* pp. 101–2.
[10] *Ibid.* pp. 105–6.
[11] *Ibid.* p. 72.
[12] *Ibid.* pp. 87–8.

'overlap' agricultural development.[1] His gloomy message to Englishmen was that while in new countries there might be 'a career of sensible advancement for centuries to come', in the 'old countries', while there might yet be 'gleams of prosperity', there was no moving of the limit set by 'the mighty tide of an advancing population'.[2] Chalmers was obsessed by his fear of a growing, 'disposable' population which, when permitted its 'full development', would double itself every fifteen years.[3] This phobia, indeed, led him to approve the repeal of the corn laws, though his support for free trade was based more upon 'moral' grounds than upon the pragmatic ones offered by the Ricardians, to whom he referred as 'mercantile economists',[4] for he did not think that free trade would 'lead to any sensible enlargement of wealth'.[5] While warning against Britain becoming dependent upon foreigners for food, he accepted imported corn as a means of providing 'a certain stretch or enlargement of external resources, whereby room and sustenance would be afforded' for an increased population. But this would only constitute 'a temporary relief'.[6] The Scottish clergyman was even ready to grant that there were 'certain transition states in the history of a nation' in which emigration might be 'a temporary expedient'. Indeed, he suggested that there might be 'a great national experiment' which would substitute emigration as a moral equivalent for the abolition of the poor laws, and urged that the government finance such an experiment, or, alternatively, that the finances might come from the parishes, which would find such an investment cheaper than poor rates.[7]

When accused in an article, written by McCulloch, in the *Edinburgh Review*, of 'one dominant and monopolizing conception', his fear of a growing population, which inhibited his ability to deal with other practical matters, Chalmers replied that he *had* recommended certain 'practicable steps', such as 'the commutation of tithes and taxes, the gradual abolition of the corn laws, and even, with certain modifications, a plan of national and organized Emigration'. By such measures, he observed, England might 'obtain a further postponement, or breathing-time', from the 'extreme pressure' of population growth.[8] What Chalmers did not stress in this reply was his view that, while such remedies might provide a breathing-time, in the long run they must inevitably compound the difficulties.

It was to be left to Wakefield to seize hold of these entirely negative elements of Chalmers' political economy and to revolutionize their spirit.

[1] Chalmers, *Political Economy*, pp. 333, 339; see also pp. 271, 314.   [2] *Ibid.* p. 258.
[3] *Ibid.* p. 234.   [4] *Ibid.* pp. 315–16.
[5] *Ibid.* p. 275.   [6] *Ibid.* pp. 149–50.
[7] *Ibid.* pp. 239–44; see also pp. 234, 236.
[8] Chalmers, *Supreme Importance*, in *Select Works*, IX, 349–50.

What Chalmers had regarded as 'temporary' and impermanent remedies—foreign trade and free trade, emigration and colonization—Wakefield, in his transformation of the landowners' economics of Chalmers into a weapon of a dynamic Radicalism, was to proclaim as the solution to the dilemma of a hard-pressed industrial society.

Edward Gibbon Wakefield

Edward Gibbon Wakefield was born into one of those talented, nonconformist, middle-class families which have made so great a contribution to nineteenth-century English life. His grandmother, Priscilla, had been a popular writer for children, and an early promoter of savings or 'frugality banks'. His father Edward, a Pall Mall land-agent, had written a highly regarded economic survey of Ireland, and was an intimate friend both of James Mill and of Francis Place. Edward Gibbon was thus born, in 1796, in unimpeachably intellectual—and Radical—circumstances. Young Wakefield was a rebel at school and his difficulties in settling down to a career were a source of frequent correspondence between his father and his father's friends, Mill and Place. In 1814, he began a career in the foreign service, first at Turin, and then at Paris. During this period he had two romantic entanglements, one temporarily successful, the other disastrous. In 1816, he made a runaway marriage with an heiress ward-in-chancery, but the young lady, unhappily, died in 1820. In 1826, seeking to repeat his stroke of a decade earlier, he enticed another heiress into a Gretna Green marriage. This time, however, he found himself sentenced to three years in prison for his daring. It was during the time of his imprisonment that he began his study of colonial affairs, and seized upon the principle of 'systematic colonization', which he began to set forth in his first book, *A Letter from Sydney*, in 1829.[1]

The 'Wakefield principle', which was to be elaborated upon in a number of pamphlets and books, was this: the selling of colonial lands at a 'sufficient price', instead of either granting them free or at a nominal price, as had been the custom, using the proceeds of sales to promote emigration to the colony concerned. The seller would be, in Wakefield's view, a private colonizing company to whom a tract of lands would be granted by the government, in exchange for their organizing such a program of colonization. The consequence of cheap or free land in the colonies had been the virtual absence

1 R. Garnett, *Edward Gibbon Wakefield; The Colonization of South Australia and New Zealand* (London, 1898); Paul Bloomfield, *Edward Gibbon Wakefield, Builder of the British Commonwealth* (London: Longmans, 1961).

of a laboring class, without which capital could not profitably emigrate or colonial economies be properly developed; it meant the scattering of the population, and the consequent failure to establish a genuine division of employments, upon which economic progress depended. If a sufficiently high price were set upon colonial lands, emigrants without sufficient capital would be obliged to sell their labor until they had accumulated enough money to purchase land, and become, in turn, employers of more recent emigrants. It was only in this way, Wakefield argued, that bond slavery would be unnecessary and that agriculture might be placed upon its most productive footing.[1]

Wakefield's project of 'systematic colonization' was an ingenious contrivance designed, as we hope subsequently to show, to answer practical Radical objections to earlier programs of colonization, and, it seems likely, to secure a career and possibly a fortune for its author when he left Newgate. In 1829, Wakefield did not endeavor to defend this program of colonization, as he was later to do, on grounds of capital glut, or even of population glut— the latter had become a familiar argument in favor of colonies during the twenties, as we shall see. Wakefield appears, at this time, to have been less troubled about surplus population or surplus capital than with the necessity of constructing an extensive trading system; nor was there any of Wakefield's later concern with establishing the British character of Australia. He was interested solely in customers for British manufactures. In *A Letter from Sydney*, he suggested the stocking of Australia with a labor force recruited from the Pacific Islands, from British India, and from China; particularly from China, for, he wrote, the Chinese had 'admirable qualities as settlers in a waste country', and 'might, within a century, convert this immense desert into a fruitful garden'. 'Would it be no advantage to British manufacturers', he inquired, 'to enjoy free trade with millions of fellow subjects of Chinese origin, and, *through them*, perhaps, with hundreds of millions of customers in the celestial empire?'[2] What Australia further needed, he declared, was 'at least, one good Political Economist at each settlement' to prevent the colonists 'from devising an Australasian tariff'.[3]

But why form colonies? Might one not trade with China's millions without troubling to colonize Australia? Wakefield had probably not read Torrens or Chalmers when he wrote this first book. He was, however, obliged to read them in order to justify a program of colonization as a

---

[1] See E. G. Wakefield, *England and America; A Comparison of the Social and Political State of Both Nations* (New York, 1834), *passim.*
[2] [E. G. Wakefield], *A Letter from Sydney* (London, 1829), pp. 218, 220–2.
[3] *Ibid.* p. 187.

national necessity. The most complete presentation of Wakefield's economics is to be found in his *Notes* upon the *Wealth of Nations*, which constituted a defense of certain strands of Smith's thought—already noted by Malthus, Chalmers, and Torrens—against McCulloch's Ricardian critique. Wakefield brought to fruition a project which Malthus had conceived, as early as 1812, to bring out an annotated edition of Smith's work;[1] the publication of the McCulloch edition in 1828 increased the need for such a 'Malthusian' edition. Wakefield attributed his insights into the 'true' principles of economics to Chalmers' *Principles*, which, he wrote, 'so abounds in novel and important speculations, that no one, who has derived his knowledge from other books on political economy, can truly suppose that he has mastered that science, even in its present imperfect state'.[2]

It was Chalmers, then—and underlying Chalmers, both Malthus and the physiocrats—who provided Wakefield with the building blocks of his system. The physiocratic groundwork of Wakefield's political economy is plainly evident: it is the 'surplus produce of agriculture, beyond what maintains the producers, that provides the means of subsistence to persons not engaged in agriculture',[3] Wakefield observed; food was the 'chief object of production', and land 'the chief element of production';[4] rent was attributed substantially to what the physiocrats had called *avances foncières*.[5] Wakefield was also critical, in the Malthusian manner, of the labor theory of value.[6] More significantly, Wakefield accepted Smith's, and Malthus', and Chalmers' view that the competition of capitalists tended to drive down the rate of profit.[7] During the war, he noted, the redundant capital had been wasted, and therefore the rate of profit had not been depressed; with the coming of peace, however, 'the more rapid accumulation of capital' had caused difficulties.[8] Wakefield quoted with approval Chalmers' view that 'profits might be sustained at any given level' by means of 'expenditures' on the part of capitalists, instead of capitalist 'investitures in trade'.[9] He was critical of the Ricardian view that profits and wages regulated each other, and that wages depended upon the proportion between the number of laborers and the wages fund; if this were true, low wages and low profits could not occur at the same time, as they had in England, or simultaneous high wages and profits, as in America. The error came from

---

[1] The Ford Collection of the New York Public Library possesses a copy of the text of a letter written by Malthus on 3 September 1812, soliciting the interest of an Edinburgh publisher in such an edition, but, evidently, the negotiations collapsed.
[2] Wakefield, *Notes upon Wealth of Nations*, I, 243 f.n.
[3] *Ibid.* I, 79.
[4] *Ibid.* I, 235.
[5] *Ibid.* I, 235.
[6] *Ibid.* I, 160–3, 170.
[7] *Ibid.* I, 243–6.
[8] *Ibid.* I, 249–50, 223–4.
[9] *Ibid.* I, 253 f.n.

the Ricardian habit of focusing attention upon the division of a constant supply when, in reality, supply was not constant, he observed, following the approach of Malthus' *Principles*.

Wakefield was convinced that the key error of the Ricardians was their neglect of the land.[1] 'The French Economists, who invented the science of political economy,' Wakefield wrote, 'treated land as the only source of wealth'; their successors, 'carried away' by Smith's labor theory, refused to even admit land as an element of production, held in thrall as they were by their worship of capital.[2] Yet nothing was truly capital, in the sense of giving employment to labor, unless the greater part of it was, 'or will purchase', food; hence production was limited not merely by capital, but also by 'the field of employment for capital itself'—the land. The simple rule was, he continued, that 'the quantity of capital which can be employed in agriculture is limited, in every society, by the quantity of land to which capital can be applied'. Labor, too, was valueless without such a field of employment and its produce depended primarily 'upon the fertility or extent of that field'.[3] and, secondarily, on the intensive 'division of employments' in agriculture, which led Wakefield to praise agricultural capitalism— the physiocrats' *grande culture*—which, he wrote, produced the greatest surplus and promoted the greatest accumulation.[4]

Wakefield suggested that wages and profits depended, not on any absolute quantities of population, capital, and land, but on 'the various proportions, whether the absolute quantities be increasing or diminishing, amongst the three elements of production'. There were several types of society. In the United States, and certain other older colonies, capital bore a large proportion to labor, and a small proportion to the field of production. These circumstances produced wages which were high, both in share and amount, and profits which, though low in share, were high in amount. A less common situation, exemplified by France at the end of the wars of the revolution, when conscription had made labor scarce, was one in which capital bore a large proportion to both labor and the field of production; here there were high wages and low profits. A third type was one in which capital bore a small proportion to both labor and the field of production; here wages were low and profits high: 'Bengal is a good example, where capital has obtained enormous profits, while wages were at the rate of about twopence a day.' A fourth type of society saw capital bearing a small proportion to labor and a

---

[1] Wakefield, *Notes upon Wealth of Nations*, I, 231–2.
[2] *Ibid.* I, 233.
[3] *Ibid.* I, 235–6, 75–6, 81.
[4] *Ibid.* I, 82 f.n., 37; compare Torrens on the division of employments, *Essay on the External Corn Trade*, pp. 69–71, 73.

great proportion to the field of production; here low wages and low profits reigned, and the profits of the capitalist provided just the slimmest 'motive for continuing to employ labourers'. There were many examples of this last condition: Genoa, Venice, Holland, 'but never was there a more striking one than that of Great Britain at the present time'.[1]

In such a society, despite increasing national wealth, the state of capitalists and laborers may grow worse, 'provided that the field of production be not extended at the same rate with the increase of people and capital'. With the end of war, great amounts of capital were accumulated in England, but as the field of production was not 'enlarged so rapidly as capital increased, more and more competition amongst capitalists' drove down the rate of profit. Improvements in medicine, especially in the care of children, resulted in a population which 'increased faster than the field of employment for increasing capital'. 'This change in proportion between two of the elements of production, and the third or chief element, while all three were rapidly increasing, explains the coincidence of rapidly increasing national wealth, with the greater uneasiness of the middle class and the greater misery of the bulk of the people.' Under such circumstances, a society was compelled to seek new land abroad if it were to avoid becoming further impoverished, even amid increasing wealth.[2]

If Wakefield agreed with his agrarian mentors that commercial states were in continual danger of becoming stationary, and even retrograde, unlike Malthus and Chalmers he did not believe that a growingly more commercial England must inevitably share this fate. Wakefield had constructed an economic model of an advanced commercial system which had turned to empire-building, an economy which was stationary as to profits and wages but 'progressive as to the extent of the field of production, the amount of capital, and the number of people'.[3] British industrialism had outgrown its 'field of employment'; it required new lands for its population and new fields in which to invest redundant capital. If England could extend its field of production, she might avoid the gloomy fate prophesied by the agrarian economists. Chalmers, Wakefield wrote, had urged expenditure; Smith, Ricardo, and McCulloch had urged parsimony. 'Neither class [of economists] admit the possibility of enlarging the field of employment for capital and labour, so as to permit, without injury to any one, and with benefit to all, for ages to come, the most rapid increase of people and capital'. Certainly 'the time is not yet come for seeking to diminish either capital or population'.[4] Wakefield urged 'all the indus-

---

[1] Wakefield, *Notes Upon Wealth of Nations*, I, 238.
[2] *Ibid.* I, 240–1.
[3] *Ibid.* I, 239.
[4] *Ibid.* I, 253.

trious classes of Britain' to 'combine to raise the general rate of profit, by enlarging the field of employment for British capital and labour'.[1] This could be done by constructing a trade empire, and by establishing colonies.

Wakefield's *England and America*, published in 1833, was a social and political analysis of an industrial England which owed its wealth to a power 'obtained from steam, which produces without consuming', an England which had by means of its manufactures, made its citizens 'the greatest commercial people in the world'.[2] Wakefield divided contemporary English society into two broad economic classes—'owners of capital and owners of labour'. In this society, money, not birth, was crucial. 'All rich Englishmen', Wakefield declared, 'belong to the aristocracy quite as much as any duke, minister, or archbishop.'[3] The working-class 'owners of labour', which was their only property, a property which they brought to a market 'overstocked with labour', realized 'what political economists call the minimum of wages', a sum 'which will barely supply the labourer with necessaries according to his estimate of what is necessary'.[4] They were the most numerous working class in the world, composed 'the bulk', 'the vast majority of the people'.[5] There was also a class which Wakefield called 'the middle or uneasy class', only part of which, however, were 'owners of capital', consisting 'of three-fourths, or rather perhaps nine-tenths', of those engaged in trades and professions. This class suffered from every kind of distress because of the generally low rate of profit caused by gluts of capital. Men with large capitals might be able to manage with a low rate of profit; they might be discontented, 'but they are not care-worn, troubled, and perplexed, like those smaller capitalists, to whom a low rate of profit brings ruin, or, at least the constant dread of ruin'.[6] Wakefield drew a picture of 'briefless barristers', of overcrowding in the medical profession and the church, of 'a swarm of engineers, architects, painters, surveyors, brokers, agents, paid writers, keepers of schools, tutors, governesses, and clerks';[7] among these uneasy classes were persons with fixed incomes—'landowners, sinecurists, public servants, and owners of government stock'.[8] While the middle classes lived in constant fear and tension, the working classes existed in such misery, that 'if the English had been a martial people', the laborers 'would

[1] Wakefield, *Notes upon Wealth of Nations*, I, 251.
[2] Wakefield, *England and America*, pp. 33–4.
[3] *Ibid.* pp. 61–3.
[4] *Ibid.* p. 47.
[5] *Ibid.* p. 40.
[6] *Ibid.* pp. 61–3.
[7] *Ibid.* p. 68.
[8] *Ibid.* p. 70.

either have destroyed the classes whom they considered their oppressors, or have perished in a servile war'.[1]

From 1688 to 1830, wrote Wakefield, continuing his analysis, England had been an 'oligarchy of borough-mongers', which protected the security of property and persons but in which there had been no justice between persons of unequal property. The French Revolution of 1789 had caused the middle classes to aspire to participate in government, and had brought them to interest themselves in the moral and educational welfare of the lower classes. The coming of the French Revolution of 1830 had revealed an England 'more or less in a state of insurrection', and it was to the fear of the mob and of barricades that the political reforms of 1832 owed their existence. However, the new English constitution, achieved in 1832, being neither oligarchic nor democratic, was, in consequence, unstable, and, Wakefield asserted, 'will not last'. The working class was determined to have universal suffrage, and 'if it were to come to a trial of strength between the two parties in open warfare (which God forbid!), the result must inevitably be favourable to the great majority'.[2]

An English social revolution, Wakefield warned, would be disastrous: anywhere else, except perhaps Holland, an insurrection of the poorer class might take place, without serious consequences, but in a complexly organized England, where 'the regular course of industry depends so much upon confidence and credit', any 'social convulsion, if it should last but a week, must produce a series of convulsions, one more violent than the other'. So universal suffrage would have to be granted to avoid such a calamity. With the advent of democracy, what would the poor want? In all likelihood, they would opt for 'a revolution of property' which would be just as disastrous to production, upon which the national well-being depended; 'capital, that was not fixed, would be moved to other countries'. Yet there was 'a way of escape': the solution was to 'render the English working class

[1] Wakefield, *England and America*, p. 42. In 1831 Wakefield wrote a leaflet on the dangers of social revolution and suggested measures to meet that impending disaster. He appealed to the 'householders', the middle classes of the English cities, not to yield to the threats of 'the populace', the rabble, common thieves, desperadoes, shady Huntites and fanatical Owenites (pp. 1–11). The passing of a Reform Bill, he wrote, would not avert the danger; householders must arm themselves: 'Guns are obtainable. They sell them at Birmingham for about twenty shillings a-piece. Put a householder and a gun together, and the householder is safe.' Indeed all the propertied had to be armed against the propertyless. 'Perhaps the richer householders, who have most property to save by this means, would subscribe to furnish with muskets those poorer householders, who belong to the working class and cannot well afford an outlay even for the protection of their wives and children' (pp. 14–16). E. G. Wakefield, *Householders in Danger from the Populace* (London, 1831?). See also Wakefield, *Swing Unmasked; or the Causes of Rural Incendiarism* (London, 1831), in which the peasantry was described as 'in the mood to commence a servile war' (pp. 18–21, 24, 45–6).

[2] Wakefield, *England and America*, pp. 93–119.

comfortable, satisfied, and as wise, at least, as the working class in America'; the poorer classes had to be persuaded to desist from demanding universal suffrage by parliament in fact legislating 'as if it had been elected by universal suffrage'.[1]

'The first step is to raise wages,' Wakefield declared. How was this to be accomplished? By extending the field for the employment of English capital and wages, by establishing a wide trading system and colonies. A free trade in corn was essential, Wakefield observed, if 'profitable investments' were to be provided 'for great masses of capital now lying idle or about to go abroad'.[2] But who was to buy English manufactured goods with their cheap corn? Wakefield turned his attention to America, and urged her to alter her method of settling the wilderness. Anticipating Frederick Jackson Turner, Wakefield attributed what he regarded as distinctively American characteristics— the frenzy at religious camp-meetings, drunkenness, impolite curiosity, bigoted patriotism, lack of regard for learning—to the frontier, and the frontier to the 'faulty mode of colonization' which had produced dispersion and isolation.[3] If the price of land in America were increased substantially, and the proceeds of land sales used to import pauper laborers from England, wrote Wakefield, applying the principles of systematic colonization to the United States, these pauper laborers, unable, now that land prices were higher, to own land until others had emigrated to take their place, could replace slave labor. When American agriculture had been organized on a fully capitalistic basis, people, 'less dispersed', would 'produce more with the same labour'.[4] With such an organization, a division of employment between England and America, of the utmost profitability to both, could be arranged: for 'with a greater produce from capital and labour, with higher profits and higher wages, the Americans would raise cheaper corn than has ever been raised; and, no longer wanting a tariff, might drive with the manufacturers of England the greatest trade ever known in the

---

[1] Wakefield, *England and America*, pp. 120–1, 123–7.
[2] *Ibid.* pp. 148, 131–45.
[3] *Ibid.* pp. 190–8.
[4] *Ibid.* pp. 220–4; see also *ibid.* pp. 201–4, 214–15. So convinced, in fact, was Wakefield of the benefits of concentration, that he, alone among contemporary English economists, was willing to endorse, though, doubtlessly, more to support his general argument than as a serious proposal, an American tariff. Not that he was convinced of any economic advantages to America of a tariff against British manufactured goods: even though 'the Americans might obtain better and cheaper manufactured goods by raising corn for the English market than by making such goods themselves', they would lose on 'the political side', for 'in America, whatever tends to keep people together is of inestimable advantage', even if purchased at an economic sacrifice. The tariff, 'by inducing so many people to become manufacturers, has prevented so many people from becoming backwoodsmen', and therefore 'counteracts in some degree the barbarising tendency of dispersion', and increases, consequently, the over-all demand for manufactured goods (pp. 226–7).

world'.[1] To help enable America to prepare for this trade, England could offer its surplus capital for investment in 'innumerable works, holding out the certainty of large profits'.[2]

China also had a role in Wakefield's scheme. The agricultural nations of the world, not desiring to have their corn paid for entirely in English manufactures, might wish, in partial payment, silver. China had an abundance of silver, yet the rulers of China, foreign Tartars, fearing lest their people, through trade and contact with foreigners, might think of rebellion, did not permit their people to buy English hardware and cottons. 'If there be any foreign restriction on the foreign demand for English manufactured goods, restrictions which it is in the power of the English government to remove,' Wakefield intoned, all the while denying any desire to employ force, 'interference for that purpose is a proper office, a bounden duty, of government.'[3] What Wakefield proposed—and what England attempted, after the Opium War, to carry into effect—was that foreigners be permitted to take over the pirate-infested islands of the China coast, to clear the seas of these pirates, and to open markets to which Chinese traders could freely and easily repair. This could be achieved without public expenditure, Wakefield counselled, for harbor dues would provide the necessary finances. If the aristocratic government of Great Britain placed difficulties in the way of this enterprise, Wakefield suggested that British merchants join American merchants in an 'Anglo-American company' which would operate under the protection of the American flag. The 'striped bunting', Wakefield declared, 'would do as well as the union jack'.[4]

To thwart an impending social revolution, Wakefield, we have observed, proposed a broad program of empire-building, designed to increase British production and wealth enormously. 'The mere division of produce between capitalists and labourers is a matter of very small moment,' Wakefield declared, 'when compared with the amount of produce to be divided.' By dwelling upon the question of distribution, 'we make bad blood between the two classes'; by examining the question of production, 'we may prove that masters and servants have one and the same interests'.[5] Through empire-building, Britain might resolve the contradictions which assailed her economy—an increasing economic polarization and the misery of the working and middle classes, growing out of the increasingly severe competition among capitalists and the consequent declining rate of profit—and

[1] Wakefield, *England and America*, pp. 224–31.
[2] *Ibid.* pp. 23–4.
[3] *Ibid.* pp. 151–6.
[4] *Ibid.* pp. 177–89.
[5] *Ibid.* pp. 82–4.

avoid the dangers of revolution and class warfare. Where Malthus and Marx saw catastrophe or the inevitability of revolution, Wakefield demonstrated a way out.

'The decline and fall of empires', Wakefield declared, had 'in great measure, been owing to the excess of two of the elements of production over the third', thus throwing 'a great part of the national wealth into the hands of an idle class', and 'producing an extreme inequality of conditions'.[1] To avoid such a result, Wakefield urged Britain's leaders to 'increase the field of production, [and to] lay hold of foreign fields, in proportion to the increase of capital and people in England'.[2] 'The whole world is before you,' he declared. 'Open new channels for the most productive employment of English capital. Let the English buy bread from every people that has bread to sell cheap. Make England, for all that is produced by steam, the work-shop of the world. If, after this, there be capital and people to spare, imitate the ancient Greeks; take a lesson from the Americans, who, as their capital and population increase, find room for both by means of colonization.' It was only in this way that England could 'escape from that corrupting and irritating state of political economy, which seems fit to precede the dissolution of empires!'[3]

Wakefield and the Radical economists: Bentham, the Mills, Scrope, Merivale

The question of Wakefield's influence upon the views of other political economists—as distinct from his undeniable influence upon the outlook of the parliamentary Colonial Reformers, as we shall see—is a difficult one to sort out. Jeremy Bentham—who was later to be claimed as a 'convert' by Wakefield, in his *England and America*—had been among the first of the political economists to engage in that 'worship of Capital' which Wakefield was determined to undermine, and Bentham's influence in political economy was powerfully exerted through his disciples, James Mill and David Ricardo. It was Bentham's early view that capital was the grand essential—that the quantity of capital, and not the extent of the market as Smith had maintained, was the great limitation imposed upon commerce and industry—which underlay Benthamite objections to the old colonial system, and provided the basis for the position which was to be identified with a later anti-colonial Cobdenism.[4]

---

[1] Wakefield, *England and America*, p. 89.   [2] *Ibid.* p. 79.
[3] *Ibid.* p. 130; see also E. G. Wakefield, *Popular Politics* (London, 1837), pp. 87–96.
[4] A fragment on 'Colonies and Navy', for example, written by Bentham in 1790 but unpublished during his lifetime, was a wholesale condemnation of mercantilism, even Adam Smith's favored Navigation Acts, and the colonial system, since the 'trade of every nation is limited by the

In an early tract, written in 1793, though not published until 1830, Bentham had insisted that it was hardly necessary to govern a people in order to sell to them or to buy from them, as England's prosperous trade with her former colonies in America had proved. The 'benefit' of a monopoly was 'imaginary', while it was 'clogged with a burthen which is real', since it propped up inefficient industries against cheaper and superior foreign products, injuring consumers and discouraging the channelling of capital and labor into the most productive areas.[1] 'I will tell you a great and important, though too much neglected truth,' Bentham declared—'TRADE IS THE CHILD OF CAPITAL: In proportion to the quantity of capital a country has at its disposal, will, in every country, be the quantity of its trade.' Without an increase of capital, 'all the power on earth cannot give you more trade: while you have the capital you have, all the power upon earth cannot prevent your having the trade you have'. 'Yes,' he repeated, 'it is the *quantity of capital*, not *extent of market*, that determines the quantity of trade.'[2] However, even as Bentham displayed the economic illogic and political immorality of empire in this tract,[3] there was a less rational element at play, also present in certain of his other writings, a special, one might almost say 'un-Benthamite', confidence in England's imperial mission.[4]

quantity of capital', and a nation could not have more trade than the capital at its disposal would justify. Jeremy Bentham, 'Colonies and Navy', in W. Stark, ed., *Economic Writings of Jeremy Bentham* (London: Allen & Unwin, 1952), I, 211–12. In a curious aside on odd sheets attached to the manuscript fragment of 'Colonies and Navy', Bentham, sounding a note similar to that of Tucker, defended pacifistic cosmopolitanism as good national policy: 'Our superiority of strength [is] not temporary,' he observed; 'it is founded partly on superiority of ports &c. [and] partly on superiority of wealth. But this superiority must go on in an encreasing ratio. Quoted in Introduction, *ibid.* pp. 47–8.

[1] Jeremy Bentham, 'Emancipate Your Colonies! Addressed to the National Convention of France, Anno 1793', in John Bowring, ed., *The Works of Jeremy Bentham* (Edinburgh, 1843), IV, 410–13.

[2] *Ibid.* p. 411.

[3] *Ibid.* pp. 408–9, 414–15; for a picture of Bentham as an anti-imperialist, see E. L. Kayser, *The Grand Social Enterprise; A Study of Jeremy Bentham in his Relation to Liberal Nationalism* (New York: Columbia University Press, 1932). Some of Bentham's later unpublished writings on colonial questions (Bentham manuscripts. University College, Portfolio no. 8, Folders no. 1–8) repeat these themes. Colonies were described as 'a net loss' to 'the people of a country', and a gain only to the 'ruling one' or 'the ruling few', whose 'sinister interest' had 'succeeded in spreading over this question such a cloud of delusive images' that most people probably believed that colonies were profitable (Folder no. 1, p. 6, dated 11 July 1818). The manuscript text of the unpublished *Rid Yourselves of Ultramaria* repeated for Spanish ears the advice given the French in 1793 (Folder no. 2, dated 1820; subsequent versions, 1821 and 1822).

[4] Bentham warned France that she could not hold her colonies against the British Navy, and urged her to sell her Indian colonies to the British East India Company: the Indians 'must have masters', he declared, and they ought to get 'the least bad ones'; 'I question whether you will find any less bad than our English company.' Bentham, 'Emancipate Your Colonies', pp. 415, 417. In 1804 Bentham observed that it was an advantage to the people of the Orient, 'to be regulated by minds such as those of Hastings's, Teignmouths, Cornwallises, Wellesleys . . . rather than those of the Tippoo's, the Wan Lan Yun's . . . or those of the disciples and associates of Thomas

There was to be a similar ambivalence in Bentham's political economy. In *The True Alarm*, in 1801, Bentham, quite surprisingly, had attacked what was becoming the orthodox view of capital and investment—the view of Turgot and Smith which he himself had espoused in 1793—from a monetary standpoint, and had emerged an advocate of unproductive expenditure.[1] An attempt to publish this tract of 1801 in English—it had already been translated into French by Dumont—was to be frustrated in 1811 by Ricardo's and Mill's strong disapproval.[2] Moreover, in his *Defence of a Maximum*, also in 1801, Bentham had written of colonies as a drain for the 'efflux of hands and mouths', and the 'efflux of capital', and suggested that 'because they are a drain' they were a 'relief'.[3] In 1804, to cite still another example, he had observed that, but for past colonization, the pressure of the population upon land in England would have caused 'a severe sense of general poverty and distress'.[4] Yet, since these views of Bentham were comparatively unknown, he was still regarded as the backbone of orthodoxy. The events of the fifteen years following Waterloo, when England was faced with what appeared to be a glut of capital, would, of course, have tended to confirm Bentham's heterodox doubts. The immediate impetus which brought Bentham back to his views of 1801 upon capital glut, and made him, in his last years, a firm advocate of colonialism—thus aligning his intellectual position with a long apparent sentimental one—came from Wakefield, who, while still at Newgate, had sent his writings to Bentham.[5]

The grounds for 'conversion' were, as noted, well prepared, and

Payne [*sic*]'. 'It would be to Egypt an advantage beyond all price, to be under the government of Britain,' he continued, and the same could be said of the 'new independent Anglo-Americans'. Bentham, 'Institute of Political Economy' (1804), *Economic Writings*, III, 356; see also M. P. Mack, *Jeremy Bentham; An Odyssey of Ideas* (London: Heinemann, 1963), p. 395. The extent of his ambivalence may be judged by a postscript to the 1793 pamphlet, which Bentham was to pen in 1829; the Utilitarian philosopher was to declare that, although he still adhered to his views of 1793 in his role as 'a citizen of Great Britain', as 'a citizen of the British Empire, including the sixty millions already under its government in British India, and the forty millions likely to be under its government in the vicinity of British India, not to speak of the one hundred and fifty millions, as some say, or three hundred millions, as the Russians say, of the contiguous Empire of China', his 'opinions and consequent wishes are the *reverse*'. Bentham, *Works*, IV, 418.

[1] See 'The True Alarm', in Bentham's *Economic Writings*, III, *passim*; see also T. W. Hutchison, 'Bentham as an Economist', *Economic Journal* LXVI (June 1956), 288–306.

[2] See Sraffa, ed., *Works of Ricardo*, III, 260–3. The French translation of this work, 'Sur Les Prix', with Ricardo's criticisms, are to be found upon pp. 269–341.

[3] Bentham, 'Defence of a Maximum' (1801), *Economic Writings*, III, 301–2.

[4] Bentham, 'Institute of Political Economy' (1804), *Economic Writings*, III, 355; yet, in an earlier passage, he described as a 'non-faciendum' the 'encreasing the quantity of land, viz. by colonization' (p. 352).

[5] [E. G. Wakefield], *Sketch of a Proposal for Colonizing Australasia, &c. &c. &c.* (n.p., 1830?), pp. 7, 42. The copy of the pamphlet in the British Museum bears the inscription: 'Jeremy Bentham [13 July 1829] Received From the unknown author/without accompanying Note.'

Wakefield was successful in winning Bentham over. In the summer of 1831, Wakefield reported that he had overcome Bentham's prejudices against colonies 'on the ground of the mischievous loss of capital which it might occasion to the mother country'. He had, he added, also liberated Bentham from a view even more prejudicial to colonies: 'it does not follow', Wakefield asserted, 'that, because labour is employed by capital, capital always finds a field in which to employ labour'. Adam Smith had understood the importance of 'the field of production, and of the market in which to dispose of surplus produce', and, now, Wakefield delighted to report, Bentham, too, had been persuaded of this case, and had come to think of colonization as 'a work of the greatest utility'.[1] Wakefield had enjoyed long discussions with Bentham upon colonial questions, and the older man had agreed to frame a charter for a society whose purpose it would be to settle parts of Australia upon the lines set by Wakefield's 'systematic colonization'. The Bentham manuscripts at University College, London, include such a charter, the title of which gave the gist of Wakefield's central idea in Bentham's unique phraseology: 'Colonization Society Proposal, being a proposal for the formation of a Joint Stock Company by the name of the Colonization Company on an entirely new principle intitled the Vicinity-Maximizing or Dispersion-Preventing principle.' This was followed by an unfolding of the Wakefield scheme in Bentham's usual manner and in his characteristic style, e.g., 'transferring individuals in an unlimited multitude from a state of indigence to a state of affluence'; as characteristic was the utilitarian philosopher's setting down of the most detailed rules of settlement, and his draft of a constitution for the new Australian colony. Bentham went so far as to specify exercises for the prospective settlers during the long voyage to Australia![2]

It is, similarly, difficult to say whether James Mill was 'converted', as the Wakefield party was subsequently to claim. In his article, 'Colony', prepared for a supplement to the *Encyclopædia Britannica* in 1820, Mill had displayed not only the usual Radical opposition to the old colonial system, root and branch, but also a recognition of the value of colonization.[3] A decade later, Wakefield was to write scathingly of Mill's 1820 article. But Mill had not been so unsympathetic to colonization, or so unsophisticated in his analysis as Wakefield was to allege. While presenting the usual Radical

---

[1] Wakefield, *England and America*, p. 252 f.n.
[2] Bentham papers. University College, Folder no. 8, dated 1831, pp. 149, 152, 161–91.
[3] James Mill, 'The Article "Colony", Reprinted From the Supplement to the Encyclopaedia Britannica' (London, 1821?), pp. 4–6, 17–18.

strictures upon the colonies as the prop of corrupt government at home, the provider of sinecures for generals and judges, and the 'grand source of wars',[1] Mill took issue with Smith's view that colonial trade turned capital out of more profitable employment, from a home to a foreign trade of slower returns, and to a much less profitable carrying trade. Critical of such physiocratic reasoning, Mill observed that Smith had overlooked the fact that one trade 'may be more conducive to a net revenue' than another, and that the foreign and colonial trade, and the carrying trade were prime producers of net revenue.[2]

Colonies, Mill also noted, might be useful as an outlet for England's surplus population. The constant pressure of population upon the land, combined with the declining returns from the land, described by Malthus, would corrode civilization in advanced countries, unless the 'redundancy of population which shows itself in modern Europe, in the effects of reduced wages, and a poor and starving people, should suggest to rulers the policy of ancient Greece, and some time or other recommend colonization'. Colonization was desirable when the land to which the colonists repaired was 'capable of yielding a greater return to their labour than the land which they leave'. Mill warned that it was important that the cost of colonization 'not be too great', which it might be if the colony were too distant, or if the population which remained at home suffered 'more by the loss of capital, than it gains by the diminution of numbers'.[3] Mill, we see, was still convinced that colonies were a drain upon the capital of the metropolis. Although Mill was originally antagonistic to 'systematic colonization', he appears, in his last years, to have allowed himself to be guided by his son's highly favorable view of Wakefield's principle.[4]

John Stuart Mill was, in the early thirties, to confess himself a disciple of Wakefield's,[5] whose 'practical conclusions', he wrote in his *Principles*, were 'corollaries from those principles' of 'the best school of preceding political economists'.[6] Mill was not to accept the Wakefield program without qualification: he wished, for example, government to take the lead

---

[1] James Mill, 'The Article "Colony"', pp. 28–9, 31–3.   [2] *Ibid.* pp. 24–7.

[3] *Ibid.* pp. 9–14. Mill also protested at the use of colonies as penal settlements. This was expensive, and 'in the great majority of cases, a voyage to New South Wales had not even the appearance of punishment'. He opted for Bentham's *panopticon* to house criminals.

[4] See D. Pike, 'Wilmot-Horton and the National Colonization Society', *Historical Studies; Australia and New Zealand* VII, no. 26 (May 1956), 206–7.

[5] See Winch, *Classical Political Economy and Colonies*, pp. 135–6.

[6] Mill, *Principles*, pp. 727–8; see *Earlier Letters of Mill*, XIII, p. 737. For similar statements, see also [J. S. Mill], 'De Quincey's "Logic of Political Economy"', *Westminster Review* XLIII, no. LXXXV (June 1845), 320; and *Earlier Letters of Mill*, XIII, p. 642.

in the formation of colonies, so that public not private interests might be foremost, and suggested that parishes make voluntary contributions sufficient 'to clear off the existing unemployed population, but not to raise the wages of the employed'.[1]

While not explicitly accepting the Malthus–Chalmers–Wakefield theory of glut, Mill sometimes argued as if it were true. The young Mill had declared, in 1824, that Say's Law was not 'a deduction of probabilities' but that 'it possesses all the certainty of a mathematical demonstration';[2] the *Principles*, however, displayed a strange ambivalence, and heterodox ideas on capital glut were interwoven with more orthodox ones based on diminishing returns.[3] 'If one-tenth of the labouring people of England were transferred to the colonies,' Mill observed in a more orthodox strain, 'and along with them one-tenth of the circulating capital of the country, either wages, or profits, or both, would be greatly benefited by the diminished pressure of capital and population upon the fertility of the land.'[4] Colonization made possible 'the good economy' of producing commodities 'where they can be produced cheapest'; if it was useful to carry goods from places where they were abundant to those where they were scarce, 'is it not an equally good speculation to do the same thing with regard to labour and instruments?' 'The exportation of labourers and capital from old to new countries, from a place where their productive power is less to a place where it is greater, increases by so much the aggregate produce of the labour and capital of the world,' Mill declared.[5]

More clearly heterodox was Mill's view that the export of British capital had accomplished 'what a fire, or an inundation, or a commercial crisis' would have brought about: 'it carries off a part of the increases of capital from which the reduction of profits proceeds'; capital export, he wrote, was 'the last of the counter-forces which check the downward tendency of profits, in a country whose capital increases faster than that of its neighbours and whose profits are therefore nearer to the minimum'. Investments in colonies and foreign countries were a precondition to the healthy functioning of advanced economies, and 'have been for many years one of the principal causes by which the decline of profits in England has been arrested', he asserted;[6] colonization, 'in the present state of the world, is the best affair of business, in which the capital of an old and wealthy country can engage'.[7]

---

[1] Mill, *Principles*, pp. 970–2.
[2] [J. S. Mill], 'War Expenditure', *Westminster Review* II, no. III (July 1824), 41; see also [J. S. Mill], 'Periodical Literature—Quarterly Review', *Westminster Review* III, no. V (January 1825), 213–32; and Corry, *Money, Saving, and Investment*, pp. 162–8.
[3] Mill, *Principles*, p. 741, and *passim*.
[4] *Ibid.* p. 742.   [5] *Ibid.* p. 970.   [6] *Ibid.* pp. 738–9.   [7] *Ibid.* p. 971

It is difficult to judge to what extent George Poulett Scrope yielded to Wakefield's influence, and to what extent he was led to adopt similar conclusions by pursuing his own lines. Wakefield, at one time, claimed him as a disciple, but Scrope denied this.[1] Scrope, the son of a prominent merchant family, M.P. for Stroud, from 1833 through 1868, became known as 'Pamphlet Scrope' because of the great number of pamphlets—estimated at some fifty—which came from his pen during this time on so many central issues of the day.[2] Like the agrarian economists, though slightly less stridently, he elevated agricultural production over industrial,[3] and insisted on the possibility of general gluts which he sometimes explained in the same way as Malthus and Chalmers, and which at other times he declared 'anomalies', introduced 'through the fraud or folly of the rulers of the social communities', and proceeding not from 'an excessive supply of goods', but from 'a deficient supply of money', a position similar to that of the Birmingham currency school.[4] Whatever the cause of glut, the solution to the problems which were its consequences was, in Scrope's view, colonization.

Like Wakefield, Scrope described 'the certain and extensive field' colonies offered for the 'profitable employment of the capital and labour of the mother country, whenever their competition at home is such as to depress the rate of profits and wages'.[5] He urged the government to provide a free passage to the colonies, securing the necessary funds from a tax upon the employers of the emigrants in the colonies.[6] Although normally a defender of the poor laws, he urged the government to refuse poor relief to all who declined to be transported to the colonies, decrying in advance the 'outcry which would be raised by some ultra-sentimentalists against such a proposition'.[7] Following the orthodox argument of James Mill, Scrope also observed that 'old states' would discover that they could not raise additional raw produce at home 'except at a sacrifice of capital and labour, which, if submitted to, must eventually lower profits and wages in every branch of industry'; as a result, millions were on the brink of starvation, 'because we have confined our growing energies too closely within

[1] See *Report from the Select Committee on the Disposal of Lands in the British Colonies*, 1836 (512) xi, 499, pp. 80–1, 90–1, 176–80.
[2] See Redvers Opie, 'A Neglected English Economist: George Poulett Scrope', *Quarterly Journal of Economics* XLIV, no. 1 (November 1929), 101–37.
[3] G. P. Scrope, *Principles of Political Economy* (London, 1833), pp. 253–6.
[4] *Ibid.* pp. 214–16. In the second edition of his *Principles*, Scrope also defended the usefulness of unproductive expenditure. See G. P. Scrope, *Political Economy for Plain People* (London, 1873), pp. 117–28.
[5] Scrope, *Principles*, pp. 374–5.
[6] Scrope, *The Common Cause of the Landlord, Tenant, and Labourer* (London, 1830), p. 11.
[7] Scrope, *Principles*, pp. 334–6; see G. P. Scrope, *Extracts of Letters From Poor Persons Who Emigrated Last Year to Canada and the United States* (London, 1832).

the narrow limits of this little island, and have been slow to avail ourselves of the prodigious facilities for enlarging the superficial area of our industrial pursuits which are afforded by our colonies'.[1] 'Expansion by colonization', for Scrope as for Wakefield, was the means of avoiding the economic difficulties with which an industrial Britain was confronted.

Herman Merivale, who was to succeed Sir James Stephen as permanent under-secretary of state for colonies, had served a term as Drummond professor of political economy at Oxford in 1837, and at this time he had delivered his noted *Lectures on Colonization*, which had revealed him a disciple of the school of Wakefield. The point towards which English industry was 'continually gravitating', notwithstanding 'all that energy and ingenuity can do towards increasing the productiveness of labour', Merivale noted in these *Lectures*, was 'the prospect of a continually increasing accumulation of capital, with a continually diminishing rate of profit in the employment of it'.[2] 'However paradoxical,' he exclaimed, citing Malthus in opposition to the Turgot–Smith–Ricardo theory of investment, 'a change from saving to spending—from productive to unproductive expenditure—may sometimes operate to relieve national industry from temporary plethora or oppression.'[3] Challenging the Manchester school's opposition to empire, Merivale declared that by possessing a colonial outlet for capital, the capitalist in 'the mother country is benefited by the warding off, for a time, of that fall in the rate of profit which must have ensued had he contented himself with employing it at home'.[4]

Merivale further insisted that 'the capital sunk in well directed emigration is speedily replaced with interest', adding that 'wherever England plants a colony, she founds a nation of customers'. England already received the profits of the trade of 'a vast confederacy', which her emigrating citizens had raised 'to an equality with the proudest empires of the earth', and empires 'as vast and wealthy' still remained to be founded.[5] 'When labourers are starving for want of employment, when capitalists are vainly stretching their ingenuity to devise some profitable investment for their wealth, or ruining each other by overstrained competition,' Merivale declared, in phrases reminiscent of Wakefield, 'he must be a most ingenious sophist,

---

[1] Scrope, *Principles*, pp. 376–8.
[2] Herman Merivale, *Lectures on Colonization and Colonies* (London, 1861), p. 179.
[3] *Ibid.* p. 183. In 1840, Merivale was to note that 'Mr McCulloch, and other writers since Ricardo', had not 'done sufficient justice' to 'Smith's views of the effect of competition among capitalists in the reduction of profit'. See [Herman Merivale], 'Wealth of Nations', *Edinburgh Review* LXX, no. CXLII (January 1840), 443.
[4] Merivale, *Lectures on Colonization*, p. 179.   [5] *Ibid.* p. 159.

who should succeed in persuading the community that its interest was to forbid the first to emigrate, or the latter to employ their capital abroad.'[1]

If Wakefield had borrowed the chief lines of his analysis from such agrarian economists as Chalmers (and behind him, Malthus), and from Torrens, whose writings were riddled with the principles and objectives of mercantilism, he was nonetheless able to persuade such beacons of orthodoxy as Bentham and the Mills of the soundness of his arguments. This in itself is testimony to the survival of outmoded, and usually unarticulated, agrarian and mercantilist assumptions in the views of the leading formulators of orthodox doctrine. Both an 'orthodox' Merivale, an admitted disciple of Wakefield, and Scrope, who largely followed his own heretical lines, were similarly to separate themselves from what has come down as conventional 'orthodox' doctrine, and to argue the necessity of colonization to a rapidly industrializing society. The arguments of this Third School in favor of colonization were to confront, in the second quarter of the nineteenth century, those of a Radical anti-colonialism, soon to become Cobdenism. During this period, there were a number of Radical disciples of Wakefield in parliament, who became known as Colonial Reformers, who were to attempt to translate Wakefield's principles into practice and, thereby, to convert the old colonial system into a system of middle-class empire.

[1] *Ibid.* p. 138.

CHAPTER 5

The Wakefield program for middle-class empire

'Upon what system', one day inquired that unwearied political student, the
Fantaisian Ambassador, of his old friend Skindeep, 'does your Government
surround a small rock in the middle of the sea with fortifications, and cram it
full of clerks, soldiers, lawyers, and priests?'
'Why, really, your Excellency, I am the last man in the world to answer
questions, but, I believe, we call it THE COLONIAL SYSTEM!'

Disraeli, *Pompanilla*

Listen, and mark yon press that wedged in close discomfort stands,
Where Labour thrusts on Capital a crowd of craving hands,
Where Capital itself is cramped, till stagnant stands the gold,
That thro' its limbs, with room to stir, a living tide had rolled . . .

Yet earth is wide enough for all, and England holds in fee
Rich prairies—broad savannahs—o'er South or Western sea,
Where virgin soils are offering their riches to the hand
That withers for pure lack of work, in this o'er-peopled land . . .

Then raise the cry, till loud and high it rise from lathe and loom,
From forge and field, from hut and hall, the cry of 'Elbow-room!'
Of elbow-room for labour, of elbow-room for life,
For mind, for means, that so may come some calm upon our strife.

Punch, 22 July 1848

Radical anti-colonialism

ONE of the most characteristic parts of the Radical creed of the last
decades of the nineteenth century was to be an opposition to
'imperialism', to the empire-building of the eighties and nineties,
climaxed by the Boer War. The views of these latter-day Cobdenites had
their origins in the anti-colonial sentiments shared by the leading men of
both parties in the England of the fifties and sixties, when colonies were
described as a millstone about the neck of the mother country, and the
colonial system as outdoor relief for the aristocracy. Because of the wide
acceptance of such views in the middle years of Victoria's reign, historians

have come to regard the entire period, roughly between the fall of Napoleon and the eighties, as a classic period of anti-colonialism.[1] It was certainly the common view during the nineteenth century, and, indeed, until comparatively recently, that the Radicals and the political economists were stalwart opponents of colonialism,[2] and there is certainly sufficient evidence for such an opinion.

The leading themes of Radical anti-colonialism were disseminated on every level. In 1824, J. R. McCulloch, in a lecture inaugurating a series founded by Ricardo's will and heard by an audience which included Huskisson, Canning, Peel, Liverpool, Lord King, Sir Henry Parnell, and Lord Lansdowne, had declared himself in favor of independence for colonies, making much of the financial burdens associated with their possession, even calling for an end to the Company monopoly in India;[3] to the end of his life, he maintained the opinion 'that extensive colonial possessions are a source of weakness rather than of strength'.[4] McCulloch's views on this question, recapitulating as they did those of earlier economists, were to become the common opinion of most Radicals. The Radical *Westminster Review*, for example, saw the colonial system as an aristocrat plot, and called for the 'emancipation' of all British colonies. The *Review* bemoaned 'that unyielding tenacity to colonial dominion which has ever been the bane and curse of the people of this country':[5] the Horse-Guards and others of the governing classes alone benefited from the colonies, not the nation as a whole;[6] the Indian empire was a means of exploiting both the inhabitants of that sub-continent, and the tea-drinkers of England, 'part and parcel of the general plot, by which the aristocracy of England are to be supported by the commonalty'.[7] It was this mood and spirit which prompted Joseph Parkes, after his brief flirtation with colonization societies, to reprint, in opposition to what he described as the 'popular outcry for war' at the time

[1] See, for example, Schuyler, *The Fall of the Old Colonial System*; also Kayser, *The Grand Social Enterprise*. A more balanced view of the Radicals and colonies is to be found in Halévy, *The Growth of Philosophical Radicalism*, pp. 510–11; and Halévy, *A History of The English People in the Nineteenth Century* (New York: Peter Smith, 1950), III, 231–2.

[2] Special notice, however, must be taken of Donald Winch's excellent recent study, *Classical Political Economy and Colonies*, which has discussed the relation of the economists to both the Wilmot-Horton and the Wakefield schemes of colonization.

[3] See Halévy, *History of the English People*, II, 193; Francis Place's notes on McCulloch's lecture of May 1824 can be found in his papers. See Francis Place Manuscripts, British Museum, Add. MSS 27, 858, vol. III, sheets 62–7.

[4] J. R. McCulloch, *A Descriptive and Statistical Account of the British Empire* (London, 1854), II, 532.

[5] 'Politics of Lower Canada', *Westminster Review* XIII (July 1830), 47–9.

[6] 'The Colonial Expenditure', *Westminster Review* XXIV (January 1836), 29.

[7] [T. P. Thompson], 'East India Trade', *Westminster Review* XIV (January 1831), 101; see also 'The British in India', *Westminster Review* IV (October 1825), 265–6.

of the Canadian revolt, Jeremy Bentham's pamphlet of 1793, *Emancipate Your Colonies*, which he described, in a letter to Francis Place, as 'perhaps the most perfect of Bentham's productions'.[1]

In the House of Commons, the leader of parliamentary Radicalism, Joseph Hume, denounced the unnecessary expenses associated with colonies as early as 1819[2], and in 1823, he urged that all colonies ought to be granted their independence: 'the commercial advantages to England would still be the same,' Hume insisted, 'for we should continue to be the principal suppliers'.[3] It was with the cry of 'economy' that the Radicals hoped to strike at the vast system of patronage embodied in the old colonial system, and in 1832, Hume presented this key Radical 'principle': 'that our colonial establishments ought, as much as possible, to be made to defray their own expenses',[4] a principle repeated, over the years, with innumerable variations.[5]

But the anti-colonialism of these Radicals was disputed within the Liberal party by the Radical Colonial Reformers. Lord John Russell distinguished between 'the Economists headed by Mr Hume', and 'the Philosophers'— that is, the Colonial Reformers—who, Russell thought, exerted more influence on Liberal colonial policy, and were 'led by Sir William Molesworth'.[6] Both Hume's 'Economists', and Molesworth's 'Philosophers', indeed, were determined that the old colonial system would have to go, but where the party of Hume (despite some early sympathy for the Wakefield system) was hostile to colonization, the Colonial Reformers were in the forefront of the fight for the Wakefield program of systematic colonization, the basis, in their view, for the transformation of the old colonial system to one of a middle-class empire. In the thirties and early forties, Wakefield's views appeared to triumph over those of other colonial projectors, and Wakefield was to receive the plaudits of Whigs like Lord John Russell,[7] and even the praise of such a fervent supporter of the old colonial system as the

---

[1] Quoted in J. K. Buckley, *Joseph Parkes of Birmingham* (London: Methuen, 1926), pp. 163–4; see also Graham Wallas, *The Life of Francis Place, 1771–1854* (New York: Burt Franklin, 1951), p. 329 f.n. In a letter to Earl Grey, dated 7 December 1853, Joseph Parkes observed that 'we should be as a Nation better off if some [of the colonies] were "moulted" [*sic*]; & which process will at no distant period come to pass. I think Rome throttled herself chiefly by a similar system, of territorial & *distant* colonial possessions.' Grey of Howick Papers.

[2] *P.D.* XL (10 June 1819), 1077–82; see also XLI (29 November 1819), 355–6.

[3] *P.D.*, N.S., VIII (25 February 1823), 250.

[4] *P.D.*, 3rd Series, XIV (23 July 1832), 648.

[5] See, for example, *P.D.*, 3rd Series, LXXIV (19 April 1844), 117–18; and *P.D.*, 3rd Series, LXXVIII (1 April 1845), 1330.

[6] Earl Russell, *Recollections and Suggestions, 1813–1873* (London, 1875), pp. 205, 201; see also pp. 202–3, 200.

[7] In an emigration debate in 1841, Russell declared that 'I have more than once expressed my concurrence in the principles' of 'Mr Wakefield'. See *P.D.*, 3rd Series, LVII (22 April 1841), 994.

Tory Sir Howard Douglas;[1] only the Manchester men seemed opposed. The second quarter of the nineteenth century, indeed, was to be one of the great ages of British colonization. By the late forties, however, the hopes of the Wakefield party were to be shattered.

Wilmot-Horton, colonization, and Wakefield

From its earliest years, the new industrialism was pursued by revolutionary violence. In the 1790s, there had been unrest among the artisan classes in the North and in London, whose democratic hopes, heightened by the French Revolution, were harshly repressed. The early years of the new century saw the machine-breaking of the Luddites, thrown out of employment by power looms and other mechanical innovations. After Waterloo, following a brief boom, England began in earnest its struggles with periodic industrial crises, which generally took the form of gluts of goods, and the consequent closing of manufactories, accompanied by the loss of employment of great numbers of seemingly supernumerary working-men, crises at times the product of, and always intensified by, deflationary factors in the economy, as some contemporaries, such as the Attwoods, understood. From 1816 to 1820, a time of economic difficulties was also the time of Peterloo and the repression of the Six Acts, when conspiracy and riot appeared endemic.[2] Trade improved with the early twenties, but prosperity was again dispelled by the panic of 1825, and a harassed peasantry revived fears of jacqueries with the rick-burnings of 1829-32, the years when mobs of working-men took to the streets to demand parliamentary reform. In the late thirties, the Chartists were to make themselves heard. Such were the circumstances in which Radicals and political economists, in the twenties and thirties, turned their attention to the formation of colonies.

Colonization—the planting of bodies of Englishmen in overseas settlements—was one of the imperial practices of the age of mercantilism of which the new age did not disapprove. The crucial spur which political economy applied to colonization, the one most readily understood by the public, was a new attitude toward population increase. Whereas for the mercantilist, population was a scarce resource to be carefully shepherded, early industrial

---

[1] *P.D.*, 3rd Series, LXXXI (18 June 1845), 807–8. See Sir Howard Douglas, *Considerations on the Value and Importance of the British North American Colonies* (London, 1831).

[2] A recent student of working-class movements has come to the conclusion that the Home Office's fears of revolution in these years were not, as had been the opinion of former scholars, a fantasy concocted by paid informers and believed by a government interested in excuses for repression, that, indeed, the Luddite and other working-class threats to government were real. E. P. Thompson, *The Making of the English Working Class* (New York: Pantheon, 1964), *passim*.

England, aided by the insights of Malthus, saw itself with a population surfeit, ever growing, and wished to discover means of ridding itself of the embarrassment. The census of 1811 revealed a British population of 12,596,803; that of 1821, an increase to 14,391,631; and that of 1831, an additional increase, once again about 15 per cent, to 16,539,318; in 1841 it was to be 18,720,394. Along with this growth in population, there occurred not only an absolute but a relative increase in poor relief: in 1801, about 9s. 1d. per capita was spent on the poor; in 1831, this sum had risen to 9s. 9d. per capita. The encouragement of emigration seemed a natural solution to the problem, and as early as 1819, parliament had voted £50,000 for sending 5,000 settlers to the Cape Colony. The twenties and early thirties were a time when there was much discussion of colonization—the subject was debated in Parliament, there were articles in the leading journals, and a number of colonial projectors competed for the accolade of putting forth a plan which would, at one blow, relieve the domestic distress believed to be due to a population surfeit, and colonize an undeveloped empire. In the twenties, the program of Sir Robert Wilmot-Horton was the starting-point for all those who concerned themselves with this problem.

In 1821, Wilmot-Horton, the Tory under-secretary of state for colonies in the Liverpool government, became the leading parliamentary advocate of colonization, most particularly in Canada, and largely upon the grounds of Malthus' argument. His plan, described in a report of a parliamentary committee in 1823, saw parishes securing loans from the government, by mortgaging their poor rates, to finance the emigration and settlement of paupers as peasant proprietors in Canada. By accepting such help, the pauper would give up all future claims to parish support.[1] Economic distress in Ireland, and Wilmot-Horton's exertions, led to a grant of £15,000 in 1823 for removing paupers to British North America; additional sums of £30,000 in 1825 and £20,480 in 1827 were voted for the same purpose. For Wilmot-Horton, colonization was, no doubt, *primarily* a means toward relieving the mother country of surplus paupers: 'Colonization abroad as a remedy for the evils of a relatively redundant population' was, he wrote in 1830, 'the best and cheapest mode of disposing of that *Abstraction* of superfluous labouring population from the general labour market, which I contend to be the *Main Remedy* for the distressed condition of the labouring classes of the United Kingdom'.[2] But Wilmot-Horton was interested not exclusively

[1] See R. N. Ghosh, 'The Colonization Controversy: R. J. Wilmot-Horton and the Classical Economists', *Economica*, N. S., XXXI, no. 124 (November 1964), 385–400.
[2] Quoted in R. C. Mills, *The Colonization of Australia (1829–42)* (London: Sidgwick & Jackson, 1915), p. 31; see also pp. 25–52 for a discussion of England's population problem.

in the emigration of paupers, as was to be later alleged by his enemies; he was also an advocate of empire-building. He was most insistent that, in so far as possible, English emigrants be prevailed upon to settle within the empire; in 1826, he described the superiority of exporting capital to British colonies rather than to foreign countries, and observed that while the United States accepted British exports to the extent of 12s. a head, Canada imported over £2 a head. Wilmot-Horton was even ready to note the advantages of the colonial 'system of our ancestors'.[1]

Wilmot-Horton's defense of colonization won the support of a number of political economists, with some of whom he was in regular correspondence,[2] while also provoking some Radical dissent. James Mill, among others, approved of Wilmot-Horton, and Torrens, when serving his first term in parliament, gave him his support.[3] An emigration, Torrens declared in 1829, which was 'founded upon the best and soundest principles of political economy', might be 'pregnant with mighty results', and 'would spread the British name, the British laws, and British influence throughout all climes of the world'.[4] Joseph Hume, on the other hand, the leading parliamentary spokesman for Radicalism during the twenties, was an opponent of emigration, colonization, and Wilmot-Horton. In 1825, he described the emigration scheme which the minister had placed before the house as 'a most wanton piece of extravagance',[5] and in March of the following year he urged that the only solution to problems of overpopulation was the limiting of reproduction.[6] Malthus himself, in the course of an extensive correspondence with Wilmot-Horton, agreed with Hume on this last point.[7] Hume's opposition was also based upon an orthodox Ricardian fear of capital loss: 'Employment must always be in proportion to capital,' he declared, 'and when so much floating capital was withdrawn from circulation'—as a result, among other matters, of allocations of money for emigration—'a proportionate quantity of employment must be withdrawn from the labouring part of the

---

[1] *P.D.*, N.S., XIV (14 March 1826), 1362–4.
[2] Wilmot-Horton pursued a correspondence with James Mill, Robert Torrens, T. R. Malthus, Thomas Chalmers, Thomas Tooke, David Ricardo, Nassau Senior, and J. R. McCulloch. See R. N. Ghosh, 'Malthus on Emigration and Colonization: Letters to Wilmot-Horton', *Economica*, N.S., XXX, no. 117 (February 1963), 62. See also Sir Robert John Wilmot-Horton, *Causes and Remedies of Pauperism in the United Kingdom Considered, Explanation of Mr. Wilmot-Horton's Bill, in a Letter and Queries Addressed to N. W. Senior Esq.*, Fourth Series (London, 1830), p. 3.
[3] See *P.D.*, N.S., XXI (4 June 1829), 1724; and *P.D.*, N.S. XIX (24 June 1828), 1503–4, 1508.
[4] *P.D.*, N.S., XVI (15 February 1827), 492–5. For Sir Robert Peel's support of Wilmot-Horton, see *ibid.* p. 507.
[5] *P.D.*, N.S., XII (15 April 1825), 1360.
[6] *P.D.*, N.S., XIV (14 March 1826), 1364; see also *P.D.*, N.S., XVI (15 February 1827), 509.
[7] See Ghosh, 'Malthus on Emigration', pp. 45–61.

community.' Hume, with none of the imperial feeling to which both Wilmot-Horton and Torrens had given expression, urged would-be emigrants to go to the United States,[1] agreeing, on this matter, with an *Edinburgh Review* article written by McCulloch in 1826.[2] The *Westminster Review* had, earlier, also urged the would-be emigrant to think only of his own interest in determining his destination, declaring that 'all new countries must be good customers to Britain', which could sell them 'goods of every description, and every quality, at the lowest price'. The *Westminster* suggested that the emigrant to the United States answer his critics in this fashion: 'if it be for my interest to emigrate to the United States, it is for the interest of my native country, as a manufacturing country, that I should emigrate thither'.[3]

Even friends of emigration and colonization found fault with Wilmot-Horton on the specifics of his program. In 1828, for example, Peel, who had given Wilmot-Horton friendly support, asserted that if men with capital would 'emigrate voluntarily', he would 'prefer such a state of society in the colonies to one composed entirely of paupers'. Peel further suggested that he would like to see men with, say, £5,000, buy land in the colonies and 'tempt' others to go as laborers; this would open 'new markets to the manufacture of the mother country'. Hume immediately supported Peel upon this point, declaring his opposition to making advances to emigrants—he called it a 'mortgage'—and urged 'voluntary' not 'coercive' emigration.[4] Some weeks earlier, in a debate, Hume had defended a Canadian company which had bought land from the government and had sold it, at a substantial profit, to emigrants—'thus the company forwarded emigration in the best possible manner', he asserted, 'without calling on the government for any assistance'.[5] The Radical *Westminster Review*, despite its cosmopolitan indifference to the destination of emigrants, was not unfriendly to Wilmot-Horton's efforts, though it urged, in 1826, that emigrants to the colonies be transported as cheaply as possible; specifically, it declared it necessary to 'transport the emigrants, not as *colonists*', as Wilmot-Horton had desired, 'but as *labourers*'.[6] In 1827, the *Westminster* described the unfortunate result of the dispersion of the Canadian population, 'a very imperfect division of employments',[7] and Alexander Baring, sympathetic to Wilmot-

---

[1] *P.D.*, N.S., XVI (15 February 1827), 510.
[2] [J. R. McCulloch], 'Emigration', *Edinburgh Review* XLV, no. LXXXIX (December 1826), 65.
[3] 'On Emigration', *Westminster Review* III (April 1825), 449–53.
[4] *P.D.*, N. S., XVIII (17 April 1828), 1556–7.
[5] *P.D.*, N.S., XVIII (27 March 1828), 1355.
[6] 'Emigration Report', *Westminster Review* VI (October 1826), 343, 370–3, 363–7.
[7] 'Canada', *Westminster Review* VIII (July 1827), 8–9; see, in addition, 'Third Emigration Report', *Westminster Review* IX (January 1828), 129–31.

Horton, in the course of a debate in the House of Commons, also inquired as to whether there was not 'too great an extension of the population in America for the purposes of civilization', praising, rather, a 'moderate degree of compression'.[1] Similarly, Michael Sadler, the Tory social reformer, in defending "home colonies" 'in the uncultivated deserts of our European empire', insisted, in 1829, that 'where men were most thinly scattered, then was their condition most wretched and degraded', and 'where they were most crowded, there were they most prosperous and happy'.[2]

The Wakefield plan of systematic colonization, previously described, was to meet virtually all the objections of both the friends and the foes of Wilmot-Horton's program.[3] It seemed almost as if Wakefield, while in Newgate, had busied himself with the *Westminster Review* and with Hansard, had taken cognizance of all the principles discussed, and then had set about, in the fashion of a creative company promoter, to formulate his scheme. Wakefield was to send a pamphlet sketching a proposal for the colonization of Australasia to Wilmot-Horton, in 1829, observing to him, in a letter, that his plan 'was originally suggested to my mind by your works on that subject'; Wilmot-Horton's writings, wrote Wakefield, had established 'that the people of this Empire are redundant, not merely in proportion to capital, according to the general theory of Mr Malthus, but, specially, in proportion to territory'. Wilmot-Horton was initially friendly to Wakefield, and was one of the original members of Wakefield's National Colonization Society, formed in 1830 to promote 'systematic colonization'. But differences soon developed. While Wilmot-Horton was ready to grant Wakefield's ideas a trial in Australia, Wakefield insisted on an unequivocal acceptance of his principle. Wilmot-Horton persuaded Torrens, Mill, and Malthus to write papers in opposition to Wakefield.[4] Torrens was later to describe how he and Malthus had at first been under the misapprehension that the Wakefield system depended on the application of labor and capital to inferior lands, which would lower profits and wages and create rent quite artificially; upon becoming convinced that this was not Wakefield's intention, Torrens joined Wakefield's colonization society.[5] There soon began a systematic denigration of Wilmot-Horton's ideas and reputation by the chief advocates of Wakefield's plan, who were later, as the Colonial Reformers, to apply the

[1] *P.D.*, N. S., XVI (15 February 1827), 503; see also *P.D.*, 3rd Series, II (22 February 1831), 895.
[2] *P.D.*, N. S., XXI (4 June 1829), 1727, 1729.
[3] A scheme much like Wakefield's, it might be added, had been proposed by a Canadian, Robert Gourlay, in the twenties. See Mills, *Colonization of Australia*, pp. 136–9.
[4] See Ghosh, 'The Colonization Controversy', pp. 390–400.
[5] *Report from the Select Committee on the Disposal of Lands in the British Colonies*, 1836 (512), xi, 499, pp. 135–6.

same techniques, for similar reasons, to assassinate the character of the permanent under-secretary to the colonial office, Sir James Stephen.

In 1830, Viscount Howick became the under-secretary of state for colonies in the new Whig government of his father, the second Earl Grey. Howick, although formerly not unsympathetic to Wilmot-Horton, was soon citing the views set forth by Charles Tennant, a member of the National Colonization Society, in this instance acting for Edward Gibbon Wakefield, who, because of his earlier excesses, found it undesirable to represent himself. On 15 January 1831, with evident exasperation, Wilmot-Horton wrote Howick that 'I was *much surprised* to hear you state yesterday that you were "Tennantish" in your views of colonization.' Tennant's views were, in Wilmot-Horton's opinion, 'utterly unsound and unpracticable'—a 'mere heresy'. Malthus, Torrens, Tooke, McCulloch, Senior, and Mill had supported his views, Wilmot-Horton maintained, and 'if *authority* is to prevail on a subject of Scientific Enquiry', he continued, he did not know 'in what quarter' the systematic colonizers were 'to apply for support'.[1] In another letter to Howick, on 17 February, Wilmot-Horton disputed the claim of the Wakefield party, apparently accepted by Howick, to having been the first to stress the advantages of 'concentration' in the settling of colonies; Wilmot-Horton presented, with a number of references, proof of his own priority. 'I am sure you will forgive my being anxious . . . that fair justice may be done to my views and opinions, & that others may not be allowed to carry away any credit which I may have earned.'[2] But Howick was unsympathetic to Wilmot-Horton's claims. In 1831, Howick oversaw the issuance of land regulations for Australia which more or less followed along the lines of Wakefield's concepts, a move which won the approval, for the moment, at any rate, as we shall see, of even so strong a Radical anti-colonizer as Joseph Hume.

Wilmot-Horton's new enmity to Wakefield's ideas made his continued presence in England an irritant, and he was named colonial governor of Ceylon, much to the pleasure of the younger Mill, one of the early Wakefield enthusiasts, who, in a letter in October 1831, noting the departure of 'our old enemy, Wilmot-Horton', was relieved that 'he no longer stands in the way of a rational scheme of colonisation'.[3] Whether because of Wakefield and his disciples, or as the fruit of previous experience of land administration, or because of a new view of England's social and economic needs, a scheme

---

[1] Letter of Wilmot-Horton to Howick, 15 January 1831. Grey of Howick Papers. On Howick, see H. T. Manning, 'Who Ran the British Empire—1830–1850?', *Journal of British Studies*, v, no. 1 (1965).

[2] Letter of Wilmot-Horton to Howick, 17 February 1831; see also enclosure, 'Observations on Lord Howick's Emigration Bill', 20 February 1831. Grey of Howick Papers.

[3] H. S. R. Elliot, ed., *The Letters of John Stuart Mill* (London: Longmans, Green, 1910), I, 19.

of 'systematic colonization' carried the day with the colonial office; for having maintained his views on colonization, Wilmot-Horton, rather plaintively, wrote in 1831, 'I might be said to have incurred the penalty of exile.'[1] In the following years, Wakefield and his disciples continued to revile Wilmot-Horton for his lack of economic sophistication, and denounced his scheme as that of, in Charles Buller's phrase, 'the shovelling out of paupers'.

The Wakefield program: advocates and critics

The Wakefield program became the positive, Radical alternative to the old colonial system. Wilmot-Horton was no Radical; indeed, he represented the old colonial system. When a young man, of unimpeachable Radical connections, developed a plan which comported with the results of the most orthodox political economy (even though its author was to set his more general grounds for empire-building in a heretical, agrarian framework), and made colonization conform, in virtually every respect, to the preconceptions of even the anti-colonial parliamentary Radicals, it was bound to attract Radical support. Stalwarts like James Mill and Stuart Mill were converted, as we have seen, as was a less orthodox, and less cosmopolitan, Bentham. The early practical objections to colonization of the parliamentary spokesman for classical orthodoxy, Joseph Hume, largely on grounds that colonization necessitated the wasteful expenditure of public funds, were, more or less, satisfied. When, in a private letter to Howick, in 1831, Hume saw the new system as preventing 'Governors and other official men appropriating to themselves very large districts of the best soil and in the most favourable situations',[2] he was reiterating Radical disapproval of a colonial system which gave the advantages associated with an imperial establishment to the aristocracy, both landed and financial, and to officeholders drawn from these classes.

The Wakefield program promised to spread these advantages to groups which had not heretofore enjoyed them. Howick—whose father's government was moving, by granting them the franchise, to enlist the support of the middle classes—acted to instil something of a new, liberal spirit of enterprise into the colonial office. While Wilmot-Horton's plans for colonization had fitted easily within the fabric of the then colonial establishment,

---

[1] Letter of Wilmot-Horton to Howick, 17 February 1831. Grey of Howick Papers. For a discussion of the circumstances which brought about the new land regulations of 1831, see Peter Burroughs, *Britain and Australia, 1831–1855; A Study in Imperial Relations and Crown Lands Administration* (Oxford: Clarendon Press, 1967), pp. 35–8 and *passim*.

[2] Letter of Joseph Hume to Howick, 24 January 1831. Grey of Howick Papers.

Wakefield sought to bypass that establishment.[1] What Wakefield proposed, indeed, was to make colonization as much a branch of private, individual enterprise as the cotton or the iron industries—was to create, through the mechanism of systematic colonization, a middle-class empire.

In the thirties and forties, there was a considerable literature—composed of pamphlets, leaflets, and broadsides, published by a number of colonization societies associated with Wakefield—to persuade would-be emigrants to make the journey to Australia. The imperial note was sounded loudly: English workers were told to 'avoid foreign countries'. The United States had slavery and 'the British are regarded as foreigners'; South America was 'inhabited by races of degenerate Spaniards and Portuguese, who are glad to get sturdy Saxons to work for them'. Most of them tellingly depicted the plight of the working-man at home:

You find trade bad; you are out of work ... things do not look as if they would improve; they may grow worse; and you feel, do all you can, working early and late, that you and those you love best may sink from the station you hold, and even starve at last.

'By many going,' British working-men were urged, 'those who remain will have more room, less competition, wages higher, food cheaper.'[2] One leaflet, praising Australian possibilities, contained such familiar phrases as 'there is not a trade or profession in the country which is not overcharged with competitors', and presented systematic colonization in these appealing terms: the cost of the passage out, the prospective emigrant was told, was defrayed by the sale of the lands to wealthier emigrants; sales created 'a labour fund,—in fact, for the benefit of the working people of England'. 'The emigrants arrive out FREE. On their arrival they find themselves in THE OPEN LABOUR MARKET.'[3]

Systematic colonization was presented as the solution to the colonial labor problem in terms of the new capitalism and its ideal of the free labor contract. As Wakefield made clear in all he wrote and said, systematic colonization was designed so that 'free' labor could play the economic role which slave labor had played in the plantations of the old colonial system. Such a use of free labor, of course, had further advantages for the new industrialism. Superfluous English laborers, at home a burden upon the

[1] See Paper presented by Sir James Stephen to Howick, 1 July 1837, in which he wrote, with considerable distaste, of the New Zealand bill of that year as the second effort, after the South Australia bill of 1834, 'to settle a Colony by the authority of Parliament'. Grey of Howick Papers.
[2] H. G. Kingston, *How the Unemployed May Better Their Condition* (London, 1848), pp. 3–6. (Published as *The Colonist*, No. 1, by the Society for the Promotion of Colonization.) See also the *Spectator* XI, no. 518 (2 June 1838), 511.
[3] J. B. Wilcocks, *Emigration, Its Necessity and Advantages* (Exeter, 1849), pp. 2, 13.

poor rates, could be more readily combinable abroad to produce wool and wheat, with an efficiency which, experience taught, was not to be expected of slave labor; and, as important, these English laborers could constitute, as slaves could not in at all the same fashion, an expanding market for English manufactures.

The question of slavery was discussed by Wakefield in a letter to the colonization commissioners, on 2 June 1835, in which the colonizer vaunted the historic role of slavery:

As the goodness of God and the progressive nature of man are unquestionable, and as God has permitted every nation to undergo the state of slavery, so we may be sure that slavery has not been an evil unmixed with good. Slavery appears to have been the step by which nations have emerged from poverty and barbarism, and moved onwards towards wealth and civilization.

In Wakefield's view, it had been slavery which had, everywhere, made possible the 'combination of labour, division of employments, surplus produce of different sorts, the power of exchanging, a great increase of capital'. 'When land is superabundant, and therefore extremely cheap, slavery seems to have been advantageous, by leading, through the greater productiveness of industry, to support for a greater number of people, and thence to such an increase of people in proportion to land, that it became easy to substitute the labour of hired workmen for that of slaves.' It had been, in Wakefield's view, the great increase of population relative to the available land which had made slavery unnecessary in Europe, but very necessary in those parts of the earth where 'land is superabundant'. The Wakefield system was proposed, therefore, as the only 'practical means of ultimately abolishing slavery throughout the world'.[1] In testimony before a parliamentary committee in 1841, Wakefield, on several occasions, referred to the state of the laborers under his system as one of 'natural slavery', of 'that natural subordination in which the greater part of mankind always have been, and probably always will be'. When Lord Stanley adverted, in a question, to Wakefield's desire to keep the emigrant 'in a state which you term one of slavery', Wakefield quickly replied, 'I said, natural slavery.'[2]

In defending the 'natural slavery' inherent in the program of systematic colonization, Wakefield presented a revealing picture of how a Radical economist might view the 'free' labor system, and Karl Marx, in his final chapter of the first volume of *Capital*, saw Wakefield's scheme as having

[1] Appendix, to *Second Report from the Committee on South Australia*, 1841 (394), iv, p. 333; see also *Report from the Select Committee on the Disposal of Lands in the British Colonies*, 1836 (512), xi, 499, p. 172 (1502).

[2] *Second Report from the Committee on South Australia*, 1841 (394), iv, p. 234 (2662, 2664); p. 238 (2696).

given the capitalist game away.[1] Indeed, middle-class prejudices, as well as interests, pervaded the Wakefield system, sometimes in a most unpleasant fashion. In vaunting his state of 'natural slavery', before the 1841 committee, for example, Wakefield described the circumstances whereby some laboring people in South Australia had clubbed together to buy land, and had established villages. They had established a 'cottier system', Wakefield said deprecatingly; through these efforts, they had achieved an 'enormous rate of wages', which, Wakefield declared, had had 'a most mischievous effect on them, and entirely corrupts them': 'they drink, they become rude and insolent, and they acquire habits of idleness; and I think ... that it would have been a very good thing if the screw had been put on tighter very soon after the founding of the colony'. Putting the screw on tighter meant, among other things, raising the price of the land, for 'the mischief that has arisen in Adelaide, has been too great a facility for the labouring classes to set up, not as miserable cottiers, with no more land than will sustain each family, but to set up as market-gardeners, and farmers, and cattle rearers, and in other ways to occupy themselves otherwise than as labourers for hire'.[2] Evidently, if Wakefield's story is to be credited, there *was* an economically effective method of colonization other than one which employed either bond slaves or 'natural' slaves; in this instance, at least, the state of natural slavery was, it would seem, in Wakefield's view, a social necessity, if the proletariat were to be raised from 'barbarism'. It was also, of course, of considerable utility to those who went to the colonies with capital.

Most appropriately, as the heart of a program to create a middle-class empire, systematic colonization was to proceed through the agency of a private company. A question, raised from the beginning, which continued to plague the various colonization societies, was whether it was not more proper to entrust such matters to government. Upon this point, George Grote, the banker, Radical M.P., and historian, speaking for Wakefield's South Australian Association, declared, in 1834, that the formation of a colony by the granting of a charter to a private company was a more British way of proceeding than the French practice of having the Crown found colonies.[3] Wakefield adopted the same position when questioned upon the

---

[1] Karl Marx, *Capital* (Chicago: Kerr, 1915), I, chap. XXXIII, 838–48; see H. O. Pappe, 'Wakefield and Marx', *Economic History Review*, 2nd Series, IV (1951), no. 1, 88–97.

[2] *Second Report from the Committee on South Australia*, 1841 (394), iv, pp. 238–9 (2696, 2701).

[3] *Ibid.*, Appendix, p. 35. Grote, Treasurer of the South Australian Association of 1834, at first approved of systematic colonization as providing for the emigration of all the classes of the metropolis, in the mode of ancient Greece. In the late thirties, he was to lose his sympathy for the Wakefield program and to favor colonial separation. See Grote's address to Exeter Hall

subject by the 1840 Committee on New Zealand. He observed, at this time, that, in surveying the history of British colonization, one would find that 'in a great number of instances the project was engendered by a company, and not by the Government', and that 'it has been the ancient practice of this country to let individuals begin, and when they have began [sic], and are ready to execute the project, then for the Government to take the necessary steps for giving them law and order'.[1] Such a position brought the inevitable charge of 'interested motives' from Wakefield's enemies.

In a parliamentary debate in 1834, Alexander Baring, of the celebrated banking family, attacked the method of colonization by private companies 'to realize the views of a set of gentlemen, whom he hoped he should not offend by calling experimental philosophers', but whose scheme was more than an academic exercise; it was 'a speculation' founded 'on interested motives', and Baring disliked seeing laborers leave England 'to promote the experiments or make the fortunes of others'.[2] The Times called Wakefield 'the philosophical emigrationist' who regarded man as 'a mere implement of husbandry',[3] and described the conduct of the Whigs in their relationship with a Wakefield colonization company as 'utterly disgraceful';[4] 'Newgate-born schemes' which provided for the sale of land by 'bubble projectors' was, in the view of The Times, 'more oppressive and unjust than any corn law', hitting as it did upon the poorest emigrants.[5] Another critic, Theophilus Heale, spoke, in exaggerated terms, of 'nearly 900,000 broad acres' granted to the New Zealand Company, one of Wakefield's companies, 'without a payment, and better still, without a condition', as 'certainly a boon of richer grace and favour than any nod which was ever given from kingly brows'.[6]

meeting quoted in [E. G. Wakefield], *The New British Province of South Australia* (London, 1838), pp. 156, 158; M. L. Clarke, *George Grote, A Biography* (London: Athlone Press, 1962), pp. 59–60; George Sutherland, *The South Australian Company, A Study in Colonization* (London: Longmans, 1898), p. 38.

[1] *Report from the Select Committee on New Zealand*, 1840 (582), vii, 447, Paper no. 74, p. 14.

[2] *P.D.*, 3rd Series, xxv (29 July 1834), 701–3.

[3] *The Times*, 5 January 1841, 4b, c.

[4] 'The Earl of Durham was fortunate enough', *The Times* reported, 'to possess himself of about a million acres' which 'cost his Lordship between 80 *l.* and 90 *l.*'; the Whigs had been 'ingenuously' told that 'as the highest rates of interest in the country are wholly unequal to the reasonable desires of godly capitalists, the disinterested and philanthropic views of the New Zealand Company, who have acquired a copartnery in the Durham speculation, are eminently entitled to Government support.' *The Times*, 13 April 1840, 4d, e.

[5] *The Times*, 4 May 1840, 4a, b; see also 16 September 1840, 4b, c, and 1 December 1840, 4c, d. Interestingly, *The Times* looked more favorably at the Wakefield High Church colony at Canterbury, an 'attempt to plant in the desert an actual offshoot of English society'; 'nothing can be more patriotic or more rational', the paper concluded. *The Times*, 23 May 1848, 4f, 5a.

[6] Theophilus Heale, *New Zealand and the New Zealand Company* (London, 1842), p. 7; see also pp. 35–6, 60–1, and *passim*.

Wakefield himself was a principal target of abuse: a journal addressing itself to a readership of those who planned to emigrate to the colonies, referred to Wakefield, in 1847, as 'that incomparable charlatan, juggler, mountebank, and humbug', and detailed how he was enriching himself by colonial jobs;[1] a similar journal, in 1849, spoke of poor working-men 'who straggled home from Wakefield Colonies, broken in spirit and in fortune', while the 'imposter' Wakefield moved profitably on from colonial scheme to colonial scheme. The latter journal described Wakefield's 'pandering to the prevalent tastes of the day': 'In 1831, he was the projector of a Republican Colony; in 1836 and 1839, of a Stock Jobbing Colony; in 1847, of a High Church feudal paternal settlement for great lords and humble serving men.' The journal grimly recalled 'the almost regal courtesy' with which Wakefield, 'in the palmy days of his grand bubble', had congratulated his 'enthusiastic victims on their fortunate prizes of "corner lots and double frontages" at Wellington and Nelson'.[2]

There was a good deal in circumstances surrounding Wakefield, his family, and his associates to make the charges appear plausible. Wakefield's father, it must be remembered, was a land-agent, and the long-lived Edward Wakefield was associated with his son's projects until his death in 1854; it is hardly surprising that during a time when speculations of various kinds were producing sizeable profits, that the Wakefields should have been attracted to speculation in colonial lands. Various members of the Wakefield family were prominently connected, in the forties, with the New Zealand Company—including Arthur, Edward Jerningham, and William Wakefield; with the exception of Arthur, killed by the Maori in 1843, they appear to have done fairly, though not outrageously, well out of their efforts at colonization, though Gibbon Wakefield did not particularly enrich himself. However, the possibilities for profit were, or appeared to be, considerable.

Some notes, in Wakefield's handwriting, appended to Bentham's 'Colonization Society Proposal' and found among the Bentham papers, listed, in the manner of a stock prospectus, the advantages which would accrue to the company and to first comers: the company would have the first choice of land; on company lands would be located the seat of government, the center of business, the sea-port and such lands would consequently rise greatly in value; the company and certain favored settlers would, during the first year, be enabled to purchase land at half the price set so that land so

---

[1] *Simmond's Colonial Magazine and Foreign Miscellany* XII, no. 46 (October 1847), 192; see also XI, no. 44 (August 1847), 443.
[2] *Sidney's Emigrant Journal* I, no. 24 (15 March 1849), 185–6; see also I, no. 25 (22 March 1849), 194; I, no. 26 (29 March 1849), 201–2; I, no. 23 (8 March 1849), 177–8.

purchased would yield a 100 per cent profit if sold the second year. 'It appears', Wakefield concluded, 'that the profits of the Company would be assured,' as would the profits of the principal settlers.[1] In testimony before a parliamentary committee in 1841, Wakefield put forward his view that there was nothing wrong with a company purchasing 'a very large block of land at the uniform price', and later 'reselling it at what may be called town improvement value' to 'other parties'. 'I cannot see how the gain of the individual was a loss to the public'; indeed, he declared, 'it was the prospect of that gain that appears to me the means by which the colony was founded at all'.[2] There seems no reason to doubt that others among Wakefield's associates had similar views and motives. It might be noted, for example, that Robert Torrens was compelled to resign as a South Australian commissioner because of his unwillingness to relinquish profits growing out of his participation in Wakefield's scheme of colonization.[3]

[1] Notes appended to Bentham papers. University College, Folder 8, pp. 192–7. An inspection of the Wakefield papers in the British Museum—consisting largely of Wakefield's letters to various members of his family over a prolonged period—confirms this reading of the 'prospectus'. For example, in a letter to his sister Catherine, dated 24 March 1853, Wakefield, in urging her and her family to join him at the Canterbury settlement, wrote: 'I hope you will come to Canterbury. If you can bring the Trust Fund you may be sure of 10 per cent on perfect security . . . Your husband would be pleased in every way with the change. Charles [a brother of Wakefield] is making a fortune without risk. He will be a member of the Provincial Parliament . . . *This letter must not be put into anybody's hands out of your own house.*' Wakefield papers. British Museum, 35, 261, folio 20.

[2] *Second Report from Committee on South Australia*, 1841 (394), iv, p. 230. Paper no. 18, in the Appendix to this report, pp. 272–3, contained this memorial of Bankers, Merchants, Shipowners and Manufacturers to Lord John Russell, which had been delivered in by E. G. Wakefield:

While it is the fitting function of a wise and benevolent government to exercise a controlling authority over the emigration of its people, and the settlement of its colonial possessions, to fix and maintain the principles on which the disposal of the public lands is to be conducted . . . the business of carrying these purposes into effect, of making known the value of colonial lands, of inviting purchasers, of collecting emigrants, and of providing the means for transporting great numbers to the most eligible spots, can only be efficiently performed by individuals or companies, conducting their affairs according to mercantile habits, and animated by the stimulus of mercantile gain.

[3] In June of 1835, Torrens had borrowed £1,000 from friends, at 5 per cent interest, over a three-year period, and had invested this amount in the South Australia Company. In October 1835 under-secretary Stephen forbade anyone holding an office in connection with the colonies—Torrens was at this time a South Australian commissioner—from having such an investment. Torrens, under the impression that this prohibition applied to the future not to the past, neither resigned nor disposed of his shares. In December 1840, however, he became aware that this double-interest must compel him to offer his resignation as one of Her Majesty's colonization commissioners. 'Up to the present time I have realized no pecuniary advantage' from the ownership of Australian land, he declared in a letter to Lord John Russell; 'part of the land', he continued, 'I gave to my son, who has gone out to the colony'. Torrens asked that his resignation be postponed until the close of a parliamentary inquiry then under way, adding, in justification of this request, that 'the colony of South Australia, devised by Mr Wakefield, was planted by me'. Somewhat to Torrens' surprise, his resignation was accepted. *Second Report from Committee on South Australia*, 1841 (394), iv, Appendix, pp. 268–72. See also letter from Lord Wellesley to Lord John Russell, 18 April 1841, suggesting a replacement for Torrens as Commissioner of the Colonial Land and Emigration Board. Russell Papers, P.R.O., 30/22, 4A.

There were other grounds for criticism of Wakefield's program. If Wakefield's support for free labor, private companies, and capitalist agriculture, seemed suited to the new economic outlook, the attempt of the colonizers to *organize* colonization *systematically* offended those adherents of *laissez-faire* who could only regard such an activity as an interference with the operations of a free market. The *Westminster Review*, under John Bowring and Perronet Thompson, both of whom had broken with the Utilitarian old guard, led by Mill after Bentham's death,[1] objected to 'any positive interference with the market for labour, or arbitrary meddling with the proportions between capital and labour even on the smallest scale', which, it declared, 'inevitably produces unpleasant and mischievous consequences'; the *Westminster* denounced the 'vain delusions'[2] of Wakefield, who was the protégé of its leading opponents, Molesworth and the Mills,[3] and his aim to plant 'slave colonies'. England, the quarterly declared, had altogether 'too many colonies, which almost overwhelm the mother country with their expenses';[4] the *Westminster* insisted, moreover, that 'backwoodsmen and squatters' constituted a kind of division of labor in colonization which it would be 'gratuitous folly' to suppress.[5] *The Economist* also condemned systematic colonization because it placed 'in the hands of the Government, by a factitious means of appropriating the capital of the capitalist, the fate of both capitalists and labourers, and giving it the power of determining, to a certain extent, the profits of capital and the wages of labour'; this the journal described as 'vicious'.[6]

J. A. Roebuck, a friend of Bentham and Mill, who wrote frequently for

---

[1] See G. L. Nesbitt, *Benthamite Reviewing; The First Twelve Years of the Westminster Review* (New York: Columbia University Press, 1934); Frank W. Fetter, 'Economic Articles in the *Westminster Review* and Their Authors, 1824–51', *Journal of Political Economy* LXX, no. 6 (December 1962), 570–96.

[2] [John Crawfurd], 'New South Australian Colony', *Westminster Review* XXI (October 1834), 446; [John Crawfurd], 'South Australian Colony', *Westminster Review* XXIII (July 1835), 239; for the *Westminster*'s highly unfavorable view of Wakefield, see 'Householders in Danger', *Westminster Review* XVI (January 1832), 223.

[3] See Halévy, *History*, III, 231–2. Mill was extremely hostile to Thompson, the proprietor of the *Westminster*, whom he described, in a letter to Carlyle in 1832, as having 'an understanding like a pin, going very far into a thing, but never covering a larger portion of it than the area of a pin's point'. Two years later, once again in a letter to Carlyle, Mill described '"philosophical radicals"' as 'narrow enough', though 'few of them are so narrow as Col. Thompson'. See Mineka, ed., *The Earlier Letters of John Stuart Mill, 1812–1848*, in *The Collected Works of John Stuart Mill*, XII, 127, 216.

[4] 'New South Australian Colony' (1834), pp. 446–8, 473–5. In this article Carey's critique of the Ricardian theory of rent—that the most accessible, as opposed to the most fertile, lands were occupied first—was anticipated, though, apparently, there was no intention of attacking Ricardo's theory.

[5] 'South Australian Colony' (1835), p. 230.

[6] *The Economist* (17 March 1849), pp. 293–4.

the *Westminster*, agreed: 'I own', he declared, 'that I look with great suspicion upon every attempt by a government to direct men in the application of their capital, and in their pursuit of wealth and happiness.' Roebuck had other grounds for criticism: Wakefield had provided that the entire land fund be applied to emigration; would it not have been wiser, Roebuck inquired, to apply some of the funds to the maintenance of a government, and to the building of roads, bridges, and wharves?[1] Like Roebuck, McCulloch criticized Wakefield's insistence that the whole amount of the sales proceeds be used for emigration, in an article for the *Edinburgh Review* in 1840. Although finding the 'Wakefield Principle' essentially 'sound', McCulloch objected to Wakefield's pretensions as a political economist, citing, particularly, the technical question of the 'sufficient price' at which land ought to be sold, and observing that Wakefield had never proved that there really existed a price which would tend toward optimal productivity; McCulloch suggested 'a uniform price, judiciously guessed at'.[2] Another economist, and a member of parliament, G. Poulett Scrope, once an admirer of Wakefield, became a critic, roughly along the lines of McCulloch. Scrope, addressing the 1836 committee on colonization, of which he was a member, described the Wakefield system 'as a specious and ingenious attempt at establishing a sort of modified white slavery'; more specifically, he disputed the principle of the sufficient price, and proposed a national fund for emigration which could be raised from taxation, from the poor-rates, or from land sales of the American variety which, he declared, was the best method.[3]

[1] J. A. Roebuck, *The Colonies of England* (London, 1849), pp. 129–41.

[2] McCulloch objected to the doctrinaire attitude of Wakefield's adherents, and was particularly annoyed by their assumption of the role of persecuted minority even while benefiting financially from their colonizing schemes. [J. R. McCulloch], 'New Theory of Colonization', *Edinburgh Review* LXXI, no. CXLIV (July 1840), 520–1, 542, and *passim*. The *Edinburgh* regarded itself an opponent of the Wakefield principle, and, in 1845, asked J. S. Mill to delete from an article he was preparing for the journal a long section of praise for systematic colonization. See Mill *Earlier Letters*, XIII, 660–1.

[3] Soon after the publication of *England and America*, Scrope had written to Wakefield reporting that 'I cannot remember ever reading any work with greater interest, or more thoroughly going along with any author in his views.' Declaring himself for 'long a zealous friend of colonization, as the one great cure of our economical evils, and a solution of all the most perplexing problems of political economy', he wrote that 'the notions which were but vaguely floating in my mind, I find methodized and arranged in a more lucid and convincing order in your work'. Scrope was later to express grave doubts. When Wakefield was called upon to testify before the 1836 committee on colonization, Scrope's earlier letter was quoted against its author by its recipient. Scrope replied that his letter had indicated agreement with the 'general scope and tendency' of Wakefield's book, not its 'every particular opinion'. *Report from the Select Committee on the Disposal of Lands in the British Colonies*, 1836 (512), xi, 499, pp. 80–1, 90–1, 176–80. Confirmation of Scrope's originality can be found in a series of letters to Howick, written in 1831, before the publication of *England and America*, in which Scrope's views on colonization appear quite fully. In a letter dated 21 February 1831, Scrope proposed a 'tax imposed on the employment of labourers in our Australian Colonies, and the expenditure of its proceeds, mortgaged in advance,

It is interesting to note that Wakefield, after emigrating to New Zealand in the early fifties, abandoned not only his original concept of the sufficient price, but even the principle of employing the revenue from land sales exclusively for emigration. He was yielding, he indicated, to special circumstances. It would appear that, in the early forties, a considerable amount of land had been bought by absentee speculators, and there was, consequently, a great number of unemployed workers; later, there was a shortage of labor when landless laborers sought their fortunes in the Australian gold fields. The balance between land and men was, under real conditions, a difficult one to maintain. Wakefield's new sufficient price was one which, it was hoped, would be high enough to make speculation difficult, and low enough to attract genuine settlers; revenues were now to be, in good part, applied to improving the market value of the land. In a word, Wakefield discovered that the leading economic objections to his principles brought to bear by such critics as Roebuck, McCulloch, and Scrope were justified by actual conditions. To the last, however, he maintained that the changes had been necessary only because his original principles had not been given a full chance to prove themselves.[1]

So considerable a body of Radical opinion attached itself to systematic colonization, indeed, that it might be maintained that an adherence to the Wakefield program constituted an important—perhaps the most important— bond among an influential group of Radicals in the thirties and forties. The Committee of the South Australian Association, a colonization society established by Wakefield in 1834, included such men as Charles Buller, George Grote, Rowland Hill, Sir William Molesworth, Dr Southwood Smith, Wolryche Whitmore, Henry Warburton, William Clay, and H. G. Ward. When the New Zealand Association, another of Wakefield's colonization societies, was launched in 1837, Lord Durham joined as a leading

in the supply of fresh labourers to meet the continually increasing Demand'. Since an increase in the labor force would lower the price of labor, Scrope added, '*the colonial capitalists would clearly be gainers*'. See also letters of 2 December 1831; 10 December 1831; 14 December 1831. Grey of Howick Papers. Scrope's brother, Lord Sydenham, succeeded Lord Durham as Governor-General of Canada. In letters, most probably to Scrope himself, which Scrope included in his biography of his brother, Sydenham denounced the Wakefield system. The system was 'utterly impracticable', Sydenham declared, since in Canada land was 'worth nothing except through the labour that is bestowed upon it'; at another time, he added: 'I told you in my last that Wakefield's doctrine won't do in Canada. To *force* concentration here is the greatest of absurdities . . . No man will go far into the woods if he can help it.' See G. P. Scrope, *Memoir of the Life of the Right Honourable Charles Lord Sydenham* (London, 1843), pp. 201, 198–202.

[1] M. F. Lloyd Prichard, 'Wakefield Changes His Mind About the "Sufficient Price"', *International Review of Social History* VIII, part 2 (1963), 251–69; see also Mill, *Earlier Letters*, XIII, 687, on absenteeism as an evil in New Zealand.

member, and, in 1839, Durham became the Governor of the Association. Wakefield played key roles in all these enterprises, though usually from behind the scenes, since he feared that his earlier escapades might bring the societies into disrepute.[1] The leading spirits of these associations—Durham, Charles Buller, a Radical barrister who served as M.P. for Liskeard, Sir William Molesworth, a Cornish baronet and Radical leader who was to edit Hobbes' works, and Wakefield himself—have gone into history as the Colonial Reformers.

The Colonial Reformers first saw in the Earl of Durham the great leader which Radicalism required. Durham's right view of colonization—he had been involved in speculation in Antipodean lands in the mid-twenties, even before Wakefield and the younger Reformers came upon the scene—was, no doubt, a pleasing part of his background, and the Earl, as noted, fulfilled their expectations not only by becoming an officer of the New Zealand Association, but by bringing both Buller and Wakefield, the latter being paid out of Durham's own pocket, to Canada with him on his famous mission; Wakefield's plan of systematic colonization was, of course, written into the Durham report. Durham, moreover, the son-in-law of the second Earl Grey, was well connected, a matter of no small importance to these Radicals who hoped to exercise a wide influence. While Durham, Buller, and Wakefield were in Canada, in 1837 to 1838, the interests of the Colonial Reformers were watched over in parliament by Molesworth; J. S. Mill, at that time the editor of the *Westminster Review*, which Molesworth had purchased from Thompson in 1834 and entrusted to Mill, gave the Durham party much needed support in the *Review*.[2]

Durham, however, died in 1840, when not yet fifty, and disappointed the hopes of his followers. The Colonial Reformers now lighted upon the heir of Earl Grey, Viscount Howick, whose activities as the under-secretary of

---

[1] In a letter, dated 2 June 1835, written to the colonization commissioners, Wakefield, referring to the large literature upon systematic colonization which had appeared since 1829, asserted: Now all of those books were written by me, and the whole of those pamphlets either by me or by friends of mine; while I also composed nearly the whole of the advertisements, resolutions, prospectuses and proposals, and of the applications, memorials, letters and replies to the Government, and other documents of any importance which were adopted by those three associations. The draft of a charter submitted to the Government by the South Australian Association, and the Act of Parliament which was substituted for the proposed charter, were drawn by a near relative of mine, under my immediate superintendence.
See *Second Report from the Select Committee on South Australia*, 1841 (394), iv, 9, Appendix, p. 332. The 'near relative' to whom Wakefield refers was most probably his brother Daniel Wakefield, a barrister and economist, and a member of the Provisional Committee of the South Australian Association in 1834.

[2] See Mill, *Earlier Letters*, XIII, 381–3; see also C. M. D. Towers, 'John Stuart Mill and the London and Westminster Review', *Atlantic Monthly* LXIX, no. CCCXI, 68, 73; see also Bloomfield, *Wakefield*, pp. 172–203, and Winch, *Classical Political Economy and Colonies*, pp. 148–59.

state for colonies in 1830–1 had been so satisfactory to their interests. On such questions as slavery, Ireland, and Canada as well, Howick's views were thoroughly acceptable. Although his attitude toward free trade had for some time been equivocal, a motion he presented to the House in 1843 revealed Howick a convert to a most advanced position.[1] Palmerston warned Lord John Russell, the leader of the Whig party, in December 1844, that Howick had plans of 'setting up business upon his own account as leader of a small party', which included Charles Buller. Buller, indeed, Palmerston reported, had been heard to say 'that Howick was the God of his idolatry'.[2]

The expectations of the Colonial Reformers were to be disappointed. Wakefield himself was in part to blame, for although his ideas and projects were initially acceptable to politicians in all political groups, Wakefield appears to have behaved in such an unattractive manner, and his efforts, and those of his followers, to press systematic colonization upon successive governments form such an unsavory record, that—especially since the early efforts at systematic colonization did not enjoy overwhelming success—in the end, all was to come to naught. The South Australian Association's solicitor, for a time, was the Birmingham Radical, Joseph Parkes, who quite soon left the Association, rather unhappy with Wakefield, whom, in 1834, he described as an 'ill judging, nasty-tempered man', and, three years later, as 'that disaffected, clever . . . scamp Gibbon Wakefield'.[3] Sir James Stephen, the permanent under-secretary for colonies, wrote, in 1845, in a private letter, that Wakefield, upon an earlier meeting, 'addressed me in such terms as to force on me the perfect conviction that I was in the presence of a man whose society was dangerous'; Stephen lamented Wakefield's 'want of truth & honour', feared 'misquotation', and rejoiced that he had 'deliberately preferred his enmity to his acquaintanceship'.[4] Although Wakefield made several efforts, in the early thirties, to press himself upon Howick, the latter kept him at arm's length, apparently not quite crediting Wakefield's assurances that he had no personal interest to further.[5]

The question of the personal interest of the New Zealand Company

---

[1] After this time, Howick worked to convert other Whigs to his position. See, for example, letters from Howick to Russell, attempting to persuade the latter to come out more vigorously for free trade. Russell Papers, P.R.O. 30/22, 4E. December 1845 (particularly, 14 and 16 December).

[2] Letter of Palmerston to Russell. 20 December 1844. Russell Papers, P.R.O. 30/22, 4D.

[3] See Buckley, *Joseph Parkes*, pp. 145–6.

[4] Letter of Sir James Stephen to Howick, February 1845. Grey of Howick Papers.

[5] See, for example, Wakefield's letter to Howick, 5 September 1831. On 3 May 1837, Wakefield observed that 'ever since 1831, I have frequently wished that some accident would give me an opportunity of verbal communication with your lordship, on a subject about which you have known & cared more than any public man—I mean the disposal of Colonial lands'. Grey of Howick Papers.

projectors helped to undermine the fairly widespread earlier confidence in the systematic colonizers. Stephen, in a letter in 1837, had written about the 'ambiguous role of the "Founders"', who 'would form a dynasty as absolute, and as completely exempt from control, as can possibly exist within the British Dominions'; by the New Zealand Act, he added, 'Parliament will have made a direct compact with the money lenders'.[1] Lord Normanby, who had been colonial secretary in the preceding Tory government, wrote to his successor, Lord John Russell, on 22 September 1839, that 'I have kept very clear of giving any countenance to that association of Durham and others who have been selling Land here before they had acquired it there.'[2] Palmerston seemed to dismiss the Colonial Reformers as mere land speculators; he was convinced that 'Charles Buller & other Persons who have engaged in Land speculations in our Colonies preach up Emigration upon a large Scale as a Cure for all our domestic Evils, because at all Events it would probably help them to turn their Lands to good account.'[3] As we have observed, Howick, too, despite his early approval of systematic colonization, joined, though more timidly, at first, in this chorus of distrust.

The correspondence of the New Zealand lobby—it must be called that— with Howick is embarrassing in the intensity with which the Wakefield program was pressed. In August 1846, for example, Charles Buller urged Howick—who had, in 1845, become the third Earl Grey, and, after Peel's resignation in 1846, was named the colonial secretary in the Russell government—to see Wakefield, whom he knew Grey disliked, on questions affecting the New Zealand Company. Wakefield 'alone can speak for the Co.', Buller wrote, rather, it would seem, forgetting whose favor was being sought, 'and if you get his assistance you have that of the Co. as a matter of certainty'; Buller, attempting to overcome Grey's 'distrust', assured the colonial secretary that Wakefield was now 'tired of conflict'.[4] Henry George Ward

---

[1] Letter by Sir James Stephen to Howick, 1 July 1837. Grey of Howick Papers.

[2] Letter of Lord Normanby to Lord John Russell, 22 September 1839. Normanby also asserted that he had warned the Wakefield group that the government maintained the right 'to question all the titles of Land' where such land 'appeared to have been acquired in excessive proportions or by fraudulent bargains'. Russell Papers, P.R.O. 30/22, 3D.

[3] Letter of Palmerston to Russell, 20 December 1844. Russell Papers, P.R.O. 30/22, 4D.

[4] Letter of Charles Buller to Grey, 3 August 1846. Grey of Howick Papers. With Buller's letter was enclosed a paper, written by Wakefield, accusing the government of having failed to live up to its promise, made by Russell, 'to give the Company an acre of land for each dollar [sic.; later defined as 5s.] of its colonizing expenditure'. Wakefield further charged the Crown with underselling the company in the land market. Wakefield urged immediate action by the newly installed Liberal government in behalf of the company: 'so as to take advantage of a tendency in the public mind to strong re-action in favour of colonizing which has been produced by the accession of some of the members of the present Government to power' (no doubt, Grey, in particular), 'which will cease upon the first disappointment of present expectations'.

and Francis Baring wrote Grey in the same fashion, and the colonial secretary was, soon, rather tired of being importuned. Edward Wakefield pursued the prime minister, Lord John Russell, with similar insistency, on behalf of the New Zealand Company.[1] The tone was that of monomania: 'While you are enjoying your rustic repose,' Buller wrote Grey, in April 1846, 'will you think once again of New Zealand?'[2] After the failure of the South Australian project, and the difficulties being encountered by the New Zealand project, Grey had strong doubts.

Grey's 'doubts' on systematic colonization undid the 'idolatry' of Buller and the Colonial Reformers, and doomed the Wakefield companies. 'It is mortifying to the last degree,' Grey wrote Buller in early 1847, clearly feeling some regret, 'but I am beginning to come to the conclusion that I can do nothing to promote "systematic colonization".'[3] Buller, on 15 March 1847, clearly shaken, warned Grey that 'If you do not succeed' in New Zealand, it will 'be a bar to your colonizing any other part of the world': 'the spectre of the New Zealand Company, destroyed in the best effort at colonization during the last 100 years, will scare every capitalist in the country from venturing in any similar enterprise'.[4] But Grey was adamant. In October 1849, in response to another plea for help, this time for the Company's Canterbury Settlement, the last of Wakefield's projects, Grey wrote, much less sympathetically, that 'the establishment of such a new settlement seems to me to be a measure more calculated to promote the interest of the New Zealand Company than that of the older settlements or of the public'. Indeed, in response to Baring's suggestion that the Company could only revive its fortunes by 'sales' in the Canterbury Colony, Grey replied that if this was so 'in spite of the very large pecuniary assistance you have received from the Govmt', specifying a large loan, at low interest, and the considerable powers of the Company, 'the objections' made 'to the whole system of giving such extensive powers to a joint stock company are well founded'; 'for the sake of attracting customers for land by the excitement of novelty,' he further observed, 'you have formed 3 or 4 different establishments with a number of settlers not more than sufficient for one'. 'There is something radically wrong in the whole system,' Grey sadly concluded.[5]

Grey's apostasy drew Wakefield's fire in his *Art of Colonization*, in 1849,

[1] See, for example, letter of Edward Wakefield to Lord John Russell, 3 December 1845. Russell Papers, P.R.O. 30/22, 4E.
[2] Letter of Charles Buller to Grey, 25 April 1846. Grey of Howick Papers.
[3] Letter of Grey to Charles Buller, 23 February 1847. Grey of Howick Papers.
[4] Letter of Charles Buller to Grey, 15 March 1847. Grey of Howick Papers.
[5] Letter of Grey to Francis Baring, 6 October 1849. Grey of Howick Papers.

which prompted Gibbon's father, in a letter to Grey, in April 1849, to apologize, 'with great pain and regret', for his eldest son's attacks, noting, with reference to Grey's past services to systematic colonization, 'the great debt which my family owe you for much which you have done'. With what appears to have been a family trait of insensitivity, however, the elder Wakefield used his apology simply as an introduction to a lengthy lobbying letter on behalf of the Company.[1] Grey replied in a pained and peremptory tone.[2]

By this time, the game was up. As a final gesture, Grey arranged to grant the New Zealand Company a sum of money in exchange for which the Company gave up its activities. Buller died in 1848; Molesworth was alienated from Wakefield, though still much under the influence of his ideas. Looking about for a new 'coming man', in the late forties—after the failures of the hopes surrounding Durham and Grey—Wakefield seems to have lighted upon the young Peelite leader, W. E. Gladstone, but this, clearly, was not to turn out as Wakefield had hoped. By the early fifties, Wakefield had become a bitter man, and a letter of his in 1852 has a paranoid ring: he denounced his former supporters, in particular, decrying 'the *immense conceit*, the *whimsicality*, the *extreme jealousy*, the *vile temper*, and the tyrannical disposition of Lord Grey'; he noted 'the turn against me of *my old, and long faithful* disciple *Molesworth*'; finally Buller, now dead, had been 'spoiled' as a colonial reformer by Grey. In 1849, the cause of colonial reform 'was dead, and was only restored to life', Wakefield observed, by the founding of the Canterbury Association.[3] The Association, which was to be Wakefield's last project, began in 1849 as a joint enterprise of the New Zealand Company and the Church of England; its president was the Archbishop of Canterbury, and its committee consisted of persons such as Bishop Wilberforce, Lord Ashley, and Lord John Manners. Despite such far from Radical plumage, it was at Canterbury that Wakefield believed his ideas were most fully set to work.[4]

[1] Letter of Edward Wakefield to Grey, 18 April 1849; see also earlier letter of Edward Wakefield to Howick, 5 December 1845. Grey of Howick Papers.
[2] Letter of Grey to Edward Wakefield, 20 April 1849. Grey of Howick Papers.
[3] Copy of Letter by E. G. Wakefield to J. R. Godley, on 7 June 1852, which had appeared in the Lyttelton *Times* of 30 October 1852. Found among Grey of Howick Papers. Wakefield, clearly, despite failures, was still much admired by his New Zealand associates in 1849. A resolution, most flattering to him in every way, passed at the Annual Meeting of the New Zealand Company on 31 May 1849, even asked 'that Edward Gibbon Wakefield, Esq., be requested to sit for his Portrait; that a Committee of Proprietors be appointed to receive subscriptions for the same' (p. 79). Minutes of General Meetings of the New Zealand Company, 1840–58, C.O. 208/179.
[4] For a full discussion of these colonization societies and their activities, see Douglas Pike, *Paradise of Dissent; South Australia, 1829–1857* (London: Longmans, Green, 1957), pp. 52–95, and *passim*; Michael Turnbull, *The New Zealand Bubble; the Wakefield Theory in Practice* (Wellington:

There was a curious flurry, in the last months of 1849, when Charles Adderley, a disciple of Wakefield, and a future Tory colonial under-secretary, made approaches to Disraeli, proposing an alliance between the protectionist party and the new colonial movement, but Disraeli turned down the suggestion, seeing in the colonial movement 'the stir of Wakefield, in whom I have little confidence'.[1] As late as 1852, Wakefield still had some hope of a political coup, as a result of Gladstone's interest,[2] and we even find him, at that time, writing to Gladstone, who, of course, was on his way to a Cobdenite position, in support of a parliamentary resolution, which had been introduced by Molesworth, to retrench imperial expenditures by withdrawing troops from various parts of the empire. In a patent attempt to win Gladstone's support for his colonization schemes, Wakefield, in agree-ment with Gladstone's own views, was critical of the role of imperial troops whose presence, he wrote, helped to promote native wars, enabled a colonial minority to govern, and corrupted colonial economies by making them dependent on military expenditure. It was the sending of troops, he declared, that had caused the problems of the New Zealand colony; if no troops had been sent, Wakefield observed, in explanation of the abject failure of the New Zealand scheme, 'the inducements to emigration would have been very great'. Indeed, Wakefield was prepared to grant, in this effort to win Gladstone's assistance, that 'if a Hume-Cobden imperial policy had pre-vailed', then 'all the main evils of New Zealand colonization . . . would have been avoided'. 'I never thought to say as much for the Manchester School,' Wakefield concluded.[3] But, evidently, even this grand concession of the old Colonial Reformer to his long-time opponents was not enough to persuade Gladstone to undertake the job of promoting a new colonization scheme. It was almost in a mood of despair that, in that same year, Wakefield himself emigrated to New Zealand, where he died in 1864.

Colonial Reformers and Exeter Hall

The Colonial Reformers cannot be regarded as mere land speculators, as Palmerston, apparently, saw them. The Wakefield party was called that of the 'Colonial Reformers' not only because they busied themselves with

Price, Milburn, 1959); Burroughs, *Britain and Australia*, pp. 12–34, 169–295, and *passim*; Bloomfield, *Wakefield*, pp. 105–59, 292–324, 349–53; Winch, *Classical Political Economy and Colonies*, pp. 111–12, and *passim*.

[1] Quoted in W. F. Moneypenny, *Life of Benjamin Disraeli*, (New York: Macmillan, 1911) III, 234.
[2] Wakefield had begun his wooing of Gladstone in the thirties. Gladstone Papers, 44, 355, f. 265; and 44, 355, f. 70.
[3] See Memorandum by Wakefield to Gladstone on Molesworth motion. Gladstone Papers, 44, 567, ff. 57b, 61, 61b, 62.

the founding of colonies by new methods, particularly in Australia and New Zealand, and with defending the interests of these infant communities before parliament, while the party of Hume and Cobden made carping jibes, but primarily because of their role, as associates of Lord Durham, in changing the basis of the government of the colonies, removing them from the centralized control of the colonial office bureaucracy, and granting them a measure of self-government. It was they who envisioned a free association of independent nations which we know as the Commonwealth, a concept that can be traced to the Durham report, which owed much to both Buller and Wakefield. Wakefield, indeed, had advocated such a program in *England and America*.

The Colonial Reformers did not wish to grant the colonies independence; even when Durham and his associates spoke of responsible colonial government, they specifically reserved for the metropolis such matters as the form of government, foreign relations, the disposal of public lands, and the regulations of all external trade, whether with England itself, another British colony, or a foreign country. The Colonial Reformers, as we shall see in a subsequent chapter, not only believed in the *necessity* of colonization, but, less imbued with cosmopolitan sentiment than the Cobdenites, wished to secure positive state action to ensure that English resources would find employment in lands which maintained allegiance to the Crown. They believed that the colonies would be more likely to maintain their loyalty to the metropolis if they enjoyed a large measure of self-government rather than if they were dependent upon a distant colonial office manned by incompetent scions of the aristocracy.

In pursuing their program of colonial expansion, the Colonial Reformers ran afoul not only of the Cobdenites, but also of the colonial office, and of nonconformist, humanitarian groups with strong ties to the Cobdenites. The weekly organ of the Wakefield party, Rintoul's *Spectator*, proved particularly useful in carrying to the country their case against the 'colonial bumbureaucracy', and against 'Mr Mother-Country', the permanent under-secretary for colonies, James Stephen. The Colonial Reformers regarded the interference of the colonial office in the affairs of overseas colonies as responsible for most difficulties; if only 'Mr Mother-Country' would not meddle, the *Spectator* observed, 'the prosperity both of the Colonies and the Central Empire may be raised to an unprecedented pitch, the Mother-country and its Colonies may become a British United States girdling the globe and leading the van in the march of civilization'.[1]

[1] 'False Alarm of the Colonial Bumbureaucracy', *Spectator* XII, no. 555 (16 February 1839), 155–6; 'Colonial Policy', *Spectator* XIV, no. 660 (20 February 1841), 180–1.

What particularly aroused the resentment of the Colonial Reformers, in the thirties and forties, was the continuous conflict over land rights between the colonists, whose parliamentary spokesmen they were, and the aboriginal races, whose interests were supported by humanitarian societies—the so-called 'missionary' interest—and by the colonial office.[1] When 'King Stephen', who was the son of a leading evangelical supporter of Wilberforce's efforts to abolish slavery, actively intervened in New Zealand, in 1845, to protect native land rights, Charles Buller, speaking for the New Zealand Company, complained 'that a sound colonizing policy has been thwarted by feeble views and narrow jealousies'. There were 'two conflicting systems of Colonial policy', Buller suggested. If the proper one were followed, England might make New Zealand 'the Britain of the southern hemisphere; there you might concentrate the trade of the Pacific; and from that new seat of your dominion you might give laws and manners to a new world, upholding subject races, and imposing your will on the strong'.[2]

In such Virgilian cadences, then, did the Colonial Reformers attack the ignoble policy of the colonial office in protecting native rights. The *Spectator* repeatedly denounced 'the humanity-mongers, the self-seeking Missionaries, and the Colonial Office',[3] citing particularly the Wesleyan Methodists who 'job in missions'.[4] In one parliamentary debate another Colonial Reformer, H. G. Ward, inquired: 'Of what avail was it to attempt to extend to savages the legal rights of civilized Englishmen?'[5]

There was a considerable body of Englishmen—principally middle-class Dissenters and Evangelicals, although they were joined by other humanitarians—who thought of themselves as possessing a philanthropic vested interest in the condition of these 'savages', and opposed the Colonial Reformers on the question of Maori land rights and similar matters, both inside and outside parliament. Following the temper of English industry, they were primarily interested in Christianity for export, and they exercised a paternal concern for their spiritual wards across the seas. Among these nonconformist missionary and humanitarian societies—generally known as Exeter Hall, from their meeting-place off the Strand—were the Anti-Slavery Society and the Aborigines Protection Society. Exeter Hall generally

---

[1] See Dandeson Coates, *The Principles, Objects, and Plan of the New Zealand Association Examined* (London, 1838), p. 41; Wakefield replied in *Mr. Dandeson Coates and the New Zealand Association* (London, 1837).
[2] *P.D.*, 3rd Series, LXXXI (17 June 1845), 669–70, 666.
[3] 'The Opposition to the New Zealand Bill', *Spectator* XI, no. 521 (23 June 1838), 585.
[4] 'Colonial Jobbers in a Flutter', *Spectator* XI, no. 520 (16 June 1838), 561.
[5] *P.D.*, 3rd Series, LXXXII (23 July 1845), 978.

found under-secretary Stephen sympathetic to its aspirations.[1] The mood of the missionary party was set forth, in the House of Commons, in 1834, by Thomas Fowell Buxton, the leader in the abolition of slavery during the previous year, who noted that 'in every place where we have established a colony, the native inhabitants, instead of being benefited, were injured by our presence among them'.[2] Standish Motte, one of the leaders of the Aborigines Protection Society, in a pamphlet published in 1840, warned England to 'be careful that in grasping the commerce of the earth we do not defraud; in acquiring possessions of territory we do not despoil; in planting new colonies, we do not demoralize, ruin, and exterminate those who by birthright are nature's lords of the soil they inhabit'.[3] The tenth annual report of the Aborigines Society in 1847 spoke of 'the struggle' 'to bring protection to the feeble families of mankind against the homicidal process which, in every instance of modern colonization, has accompanied the diffusion of our Anglo-Saxon Race'.[4]

But, as Buxton insisted at a meeting at Exeter Hall in 1839, the societies of Exeter Hall did not oppose colonization; they simply wished 'to render the spread of British colonies beneficial, not ruinous, to the Aborigines'.[5] Exeter Hall not only regarded colonization as useful to the performance of such good works as the extirpation of slavery and the spread of Christianity; many of the humanitarian leaders saw the usefulness of colonies to an industrial Britain in much the same light as did the Colonial Reformers. Standish Motte, for instance, urged, simply, that in planting colonies to open 'new fields for British capital and enterprise, and creating a vent and employment for that industry and intelligence which is stagnant at home', England had to observe the rules of justice to all races, if her colonies were to flourish.[6] The same spirit was apparent in the 1847 report of the Aborigines Protection Society, which subscribed to the statement of one of its leaders, J. J. Gurney, of the famous Quaker banking family, that a nation which acted in a Christian manner—which would 'proclaim the principles of universal peace, suffer wrong with condescension, abstain from all retaliation,

---

[1] See Paul Knaplund, *James Stephen and the British Colonial System: 1815–1847* (Madison: University of Wisconsin Press, 1953), *passim*; see also B. Semmel, *Jamaican Blood and Victorian Conscience* (Boston: Houghton Mifflin, 1963), pp. 18–22.
[2] *P.D.*, 3rd Series, XXIV, (1 July 1834), 1061.
[3] Standish Motte, *Outline of a System of Legislation, For Securing Protection to the Aboriginal Inhabitants of All Countries Colonized by Great Britain* (London, 1840), pp. 6–7; see also *Report from the Select Committee on Aborigines* (British Settlements), 1836 (538), vii, 1, p. 455 (3877–9), and *passim*.
[4] *The Tenth Annual Report of the Aborigines Protection Society* (London, 1847), p. 9.
[5] *The Second Annual Report of the Aborigines Protection Society* (London. 1839), p. 21.
[6] Motte, *Outline*, pp. 9–10.

return good for evil, and diligently promote the welfare of men'—would 'be blessed with eminent prosperity, enriched with unrestricted commerce, loaded with reciprocal benefits, and endowed for every good and wise and worthy purpose with irresistible influence over surrounding nations'.[1] Louis Chamerovzow, the Polish-born secretary of the Protection Society, in 1847, constructed this benign, if incomplete, syllogism: 'The prosperity of Great Britain is intimately connected with that of her Colonies; the Prosperity of these with that of the native population.'[2] It was with the second term of the syllogism that the Colonial Reformers had quarreled.

It would appear, then, that even the struggle of the Colonial Reformers for responsible government in the Colonies may be subject to a pejorative interpretation. The white settlers in New Zealand and Australia, it might be easily argued, wanted to handle the natives according to their own, far from benign, lights, free of interference from 'Mr Mother-Country' of the colonial office; we are not unfamiliar, today, with similar colonial demands. Would Palmerston's hostile view of the Wakefield party apply here, as well? The Colonial Reformers were, as Russell labeled them, indeed, the 'Philosophers', intellectuals attracted to an elaborate and doctrinaire program, the practical import of which might be directed toward enriching themselves, as they probably saw it, while benefiting their country and their hard-pressed or impoverished fellow citizens, hurting none, except perhaps some savage Maori. While a Wakefield or a Torrens, or even Charles Buller, might require, even urgently in the case of Wakefield and his family, the profits of speculation in colonial lands, this could hardly be the case with great landowners such as Molesworth or Durham, to whom such speculation was hardly a necessity—even though, as we have noted, Durham had invested in Australasian lands as early as the twenties.

Certain Methodist gentlemen of the Exeter Hall party had gone so far, in their presumption, to suggest that if land were needed to settle redundant Britons or Irishmen, the estates of Sir William Molesworth, or Lord Durham, might readily be made available for this purpose by act of parliament. The *Spectator* was indignant at Exeter Hall's distorted values:

So, the thinly-scattered savages of New Zealand—a diminishing population less than that of a single district of London, spread over a surface of many thousand miles—have the same title to the millions of uncultivated and unappropriated acres in their country, that an English nobleman has to his estate! Parliament may

[1] *Tenth Annual Report of Aborigines Protection Society*, p. 29.
[2] L. A. Chamerovzow, 'England and New Zealand', *The Colonial Intelligencer; or Aborigines' Friend* x (December 1847), 170–1.

deal with the land in Cornwall, Essex, or Durham, as with the wilds of South Australia and New Zealand! Truly this is a pretty doctrine, and beautifully illustrates the fitness of its authors for the government of a colony.[1]

The weekly's statement illustrates, further, the basis for the Palmerstonian view of the Wakefield party.

On colonial questions, Exeter Hall would have the sympathy and assistance of the party of Hume and Cobden, who, unlike the missionary party, had no interest in appearing fit for colonial government, as we have seen, but whose imagination had been captured by an imperial vision of another sort. In adapting the trade theories of the classical economists, they became the champions of preserving and extending the nation's industrial predominance —the British Workshop of the World.

[1] 'Colonial Jobbers in a Flutter', *Spectator* XI, no. 520 (16 June 1838), 561. It may have been J. A. Roebuck's colonial background which led him to adopt a similar position. Roebuck, *Colonies of England*, p. 138. 'I say, that for the mass, the sum of human enjoyment to be derived from this globe which God has given to us,' Roebuck declared, 'it is requisite for us to pass over the original tribes that we find existing in the separate lands which we colonize.' 'When the European comes in contact with any other type of man,' he continued, 'that other type disappears.' Roebuck was not upholding the white man's burden but the standard of a premature, imperialist social-darwinism. 'Let us not shade our eyes, and pretend not to see this result,' he concluded. That would be 'hypocrisy'.

CHAPTER 6

Parliament, political economy and the Workshop of the World

That age of economical statesmanship which Lord Shelburne had predicted in 1787, when he demolished, in the House of Lords, Bishop Watson and the Balance of Trade, which Mr Pitt had comprehended, and for which he was preparing the nation when the French revolution diverted the public mind into a stronger and more turbulent current, was again impending, while the intervening history of the country had been prolific in events which had aggravated the necessity of investigating the sources of the wealth of nations. The time had arrived when parliamentary pre-eminence could no longer be achieved or maintained by gorgeous abstractions borrowed from Burke, or shallow systems purloined from De Lolme, adorned with Horatian points, or varied with Virgilian passages. It was to be an age of abstruse disquisition, that required a compact and sinewy intellect, nurtured in a class of learning not yet honoured in colleges, and which might arrive at conclusions conflicting with predominant prejudices.

Disraeli, *Coningsby*

The mysteries of economical science are mysteries no longer; the recondite wisdom of the Smiths, Says, and Ricardos has become the diffused convictions, the common sense of society.

Philip Harwood, Lecture delivered at the
London Mechanics Institution, Chancery Lane, 1843

The science of political economy, as expounded by the most learned pundits of the day, is a very abstruse and arbitrary system. It partakes of the mysteriousness of theology and the glorious uncertainty of the law.

The Times, 19 March 1847

IN the last two decades of the eighteenth century, the Industrial Revolution had taken hold in Great Britain, as we have noted earlier, and Britain was well on its way toward becoming the world's first industrialized country. It was during the first three to four decades of the nineteenth century that the greatest structural change occurred, most particularly in the two decades following Waterloo. In 1801, approximately 35 per cent of the British labor force was in agriculture, forestry, or fishing, and about

130

30 per cent in manufacturing and mining; by 1841, these figures were 22 per cent and 40 per cent respectively. England was rapidly becoming urbanized, as well, and by 1841, more than one out of every three persons in England and Wales was living in towns of over 20,000 population. The staple manufacture of the newly industrialized England was no longer wool, but cotton. At the beginning of the eighteenth century, manufactured woollens had constituted two-thirds of the value of all British domestic exports; by 1815, the value of exported cotton goods—the product of the new industrial system—was twice that of exported woollens, and constituted 40 per cent of the declared value of all British exports. By 1830, cotton accounted for about one-half of the value of domestic exports, and the textile and dress industries together provided about three-quarters of such exports. Between 1800 and 1830, the value of British exports quadrupled, and it was clear that the expansion of overseas trade played a strategic role in setting the pace for the expansion of the economy.

In 1822, in speaking to his constituents, the electors of rural Huntingdon, Lord John Russell, a son of the Duke of Bedford, one of the great landowners of England, declaimed against the practitioners of the pretended science of political economy 'who wish to substitute the corn of Poland and Russia for our own'. Their principle was 'to buy where you can buy cheapest', and they were not concerned about the difference 'between an agricultural and manufacturing population in all that concerns morals, order, national strength and national tranquillity'. Wealth was the 'only object of their speculation', nor did they consider the millions who might be 'reduced to utter beggary in the course of their operations'. This they call 'diverting capital into another channel'. Their reasoning lies 'in abstract terms, their speculations deal so much by the gross, that they have the same insensibility about the sufferings of a people, that a General has respecting the loss of men wearied by his operations'. Political economy was 'now the fashion', Russell concluded, and 'the Farmers of England, are likely, if they do not keep a good look out, to be the victims'.[1]

In his memoirs, published toward the end of his life, Russell did not mention this early effort in political speech-making, but did recall a speech he had delivered in the 1840s to a new set of constituents, the electors of the City of London. 'I said', Earl Russell recollected, that 'it was barbarous to prevent the manufacturer of Lancashire from sending his yard of cotton cloth to Ohio, or to prevent the farmer in Ohio from sending his bushel of corn to Lancashire'. The population of Great Britain was 'so cabined,

[1] Quoted from *Morning Chronicle* of 18 January 1822 by Sraffa, *Works of Ricardo*, IX, 155 f.n.

cribbed, confined to the land of the British Isles, that our manufacturing towns will always be very populous', Russell had continued, and there would 'exist for a long time vast territories in North and South America, in the plains of Buenos Ayres, in the hills and dales of Australia and New Zealand, whose herds of cattle may find plentiful pasture, and the grower of corn receive an ample remuneration for his labour'. The 'evil genius of protection' which prevailed in so many parts of the world 'must be overcome', Russell had declared.[1]

This rather remarkable revolution in sentiment was not confined to Lord John Russell. Halévy wrote of the struggle between two Englands, the old agrarian England, attempting to maintain some sort of economic parity with the new economic forces which threatened to overwhelm it—whose spokesmen among the economists, as we have seen, were Malthus and Chalmers—and the new industrial England which, with the support of economic orthodoxy, was striving to make England the Workshop of the World. Years before the abolition of the corn laws, free trade was to triumph in all important food imports other than corn, and in 1842, Peel was even to arrange for the free admission of empire corn; by 1846, much of the landed aristocracy, which composed the greater part of both houses of parliament, had come to see that the repeal of the corn laws would not, after all, be so very injurious to them, and indeed, that it might prove an advantage. But it took a good deal of time and debate before such a point of view could prevail, and the dissemination of the principles of the political economists played some role in securing that outcome. Of course, changing economic and political realities played a more significant role.

England, more and more an industrial country, was faced with the need to feed an increasing population, which, having attained a wheaten loaf by the middle of the eighteenth century, appeared determined to avoid a decline in its standard of living to coarser grains, or, even worse, to potatoes. English agriculture was to prove unable to meet this challenge: G. R. Porter calculated that while in the decade 1811–20, despite the great expansion of wheat growing, 611,437 Britons were fed on foreign wheat, the decade of 1841–50 saw 3,451,608 in that condition.[2] It was in 1815 that the sliding scale tariff which had protected wheat growers, though high wartime prices had kept it inoperative, was abolished in favor of an absolute prohibition until the price of 80s. a quarter, a virtual famine price, had been reached. In that year, the new class of factory owners, emboldened by their growing economic strength and aided by the lower classes, had opposed the corn laws:

[1] Russell, *Recollections and Suggestions*, p. 247.
[2] G. R. Porter, *The Progress of the Nation* (London, 1851), p. 143.

there had been rioting by mobs of London working-men against what Francis Place, the Westminster Radical who had helped to organize the opposition, called 'this atrocious Bill', passed 'behind immensely strong double barricades of timber which blocked up the street and other avenues to the House under the cannon of the artillery, the swords of the cavalry, and the bayonets of the infantry'.[1] With the end of wartime demand, an expanding British industry found itself, despite Say's Law, with the need to find new markets for its rapidly increasing production; the factory owners, already feeling hampered by the commercial restrictions of the old system, became particularly resentful of the corn laws, which, they were convinced, by artificially raising wheat prices in the interest of the agricultural classes, necessitated higher labor costs and thereby limited the ability of British industries to compete for wider markets, which, they believed, had to be procured if economic crises were to be avoided.

Even though the political economists were not united on this question, the middle classes rested their arguments for a free trade in corn upon the 'science' of political economy—'all free traders are, *ex vi termini*, political economists', *The Times* was to observe in later years[2]—and, consequently, the landed classes decried political economy and praised the 'system of our ancestors'. Yet, from the beginning, even opponents of 'abstract science' found themselves employing the dicta of political economy, when able to do so, and during a period of about thirty-five years, from 1815 to 1850, the halls of parliament were filled with discussions, some on a high level, concerning the nature and validity of the new political economy, and the ways in which it ought or ought not to be used in determining policy. During the first twenty years of debate—a time when such political economists as Horner, Brougham, Ricardo, Torrens, and Lauderdale were in parliament—political economy was treated with scorn by its opponents, and even its adherents maintained, in public, a reserved and somewhat critical attitude. By the late thirties and the forties, the new political economy had taken hold; its ideas had been successfully applied in legislation and free traders were present in sizeable numbers in the lower house. By this later time, the disciples of the new economics were more and more inclined to speak of the principal writings of the political economists as if they constituted the Pentateuch, and its opponents were compelled, in the manner of their contemporaries of the higher criticism, to point out inconsistencies in the text.

[1] Quoted in Wallas, *Francis Place*, p. 57 f.n.
[2] *The Times*, 18 November 1845, 4c.

The ideas of the earlier political economists—of Adam Smith, of Josiah Tucker, of David Hume—had been on the whole acceptable to the practical men who sat in the British parliament during the days of Shelburne and Pitt, who, indeed, nearly succeeded in committing England to a 'liberal' trade program in the 1780s, convinced as they were that free trade was in the national interest. This Pittite outlook persisted into the early decades of the new century, among persons like Lord Grenville, whom we find, in 1810, angrily condemning the Orders-in-Council, and observing that the concept of the balance of trade was 'a doctrine so antiquated, and so proscribed by all men of enlightened views, that it was only fit for dark ages'.[1] During the last years of the war, Henry Brougham, and Alexander Baring, an heir to the noted financial and commercial house which bore his family's name, also fought against the Orders-in-Council, and, after the war, both these men continued to denounce all restrictions on commerce. In a debate in March 1817, Brougham presented a motion which, noting the distress in the country, declared that it was 'absolutely necessary to enter upon a careful but fearless revision of our whole commercial system', if this distress were to be lessened. The 'old mercantile system has long been exploded', Brougham declared, yet many still clung to the shattered wreckage; indeed, 'the practical results of this extirpated heresy are interwoven with our whole commercial policy'. Alexander Baring rose to support Brougham, as in years past, and even the president of the board of trade, F. J. Robinson, declared Brougham's remarks on the commercial system to have his 'entire concurrence', observing that 'it was true, in a considerable degree, that the prohibitory system operated to produce the present distress of the country'. Castlereagh, the foreign secretary, also agreed with this view.[2]

This Pittite commitment to free trade was, however, undermined within the ranks of the Tory party by the controversy concerning the corn laws, an issue which would see even Baring change his course. When Lord Archibald Hamilton, in an 1814 debate upon the corn laws, spoke out for full freedom of trade,[3] William Huskisson, who had been a member of Pitt's government, and was certainly no friend to the old commercial system, declared that Hamilton's appeal 'to general and abstract principles of political oeconomy totally failed; because the whole of our commercial and oeconomical system was a system of artificial expedients'.[4] Were there not, after all, special reasons for the defense of a virtual monopoly for British agriculture in the supply of corn? Would it not be dangerous to depend upon

[1] *P.D.*, 8 February 1810, pp. 346–8.
[2] *P.D.* xxxv (13 March 1817), 1005, 1013, 1018–19, 1024–8, 1038, 1044–6, 1051–5, 1066, 1069.
[3] *P.D.* xxvii (16 May 1814), 895–8.   [4] *Ibid.* pp. 920–1.

the foreigner for food? Still, those who wished to remove restraints imbedded in commercial legislation found friends in Lord Liverpool, and in the group of Pittites who dominated his cabinet in the twenties. All of them—Canning, Robinson, and, most particularly, Huskisson—despite their denials to assuage the feelings of fellow Tories ever hostile to abstract 'theory', were heavily indebted to the new political economy.

A petition of London merchants, drawn up by Thomas Tooke, an economist and a friend to Ricardo, Horner, and Huskisson, with Liverpool's approval and support, and presented by Alexander Baring to the House of Commons on 8 May 1820,[1] declared that foreign commerce was 'eminently conducive to the wealth and prosperity of a country', and that 'freedom from restraint' was 'calculated to give the utmost extension to foreign trade, and the best direction to the capital and industry of the country'. The petition exalted 'the maxim of buying in the cheapest market, and selling in the dearest' as 'the best rule for the trade of the whole nation', and held that if certain English productions were disadvantaged by a system of freedom, others 'to which our situation might be better suited' would be benefited, with 'probably a greater, and certainly a more beneficial employment to our own capital and labour'. The petitioners insisted that the 'restrictive system' had 'aggravated' the 'distress which now so generally prevails'. Other nations were looking toward England as a model for their own behavior: 'they insist upon our superiority in capital and machinery, as we do upon their comparative exemption from taxation, and with equal foundation'. While, if possible, it would be useful not to remove particular restrictions until the government obtained reciprocal action by foreign governments, the petitioners nonetheless declared that 'our restrictions would not be the less prejudicial to our own capital and industry, because other governments persisted in preserving impolitic regulations'.[2]

A Select Committee on the Means of Maintaining and Improving the Foreign Trade of the Country took up the cry of the petition, and the Liverpool government moved to give effect to the demands of the merchants. The report of the Committee, in July 1820, declared 'that the skill, enterprise, and capital of British merchants and manufacturers require only an open and equal field for exertion', and that 'the most valuable boon that can be conferred on them, is, as unlimited a freedom from all interference' as was 'compatible' with the requirements of certain 'vested interests' and 'the

[1] Halévy, *History*, II, 122.
[2] Reprinted in *The Annual Register, 1820* (London, 1820), part II, pp. 770–3. In reply to the petitions, Robinson described 'the restrictive system' as 'founded on error and calculated to defeat the object for which it was adopted'. *P.D.*, N.S., I (8 May 1820), 182–3.

safety and political power of the country'.[1] It was in this spirit—that of Pitt, Shelburne, and Tucker—that the government moved in the years ahead. F. J. Robinson, at the board of trade, with Thomas Wallace as his vice-president, proceeded to make useful relaxations of the Navigation Acts. When William Huskisson succeeded to the presidency of the board of trade, in 1823, he altered even more profoundly the character of the old commercial system, particularly modifying the restraints which clogged the colonial trade. Prohibitions upon imports were replaced by duties; duties were substantially reduced, especially upon raw produce; and a general duty of 50 per cent on manufactured imports was lowered to 20 per cent.

The Earl of Liverpool, the prime minister, in an address to the Lords in 1822, declared, in the best spirit of liberal political economy, that 'any measure which tended to increase the wealth of foreign nations was calculated to produce an increase of our own', adding that the 'increase of the trade of foreign countries offered the best security against the distress of our manufacturers'.[2] Wallace, more in the spirit of Tucker, observed, in early 1823, that if Britain removed 'the greater part' of her prohibitory laws and restrictions, she could take the fullest advantage of the 'chances and contingencies which the state of the world seemed ready to open to the commercial skill and enterprise of England'.[3] In 1825 William Huskisson agreed with the 'great commercial and political truth', that 'an open trade, especially to a rich and thriving country, is infinitely more valuable than any monopoly'.[4]

Though Huskisson and Robinson had, of necessity, to move cautiously with respect to corn trade, even here their sympathies were with those who wished to modify substantially the virtual prohibition against corn imports which the legislation of 1815 had imposed; and in this delicate matter, as well, they had the support of Liverpool. In a parliamentary debate on the introduction of a sliding scale for corn imports, in February 1822, the prime minister, while acknowledging the importance of the landed interest, reminded his audience of peers that the agricultural was not 'the *only* interest in Great Britain', that, indeed, it was 'not even the *most numerous interest*'. Cheaper food prices, he declared, would benefit the majority of the community.[5] In 1828, after a lengthy debate—replete with innumerable references to economic principles, this despite the insistence by the government that it was acting on grounds of common sense rather than of abstract

---

[1] See *Annual Register* (1820), p. 773.
[2] *P.D.*, N.S., VII (17 June 1822), 1121.
[3] *P.D.*, N.S., VIII (12 February 1823), 101.
[4] *P.D.*, N.S., XII (21 March 1825), 1111–12, 1098, 1104, 1107.
[5] *P.D.*, N.S., VI (26 February 1822), 709–10.

doctrine—a sliding scale for corn was set up which provided for a duty of 23*s*. per quarter until the price of corn reached 64*s*.; of 16*s*. 8*d*. until the price reached 69*s*.; and 1*s*. when the price was at or above 73*s*. This was to be the state of the law for over a decade. Sir Thomas Gooch, an advocate of the landed interest, had complained, a year earlier, that he had heard 'so much of political economy' in connection with the corn laws that he was 'heartily sick of political economists altogether', and wished that a clause be 'inserted in the present bill, enacting that every vessel laden with foreign corn destined for this country should take back, instead of ballast, a cargo of political economists'.[1]

The role which the writings of Tucker and Smith had played in helping to bring about the Irish proposals and the French treaty in the 1780s was filled during the 1820s by the works of David Ricardo. In a letter to his wife, in January 1819, William Huskisson, who was to play the central role in the commercial reform of the twenties, asked his wife to procure for him a copy of Ricardo's *Elements of Political Economy* or the issue of the *Edinburgh* in which the book had been reviewed, so that he might prepare himself for a debate in the House.[2] Huskisson and Ricardo, who had secured a seat in the House of Commons in 1819, served together upon the Committee on The Agriculture of the United Kingdom in 1821; Ricardo reported in a letter that he had 'worked very hard', and hoped that he had not been 'without effect in correcting mistaken principles'.[3]

In committee, Huskisson and Ricardo seemed to have agreed on almost every matter—this, at least, was Ricardo's view. One witness, Thomas Attwood, the Radical leader of the so-called Birmingham currency school, described them as the two guiding spirits of the committee—'as sharp as *needles* and as active as bees'.[4] It was Huskisson who wrote the committee's report, although the influence of Ricardo was clearly discernible, and the law of rent was one of its foundations. The committee, however, 'abstained' from recommending a free trade in corn—even though 'those general principles of freedom of trade' were 'now universally acknowledged to be sound and true'—this so as 'to spare vested interests', and 'to deal tenderly with those obstacles to improvement which the long existence of a vicious and artificial system too often creates'.[5] It is interesting to note that, in the

[1] *P.D.*, N.S., XVII (2 April 1827), 198.
[2] Quoted in C. R. Fay, *Huskisson and His Age* (London: Longmans, Green, 1951), p. 198.
[3] In Sraffa, ed., *Works of Ricardo*, VIII, 369.
[4] *Ibid.* p. 370 f.n.
[5] *Report from the Committee on The Agriculture of the United Kingdom*, 1821, (688), ix, 1, pp. 18–20, 24.

twenties, Sir Henry Parnell, the Irish baronet and economist, who had been chairman of an 1813 committee which had urged agricultural protection, reversed his position, converted, he declared in parliament, by the Ricardian theory of rent.[1]

Yet, throughout, the liberal Tories strove to avoid any appearance of a doctrinaire commitment, and persistently disclaimed all ties to political economy. In 1823, Lord Liverpool had proclaimed before a dinner of the Ship-Owners Society against 'fanciful and impracticable theories'; Ricardo, understanding the limitations under which the politicians worked, held him not to have spoken his 'real sentiments'. Lord Goderich, the former F. J. Robinson, whom Ricardo, in 1823, had described as 'a tolerable political economist, and well inclined to liberal principles of trade',[2] when prime minister in 1827, was to declare, superciliously, that he had never 'subscribed' to the 'doctrines' of political economy, though admitting that 'he might, perhaps, occasionally puzzle himself with the essays of the political economists, which, he believed, likewise puzzled their authors'.[3] Even Lord King, an author of an early work on currency, and the biographer of Locke, who was to be the chief spokesman for the opponents of the corn laws in the upper house during the twenties, felt compelled to deny, in reply to a gibe, that he was 'one of the political metaphysicians', and to assert that he 'would readily give to the Devil all the Scotch metaphysicians that ever existed'. Nevertheless, foreshadowing the mood of a later Cobdenism Lord King described 'true faith' to be 'to allow free trade in every thing'; that, indeed, was 'not only true faith, but good works'.[4]

Even in this early period, however, the parliamentary opponents of 'abstract doctrine' nonetheless advanced the views of older schools of economics regarded as more sympathetic to agriculture. When a country gentleman spoke up in debate, in 1815, on behalf of the physiocratic school,[5] Francis Horner, on the following day, proclaimed his astonishment that men 'by whom theorists had been decried', had become proponents of French physiocratic economics; appealing to national sentiment, Horner asked why such opponents of political economy treated with 'levity' Adam Smith, whose opinions had been recommended by 'our most distinguished statesmen', Pitt and Burke. 'But as to political economy,' Horner concluded, 'upon what ground could gentlemen pretend to depreciate its character, unless they mean to depreciate the exercise of reasoning?'[6] In a debate in

[1] *P.D.*, N.S., XVI (9 March 1827), 1102–5.
[2] Sraffa, ed., *Works of Ricardo*, IX, 269 and 269 f.n.
[3] *P.D.*, N.S., XVII (15 May 1827), 805.   [4] *P.D.*, N.S., XIX (13 June 1828), 1345–6.
[5] *P.D.* XXIX (22 February 1815), 980.   [6] *P.D.* XXIX (23 February 1815), 1031–2.

1834, Sir James Graham made a similar appeal to the physiocrats, which prompted a Liberal M.P. to observe that he had not expected to hear the 'exploded doctrine of the French economists revived at the present time'.[1] In 1827, the protectionist Lord Redesdale, in more patriotic fashion, turned for support to proper English economics—to Sir Richard Steele, who, as his writings in the old *Spectator* had revealed, Redesdale declared, 'knew more of political economy than ever Mr M'Culloch did', and to the writings of 'another of the old writers, Sir W. Dugdale', in order to prove that it was not the fertility of the land, as the Ricardians claimed, but the improvements upon the land which gave them value; his speech was praised by the Earl of Lauderdale, a political economist himself, and a defender of the corn laws, as containing 'the soundest' doctrine.[2]

The admission to the franchise of a middle-class electorate in 1832, even though the new voters, on the whole, turned to landed aristocrats to represent them in parliament, helped to further the cause of political economy and of free trade, as did the continued expansion of industrial production. (Between 1832 and 1850, pig-iron production advanced from 700,000 tons to 2,250,000 tons; coal from 26,000,000 tons to 60,000,000 tons; the weight of cotton consumed rose from 259,000,000 lb. to 588,000,000 lb.) A force in the same direction was the distress among the lower classes, both rural and urban, a distress which was converted into a revolutionary threat by Chartism, in the late thirties and the forties, and which the Anti-Corn Law League, at hundreds of meetings throughout the United Kingdom, was to attribute to the corn laws.

By 1846, moreover, a substantial part of the landed aristocracy had been converted to free trade: some out of sympathy for the distress, others because of fear of revolution, still others, and not the least part of the aristocratic supporters of corn law abolition fell into this grouping, because they had sufficiently diversified their interests so that they might readily believe they had much to gain from the growing prosperity of an industrial England. By marriage and investments, the aristocracy and the gentry had become connected with mercantile and industrial enterprise; moreover, the gentlemen upon whose lands the cities of an industrial England were encroaching were anticipating the rising values and rents which must result from industrial development, and others who owned coal, or iron, or lead mines were in a similarly agreeable situation.

By the forties, while the corn laws still afforded some measure of comfort to the English wheat-grower, it was the tenant farmer, not the landlord, who had most to lose by repeal. Some aristocrats no doubt defended the

[1] *P.D.*, 3rd Series, XXI (7 March 1834), 1267.   [2] *P.D.*, N..S, XVII (15 May 1827), 792–4, 809.

corn laws as a matter of economic necessity; others did so largely because they felt a gentlemanly obligation to stand by their tenants—and those tenants did what they could, in the forties, to press that obligation upon their landlords.[1] Moreover, the corn laws were a symbol of the old aristocratic predominance, and as such had a high emotive value. Still, the corn laws were to be repealed, thanks, in good part, to aristocratic defection, and the growing acceptance of the 'science' of political economy played no small part in this breaching of the outer walls of the landowner's castle.

The movement toward the rationalization of commercial legislation, begun by Pitt, and furthered by Huskisson, was joined, in the forties, by the Whigs, operating upon the advice of Nassau Senior. In 1841, the Melbourne government, with Lord John Russell as its leading figure in these matters, proposed to modify the timber and sugar preferences, so advantageous to Canadian and West Indian interests, yet such a nuisance to an England determined to make no further sacrifice on behalf of its colonies, and to buy, in accordance with the best economic precepts, in the cheapest markets. In addition, the Whig budget proposed to impose a fixed duty of 8s. a quarter upon corn to replace the sliding scale of 1828, abridging, still further, the force of the corn laws.

In this, the Whigs had the posthumous support of Ricardo who, though he had on one occasion in parliament advocated an entirely free trade in corn,[2] was later, in a letter to McCulloch in March 1821, to speak of 'a countervailing duty', to compensate the agriculturist for the 'peculiar taxes' to which he was subject, and was even ready to grant a drawback upon the exportation of corn.[3] In a pamphlet, published subsequently, Ricardo suggested a duty on imported corn of 20s. a quarter, which would be reduced by 1s. each year until it reached 10s., and a 7s. drawback upon exportation; he noted that 10s. was probably too high a countervailing duty, and declared that he 'would rather err on the side of a liberal allowance than of a scanty one'.[4] McCulloch had agreed with Ricardo, and continued to maintain this position after Ricardo's death.

The leader of the opposition, Sir Robert Peel, while proclaiming himself

---

[1] See W. O. Aydelotte, 'The Business Interests of the Gentry in the Parliament of 1841–47', Appendix to G. Kitson Clark, *The Making of Victorian England* (Cambridge, Mass.: Harvard University Press, 1962), pp. 290–305. See also G. Kitson Clark, 'The Repeal of the Corn Laws and the Politics of the Forties', *Economic History Review*, 2nd Series, IV, no. 1 (1951), 12, 13.

[2] *P.D.*, N.S., IV (27 February 1821), 945.

[3] Sraffa, ed., *Works of Ricardo*, VIII, 355–60.

[4] David Ricardo, M.P., *On Protection to Agriculture* (London, 1822), pp. 56, 81–5. Mill, in an article on the corn laws for the *Westminster Review*, wrote that it was only 'with the greatest hesitation' that 'we presume to differ from so great an authority' as Ricardo. ('The Corn Laws',

a free trader and a follower of Huskisson, insisted that corn and sugar were special cases. Peel proposed a revision of the sliding scale, instead of Russell's fixed duty, in the case of corn, and argued that sugar produced by free labor in the British West Indies ought to receive some preference over Brazilian or Cuban sugar produced by slave labor. (The West Indian sugar producers were not to lose their preference until 1854.) The Whig government fell on these issues, and Peel came to office.

It was now for Peel to prove his boast that he was a free trader. As early as 1842, a year after assuming office, Peel, who had demonstrated his *bona fides* as a political economist in his alliance with Ricardo in behalf of resumption of specie payment in 1819, assumed the mantle of Huskisson. In March of that year, the prime minister proposed a considerable reduction of all duties on the raw materials needed in manufacturing, of all duties on goods partially or wholly manufactured, of duties on timber, and all export duties. Since England was, at this time, overwhelmingly dependent upon such duties for revenue, Peel, following the precepts of the liberal economists, proposed a direct tax, an income and property tax of 7*d.* per pound, to replace these indirect taxes which had impeded commerce. In 1844, the duty on wool was abolished; in 1845, that on cotton was removed, as were many others, including the export duty on coal; in 1846, the protective duties on linen, woollen, and cotton manufactured goods were reduced from 20 to 10 per cent, and there were reductions on other duties upon manufactures. Between 1841 and 1846, Peel repealed 605 duties and reduced 1,035 others. Peel, 'wearied with our long and unavailing efforts to enter into satisfactory commercial treaties with other nations', resolved 'to consult our own interests', and proceeded with a program of unilateral advance toward free trade.[1]

In 1829, Joseph Hume, in presenting a petition of the woolcombers of Kidderminster, had brought laughter to the House when he reported that the petitioners 'had carefully considered Colonel Torrens' "Essay on the external Corn-trade"', and "The Catechism of the Corn Laws"'. The laughter led Hume to urge his fellow members to read, at least, the 'Catechism', which, he informed them, they could obtain for 6*d.*[2] In the years

---

Westminster Review III, no. IV (April 1825), 394–420.) In another article ('Corn Laws', *Westminster Review* VI, no. XII (October 1826), 373–404), 'with due deference to Mr. Ricardo', Mill suggested that the proper remedy was to equalize taxation rather than to compensate the landowner for an unjust system. He added, more belligerently, that 'the extra taxation on agriculture, at the present time, is not sufficient to justify a duty of more than 2*s.* 6*d.* per quarter', rather than Ricardo's 10*s.*

[1] See Leone Levi, *The History of British Commerce and of the Economic Progress of the British Nation, 1763–1878* (London, 1880), pp. 264–8.

[2] *P.D.*, N.S., XXI (8 May 1829), 1165.

ahead, it seemed that many had taken his advice to become acquainted with the arguments of the economists. By 1841, Lord Ashburton, the former Alexander Baring, who had altered his earlier opinions sufficiently to have become a strong proponent of the corn laws and an enemy of the political economists, felt obliged to concede that the theories of political economy were 'entitled to this degree of respect—that those who departed from them ought to be called on to show the grounds of their departure'.[1] By 1842, indeed, the fathers of political economy had become so well established that W. B. Ferrand, a member of Disraeli's small party of Tory democrats, spoke almost reverently of Adam Smith, Ricardo, Malthus, McCulloch, while condemning their doctrinaire epigones.[2]

As early as the late thirties, when Cobden, Villiers, Clay, Hume, and their colleagues began to demand unconditional repeal of agricultural protection, the advocates of the corn laws responded by citing Ricardo, McCulloch, and Smith, who had, after all, never supported such a policy. The protectionists repeatedly referred to Ricardo's and McCulloch's remarks on the 'peculiar burdens' of agriculture. Speaking before the House of Lords in 1840, Lord Ashburton reminded the peers that McCulloch had admitted that the corn-grower was 'entitled to a protection equivalent to the peculiar charges' imposed upon him.[3] When, in 1842, Peel, concerned about the recent famine, made an effort to modify the scale of 1828, he defended his moderate protection to corn-growers by declaring that the ideal scale drawn up, twenty years earlier, by Ricardo—'no particular friend to the agricultural interest'—was yet more generous to agriculture.[4] The protectionist opposition became positively fond of political economy,[5] and a follower of the young Disraeli, having been told by Cobden to study the political economists, emerged, as he told the House of Commons, with the news that

[1] *P.D.*, 3rd Series, LVIII (24 May 1841), 705. But, on the following day, Ashburton added that he did not wish to see the professor of political economy brought from Oxford 'to Downing-street to govern us'. *P.D.*, 3rd Series, LVIII (25 May 1841), 733.

[2] In this difficult and obscure subject, he sneeringly declared, 'it was reserved for the hon. Member for Wolverhampton (Mr Villiers) to dispel the clouds, it was left for the hon. Member for Bolton (Dr Bowring) and the hon. Member for Stroud (Mr Scrope) to become bright constellations, it was destined for the hon. Member for Dumfries (Mr Ewart) to become the evening star: ever singing, as he twinkles," the blessings of free trade"'. *P.D.*, 3rd Series, LV (14 February 1842), 431.

[3] *P.D.*, 3rd Series, LIV (11 June 1840), 1029; see Peel on this question, *P.D.*, 3rd Series, LX (21 February 1842), 729; see also *P.D.*, 3rd Series, LXI (14 March 1842), 552–3; also *P.D.*, 3rd Series, LXXXV (26 March 1846), 111, 113. (In 1841, so unlikely a personage as the Duke of Wellington informed the lords that Adam Smith had excepted corn from his ideas on free trade, only to be chided by Earl Fitzwilliam who suggested that 'it would, perhaps, be necessary for both his noble Friend and himself to read Adam Smith again'.) *P.D.*, 3rd Series, LVIII (11 May 1841), 184.

[4] *P.D.*, 3rd Series, LX (23 February 1842), 966–7.

[5] See, for example, *P.D.*, 3rd Series, LXXXIII (9 February 1846), 584–5.

'there was not one of them who did not agree' that 'for the benefit of all classes in the country, it was necessary to give a preponderating influence to the affairs of the land'.[1] The Whig Lord John Russell, in 1843, subscribing, in general, to this sentiment, proposed a 'compromise' position based upon 'the doctrine held by Mr Ricardo, a great theoretical philosopher', and cautioned the House not to 'rush from one extreme to another' when making 'a change with regard to interests that had been long established'.[2]

The Cobdenites ignored such appeals to authority, and the Anti-Corn Law League demanded immediate and absolute repeal of the corn laws.[3] Charles Villiers, a former friend of Bentham and the Radical M.P. from Wolverhampton, one of the leading parliamentary spokesmen for free trade, suggested that Ricardo had spoken in terms of conditions 'as they existed twenty years ago',[4] and therefore could be safely disregarded. Cobden, no doubt tiring of hearing the opposition's appeal to McCulloch's writings, excoriated Ricardo's leading disciple, in an address to the Commons in 1845, as 'a painstaking statistician' who had not contributed 'a single new idea' to the science of political economy—and, furthermore, 'had a strange facility in shifting his views to the exigencies of parties and politicians'.[5] A protectionist member from Somersetshire suggested, in 1846, that Adam Smith—and he might have mentioned the other leading economists as well—was an 'authority always quoted on the other side when it served their purpose', but his work, when their purpose was not served, 'was treated as an old almanac'.[6]

During this time, from 1841 to 1846, when the agitation of the Anti-Corn Law Leaguers was at its peak, Sir Robert Peel was the Tory prime minister. Peel's mind had 'a natural leaning towards politico-economical truths', Cobden wrote in 1846; 'I have not the same confidence in Lord John and the Whigs.'[7] In the twenties, Peel had devoted much time to the study of political economy, particularly to reading Smith, Hume, and Ricardo. 'I have read all that has been written by the gravest authorities on political economy on the subject of rent, wages, taxes, tithes,' he told the House in 1839.[8] Certainly, from 1841 onwards, Peel, in battling Cobden

---

[1] *P.D.*, 3rd Series, LXXXIV (3 March 1846), 549–50.
[2] *P.D.*, 3rd Series, LXIX (11 May 1843), 229–33.
[3] For Russell's opinion on these differences in view, *P.D.*, 3rd Series, LXXV (25 June 1844), 1427.
[4] *P.D.*, 3rd Series, LXIX (15 May 1843), 406.
[5] *P.D.*, 3rd Series, LXXX (3 June 1845), 1414–15.
[6] *P.D.*, 3rd Series, LXXXIII (13 February 1846), 891. That same year, C. N. Newdegate of Warwickshire noted that whereas Peel and Graham had now accepted Smith and Ricardo on the subject of free trade, they did not regard the economists as such great authorities on monetary questions. *P.D.*, 3rd Series, LXXXVI (12 May 1846), 426–7.
[7] Quoted in Morley, *Cobden*, p. 366.   [8] *P.D.*, 3rd Series, XLVI (15 March 1839), 777.

and the Anti-Corn Law League, did not maintain the position of diehard agricultural protection. Rather, relying on Ricardo and McCulloch, and displaying considerable sophistication in his arguments, he urged that a countervailing duty be established to compensate agriculture for its peculiar burdens.

But, as we learn from his memoirs, all the while the logic of political economy, and his sensitivity to the climate of opinion, were driving Peel towards abolition. Having become convinced that lower corn prices would not drive down wages, a view which Cobden and the League were furthering, as we will see, in contradiction of Ricardo, and that, therefore, repeal would add to the 'health, morals, tranquillity and general prosperity' of the country, he was experiencing, by the forties, an 'increasing difficulty' in resisting 'the application to articles of food of those principles which had been gradually applied to so many other articles'.[1] Peel's position was an awkward one. He had come to power to protect corn laws, yet he, his home secretary, Sir James Graham, the author of a tract on *Corn and Currency*, and his president of the board of trade, W. E. Gladstone, also converts to political economy, while directing oratorical jibes in parliament against free trade in corn, proceeded to whittle away at the corn laws. The Anti-Corn Law League, using the technique of the carrot and the stick, while endeavoring to intimidate Peel by the threat of a popular revolt, in the process subjecting him to an intense personal attack—Cobden at one point suggested the usefulness of his assassination—offered Peel eternal fame as the savior of his country and the father of a more prosperous Britain.

Peel saw England as facing the most bloody of revolutions. The 'hungry forties' were a time of severe distress and unrest, and the Anti-Corn Law League, on one side, and a growingly socialist Chartism, on the other, were spurring the working classes to act decisively. Sir James Graham, Peel's chancellor of the exchequer, wrote to Peel, in October 1845, that anti-corn law 'pressure is about to commence', and that it would be the 'most formidable movement in modern times'. 'Everything', Graham declared, 'depends on the skill, promptitude, and decision with which it is met.'[2] At the same time, Chartist agitation was mounting, and, finally, in October 1845, Peel had become convinced of the immediacy of famine in Ireland. When J. W. Croker, the editor of the *Quarterly Review*, a protectionist and a Tory stalwart, attempted to steady the prime minister's resolution and urged him to reaffirm Croker's own conviction that the landed interests were the only 'foundation on which the country can stand', Peel, in August

---

[1] Quoted in C. S. Parker, *Sir Robert Peel* (London, 1891–7) III, 220–1.
[2] Quoted in *ibid*. p. 224.

1845, suggested that 'the maintenance—if possible the steady increase—of commercial prosperity' was 'absolutely essential' to the 'real welfare' of the landed interest. 'I should shudder at the recurrence of such a winter and spring as those of 1841–2,' he observed in conclusion.[1] Later, in a letter to Graham, on 2 September 1846, after repeal, Peel was to declare that 'I am fairly convinced that the permanent adjustment of the Corn Laws has rescued the country and the whole frame of society from the hazard of very serious convulsion.'[2]

In December 1845, Peel, having adopted what Disraeli was to deride as 'the more vigorous, bustling, popular and progressive' doctrine,[3] presented his proposals for repeal of agricultural protection to his Cabinet, only three members of which backed him. Peel decided to resign, but Tory fears that, in the words of Lord Heytesbury, this would mean 'entrusting the reins of government to men so thoroughly reckless as Lord Grey and Mr Cobden',[4] resulted in the decision of most of his colleagues to continue in support. (Arbuthnot, a confidant of the Duke of Wellington, writing to Peel on Boxing Day of 1845, gasped his 'relief' at Peel's decision to stay. Had Peel resigned, Arbuthnot 'contemplated nothing short of revolution', adding that 'you can have no notion how much the Duke suffered when he thought we were to be cursed with a Whig-Radical Government'.)[5] In January of 1846, Peel submitted his bill to introduce a much modified system of protection for agriculture, which was to last until 1 February 1849, after which time all grain would be admitted at a fixed duty of 1s. per quarter. After a considerable debate, and a split within the Tory party, the bill passed. Because of famine conditions in Ireland, even these minimal duties were suspended between 1846 and 1849 so that, in effect, the United Kingdom enjoyed a free trade in corn beginning in 1846.

Political economy had triumphed, and political economy, particularly as it affected the corn laws, had become a species of holy writ. The Bishop of Oxford, in defending repeal, declared, in 1846, that 'of this whole matter

---

[1] Quoted in *ibid*. pp. 193–4.
[2] Quoted in C. S. Parker, *Life and Letters of Sir James Graham, 1792–1861* (London: John Murray, 1907) II, 51. In May 1846, after Peel had determined to seek repeal, a protectionist M.P. compared the prime minister to Turgot, and had suggested that Peel was precipitating a revolution by adopting Turgot's principle of free trade. 'Does my hon. Friend not feel', Peel replied, 'that if the doctrines of Turgot had been applied at an earlier period—that if the aristocracy had not insisted on maintaining their privileges—that the revolution of France would not have been precipitated, and that the evils of that eventful period would have been diminished? Does not my hon. Friend feel that it was the unjust maintenance of bygone privileges that led to the revolution, rather than the doctrines of Turgot?' *P.D.*, 3rd Series, LXXXVI (4 May 1846), 64, 66.
[3] *P.D.*, 3rd Series, LXXXVI (15 May 1846), 675–6.
[4] Quoted in Parker, *Peel* III, 290.
[5] Quoted in *ibid*. pp. 290–1.

the very alphabet is to be found in the science of political economy'; 'on the surest principles of political economy,' he continued, 'so far as I have been able to understand them, I approve of this measure'.[1] Addressing the Lords, two weeks earlier, Earl Grey had spoken of 'Dr Adam Smith's immortal work', and of the 'authority of those maxims of commercial wisdom which had long been received as infallible by philosophers in their closets', and which now 'began also to be recognized in the councils of the nation'.[2] The Marquess of Lansdowne, a descendant of Shelburne, speaking in a similar vein, piously reminded the peers that Pitt had 'studied political economy', and had 'always endeavoured to avail himself of it, and did so with great success'.[3]

Yet Disraeli was no doubt correct when, in May 1846, he declared that Richard Cobden 'knows very well there is no chance of changing the laws of England with abstract doctrine'.[4] Men did not generally follow the dictates of abstract truth, the leader of the Tory protectionists suggested, no matter how 'scientifically' demonstrated, unless impelled by other, more substantial forces. The science of political economy was enabled to play its by no means unimportant role in bringing England to the utopian ideal of Adam Smith, because it had become even clearer, after 1815, what had seemed sufficiently evident in the 1780s, that Free Trade had become the national interest. From the end of the Napoleonic Wars onward, the dream which presented itself to Englishmen of the industrial classes was that of a British Workshop of the World, a dream which might be realized, they believed, through the dissemination of free trade principles.

In the decade and a half following Waterloo, the possibilities of a new commercial empire based upon England's industrial predominance, so glowingly depicted by Robert Torrens, was a frequent subject of parliamentary discussion. The arguments, borrowed from economists, had a twofold theme: that general trade restrictions were an obstacle to the realization of such a goal, and, more specifically, that the corn laws, both because they raised the price of British manufactures, thereby stimulating foreign industrial rivals, and because, by blocking the exports of agricultural countries, they limited the market for British manufactures abroad, had to be repealed if British industrial predominance were to be maintained.

These arguments were presented in the earliest debates on the corn laws.

[1] *P.D.*, 3rd Series, LXXXVII (12 June 1846), 322–3.
[2] *P.D.*, 3rd Series, LXXXVI (28 May 1846), 1319–20.
[3] *Ibid.* p. 1343.
[4] *P.D.*, 3rd Series, LXXXVI (15 May 1846), 658.

In 1814, for example, Earl Stanhope, a corn law opponent, had declared that if British manufactures 'were enhanced by the high price of provisions and of labour, steam-engines would be set to work in other countries' to rival and injure British manufactures and commerce, 'the only foundation upon which rest the strength and glory of our navy'.[1] One of the first Radical M.P.s, George Philips, in 1816, before the Commons, quoted Malthus and Smith upon the necessity of purchasing in the cheapest market, and added that since the importation of corn meant the exportation of manufactures, restrictions on corn imports were 'at variance with the best principles established in the science of political economy', and 'had produced injury rather than advantage to the empire'. 'If Holland, Venice, and Hamburgh, had declined a dependence upon foreign countries for their support,' Philips continued, 'they would always have remained perfectly inconsiderable states, and never could have risen to that pitch of wealth, power, and population, which distinguished the meridian of their career.'[2] Francis Horner, a few days after Philips' statement, suggested that 'no rich country was ever a great exporter of corn'; 'the poor country', he declared, was 'always the exporter of that article to the rich, for which she received manufactures in return'.[3] Sir Robert Peel anticipated his later sentiments by warning, at this time, of the danger to British manufacturing of dear corn.[4] C. C. Western, a well-known sheep breeder, writer on economic questions, and a spokesman for the agricultural interest, was both pained and astonished that Philips and those who supported him seemed 'to have contemplated, with great composure, the absolute destruction of the agriculture of a great part of the country'.[5]

Joseph Hume was the most persistent advocate of making England the Workshop of the World, during this period. In 1821, for example, Hume declared that 'with our capital, the proposed alterations' in the trade system which were being proposed by Huskisson and his lieutenants 'must give us the advantage over every other country'.[6] Hume extended the vision when, in 1829, while making a proposal for a completely free trade in corn, he observed that the 'greater part of the world' was 'dependent upon us for manufactures', even though, because of the corn laws, high labor costs had caused British manufacturers to enter the world market 'under great disadvantages'. Indeed England would have lost every market, Hume

[1] *P.D.* XXVII (6 June 1814), 1066.
[2] *P.D.* XXIX (17 February 1815), 817–18.
[3] *P.D.* XXIX (23 February 1815), 1036.
[4] *P.D.* XXIX (27 February 1815), 1060.
[5] *P.D.* XXIX (17 February 1815), 822–3; see also pp. 833–4.
[6] *P.D.*, N.S., V (25 June 1821), 1310.

continued, had she not possessed 'in the better division of our labour and in the superiority of our enterprise, machinery, fuel, and roads, advantages which counterbalance the fearful odds which the disparity in the price of food produced against us'. Hume urged that Great Britain follow the example of Venice and exchange her manufactured goods for foreign corn: corn ought not to be permitted to rot in Poland, while British manufactures were 'sunk in depreciation at home'. 'Everything which the world produced was at our command,' Hume proclaimed; by extending her foreign commerce, England could 'render all the world tributary to us'.[1] In the vote which followed, only twelve members voted for Hume's proposal.[2] In 1833, Hume spoke out even more determinedly in behalf of an England devoted to manufacturing: once the corn laws were repealed, and England could purchase foreign raw commodities, the world would exert such a demand for British manufactures that 'there was no limit to the increased employment of hands in manufactures'.[3] No doubt somewhat disappointed by his failure to convince the House in the previous twenty years, Hume warned the Commons in 1843 that though it was growing late, 'there was still time to repent'. Other countries were encroaching upon England's industrial predominance: 'of late years Belgium had made rapid advances', Germany was similarly 'in a state of progress, and America also, had made considerable strides'. Yet—if only the corn laws were abolished—Hume was 'perfectly confident, that in the end our capital must triumph'.[4]

Nor was Hume alone in presenting such views. A number of parliamentary Radicals had similar hopes and fears. Robert Torrens, in an 1826 debate, told the House of Commons that 'if there was a free trade tomorrow, our manufacturers might meet all the world; and their knowledge and skill, their capital and their machinery, would give them a decided advantage'; as it was, 'the prosperity of England stood but on a foundation of sand'.[5] In 1834, Torrens proclaimed that 'there was no possible limit to the prosperity of England, if the ports were only thrown open to foreign corn'.[6] While

---

[1] *P.D.*, N.S., XXI (19 May 1829), 1464–78. A good Ricardian, Hume denied that there was 'overproduction' in England, for overproduction could not exist 'generally'—there might be a 'temporary over-production in one article, but it could not exist in all'; if there were gluts, it was because of restrictions upon trade.

[2] *Ibid.* p. 1487.

[3] *P.D.*, 3rd Series, XVII (17 May 1833), 1359. Hume's argument frequently ran along mercantilist lines. For example, he declared it fortunate for England that 'all her imports were raw materials'; 'the cost of the raw material, generally speaking, was not more than nine, ten, or at the outside, twenty per cent of the finished article'—'all the rest was the profits of capital and wages laid out in this country'; see also *P.D.*, 3rd Series, XXI (6 March 1834), 1210.

[4] *P.D.*, 3rd Series, LXIX (12 May 1843), 271–2.

[5] *P.D.*, N.S., XVI (30 November 1826), 207.

[6] *P.D.*, 3rd Series, XXI (6 March 1834), 1222.

Poulett Thomson, a scion of a prominent merchant family, who had served as president of the board of trade, might, in 1834, proudly, and more sanguinely, observe that the British manufacturer was already sending his produce 'to distant' and 'foreign climes', even into the interior of Africa, and proclaim that Great Britain had already become 'in a manner the manufacturing work-shop of the World',[1] others saw such a development possible only after corn law repeal. In the corn law debate of 1842, the Whig essayist and historian T. B. Macaulay declared that if the corn laws were repealed, 'we might supply the whole world with manufactures, and have almost a monopoly of the trade of the world', while 'other nations were raising abundant provisions for us on the banks of the Mississippi and the Vistula'.[2] A British emissary, returned from a fact-finding expedition to the Continent, reported to the House of Commons Metternich's declaration: 'Take our corn and we will take your manufactures.'[3]

By the late thirties and early forties, the repealers felt the need for haste. A *Zollverein* had been formed among the German states, a tariff league behind whose walls a great industrial machine was being constructed; the purpose of the *Zollverein* was, in Villiers' words, 'to oppose what was called our "commercial despotism"'.[4] Lord Lyndhurst, an American-born barrister who had served as lord chancellor in the late twenties, warned the peers in 1838, not only of 'a decrease of the exports of this country' to Germany, but that 'manufacturing establishments had started up in central Germany' which now competed with British industry in the United States, 'which was always considered our own especial market'; indeed, in the United States, 'the cottons of Germany, and the hardware of Germany could now be purchased at a lower price than similar articles the manufacture of this country'.[5] Poulett Scrope pressed the prime minister in 1843 to 'secure and preserve for us the immense markets of America' by means of more liberal trade policies.[6]

It was not to be the vision of a cosmopolitan world economy of Cobden's dream, but rather that of preserving an industrial predominance—'almost a monopoly', in Macaulay's words—as proclaimed by Hume, Torrens, and others, which helped to move Peel to action in 1845 and 1846. Peel saw free trade as essential to England's position as the Workshop of the World. 'During war,' he told the Commons, in January 1846, 'we commanded the

[1] *P.D.*, 3rd Series, XXI (7 March 1834), 1287–8.
[2] *P.D.*, 3rd Series, LX (21 February 1842), 754.
[3] *P.D.*, 3rd Series, XXXVII (16 March 1837), 595.
[4] *Ibid.* p. 591.
[5] *P.D.*, 3rd Series, XLIV (14 August 1838), 1177.
[6] *P.D.*, 3rd Series, LXIX (15 May 1843), 357.

supply of nations.' Now England was encountering difficulties. The continuance of England's 'manufacturing and commercial pre-eminence', however, might be ensured by cheap and abundant food which would promote the increase of British capital 'by which we can retain the eminence we have so long possessed'. Though there was no guarantee that other nations would, in reciprocity, lower their tariffs, England might 'depend upon it', Peel assured the House, that 'your example' in undertaking free trade 'will ultimately prevail'.[1] In February 1846, in a magnificent piece of oratory, the prime minister asked the Commons to select the motto to characterize future English commercial policy: 'Shall it be "advance" or "recede"'; 'which is the fitter motto for this great Empire?' He urged the House to 'consider the advantage which God and nature have given us, and the destiny for which we are intended'. England stood as 'the chief connecting link between the old world and the new'. She enjoyed 'maritime strength and superiority'. 'Iron and coal, the sinews of manufacture,' gave England 'advantages over every rival in the great competition of industry'; 'our capital far exceeds that which they can command'; 'in ingenuity—in skill—in energy—we are inferior to none'. 'Our national character', and 'the free institutions under which we live', when combined with 'our natural and physical advantages', placed England 'at the head of those nations which profit by the free interchange of their products'. 'And is this the country to shrink from competition?' Peel inquired. England must 'determine for "Advance"'. The ghosts of Pitt and Tucker, now content, could cease their rattlings.[2]

The Economist, established in 1843 to do battle for free trade, described England's formal colonial empire, in 1848, after the repeal of the corn laws, as 'little more than a repetition of the old attempt, so often renewed and so generally ending in calamitous ruin, to establish a species of universal empire, and be the selfish and almost undisputed masters of the globe'; the journal, however, noted that England's informal trading system was, on the other hand, 'founded to obtain a commercial end, and secure, by controlling political action, the benefits of trade'. Its benign character, *The Economist* remarked, was assured since 'our ultimate controlling power' was 'not an Alexander, not a colonial secretary, but the Parliament that represents and gives effect to the views and wishes of our commercial people'.[3] This view of a cosmopolitan trading association, profitable to all

---

[1] *P.D.*, 3rd Series, LXXXIII (27 January 1846), 241, 246, 276–80.
[2] *P.D.*, 3rd Series, LXXXIII (16 February 1846), 1041–2.
[3] *The Economist* VI (29 July 1848), 844.

participants, a 'universal empire', in *The Economist*'s phrase, presided over by the free parliament of a 'commercial people' devoted to the peaceful and profitable commercial intercourse of all nations in accordance with the principle of the international division of labor, is frequently encountered in the nineteenth century and afterward. A number of leading Radicals, Cobden being perhaps the foremost, strove to realize this vision.

When other Radicals spoke in more vigorous terms of maintaining an industrial predominance, of Britain maintaining its position as the metropolis of a commercial 'empire' and as the Workshop of the World, and of other nations as in a 'tributary' relationship, were all these mercantilist phrases simply designed to appeal to the atavistic sentiments of Whigs and Tories, who would otherwise be reluctant to enter into a cosmopolitan trading system? There is evidence to suggest that many leading Radicals, far from being devoted to the Cobdenite ideal of a pacifistic cosmopolitanism, stood ready to follow up vigorous language by vigorous action, when the expansion of British commerce was at issue. Indeed, it would appear that the Tory Canning, known for his bustling foreign policy, and the fiery Whig Palmerston, hardly a Cobdenite, might, on occasion, be more conciliatory, less provocative, and, as a subsequent generation might describe it, less 'jingoistic' than such leading Radical spokesmen as Hume, Buller, and the *Manchester Guardian*.

This 'imperial' mood was apparent as early as 1824, when Sir James Mackintosh, a barrister and law reformer, the friend and ally of Bentham and Romilly, in presenting a petition of the City of London for the recognition of the independence of the South American states, addressed the House in terms which were to become familiar a little over a half-century later. Mackintosh urged the government to act forcefully, if necessary, to secure the repayment of loans being made by English financial houses to South American governments. Though granting that the interests 'at stake' might be said to be 'rather individual than national', he insisted that 'the mass of private interest engaged in our trade with Spanish America, is so great as to render it a large part of the national interest'. Mackintosh, in proof, listed a hundred English houses of trade, established in various parts of South America, and cited the great numbers of English technicians and scientists who had gone to the newly independent countries, calling these missionaries who would open 'new markets for the produce of British labour'. It was a 'great national interest as well as duty to watch over the international rights of every Briton, and to claim them from every government': states must treat the wrongs of their subjects as 'public injuries'; 'a wrong done to the humblest British subject,' he declared, 'an insult offered to the

British flag flying on the slightest skiff, is, if unrepaired, a dishonour to the British nation'.[1] The Tory foreign secretary, Canning, rejected such a view, asserting that British financiers, in their dealings with foreign states, 'ought not to carry with them the force and influence of the British government, in order to compel foreign states to fulfil their contracts'.[2]

In 1839, to cite another example, some members of the House protested at the interference of French authorities in West Africa with British merchantmen. Stephen Lushington described the 'insult . . . offered by a French naval officer to the British nation, in the person of the British merchants', and asked for redress; he was supported by George Grote, who spoke of 'the very serious and permanent damage' of having the West African trade 'for ever interdicted to English capital and enterprise'. Another member noted the 'sense of the whole mercantile community' that such 'aggressions' might properly lead to war. Joseph Hume taunted the Whig foreign minister for his overly conciliatory attitude, prodding him to behave more forcefully: while granting that every public officer ought to exercise a 'degree of patience', Hume proclaimed that in his unduly patient behavior 'the noble Lord was not dealing fairly with the merchant', and asked for immediate naval protection for English merchant ships.[3] The foreign secretary whom Hume was thus chiding for pusillanimity was Palmerston.

With the Opium War, the Whig government was at last taking the firm action, so long demanded by the Radicals, to extend trade. In 1839, the Chinese government had ordered the confiscation of quantities of opium which, contrary to previous understandings, were being smuggled into China from India by British merchants, and the government of Lord Melbourne made war in defense of the smugglers.[4] The Tory opposition—led by Peel and Sir James Graham—denounced the war,[5] although, with but few exceptions, the tone of their statements might suggest that motives of party rather than principle were paramount. W. E. Gladstone, however, still a Tory, anticipated his later 'Cobdenism', by unequivocally denouncing the policy of 'force and violence'; 'I do not know, and I have not read of', he declared, a more 'unjust and iniquitous war'.[6]

---

[1] *P.D.*, N.S., XI (15 June 1824), 1359, 1380–1, 1387–8.   [2] *Ibid.* p. 1404.

[3] *P.D.*, 3rd Series, XLVII (2 May 1839), 721–34. Hume, it might be noted, had, in the first decade of the century, been an army surgeon with the forces of the East India Company in the Mahratta war, and when he retired from the service in 1808, it was with £40,000, all the product of his Indian adventure.

[4] See D. E. Owen, *British Opium Policy in China and India* (New Haven: Yale University Press, 1934), pp. 146–75, on 'the crisis of 1839'.

[5] See, for example, *P.D.*, 3rd Series, LIII (7 April 1840), 672, 703–4, 670–1.

[6] *P.D.*, 3rd Series, LIII (8 April 1840), 816, 818–19.

The Liberals and Radicals, on the other hand, made a spirited and virtually unqualified defense of the war, and even of the opium traffic.[1] Lushington, a pillar of Exeter Hall, made a moral defense: he described Chinese behavior as 'a grievous sin—a wicked offence—an atrocious violation of justice, for which England had the right, a strict and undeniable right', by 'the law of God and of man', 'to demand reparation by force if refused peaceable applications'.[2] Sir J. C. Hobhouse, Byron's travelling companion and literary executor, who had been the Radical M.P. for Westminster in the twenties and at this time represented Nottingham, protested at efforts to 'damp and discourage the efforts of our gallant troops in that great enterprise', and insisted, in a cosmopolitan spirit, that England was not pursuing purely selfish trade ambitions; rather she was fighting for the opening of trade for all nations.[3] More practically, Charles Buller declared the war essential if Britain were not to 'lose for ever or for a long time, the very large and lucrative trade that had for more than a century been carried on with China'; the war, Buller concluded, following Wakefield's phrases in *England and America*, must be seen as an opportunity 'to place that trade on an entirely new, secure, and progressive footing', so that the full benefit from 'a really free intercourse' between England and China's 'three hundred millions of civilised and industrious people' might be reaped.[4] H. G. Ward, another Colonial Reformer, declaring the evils of the opium trade 'very considerably exaggerated', inquired why the lucrative Chinese trade ought to be allowed to fall to America. 'We are the strongest power,' he declared.[5]

Finally, Joseph Hume, addressing the House in July 1840, insisted that the British merchants whose stocks of opium had been seized were entitled to government compensation, and proclaimed that the government ought to protect the lives of British subjects abroad under all circumstances. 'From the moment British subjects at Canton', Hume declared, 'were placed in prison to the danger of their lives the Chinese became the aggressors'; moreover, he concluded, 'considering the vicinity of China to the Burmese empire', it was evident that the 'peace of India greatly depended on our vindicating British supremacy before China'.[6] (When war came to the Punjab in 1849, Joseph Hume's reaction was to be a similar one.)[7]

The *Manchester Guardian*, the Radical organ of the North, also supported the Ministry during the Opium War, and 'particularly' directed the 'attention

---

[1] See, for example, Macaulay's defense of the opium traffic. *P.D.*, 3rd Series, LIII (7 April 1840), 719–20; see also p. 742.

[2] *P.D.*, 3rd Series, LIII (9 April 1840), 865–6.

[3] *Ibid.* pp. 886, 898.

[4] *P.D.*, 3rd Series, LIII (8 April 1840), 781–2.

[5] *Ibid.* pp. 824, 828, 830.

[6] *P.D.*, 3rd Series, LV (27 July 1840), 1051–2.

[7] *P.D.*, 3rd Series, CIII (5 March 1849), 168; see also CIV (24 April 1849), 752–3.

of our readers to the admirable speech of Lord Palmerston' in support of the war.[1] In a subsequent article, the *Guardian* justified the war as one which was attempting 'to obtain redress for past and security against future outrages by the Chinese authorities' against British trade.[2]

In 1846, Earl Derby and Benjamin Disraeli became the leaders of those Tories who remained faithful to the corn laws, and directed venomous attacks against the prime minister and against political economy; they especially ridiculed the vision of a British Workshop of the World. Disraeli jibed at the theories of the political economists which, he declared, Peel and the Cobdenites had swallowed whole, and warned Peel that, by repeal, 'you bring about that social revolution' which Peel had, in the past, 'always reminded us would be the consequence of following the policy of the school of Manchester'.[3] Disraeli declared that Peel, long held in thrall by political economy, had begun his career by stealing the ideas of Francis Horner, and was ending it by stealing those of Richard Cobden.[4] In former years, Disraeli himself had seemed friendly to the policy of relaxing the corn laws, and, in his novels, he had not only praised political economy, but had ridiculed the old colonial system, indeed, had tauntingly reminded the Liberals that it had been the Tories—first at Utrecht, in 1713, and then under Pitt and Huskisson—who had fought for free trade against protectionist Whigs.[5] Supporters of the prime minister suggested that it had been Peel's refusal to offer Disraeli a suitable office which had sent him into the arms of the protectionists. By 1846, Disraeli had been so entirely 'converted' as to eulogize the old colonial system, because of which, he asserted, the merchants of England had enjoyed 'more secure markets and larger profits'. After the American Revolution, Disraeli conceded, Pitt had been forced to establish a new commercial system—'a large system of commercial intercourse on the principle of reciprocal advantage'; England had returned to this system under Huskisson and Liverpool. But Peel was, now, in neglecting the principle of reciprocity and moving toward a unilateral free trade, turning against the system of Pitt and Huskisson.[6]

As for the dream of making Great Britain the Workshop of the World, Disraeli had declared such an empire impossible to achieve as early as

---

[1] *Manchester Guardian*, 11 April 1840, 2h.
[2] *Manchester Guardian*, 18 April 1840, 2e.
[3] *P.D.*, 3rd Series, LXXXVI (4 May 1846), 85–7.
[4] *P.D.*, 3rd Series, LXXXVI (15 May 1846), 675–6; Disraeli made the same charges against Peel in his *Lord George Bentinck* (London, 1872), p. 306.
[5] See, for example, quotations from *Sybil*, *Pompanilla*, and *Coningsby* which introduce chapters 2, 5, 6, *supra*.
[6] *P.D.* LXXXIII (20 February 1846), 1335–40.

1838. It was 'a delusion', he had observed, at that time, to suppose that if only England adopted a free trade in corn, the Continent 'would suffer England to be the workshop for the world'.[1] Two years later, in 1840, Disraeli had noted that the Dutch had once regarded all Europe as 'their farm', an expression which Disraeli regarded as 'an appropriate pendant to one which we were much in the habit of using in this country—to make Britain the workshop of the world'. The English free traders were stimulated by 'the same arrogant aspirations', which were founded on a 'profound ignorance of human nature'. 'However we might modify our own tariff, the industry of other nations would ramify into various courses,' Disraeli had concluded.[2]

Other Tories had spoken similarly. The Earl of Darlington, in 1839, had chided those who 'not content with the extent, great as it was, to which this country pushed her manufactures', desired only 'to make this country manufacture for every other country in Europe, if not the whole world'; even if such a situation 'were possible', Darlington declared, 'it would not be just'.[3] In the debate upon the Navigation Acts, in 1849, G. R. Robinson was to warn the Manchester men that 'it was in vain for them to strive against the stream': 'every year—experience demonstrated it—those great commercial States that were growing up were attaining a better position to enable them to rival us'; America, France, Belgium, Germany, and even Italy, were 'every year becoming more and more capable of dispensing with English manufactures'. The Cobdenites, he was to conclude, were inviting disaster by persisting 'in the vain hope of making this country, what she could never be, the great workshop of the world'.[4]

Reverting to the Malthusian argument of some decades earlier, Disraeli proclaimed, in 1846, that 'the first duty of the Minister, and the first interest of the State', was 'to maintain a balance between the two great branches of national industry'; neither agriculture nor industry ought to be permitted to dominate to the great loss of the other. Whereas Malthus had presented an economic justification for such a balance, Disraeli, in an argument similar to one Chalmers had employed, insisted that England, indeed, ought to give a 'preponderance, for that is the proper and consti-tutional word, to the agricultural branch', because 'in England we have a territorial Constitution', and such a constitution was 'the only barrier against that centralising system which has taken root in other countries'. Disraeli warned his listeners that corn law repeal meant a subjection to 'the

[1] *P.D.*, 3rd Series, XLI (15 March 1838), 940.
[2] *P.D.*, 3rd Series, LIII (1 April 1840), 383-4.
[3] *P.D.*, 3rd Series, XLVI (13 March 1839), 495.
[4] *P.D.*, 3rd Series, CIV (23 April 1849), 640.

thraldom of Capital'. It was the land of England, which ought to receive the protection of government, Disraeli observed in a peroration unwittingly praising, in the manner of Balaam, what he had come to curse, the land of 'that country which is the metropolis of the world', and which 'receives the tribute of the world'.[1]

But victory was not to rest with agrarian scoffers, and the Radical middle classes succeeded in persuading parliament to reject the balanced economic development urged by agrarian economists, in an effort to make Britain the Workshop of the World. The mood of the country was that of the Radical Henry Labouchère, the president of the board of trade, who, in 1840, had rushed to the defense of British manufacturing against Disraeli's attacks. 'The hon. Gentleman might call this an arrogant aspiration', he declared, but he 'looked with hope to that British energy' which 'had raised us to that pitch of manufacturing greatness', which 'was the real talisman of this country', and from which 'we could not now descend, he would not say with honour, but even with safety'. Labouchère pictured an England compelled by its economic circumstances to maintain its predominance; 'it was their duty', he concluded, 'to foster, extend, and encourage the manufactures of this country'.[2] In 1846, the year of repeal, Poulett Scrope ridiculed the protectionist view that 'we should be better off' if 'Berkeley's famous wall of brass surrounded the island, instead of the sea', better off if England were 'confined to her own narrow limits, and to the consumption of what she can produce within herself'. 'The acknowledged source of Great Britain's wealth, power and greatness', Scrope declared, was 'her foreign commerce'. Through her commerce, Britain had become 'queen of the ocean', 'making every corner of the globe tributary to her wants'.[3]

There is no question but that England, during the first half of the nineteenth century, possessed, in Peel's words, both a 'manufacturing and commercial pre-eminence'. During the middle decades of the nineteenth century, Great Britain was the most important trading nation, and the volume of Britain's international trade was growing at the remarkable rate of 4.5 per cent annually during much of this period. The rate of expansion of Britain's industry was closely tied to the expansion of British trade, the importation of raw materials and the sales overseas of manufactures; and it was the recognition that British exports were necessarily limited by the purchasing power of other countries, as we have seen, which helped to spur the abolition

[1] *P.D.*, 3rd Series, LXXXIII (20 February 1846), 1335–40, 1346–7; for a sharp discussion of 'Mr D'Israeli's Political Philosophy', see *The Economist* IV (23 May 1846), 659–60.
[2] *P.D.*, 3rd Series, LIII (1 April 1840), 385–6.
[3] *P.D.*, 3rd Series, LXXXIII (20 February 1846), 1273, 1275, 1281.

of hundreds of tariffs, including those on imported corn, during the forties. (It is interesting to note, however, that even in this period of industrial predominance, Britain achieved a balance of payments surplus not by virtue of her trade balance but because of 'invisible' items, such as dividends from overseas investment, fees from shipping services, etc.; indeed, during the period from 1800 to 1850, these invisible items constituted about 25 to 30 per cent of British receipts from the rest of the world, and in subsequent years this figure was to increase.) The total imports, in these middle decades, amounted to more than one-third of the national income: textiles were, as we have observed, central to British trade, and about 30 per cent of all British imports, in the forties, were raw and semi-manufactured materials necessary for the textile industry; food, drink, and tobacco constituted an additional 40 per cent of imports. In the early fifties, the Workshop of the World's share of the world export trade in manufactures was probably more than 40 per cent. In the export trade of certain manufactures, such as textiles, English industry enjoyed a virtual monopoly position, and it was this position which English statesmen wished to retain and indeed to strengthen against foreign rivals.

We have seen the distillation and dissemination of the principles of political economy among all the parties in both houses of parliament, most particularly during the thirties and forties. It was under the banner of the new 'science' that men rushed to the support of free trade, as well as to oppose it, though, of course, it was the free traders who fully partook of its authority. Armed with that authority, the parliamentary free traders, as we have seen, strove not so much to achieve a cosmopolitan system, such as was to be associated with Cobden, but to preserve Britain's industrial predominance, and, if possible, to achieve a virtual industrial monopoly for a British Workshop of the World. (In the interests of trade, they were even ready, like the mercantilists of the preceding century, to urge their governments to use force and to make war.) In promoting such a goal, they carried forward the argument of Josiah Tucker that by a system of free trade, a richer manufacturing nation could maintain its superiority over poorer agricultural nations. Tucker's argument had converted Pitt; supplemented by the somewhat diluted principles of classical political economy, it was to convert Peel over half a century later. The defeated opposition, led by Disraeli, had to make do with the position outlined in the middle of the eighteenth century by David Hume, supplemented by certain principles of the agrarian economists.

CHAPTER 7

Cobdenism and the 'dismal science'

IT was probably, as we have seen, the specifically anti-colonial sentiments and phrases of the party of Hume and Cobden, which, in the cosmopolitan heyday of free trade, many Britons were to share and to mouth, which have for so long made historians view an age of colonization as one merely of the dismantling of colonial empire; it was the liberal and even democratic vocabulary of 'responsible self-government' of the Radical Colonial Reformers which permitted later generations to sympathize with their attack on 'Mr Mother-Country' Stephen, while either ignoring or viewing with a secularist suspicion the pleas of the 'missionary interest'. Similarly, it was Cobden's benign view of a cosmopolitan and pacific international division of labor, erected upon the most liberal principles of political economy, which led historians for so long, to ignore the voluminous evidence that another, less cosmopolitan vision of empire, one derived from England's mercantilist past, was prevalent, probably predominant, not only in the parliament as a whole, but also among parliamentary Radicals; it was probably this as well which led historians to pass over the very unpacific jingoism of the leading Radicals, both anti-colonial and colonizers, when matters concerning the expansion of trade were at issue. Finally, it was the victory of an optimistic Cobdenism (the temper of which was reinforced by the prosperity of the fifties and sixties), with its vision of the smooth passage of industrialism, based on an almost religious conviction of the spiritual and moral truth of free trade, as we shall see, which has made us forget the existence of a full-scale theory of capitalist imperialism, which, following the pessimistic principles of the heterodox agrarian economists and of Wakefield, saw the *necessity* of a continually expanding foreign trade and of colonization to a developing industrialism.

We are confronted, indeed, by two different systems of political economy: a roseate, watering-down of orthodoxy, and a black analysis of the inner contradictions of Britain's industrialism, a Pelagian Cobdenism, and an Augustinian 'Wakefieldism', convinced of the inevitable deficiencies of an economy born in the sin of those who had departed from an agrarian godliness. We have already seen the development of Wakefield's analysis;

in this chapter, we will see that analysis wielded by many different hands, for the leading Colonial Reformers were not only adherents of Wakefield's systematic colonization, but of his political economy which saw the necessity of colonization. Born of the 'dismal science', the theory of capitalist imperialism, set in an analytical context which our century would describe as quasi-Marxist, had many advocates in England during the thirties and forties, before it was overwhelmed by the more harmonious views of Cobdenism.

Cobdenism

Richard Cobden saw free trade as inexorable truth, proceeding as it did, logically, from the principles of the science of political economy, and as so universally beneficial that to oppose it was the devil's work. For Cobden, free trade was virtually a scriptural principle, and much of English nonconformity shared his view. With the repeal of the corn laws, the former Manchester manufacturer—Cobden had given up his business to campaign for free trade—became the leader of the advanced wing of Liberalism, a position which he, supported by his ally, the Quaker John Bright, retained until his death in 1865. Cobden's views upon a wide variety of questions— his cosmopolitanism, pacifism, anti-colonialism—were, as we know, to become the hallmarks of Radical policy from the late forties until the war of 1914, and well into the twentieth century Radicals happily accepted the label of 'Cobdenites'. Indeed, Englishmen, generally, were to accept the Cobdenite defense of free trade—combining as it did the force of 'science' with that of religion.

The principal features of this 'Cobdenism' had appeared as early as 1835 and 1836, when Cobden published, anonymously, two pamphlets in which he set forth his views on colonies, emigration, Ireland, the Eastern Question, and relations with the United States. Cobden, a pacifist, regarded free trade as the essential foundation for an era of universal peace. 'The middle and industrious classes of England can have no interest apart from the preservation of peace,' he asserted; 'the honours, the fame, the emoluments of war belong not to them; the battle-plain is the harvest-field of the aristocracy, watered with the blood of the people'.[1] Cobden revealed himself a friend of Ireland, warning of the consequences of continuing to allow Ireland to operate 'like a cancer in the side of England', and urging Englishmen to export capital to Ireland in order to improve Irish agriculture, and to equip her with a system of manufacturing and commerce. Cobden,

[1] Richard Cobden, *England, Ireland, and America* (Edinburgh, 1836), p. 11.

interestingly enough, approved of emigration to help solve the problems of Ireland, while regarding with 'suspicion' attempts 'to expatriate' Englishmen.[1] In these early tracts, Cobden set the lines of Radical thinking upon the Eastern Question, when, in opposition to the dominant view of his day, he expressed the wish that Turkey would fall to Russian arms,[2] for the Russians, as opposed to the Turks, were, growingly, a commercial people, and 'wherever a country is found to favour foreign commerce,' Cobden wrote, 'it may infallibly be assumed, that England partakes more largely of the advantages of that traffic than any other state'. England, consequently, 'would be found at Constantinople, as she has already been at St Petersburgh, reaping the greatest harvest of riches and power, from the augmentation of Russian imports'.[3] Finally, in his 1835 tract, Cobden displayed his fervent anti-colonialism. He pointed to Spain—'a miserable spectacle of a nation whose own natural greatness has been immolated on the shrine of transatlantic ambition'—and gravely inquired, 'may not some future historian possibly be found recording a similar epitaph on the tomb of Britain?' Colonies were useless to the mother country, and, indeed, harmful, since they were the occasion for much unnecessary expense, since, 'provided our manufactures be cheaper than those of our rivals, we shall command the custom of these colonies by the same motives of self-interest which bring the Peruvians, the Brazilians, or the natives of North America, to clothe themselves with the products of our industry'.[4] Cobden shared Wakefield's view of the advantage of the American trade, and even perceived that, in the not distant future, 'by the successful rivalry of America, shall we, in all probability, be placed second in the rank of nations'.[5] Nor did such a prospect appear seriously to offend him.

But even a cosmopolitan Cobden did not fail to understand, in the mid-thirties, the nature of England's predominant position, which, as a good Englishman, he desired to see maintained. He was proud that England enjoyed a commerce which cast into 'comparative obscurity, by the grandeur and extent of its operations, the peddling ventures of Tyre, Carthage, and Venice'. 'No country', Cobden boasted, 'can carry on great financial transactions except through the medium of England'; 'London is the metropolis of the moneyed world.'[6] If English predominance was unrivalled

---

[1] Cobden, *England, Ireland, and America*, pp. 21–5.   [2] *Ibid.* p. 8.
[3] A Manchester Manufacturer [Richard Cobden], *Russia* (Edinburgh, 1836), p. 9.
[4] Cobden, *England, Ireland, and America*, pp. 6–7.
[5] *Ibid.* pp. 25–33. Cobden was, later, to back this highly favorable view of America's future by heavy investments in U.S. railways; he was a shrewder judge of the long run than of the short run, it would seem, for he did not do well. See E. H. Cawley, ed., *The American Diaries of Richard Cobden* (Princeton: Princeton University Press, 1952), pp. 41–58.
[6] Cobden, *Russia*, pp. 8–9.

in finance and commerce, however, there were challenges to her industrial leadership: Germany, France, Switzerland, and virtually every other continental nation, had excluded British textiles from their markets by protective duties in order that they might establish their own manufactures; Prussia was completing 'a wall of tariffs' which would 'more effectively than did Napoleon, exclude us from the German market—Prussia, for whom we bled, and for whose subjects we are still taxed!' The British ministers at the Congress of Vienna, Cobden complained, in perhaps un-Cobdenite fashion, 'might have stipulated for, and might have commanded a trade with all Europe, as some indemnity for our expenditure', but they had disregarded the interests of British manufacturers.[1] Only the adoption of free trade, which Cobden insisted was a question of 'absolute state necessity', could prolong England's industrial predominance: free trade would lower British corn prices and simultaneously raise the corn prices in the rest of the world, producing 'a shock' for England's rivals. If a simple revenue duty, rather than a protective one, had been set in 1815, the factory system would not, 'in all probability', have 'taken root' in America and on the Continent; it certainly could not have 'flourished, as it has done' through 'the fostering bounties which the high-priced food of the British artisan has offered to the cheaper fed manufacturer of those countries'.[2]

Of all the politicians on either side of the corn-law question, Cobden was among the least in awe of economic 'science', despite his protestations to the contrary. We have observed that in 1835 Cobden had strongly implied the Ricardian argument that if corn were cheaper, wages might be lowered, and English manufacturers might consequently be more competitively priced. During the course of the anti-corn law campaign, this Ricardian argument, most unpopular with the working classes, was dropped, and its validity denied by Cobden. The 'rate of wages' had 'no more connection with the price of food than with the moon's changes', Cobden was to proclaim in 1841.[3] The campaign of the Anti-Corn Law League, indeed, while it beatified and sanctified Adam Smith, owed little to the Ricardian mainstream, and Cobden's parliamentary denunciation of McCulloch on 'the peculiar burdens' of agriculture must be recalled. A view of class harmony between manufacturer and working-man rather than the Ricardian view of class conflict was adopted by Cobden, and the League, which, in its literature, followed Cobden's line of argument, even suggested that repeal would raise real wages.[4] While orthodox political economy produced insights of altogether

[1] Cobden, *England, Ireland, and America*, pp. 35–6.   [2] *Ibid.* pp. 36–9.
[3] John Bright and Thorold Rogers, eds., *Speeches on Questions of Public Policy by Richard Cobden, M.P.* (London: Macmillan, 1870), I, 7.
[4] See Blaug, *Ricardian Economics*, pp. 202–9.

too gloomy an order, Frederic Bastiat, whom Cobden met in 1845, filtered the 'dismal science' through a rosy prism, producing just the message Cobden desired to hear—that with the adoption of free trade, all problems would be resolved. Cobden, writing to his disciple John Bright, in 1851, noted that 'wherever the deductions of political economy lead, I am prepared to follow', but, he asked Bright, 'have you had time to read Bastiat's partly posthumous volume, "Les Harmonies Economiques"?' 'If not, do so; it will require a studious perusal, but will repay it. He has breathed a soul into the dry bones of political economy, and has vindicated his favorite science from the charge of inhumanity with all the fervour of a religious devotee.'[1]

It was with the fervor of 'a religious devotee' that Cobden approached the question of free trade. The arguments of the economists left him comparatively cold; although he was willing to employ them if they seemed useful, somehow they made free trade appear sordid. 'My friends,' he told a London meeting of the Anti-Corn Law League, in May 1843, 'freedom of trade, rightly understood, has nothing sordid about it. It is a benign principle.'[2] For Cobden, and, indeed, for the men of Manchester generally, the fight for free trade was a fight for all that was good, true, and just. 'Our object', he told the House of Commons in 1843, 'is to make you conform to truth, by making you dispense with your monopolies, and bringing your legislation within the bounds of justice.'[3] John Bright, Cobden's chief disciple, in a speech before the House in 1845, declared that he spoke on behalf of those people 'into whose hearts free-trade principles had sunk, and become, verily, a religious question'. There were cries of 'Oh, oh.'[4] Defending repeal of the corn law in 1846, Cobden denied 'anything selfish' or 'discordant with Christian principles' in the maxim, 'to buy in the cheapest market and sell in the dearest'. 'What is the meaning of the maxim?' he asked. 'It means that you take the article which you have in the greatest abundance, and with it obtain from others that of which they have the most to spare, so giving to mankind the means of enjoying the fullest abundance of earth's goods, and in doing so carrying out to the fullest extent the Christian doctrine of "Do ye to all men as ye would they should do unto you".'[5] It was this view of free trade as a moral or religious goal, a

---

[1] Quoted in Morley, *Cobden*, p. 561; see also pp. 206–9; see also Bright and Rogers, *Speeches by Cobden*, I, 471.
[2] 'Speech of R. Cobden, Esq., M.P., at a Meeting of the Anti-Corn Law League, held at the Hall of Commerce, London, May 29, 1843' (n.p., n.d.), p. 4.
[3] *P.D.*, 3rd Series, LXIX (15 May 1843), 400.
[4] *P.D.*, 3rd Series, LXXXI (10 June 1845), 349.
[5] Quoted in Levi, *History of British Commerce*, pp. 294–5.

panacea for a distressed England, which distinguished the Cobdenite outlook[1] from the more pragmatic and distinctly less optimistic views of the Colonial Reformers, and even of such spokesmen for a Workshop of the World as Joseph Hume.

At the moment of victory, there remained evidence of Cobden's earlier pride in England's economic pre-eminence. In an address to 'the aristocracy of England', Cobden declared that 'this is a new era'; 'the age of improvement', 'the age of social advancement', 'a mercantile age, when the whole wealth of the world is poured into your lap'. 'You cannot have the advantages of commercial rents and feudal privileges,' he told England's landed gentlemen, 'but you may be what you always have been, if you will identify yourselves with the spirit of the age.'[2] England was fortunate in that its advantages lay in promoting 'the spirit of the age', and in advancing such a grand spiritual and scientific truth as free trade.

The 'Cobdenism' of the Anti-Corn Law League

If, despite occasional lapses in which even he was carried away by his desire to ensure the continuance of England's industrial predominance, we can call Cobden pretty much a 'Cobdenite', and most certainly a Cobdenite if we think of Cobdenism as a highly optimistic, quasi-religious view of free trade as natural law and the chief foundation for a harmonious world order, of an almost utopian cast, it is difficult to regard the campaign of the Anti-Corn Law League, and of the various pamphleteers associated with that campaign, as Cobdenite. Indeed, a student of the literary outpourings of the great effort to turn Great Britain to a free trade in the 1840s would have a hard time distinguishing the line taken in the hundreds of leaflets and pamphlets issued at that time from that of the attempts of the Fair Trade League, in the 1880s, or of the Tariff Reform League, in the decade before the War of 1914, to bring Great Britain back to a system of protection and imperial preference. It is not surprising to learn that the Tariff Reform League did seek to model its campaign activities after that of its highly successful free trade predecessor; it is, perhaps, surprising to observe that the protectionists might easily have borrowed the full texts of the earlier

---

[1] See, for example, Rev. Edmund Kell, *The Injurious Effects of the Corn Laws on All Classes of the Community* (London, 1840), p. 43; also 'Christian Thoughts on Free Trade', in *The Economist* 1 (30 December 1843), 339. *The Times* had opposed the corn laws as 'repugnant to the first principles of humanity' as early as 1814. See *The Times*, 2 September 1814, 3c; see also 18 January 1839, 4b, c.

[2] *P.D.*, 3rd Series, LXXVIII (13 March 1845), 809-10; see also letter quoted in Morley, *Cobden*, pp. 634-5.

free trade broadsides, merely substituting a call for 'protection and preference' for that of the 'repeal of the corn laws'.[1]

Free trade had for some decades, even before the Anti-Corn Law League
had come to dominate the free trade movement, been presented to the low-
paid, or unemployed working-man, among whom Chartism was sowing
revolutionary discontent, as the solution to England's industrial crises.[2]
The message of the orthodox free traders, therefore, possessed a somewhat
optimistic appearance, distinguishing it from the views of the Colonial
Reformers, for whom capitalist crises were persistent and chronic. Yet, there
was a sterner aspect assumed by the free trade argument before the Anti-
Corn Law League took the field. The orthodox view had long been that if
corn prices were lowered by free importation, then wages would decline,
and British manufacturers would be better able to compete in the world
market.[3] As late as 1839, in a pamphlet in the form of a letter addressed to
the Manchester Chamber of Commerce, a free trade spokesman declared
that 'the wages of our artisans are more than double those given to foreign
workmen of the same class: with a free trade in corn, they would approximate
more nearly'.[4] The protectionists were only too ready to accept this bit of
economic reasoning,[5] since such a prospect only alienated large sections of
the working classes.

The opposition of the free traders, in the twenties and thirties, to factory
reform had already disaffected much of the working-class leadership. Free
trade and social reform were ambiguously linked by Joseph Hume, and
others, when they defended the factory owners against the charges of, in
Hume's words, 'avarice' and of 'wanton cruelty' which had been levelled
against them because of their opposition to factory reform. Any immediate improvement in the conditions of work would, Hume and his associates
believed, by raising costs, undermine Britain's competitive position. Free

[1] For a discussion of the Fair Trade movement, see B. H. Brown, *The Tariff Reform Movement in Great Britain, 1881–1895* (New York: Columbia University Press, 1943), *passim*; for the campaign of Chamberlain's Tariff Reform League, see Bernard Semmel, *Imperialism and Social Reform* (Cambridge, Mass.: Harvard University Press, 1960), pp. 100–27, and *passim*.

[2] See, for example, William Mann, *Letters on the Corn Laws* (London, 1828), p. 3; see also T. P. Thompson, *A Catechism on the Corn Laws* (London, 1827), 3rd edition, p. 23, and *passim*; also the equally popular pamphlet, also by Thompson, *Corn Law Fallacies: With the Answers* (London, 1839).

[3] See, for example, A. Hammerman, *Letter to the Hon. Mr. Baron Hepburn* (Edinburgh, 1814), p. 13.

[4] W. Wolryche Whitmore, *A Second Letter on the Corn Laws to the Manchester Chamber of Commerce* (London, 1839), pp. 10–11.

[5] See, for example, statement of Lord George Bentinck, after the repeal of the corn laws, *P.D.*, 3rd Series, XCIX (9 June 1848), 595–6.

trade was the ultimate remedy, Hume observed, for 'let this corn monopoly be reduced, and not only the distress of the manufacturers would be alleviated, but also the hard treatment which factory children undergo would be put an end to'.[1] Such arguments did not prove very inspiring to the working classes.

The Anti-Corn Law League, following its leader Cobden, took a considerably more optimistic view than had the earlier free traders, or the economists upon whose writings both generations of free traders had claimed to be basing their views.[2] It was this optimistic view which was to be so widely disseminated—in weekly newspapers, pamphlets, and broadsides. Cobden and the men of the League denied what any Ricardian would have found unexceptionable. 'This fallacy of wages', Cobden declared in the forties, was 'at the bottom of all opposition to the repeal of the Corn Laws'.[3] Consequently, during the distress of the forties, the Cobdenites substituted for this 'fallacy' another argument, which, in various forms, became the chief theme of the anti-corn law literature: Great Britain, the argument ran, could only be assured of foreign markets if she provided agricultural nations, potential consumers of British hardware and cloth, with a market for their exports of food and raw materials.

'Foreigners are standing begging for our manufactures, on the sole condition of our taking in return what *we want*, and *they have to give*,'[4] wrote Perronet Thompson; 'the laws that regulate trade', wrote another pamphleteer, 'are those of nature; there will be no imports without exports'.[5] G. R. Porter, the board of trade statistician, said much the same in his *The Many Sacrificed to the Few*,[6] and a prize-winning essay, published by the League in 1842, warned that 'an immense proportion of our population must inevitably be starved off through famine', unless England were prepared to take in payment for her manufactures, 'American flour, Dantzic wheat, Baltic timber, and Brazilian sugar'.[7] The picture of 'golden fields of harvest' in America which Manchester and Birmingham might purchase with their manufactures was depicted by still another pamphlet.[8]

---

[1] *P.D.*, 3rd Series, xv (26 February 1833), 1161–2; Torrens, at this time, spoke in similar terms. See also R. Torrens, *Three Letters to the Marquis of Chandos on the Effects of the Corn Laws* (London, 1839), pp. 8–10.

[2] In 1841, however, McCulloch was to reverse his earlier position on this question, and bring it into line with Cobden's. See J. R. McCulloch, *Statements Illustrative of the Policy and Probable Consequences of the Proposed Repeal of the Existing Corn Laws* (London, 1841), p. 28.

[3] Bright and Rogers, *Speeches by Cobden*, I, 6.

[4] Thompson, *Corn-Law Fallacies*, p. 2.

[5] Anon., *American Corn and British Manufactures* (London, 1845), p. 34.

[6] [G. R. Porter], *The Many Sacrificed to the Few; Proved by the Effects of the Food Monopoly* (London, 1841), p. 11.

[7] George Hope, *Agriculture and the Corn Law*, *Prize Essay* (Manchester, 1842), p. 15.

[8] [J. S. Bartlett], *A Letter to the Right Honourable Baron Ashburton* (New York, 1842), p. 7.

It was in this way that the conception of the Workshop of the World was presented to the working classes. If the worker was not sufficiently attracted by the carrot, inviting him to participate in the Empire of Free Trade, he might also be belabored by the stick, carved from a tree, many centuries old, whose roots were far from dead. It was a far from cosmopolitan message, one curiously similar to that of a later Tariff Reform neo-mercantilism, which filled the literature of the Anti-Corn Law League: it was a concern, crudely expressed, with maintaining Britain's industrial monopoly or, at least, her industrial predominance, another of the legacies of mercantilism. If England did not act quickly to capture foreign markets by abolishing the corn laws, Thompson, the most popular of the publicists for free trade, declared, the foreigner would set up to manufacture for himself, and be forever lost as a customer.[1] The first item of the first issue of the *Struggle*, a free trade paper published for the North of England working-man, warned that 'While *Whigs* and *Tories* are contending for power, *Foreigners* are stealing our *Trade*—the *heart* and *vitals* of our country.'[2] Even if the foreigner did not become a manufacturer, the *League*, a paper published weekly by the Anti-Corn Law League, declared that the English capitalist would seek the advantages available abroad;[3] a 'vast number' of English manufacturers had already emigrated to the Continent and erected factories there, the *Struggle* observed, 'giving employment to the Swiss, Belgians, and Dutch, and taking it from you'.[4]

A considerable number of protectionist pamphlets were issued to combat the arguments of the free traders, many of them designed to undermine the faith in commerce and manufacturing, and in the ability of Britain to maintain its commercial and industrial predominance, upon which the free traders had erected their entire system. Agriculture was a 'certain dependance', a pamphlet declared, commerce highly uncertain; was it 'in the nature of things that we are to continue always to manufacture for the rest of the world'?[5] 'All the world cannot be agricultural; and England alone manufacturing,' observed another pamphlet in 1844.[6] If England neglected its agriculture in order to follow the example of 'mere mercantile states' such as Holland, Venice, and Genoa, it faced ruin, still another pamphlet

---

[1] Thompson, *Corn-Law Fallacies*, p. 2.
[2] *The Struggle*, 1842, no. 1, p. 1.
[3] See, for example, *The League* II, no. 97 (2 August 1845), 707; see also W. Wolryche Whitmore, *A Letter to the Electors of Bridgenorth Upon the Corn Laws* (London, 1826), pp. 27, 29.
[4] *The Struggle*, 1842, no. 24, p. 3.
[5] John Robinson, *The Whole Scheme of the Corn Law Abolitionists Unmasked* (London, 1841), pp. 3-5.
[6] E. S. Cayley, M.P., *Reasons for the Formation of the Agricultural Protection Society* (London, 1844), p. 19.

noted.[1] This, with numerous variations, was a much repeated theme.[2] What England required, the protectionist writers insisted, was a balanced development of her economy;[3] an '*intermixture* of commerce and agriculture' was the 'best security', 'the most effectual antidote provided to the evils with which either, when existing alone, is so prone'.[4] (The protectionist pamphleteers were highly critical of the 'hard-hearted theorists'[5] of orthodox political economy, who readily defended a manufacturing system, whose 'peculiar feature' was not only 'the over production of manufactures, but the gradual casting off of adults', not only in times of distress 'but in the ordinary and vigorous exercise of commercial pursuits'.[6])

While the protectionists insisted on the impossibility of preserving an industrial monopoly, and decried the heartlessness of those who were vainly attempting to do so, even McCulloch, that supposedly inveterate enemy of mercantilist heresies, could say in a pamphlet written in 1841, that 'the preservation of the wealth, power, and prosperity of the empire depends essentially on our being able to maintain our manufacturing and commercial ascendancy'.[7] Without free trade, the *Manchester Guardian* declared, more moderately, Britain's commerce would dwindle; 'the greatness, the prosperity, and even the national independence of Great Britain are bound up in its commercial eminence'.[8]

There was another, highly significant mercantilist assumption which underlay the campaign of the Anti-Corn Law League—the view that a nation might grow wealthy only by foreign trade, only by extracting a profit from abroad, a view whose appearance we have already noted in the early writings of James Mill and Torrens. The agrarians were only following the physiocrats and Adam Smith when they praised the home market. Were not the home market and the colonial market far superior to 'fluctuating and uncertain' foreign markets, a protectionist pamphleteer inquired,

---

[1] Lord Stourton, *Two Letters to the Right Honourable the Earl of Liverpool* (London, 1821), p. 83.
[2] See, for example, Lord Western, *The Maintenance of the Corn Laws* (London, 1839), pp. 20–1.
[3] See, for example, anon., *Thoughts on the Policy of the Proposed Alteration of the Corn Laws* (London, 1827), pp. 12, 14, 56.
[4] Archibald Alison, *Free Trade and Protection* (Edinburgh, 1844), p. 40.
[5] Arthur Ashpitel, *A Few Facts on The Corn Laws* (London, 1839), p. 25; see also Edinburgh Evening Post and Scottish Standard, *Ought the Corn Laws to be Repealed* (Edinburgh, 184?), pp. 3–4, 7–8; and Philip Henry Stanhope, *A Letter from Earl Stanhope on the Corn Laws* (London, 1826), p. 20.
[6] G. C. Holland, *The Millocrat* (London, 1841), no. VI, pp. 5–6; for a highly sentimentalized version of this charge, see Ashpitel, *Facts on the Corn Laws*, p. 25.
[7] J. R. McCulloch, *Statements on Policy and Probable Consequences*, p. 3.
[8] *Manchester Guardian*, 3 January 1844, 4c; see also 1 January 1845, 4d; see also Arthur Morse, *Agriculture and the Corn Law, Prize Essay*, p. 16.

warning that the home market would seriously deteriorate if the corn laws were repealed;[1] 'why are the natives of Sweden to be preferred to the inhabitants of Staffordshire or Wales?'[2] An anti-corn law pamphleteer replied that 'in the infant state of manufacture', up until that time 'when the supply does not exceed the demand', the home market was the best. But, then, glut appeared, and the foreign market had to be appealed to; it was not the home but the foreign market which was 'unlimited and never glutted'.[3] The *Struggle* observed that 'while there is one bare back in the universe, wishing for English goods on terms of fair exchange, *there cannot be an over production of cotton or woollen cloth*'.[4] Perronet Thompson had strong doubts concerning the validity of Say's Law,[5] and urged the necessity of overseas markets. Thompson declared that 'the good market is the market that gives most', adding that 'if the home market is to be the best, let it prove it'.[6] Elsewhere, more brutally, Thompson maintained that for every customer lost at home, 'ten twice as good would be acquired' abroad.[7]

There was some discussion of these questions among the Chartists. William Lovett was an earnest free trader of the Cobdenite sort, but, according to Gammage, the 'largest' party among the Chartists, one headed by Bronterre O'Brien and Feargus O'Connor, was opposed to Cobden's free trade proposals, though they were not all necessarily opposed to the principle of free trade. O'Connor, of course, sympathized with the landed interest, and was an all-out protectionist; in the usual protectionist manner, he vaunted the 'home market', and was suspicious of foreign trade. O'Brien, on the other hand, while holding that the monied class was more pernicious than the landlords, regarded both forms of property as the enemy of the working-man. O'Brien did not object to free trade, but believed that a general adjustment of incomes was necessary before the change to free trade could be made equitable; otherwise creditors and those living on fixed incomes would benefit unfairly by cheapening prices, and, consequently, the non-producing classes would obtain a greater share of the product of industry at the expense of the producing classes. This last, Gammage tells

---

[1] Alison, *Free Trade and Protection*, pp. 41–4.
[2] Stourton, *Two Letters*, pp. 152–3.
[3] Kirkman Finlay, *To the Right Hon. Lord Ashley, &c., &c.* (Glasgow), p. 7 f.n. The chief purpose of Finlay's pamphlet was to denounce the Ten Hours Bill, which he described as a bill 'to Transfer the Cotton Manufacture of Great Britain and Ireland to Foreign Countries' (p. 9 f.n.).
[4] *The Struggle*, 1842, no. 2, p. 6.
[5] See T. P. Thompson, *An Exposition of Fallacies on Rent, Tithes, &c.* (London, 1826).
[6] T. P. Thompson, *Exercises, Political and Other* (London, 1842), v, 20.
[7] Thompson, *Corn-Law Fallacies*, p. 2.

us, became the dominant Chartist argument on the corn laws.[1] In proposing such a general adjustment of incomes, the Chartists, apparently, sought a middle course: they favored the expansion of foreign trade by the abolition of the corn laws, but also desired a simultaneous expansion of the capacity of the home market, to be brought about by a redistribution of income.

The Wakefield party

When Cobden came to parliament in 1841, as the leader of the anti-corn law forces, he became, as well, a leading spokesman for the anti-colonial cause. The *Spectator*, devoted to systematic colonization, observed, unhappily, in 1843, that 'Mr Cobden has stepped out of his legitimate avocation, as a Free Trade agitator, to be an Anti-Colonial agitator.'[2] There were a number of sharp collisions between the Cobdenites and the Colonial Reformers. Somehow, during the forties, the men of Manchester had come to believe that emigration to the colonies was being set forth as an *alternative* to free trade. This they regarded as intolerable. The corn-law repealer Villiers declared, during the emigration debate of 1840, that it was the corn laws alone which were the cause of distress, and which 'gave rise to the notion of redundancy of labour'. 'There was no necessary redundancy,' he insisted. Meanwhile, Villers urged, let the working class, made wretched by the corn laws, remain in England to terrify the landlords into reform.[3] In 1843, Joseph Hume, although not entirely opposing emigration, insisted that it provided only the smallest relief. Why should we 'send our capital and labour abroad'? he inquired. 'Let the country have free-trade, and the necessity of emigration as a means of relief would be done away with,' Hume concluded.[4]

The Colonial Reformers, on the other hand, always following Wakefield, to whose analysis and even to whose phrases they were faithful, insisted that free trade by itself was not a sufficient remedy for England's distress. The first effect of the repeal of the corn laws, Rintoul's *Spectator* observed, would be 'to give an impulse' to trade and manufacturing, but England had 'already manufacturing-power enough to supply the world'. This period of 'renewed activity', under 'existing circumstances as to population, must produce a new glut'. With free trade, indeed, there would be 'more

[1] R. G. Gammage, *History of the Chartist Movement* (1837–54) (Newcastle-on-Tyne, 1894), pp. 102–4; P. W. Slosson, *The Decline of the Chartist Mouvement* (New York, 1916), pp. 47–9, 51. On working-class praise of the home market, see E. P. Thompson, *The Making of the English Working Class*, p. 776.
[2] 'Colonies, Their Cost and Profit', *Spectator* XVI, no. 772 (15 April 1843), 347.
[3] *P.D.*, 3rd Series, LIV (2 June 1840), 873–5.
[4] *P.D.*, 3rd Series, LXVIII (6 April 1843), 581.

capital competing in the market to crush the small capitalist' and 'more people to be thrown out of employment'. Emigration would then have to be undertaken, under the pressure of even greater distress than existed before repeal: 'emigration, in fact, is a necessary auxiliary to Corn-law Repeal', the *Spectator* concluded—emigration and systematic colonization. Only systematic colonization could 'save the projectors' of the corn-law repeal 'from the disgrace of disaster arising from their nostrum—Corn-law Repeal *and nothing else*'.[1] 'It is not bread alone that is wanted in England,' the *Spectator* declared, 'but elbow-room.' 'Mr Cobden cries out for bread, but thinks the elbow-room may be dispensed with.' 'Free trade alone will not do.'[2]

So, while the party of Hume and Cobden defended free trade as the one grand remedy for all Britain's problems, following, in this, certain arguments, with modifications, of Tucker, Smith, and Ricardo, the 'Philosophers' of the Wakefield school insisted upon the need for both free trade and a continuing program of colonization if England were to avoid the calamities which threatened an advancing industrial and commercial system. If the party of Hume and Cobden could optimistically view an international free trade as fulfilling the conditions for the harmonious operation of Say's Law, the school of Wakefield, following the more physiocratic strains of Smith, Malthus, and Chalmers, saw the continuing necessities for empire-building if a stultifying glut of goods, men, and capital, were to be overcome. Despite a jarring personality, Gibbon Wakefield was able to persuade some of the foremost Radical politicians and theorists of his time of the soundness of his analysis of industrial society. In the phrase of a journal of the day, one rather hostile to his views, Wakefield had made the leading young Radical politician of the period—Sir William Molesworth—one of his 'speaking-trumpets',[3] and, indeed, the same might have been said, as we have seen and shall see further, of Charles Buller, H. G. Ward, W. W. Whitmore, George Grote, and R. S. Rintoul. Wakefield's theory of capitalist imperialism was founded upon a distinctive critique and analysis which, apparently, enabled the young Colonial Reformers of the thirties and forties to understand the profound changes which England was experiencing, and which, furthermore, provided them with a practical program to deal with England's new circumstances. The familiar phrases of Wakefield's *England*

---

[1] 'Emigration and Its Fraudulent Detractor', *Spectator* XIV, no. 702 (11 December 1841), 1189; see also 'Emigration and Free Trade', *Spectator* XIV, no. 703 (18 December 1841), 1210–11.

[2] 'Give Us Bread and Elbow-Room', *Spectator* XVI, no. 784 (8 July 1843), 635; for a similar rejoinder to Cobden from the Tory Reformer Richard Oastler, see *Richard Oastler's Reply to Richard Cobden's Speech; At Leeds, 18th December, 1849* (London, 1850), pp. 18–19, and *passim*.

[3] *Sidney's Emigrant Journal* I, no. 26 (29 March 1849), 202.

and America were continually in use in the parliament and its committees.

W. W. Whitmore, M.P., Chairman of the South Australian Association, for example, in testimony before a parliamentary committee in 1836, urging the need for colonization, spoke of the 'abundant and overflowing' capital of England, and the need for an expanding 'field of employment' not only for the poor but for lawyers, physicians, and middle-class spinsters. Since 1815, he declared, 'without the drain of war', we do not find 'a full employment for all our talent, our labour, or our capital'. How could England find such 'a full employment'? 'By colonization,' Whitmore asserted, 'by extending your empire; by causing the surplus of capital, as well as people, to spread themselves over a field boundless in point of extent; capable of producing articles required in this country' both 'for immediate consumption' and as the 'raw materials of your manufactures'. Such colonies— possessing 'a population of British origin, governed by the same laws, speaking the same language, and having nearly the same wants and feelings as the parent state'—will remain attached to the mother country through the bond of trade, exchanging their raw products for the manufactured goods they 'will for centuries require' from England. 'By colonization,' he concluded, 'I mean the extension of the British empire, whereby its commerce, its wealth its shipping and power, may be augmented, its rate of profit raised. and the general welfare and happiness of all classes of its subjects promoted.'[1]

In an address before the House of Commons, in June 1839, to cite another example, the Colonial Reformer, H. G. Ward, the M.P. for Sheffield, whose youth had been spent in the diplomatic service and who was to end his days as a colonial governor in India, set forth the same doctrine from still another point of vantage. Chartism ('an agitation against property—against law— against society itself'), Ward observed, was rampant. It was a 'knife and fork question'; in no part of the world did there exist 'such a fearful distinction between the richer, and poorer, classes, as here', and, consequently, Chartist revolutionary principles, appealing to class hatred, were particularly dangerous. Parliament could deal with Chartism only by 'going to its source, and by removing, or mitigating, the pressure, which occasions it': this pressure could 'be traced clearly to the disproportion between our population and the field for the employment of labour', a disproportion which affected all classes—'the Church, the Bar, the Army, the Navy, trade'— for 'every department is overstocked'. The remedy was 'the proper disposal of the waste lands in our colonies'. The government persisted in regarding

[1] *Report from the Select Committee on the Disposal of Lands in the British Colonies*, 1836 (512), xi, 499, pp. 1–8.

the empire as a 'field for patronage', but the waste lands 'are emphatically public lands, the inheritance—the patrimony of every poor man in England, Ireland, and Scotland, who pays allegiance to the Crown—and as such I claim them', Ward declared. After eulogizing Wakefield's *England and America*—its 'admirable clearness', 'the vast array of facts', 'the great practical results, to which it must lead', 'all the offspring of one man's mind', 'an honour to the country, and the age'—Ward observed that, 'in preaching this doctrine of colonization, I do not look to any barren extension of territory; I look to a great impulse being given to our manufactures and trade—a relief from pressure here—a rapid increase in our colonies in consequence of that very relief'. Colonial markets were 'the best and least fluctuating of markets', which would survive 'the convulsions of war or Revolution itself'. 'There are some people,' Ward concluded, 'who say we don't want to extend our colonies—we have "colonies enough". I ask in return, have we markets enough? Have we employment enough? Are wages high enough, and profits high enough? Is there no political discontent—no physical suffering?' British trade was diminishing; 'foreign competition is growing up'. 'Is it not desirable, and wise, to open a safety-valve', to 'promote the welfare of many millions of human beings, and to enlarge the sovereignty of the British Crown', all at the same time?[1] In seconding Ward's motion, Sir William Molesworth also paid tribute to the author of *England and America*, and pictured the great commercial opportunities which Australasia offered Great Britain as compensation for those 'we are on the eve of losing in the Old World'—provided only that 'those fair and fertile portions of the earth's surface were peopled with men of the British race'.[2]

Charles Buller's acceptance of the Wakefield analysis was evident in his address to the House of Commons, in April 1843, also on the subject of colonization. The present distress, Buller began, was not due to 'partial' or 'temporary' causes. There had been 'overproduction', 'there never was so much money lying idle', and workhouses were 'getting crowded with able-bodied men, who could not get employment'. There had also been distress in the United States, but hardly as severe as the English troubles; in England, 'there is a permanent cause of suffering in the constant accumulation of capital, and the constant increase of population within the same restricted field of employment'. The result was that 'every kind of business is more and more passing into the hands of great capitalists, because they can afford, on their large amounts, to be content with a rate of profit, at

[1] *P.D.* XLVIII (25 June 1839), 841–8, 866–8.
[2] *Ibid.* pp. 872, 887–8.

which the smaller capital would not produce a livelihood'. 'In this country there are seen side by side, in fearful and unnatural contrast, the greatest amount of opulence, and the most appalling mass of misery.' This constituted a danger to 'property and order'. The cry of fair wages had to be answered 'if you wish to retain your own great advantages of position and property', he told the members of the House. What was required was 'a wider field of employment'; colonization was the 'remedy against the distress of the country'. 'I propose colonization', Buller declared, 'as subsidiary to Free-trade', as a 'surer' remedy, less liable to 'interruptions from the caprice of others, as trade with foreign nations must always be subject to'. Furthermore, Buller observed, Britain could readily maintain control of the fiscal policy of her colonies, and would see to it that they would erect no tariffs hostile to England. On this occasion, Buller, too, paid public tribute to Edward Gibbon Wakefield.[1]

Sir William Molesworth, the Radical baronet, and a leading spokesman for the Wakefield party on colonial questions, was, like others of the Wakefield party, disabused by the failures of practical efforts at 'systematic colonization'. In the forties, he, more and more, looked toward Cobden for leadership,[2] and became one of the spokesmen for corn-law repeal.[3] Though Wakefield believed him lost as a disciple, Molesworth's corn-law speeches continued, to the end, to bear, unmistakably, the Wakefield imprint. He was still in the Wakefield camp, in 1837, when, in supporting Sir William Clay's resolution for repeal, Molesworth observed that laborers and capitalists both suffered from 'hurtful competition', because of 'a tendency in labour and capital to augment more rapidly than the means of employing them'. Labor and capital were 'superabundant' compared to land, and consequently both wages and profits were low; 'a free importation of corn would be equivalent to the addition of so much land to this country', he observed, and 'we might perpetually import food from other countries in return for our manufactures'. Corn-law repeal was necessary, Molesworth insisted, in virtual direct quotation of his master, 'to render the inevitable progress of democracy in this country as safe and peaceable as it is in America'.[4] In seconding Villiers' resolution of 1838 calling for repeal, Molesworth declared that competition and the 'general fall of profits' was bringing about the ruin of the 'smaller capitalists', who would be 'absorbed in the labouring class' until 'the community would ultimately consist only of two

[1] *P.D.*, 3rd Series, LXVIII (6 April 1843), 486–505, 513.
[2] See, for example, letter of Richard Cobden to Walmsley, dated 8 July 1848. Miscellaneous Papers, N.Y. Public Library.
[3] See *The League* III, no. 110 (1 November 1845), 55.
[4] *P.D.*, 3rd Series, XXXVII (16 March 1837), 597–601.

classes—labourers and the possessors of immense capitals'. The alternative to such a dire outcome was to 'augment . . . the field of employment' by, first of all, repealing the corn laws.[1]

By the late forties, Wakefield regarded Molesworth as lost to the cause of colonization; and, indeed, Molesworth was to adopt some of the anti-colonial slogans of a victorious Cobdenism. Yet the Wakefield inheritance was to persist. In a speech on colonies in 1848, for example, Molesworth observed that 'all the benefit which, as far as trade is concerned, we derive from the sums which we expend on colonial dominion, consists in the power we thereby possess of averting the possibility of the colonies enacting hostile tariffs against our produce and manufactures', and that this gain was not worth the expense of governing the colonies; however, the old Colonial Reformer added that if England adhered to 'the principle of responsible government', leaving her colonies to manage their own affairs 'uncontrolled by the Colonial Office', she would not have the expense of government, and the colonists would continue 'our fellow subjects', and valuable trading partners. There were, moreover, other, very substantial, reasons for colonization, in Molesworth's view, and in describing these, Wakefield's phrases came easily to his tongue. If only England would make her colonies 'what the backwoods are to the United States', he declared, the most difficult economic problems of England and Ireland might be solved. 'If the colonies were properly planted', then 'our kinsmen and friends, instead of overstocking the liberal professions', and 'overcrowding the Army and Navy', would 'seek their fortunes in the colonies and prosper'. 'For we are by nature a colonising people,' Molesworth intoned; it was England's destiny, with respect to the sparsely settled countries, 'to convert their wastes into the happy abodes of the Anglo-Saxon race'.[2]

The differences between Colonial Reformers and the cosmopolitan opponents of colonization, though both Radical groups were now united under Cobden's leadership, persisted, we see, for a while at least. In 1849, in the House of Commons, Molesworth again paid tribute to the 'distin-

---

[1] *P.D.*, 3rd Series, XLI (15 March 1838), 923–32. In this address, Molesworth also observed that it was upon the existence of an agricultural surplus that all civilization depended, and that it was to this surplus that England owed, he continued, using Chalmers' term and argument, her 'disposable population': 'You would be rich and powerful in proportion to the amount of your disposable population'; with such a population, 'you might stud the seas with your ships, cover the land with your armies, set at defiance any one nation, or any combination of nations, which might be leagued in hostility against you, and carry on in security an extended commerce with every other portion of the globe'. A 'vast disposable population' would be 'consequent upon unrestricted trade in corn'. See also *P.D.*, 3rd Series, XLVI (13 March 1839), 442–4, 448, 451–6, 460, 462.

[2] *P.D.*, 3rd Series, C (25 July 1848), 830–3, 853–4, 856–7.

guished men' who had 'attentively studied the subjects of colonisation and emigration, with the view of relieving the economical difficulties of the united kingdom', citing Wakefield as 'the most eminent' among these, a man, who, by his writings, Molesworth concluded, had 'produced a profound impression on the minds of some of the ablest men of our day'. Molesworth offered J. S. Mill and George Grote as examples of the men upon whom Wakefield had produced 'a profound impression'.[1]

Although allied in so much, the Cobdenite and the Colonial Reformers (the advocates of a more dismal science), were moved by substantially different principles, as we have seen. While operating on these different economic preconceptions, Molesworth and Cobden, and their numerous followers might, nonetheless, all defend the necessity of free trade. One member of the Wakefield school, however, followed its principles to another conclusion. Robert Torrens, in the forties, challenged the view that a unilateral free trade would be useful to Great Britain. Torrens saw not only the need for colonization to prevent a free trade from compounding England's difficulties, but also insisted on the necessity of securing reciprocal tariff advantages from foreign countries. In his analysis and proposals, he anticipated much of the neo-mercantile imperialism to be advocated by Joseph Chamberlain, over half a century later. The victory of Cobdenism was to see still another former Radical and free trader, Lord Brougham, revert to certain of the leading principles of the old commercial system, to which he had already demonstrated a clear attachment nearly a half-century earlier.

[1] *P.D.*, 3rd Series, CVI (26 June 1849), 940.

CHAPTER 8

Mercantilist revival

Envy bars out truth; in recommending free trade England is suspected to have a sinister object in view ... Were Englishmen hostile to the prosperity of the continent, as continental politicians frequently assert, instead of urging free trade on its acceptance, we should keep it carefully to ourselves. We should guard it as the secret of our future greatness. We should prevent our neighbours, if we could, from sharing its manifold advantages.

The Economist, 11 September 1847

We shall urge finally, that the high place which England occupies, as the first among the commercial nations of the world, has been assigned to her in the order of providence, not by a fortuitous concurrence of events ... but as the natural and proper consequence of her possessing in a superior degree, the elements of industrial greatness ...

Foreign and Colonial Quarterly Review, I, No. 1, July 1843

Though he could not believe with the author of an able pamphlet (Col. Torrens) that the sun of England was set, that the commerce of England would continue to decrease, that wages would continue to decline, that the operatives would have to learn to live on inferior food: though he would not bring himself to believe all this, yet he was compelled to admit that there was great room for anxiety.

Gally Knight, House of Commons, 6 April 1843

IN the years since the corn laws of 1815 were first debated, many members of both Houses of Parliament, as we have observed, had proclaimed, as had Dean Tucker over half a century earlier, the advantages a manufacturing country enjoyed over an agricultural one, and had declared that free trade was the policy by which an advanced economy might preserve such advantages. However, when foreigners repeated these assertions, many of the advocates of free trade felt grossly misunderstood: a territorial division of labor, they argued, would leave industrial activities to those best suited for them, that is, Britain; an international free trade, they insisted, would promote the universal good, and was, indeed, simply sound Christian ethics. The so-called "national" school of political economy, on the Continent and in the United States, speaking in support of local industrial interests, denounced free trade as the instrument by which England planned to maintain her industrial monopoly, to perpetuate her exclusive enjoyment of the immense productive capacities of the new machinery. The 'science' of political economy, with its pretended 'cosmopolitanism', they declared, was designed to keep the non-British world in the humiliating and economically inferior position of serving as suppliers of food and raw materials— mere hewers of wood and drawers of water—to a British industrial metropolis. Like the mercantilists of the preceding century, the 'national' economists insisted that a manufacturing country must not only be more powerful than an agricultural country, but considerably more prosperous, and urged the protection of infant manufacturing plants by tariffs. In a letter, in 1856, Richard Cobden, disheartened by attacks on free trade by protectionists in Germany and the United States, was to declare, with some disgust, that 'the less we attempted to persuade foreigners to adopt our trade principles, the better'.[1]

The national economists

In 1790, perhaps the first of the 'national economists', the American secretary of the treasury, Alexander Hamilton, had presented a *Report on Manufactures* to the United States Congress. Writing nearly forty years before Senior's statement of the law of increasing returns in industry, Hamilton noted that 'the labor of artificers being capable of greater subdivision and simplicity of operation than that of cultivators' was 'susceptible, in a proportionately greater degree, of improvement in its productive powers, whether to be derived from an accession of skill or from the application of ingenious machinery'.[2] Under such circumstances, 'the substitution of foreign for domestic manufactures is a transfer to foreign nations of the advantages accruing from the employment of machinery'.[3] Moreover, Hamilton continued, the inherent nature of trade between an agricultural and a manufacturing country placed the former at a considerable disadvantage.[4] Foreign demand for agricultural products was 'rather casual and occasional, than certain or constant'; the variety of the goods Europe was prepared to sell, the distance from Europe, and the high transport costs caused by the greater 'bulkiness' of raw produce, were other factors

---

[1] Quoted in Morley, *Cobden*, pp. 309–10.
[2] Alexander Hamilton, 'Report on Manufactures', in *Papers on Public Credit, Commerce and Finance* (New York: Columbia University Press, 1934), p. 182. It is the view of H. R. Syrett and J. E. Cooke, editors of *The Papers of Alexander Hamilton* (New York: Columbia University Press, 1966), vol. x, that Hamilton's opinions on these questions were mostly derived from Postlethwayt, Necker, and Steuart (pp. 1, 7, 242, 261, 338–9, and *passim*).
[3] *Ibid.* p. 192.
[4] *Ibid.* pp. 200–1.

which would put the American terms of trade at a chronic disadvantage.[1] Hamilton, therefore, called upon the Congress to establish a system of protective duties, prohibitions, bounties, and drawbacks to industry[2] to 'the degree in which the nature of the manufacture admits of a substitute for manual labor in machinery'.[3] The United States ought not to be dependent upon Europe for manufactures; a country ought to aim, Hamilton concluded, at possessing 'all the essentials of national supply'.[4]

Other Americans followed in Hamilton's steps. Individual interests were 'perpetually at variance' with national interests, a Baltimore lawyer Daniel Raymond wrote in 1823; while it might be 'beneficial' to Southern planters to import cheap textiles from England, because they found a market for their own produce there, it certainly was not beneficial to the country.[5] Because of the 'superior skill' of the English, it was 'utterly impossible' to compete 'upon equal terms'.[6] 'Although it may be more beneficial for the time being, for a nation to import, than to manufacture its own comforts of life,' he observed, 'how will it be fifty years hence?'[7] Raymond, too, called for the framing of a protective tariff.

Friedrich List was a Swabian bureaucrat, turned professor of political economy at Tübingen, whose experiences in Germany and then in the United States of the early part of the nineteenth century (where he became familiar with the writings of Hamilton, and, probably, of Raymond)[8] had convinced him that free trade, although it might be good national policy for England, was bad policy for less industrially advanced countries. Eloquently, if not fully accurately, List described England's Empire of Free Trade:

In all ages there have been cities or countries surpassing others in manufactures, trade and navigation; but the world has never witnessed a supremacy to be compared with that existing in our time. In all ages states have aspired to domination, but no edifice of power has ever been constructed upon so broad a base. How miserable appears the ambition of those who attempted to establish universal domination upon the power of arms, in comparison with the great attempt of England to transform her whole territory into an immense manufacturing and commercial city, into an immense port, and to become to other nations what a vast city is to the country, the center of arts and knowledge, of an immense commerce, of opulence, of navigation, of naval and military power; a cosmopolitic

[1] Alexander Hamilton, 'Report on Manufactures', pp. 197–8, 201, 225, 228–9.
[2] *Ibid.* pp. 234–5; see also pp. 223–4.
[3] *Ibid.* p. 249.
[4] *Ibid.* p. 227.
[5] Daniel Raymond, *The Elements of Political Economy* (Baltimore, 1823) II, 225–6, 228–9, 240–3, 231–2.
[6] *Ibid.* pp. 245–6; see also pp. 240–3.
[7] *Ibid.* p. 250.
[8] For a comparison of the ideas of Raymond and List, see C. P. Neill, *Daniel Raymond: An Early Chapter in the History of Economic Theory In the United States* (Baltimore, 1897), pp. 46–63.

country supplying all nations with manufactured products, and asking in return from each country, its raw materials and commodities; the arsenal of extensive capital, the universal banker, regulating, if not controlling the circulating money of the whole world, and making all nations tributary to her by loans and the payment of interest.[1]

Orthodox doctrine, List continued, was based upon a 'chimerical *cosmopolitanism*' which had 'no regard for national interests', and upon 'a disorganizing *individualism*', which thought entirely of the profits of the moment and which took account 'neither of the moral nor of the political interests' of the future, 'nor of the productive power of the nation'.[2] List grounded his doctrine upon a theory of productive powers; 'the power of creating wealth', he was convinced, was 'vastly more important than wealth itself'.[3] List lauded manufacturing and opposed 'that insane doctrine' which sacrificed the interests of agriculture and manufacturing to the 'pretensions of commerce,—to the claims of absolute free trade'; the doctrine that regarded the whole world as 'a republic of merchants, one and indivisible'.[4]

Henry Carey, the son of the protectionist publisher, Matthew Carey, and nineteenth-century America's outstanding economist,[5] the heir of Hamilton, Raymond, and List, set forth a more emotional, even, it might be said, hysterical, picture. The British policy of free trade aimed, he wrote, at perpetuating the economic subservience of America, indeed of all the world, to Great Britain, and Carey appealed to 'all the agriculturists of the world' to recognize their 'solidarity of interest' against the British trading colossus. Carey maintained that England had been warring against 'the agricultural communities of the world, for the reduction of the prices of their rude products'.[6] 'The system which looks towards making Britain "the workshop of the world"', he declared, 'is, of all the forms of tyranny ever devised, the one that, *par excellence*, tends to the establishment of slavery as the normal condition of the man who needs work.'[7] Free trade

[1] Friedrich List, *National System of Political Economy* (Philadelphia, 1856), chap. 33, intro.
[2] *Ibid.* p. 262.
[3] *Ibid.* p. 208.
[4] *Ibid.* p. 341.
[5] See A. D. H. Kaplan, *Henry Charles Carey: A Study in American Economic Thought* (Baltimore: Johns Hopkins, 1931). For a detailed outline of Carey's economics, see H. C. Carey, *Principles of Social Science* (Philadelphia, 1858), 3 vols.
[6] H. C. Carey, *Letters to the President on the Foreign and Domestic Policy of the Union and Its Effects as Exhibited in the Condition of the People and the State* (Philadelphia, 1858), pp. 126, 131; see also pp. 79–86.
[7] H. C. Carey, *Review of the Decade 1857–67* (Philadelphia, 1867), pp. 15, 17, 26–7, 31, 35. See also H. C. Carey, *Commerce, Christianity, and Civilization, Versus British Free Trade: Letters in Reply to the London Times* (Philadelphia, 1876), pp. 10–11, 35–6; H. C. Carey, *The Harmony of Interests, Agricultural, Manufacturing, and Commercial* (Philadelphia, 1851), p. 71.

policy aimed to secure to England the '*monopoly* of machinery'; protection, on the other hand, 'seeks *to break down this monopoly*'.[1] Carey saw England as having 'passed her zenith', because her lop-sided development had compelled her to neglect the home market, which, as Adam Smith and Mirabeau understood, Carey added, was the best of markets.[2] The future, Carey declared, belonged to Germany, Russia, and the United States.[3]

The English political economists, generally, regarded the writings of the national economists as reversions into a pre-scientific mercantilism, and consequently beneath professional consideration. John Austin, the political theorist of utilitarianism, writing upon Friedrich List for the *Edinburgh Review* in 1842, found that, 'considered as a system of international trade', List's 'treatise is unworthy of notice', and was, in fact, the 'work of a zealous and unscrupulous advocate'.[4] *The Times*, in 1847, denounced List and his followers for disseminating 'the most erroneous and absurd notions of the policy of this country', and described their political economy as 'extravagant fictions'.[5]

Yet the arguments of the 'national' school were not devoid of merit. In certain instances, indeed—in the case, for example, of Hamilton's view of the terms of trade—economists of the national school appear to have anticipated many elements of the later analysis of English political economy. The policy of tariff protection, urged by these economists, had been the one recommended by Tucker, in the previous century, in his private rebuttal to Hume, as the means by which poor, agricultural nations might defend themselves against the economic advantages possessed by richer, more advanced nations. Tucker, too, had argued that variations in wealth tended, under conditions of free trade, to perpetuate themselves; and so had, in the years following, James Mill, Torrens, Brougham, and Ricardo, all of whom had also written of the considerable advantages a manufacturing nation possessed over an agricultural one. Of course, parliament was to hear many speeches, as we have already noted, agreeing with the view of the national economists that free trade would help to maintain England's industrial monopoly. Parliament was also to hear, in the early stages of Great Britain's

---

[1] Carey, *Harmony of Interests*, p. 72.

[2] See Carey, *Review of the Decade*, pp. 37–9; Carey, *Harmony of Interests*, pp. 227–9; Carey, *Commerce, Christianity, and Civilization*, p. 6. Writing in 1867, Carey prophesied the further decline of Britain if 'success attend the present efforts at substituting fluid hydro-carbons, readily susceptible of transportation' for British coal. The first oil well had been drilled in Pennsylvania a decade earlier. (Carey, *Review of the Decade*, p. 36).

[3] *Ibid.* p. 39; and H. C. Carey, *The Way to Outdo England Without Fighting Her* (Philadelphia, 1865), p. 165.

[4] [John Austin], 'List on the Principles of the German Customs Union. Dangers of British Industry and Commerce', in *Edinburgh Review*, no. CLII (July 1842), 521–2.

[5] *The Times*, 16 January 1847, 4b.

effort to become the Workshop of the World, a number of Englishmen, among them certain of the chief formulators of the new political economy, who, in a far from liberal spirit, were to display, even more crudely, forms of economic thinking of an entirely nationalist and mercantilist order, even while they fought for a 'cosmopolitan' free trade.

The exportation of machinery and capital

Of perhaps the greatest interest in this connection was the antagonism of many free traders to the sale of British-produced machinery abroad.[1] During the parliamentary session of 1825, Joseph Hume, prompted by Francis Place, endeavored to abolish the laws whose purpose it was to protect England's lead in manufacturing by prohibiting the export of machinery. The Tory government, although sympathetic, decided that, given parliamentary resistance, it would be wiser to have machinery-export arranged by special licenses, rather than attempt abolition of prohibitory laws.[2] In May 1826, Hume resumed his effort, suggesting that the manufacture of machinery for export would 'give employment' to many workmen; but the response, again, was not favorable.[3] In December, Hume tried once more, supported by Sir Henry Parnell, who declared that 'the use of that machinery would enable other countries to increase their wealth, and we should ultimately derive a proportionate benefit from such an increase'.[4]

This statement prompted Robert Torrens, elected M.P. for Ipswich the previous month, to announce his opposition. Torrens insisted that he was, 'generally speaking, a friend to free trade'; however, 'in every science, there must necessarily be exceptions'. Since 'we made better machinery than our rivals', English manufactures were 'cheaper and better'. Why, then, he asked, should we 'give up our exclusive advantage'? Torrens proclaimed that England, 'with a firm hand', ought to keep all her 'exclusive advantages', because they 'evidently ministered to the wealth and the prosperity of the country'. Indeed, Torrens urged England to restrict the export of her cheap coal, without which French manufacturers could not operate steam-engines to advantage, and he suggested a duty of 50 per cent on all coals exported to the Continent. (In 1825, only about 1.4 per cent of the 21.9 million tons of coal produced in England was exported; by 1840, the figure was to be 4.8 per cent of 33.7 million tons, and coal exports

[1] See account in Wallas, *The Life of Francis Place*.
[2] Francis Place Papers. British Museum Add. MSS 27,798, Sheets 65, 67.
[3] *P.D.*, N.S., xv (11 May 1826), 1118–21.
[4] *P.D.*, N.S., xvi (6 December 1826), 291–2, 295.

were to climb steadily until, in 1913, they were to amount to about 32.8 per cent of 287.4 million tons.)

'It had been for so long a time the habit to look upon any man as a Goth who dissented from the modern doctrine of political economy', said Alexander Baring, after Torrens' speech, that he was especially delighted that Torrens had taken the position that England ought to protect her 'ingenuity and skill'. Sir Robert Peel also expressed his sympathy with Torrens 'respecting the true principle on which our commercial policy should rest', as did Henry Bright, who 'trusted that, in the present session, the true principles of political economy would be better understood'. An M.P. from Stafford-shire reminded the House that a memorial of the Manchester Chamber of Commerce had come out against the 'indiscriminate exportation' of machinery. This information caused Henry Warburton, a timber merchant who was a member of Bentham's circle, and who was to become a prominent member of the Anti-Corn Law League, to express his 'surprise, that the people of Manchester, who had been the first to petition for a free trade in corn, should have lent themselves to the getting up of such a memorial'.[1]

Although William Ellis,[2] a friend of J. S. Mill, and an economist who was to found the Birkbeck Schools, and the remarkable Charles Babbage,[3] known primarily for his invention of a 'calculating engine', had written of the economic advantages of exporting machinery, a much more highly regarded political economist, Nassau Senior, writing, in 1830, from his position as the first occupant of the Drummond professorship of political economy at Oxford, provided a theoretical underpinning for the position taken by Torrens, Baring, Peel, and the Lancashire cotton manufacturers. In mining countries, Senior argued, the general rate of wages was determined by the cost of producing the precious metals: 'the mine worked by England is the general market of the world: the miners are those who produce those commodities by the exportation of which the precious metals are obtained'. It followed, consequently, 'that the amount of the income in money of each individual depends on the prosperity of our foreign commerce', and England's foreign commerce rested upon the improved efficiency of labor in manufacturing. It was, then, the 'inventions of Arkwright and Watt' which made English labor 'more than ten times as efficient in the production of exportable commodities' as, for example, India, and which enabled Englishmen to obtain foreign products 'not merely at the expense of less labour than it would cost to produce them, but often at the expense

[1] P.D., N.S., XVI, (7 December 1826), pp. 294–8.
[2] [W. Ellis], 'Exportation of Machinery', Westminster Review III, no. VI (April 1825), 387–9, 391–4.
[3] Charles Babbage, On the Economy of Machinery and Manufactures (London, 1832), pp. 292–306.

of less labour than they cost in the producing countries'. England's 'superior productiveness' then, was due, not to 'peculiar local advantages', the conventional explanation, but principally to 'our comparatively greater and more skilful use of machinery and our better division of labour', which indeed gave hope of ever increasing returns.[1]

Many economists had maintained that if continental nations manufactured cotton goods more cheaply, England could purchase her cottons from them and devote herself to other manufactures. 'These opinions have such an appearance of liberality,' Senior wrote, 'that I am sorry to dissent from them.' England and the Continent were competitors in the general market of the world and 'such an alteration would diminish the cost of obtaining the precious metals on the continent, and increase it in England'; under such circumstances, England 'might find it easier to obtain cottons, but we should find it more difficult to import everything else'. In an appended footnote, Senior added that 'this reasoning bears materially on the question as to the exportation of machinery'.[2]

The protectionists of the 'national' school would have entirely agreed with Senior in this matter—Hamilton, we recall, even anticipated him in part—and List and Carey would also have recognized, bitterly, the 'truth' of his view of the international division of labor: 'when a nation in which the powers of production, and consequently the wages of labour, are high, employs its own members in performing duties which could be as effectually performed by the less valuable labour of less civilized nations,' Senior observed, 'it is guilty of the same folly as a farmer who should plough with a race-horse'.[3]

But Senior, of course, was an advocate of free trade, and, like the Manchester manufacturers, protested against the 'barbarous policy' which made the prices of raw materials higher in England than elsewhere;[4] other free traders closely followed Senior's arguments. In March 1830, for example, Lord King, in presenting a resolution for a free trade in corn to the upper house, asserted that England was in 'possession of an unbounded supply of coal, of the most ingeniously contrived machinery, and of a very extensive amount of capital'. With such advantages, 'the produce of England would always exchange against a greater amount of the produce of any other country not possessing the same advantages'. If we 'suppose, for instance', Lord King continued, 'that the labour of four Englishmen

[1] Nassau Senior, *Three Lectures on the Cost of Obtaining Money and on Some Effects of Private and Government Paper Money* (London, 1830), pp. 11–16, 18–20, 23–4; see also p. 1.
[2] *Ibid.* pp. 25–6.
[3] *Ibid.* p. 30.
[4] *Ibid.* p. 24, 33–5.

aided by machinery, would produce manufactured produce which would exchange against the produce of the labour of eight Russians when applied to the soil, was it not palpably to the advantage of England to make this exchange, since the result was double profits to the capital of England'. With such clear advantages, which would necessarily accrue to a country which exported manufactures, under the conditions of the new technology, King found it to be 'the true policy of England to encourage the full development of her most productive industry'. The corn laws of 1815, King's resolution continued, had, in some degree, 'destroyed the advantages which nature and industry had bestowed upon us', and, 'by the most perverse policy', had 'compelled our natural customers to become our competitors, our rivals, and almost our enemies'.[1]

The antagonism of many free traders to capital export would also have served to confirm the prejudices of the national economists. Adam Smith had been seriously concerned lest the colonies drain the mother country of much-needed capital, and Ricardo had written of the reluctance of Englishmen to see their capital go beyond the British borders, a fact for which he was grateful.[2] The men of Manchester were following sound authority when, bemoaning the growing export of capital, they saw capital not as glutting the market, but as the provider of desperately needed employment, and in chronically short supply. The corn laws were blamed for the growth of capital export. The Committee upon Import Duties, as late as 1840, elicited testimony upon the subject from a leading associate of Cobden, J. B. Smith, who was much disturbed that 'one-half the capital for making the railway from Rouen to Paris has been recently subscribed in England'—failing to understand, as we shall observe, how rewarding to British industrial growth investments in overseas railroad construction might prove to be—and from another corn-law repealer who described, not too accurately, British capital 'going into Belgium, France, and Germany to a very great amount' as 'employed there producing manufactures which meet us in the markets' of the world. British capital was invested in foreign manufactories because of 'the cheapness of provisions' abroad; unless the corn laws were repealed, these men believed, England would continue to be drained of much-needed capital to the advantage of the foreigner. James Deacon Hume, a long-time permanent official of the board of trade, gravely warned the committee that 'the day of trial is not now so distant' as England had, until recently, believed.[3]

[1] P.D., N.S., XXIII (29 March 1830), 969-70, 973-4.
[2] D. Ricardo, The Principles of Political Economy and Taxation (London: Dent, 1937), p. 83.
[3] Report from the Select Committee on Import Duties, 1840 (601), V, 99, pp. 164 (No. 2083), 83 (No. 1046).

On several issues then—on capital-export, the export of coal, and the export of machinery—Radicals and political economists wrote and acted in contradiction to the ideal of a free international economy, which they praised so highly when the question concerned the need to repeal the corn laws and to reduce foreign tariffs. In the end, no action was taken to impose a tax on ever growing coal exports. The repeal of the corn laws was, moreover, not followed by a decline in overseas investment. In the forties, furthermore, the requirements of ideological consistency, and the pressures of the engineering industry, were even to topple the obstacles to the export of machinery.[1] Though the exports of machinery, by special license, rose from £60,028 in 1831, to £387,097 in 1840, the manufacturers of Manchester persisted in opposing the lifting of the prohibition, and were not much impressed when Hume argued, in February 1841, that if the prohibition had been repealed in 1825, 'the manufacturers of machinery in this country would have been in possession of the whole continental trade for tools as well as machinery—the most lucrative trade, perhaps, in the world'; Muntz, the M.P. for Birmingham, which manufactured much of this machinery, of course, supported Hume.[2] In June 1841, the weekly *Spectator* complained that the Manchester manufacturers 'appear to have been ... exceedingly slow to embrace in practice the creed, the profession of which just now is so fashionable'; 'it is idle', the journal declared, for the commercial classes 'to cry for a repeal of the Corn-laws and to propound the dogmas of perfect Free Trade, unless they are prepared to abide by those dogmas through good and evil'.[3] Two years later, a new committee was appointed to inquire into the subject, and, in the following year, 1844, the export of machinery was at last set free.

Not only Senior, but John Stuart Mill found himself confirming certain of the propositions of the national economists, especially in his analysis of the terms of trade. In an essay written in 1829, though not published until 1844, Mill observed that England probably drew to herself the 'largest share of the gains of international commerce', because her exports were 'in universal demand', and were of the kind 'that the demand increases rapidly as the price falls', that is, a highly elastic demand. 'Countries which export food', he added, 'have the former advantage, but not the latter.'[4] Moreover, in his *Principles*, Mill noted the advantages to a nation when its exportable products 'contain greatest value in smallest bulk', the point made by Hamilton half a century earlier. England was enabled to obtain her money,

[1] L. Levi, *History of British Commerce*, pp. 270–1.
[2] *P.D.*, 3rd Series, LVI (16 February 1841), 670–82, 689, 691.
[3] 'Export of Machinery', *Spectator* XIV, no. 677 (19 June 1841), 592–3.
[4] J. S. Mill, *Essays on Some Unsettled Questions of Political Economy* (London, 1844), p. 45.

i.e., precious metals, more readily than other countries because of 'the great demand in foreign countries for the staple commodities of England', and because of 'the generally unbulky character of those commodities, compared with the corn, wine, timber, sugar, wool, hides, tallow, hemp, flax, tobacco, raw cotton, & c., which form the exports of other commercial countries'.[1] (Further concessions to the arguments of the national school concerning the plight of the exporter of raw produce were made by Mill's disciple, Cairnes, in 1874,[2] and Robert Giffen, a board of trade economist, supplied data, of a similar character, in an article the following year.)[3] Mill was ready even to yield to the national economists upon the question of protecting an 'infant industry': since the 'superiority of one country over another in a branch of production often arises only from having begun it sooner', he wrote, he was willing to justify duties 'imposed temporarily (especially in a young and rising nation) in hopes of naturalizing a foreign industry, in itself perfectly suitable to the circumstances of the country'; indeed, a protective duty, 'continued for a reasonable time', might 'sometimes be the least inconvenient mode' for a nation to tax itself to support such an 'experiment'.[4] When American or Australian protectionists defended the erection of tariffs upon his authority, however, Mill sought to qualify strongly this statement.[5]

On the disadvantages of unilateral free trade : Mill, Torrens, Longfield, Scrope

There were political economists, with roots in orthodoxy, who nonetheless concluded that the policy which urged England to move *unilaterally* toward a completely free trade threatened the destruction of her predominance. Robert Torrens, whose mercantilist proclivities have already been observed, was the foremost of these, and his analysis was derived from such relatively unexceptionable sources as J. S. Mill, and Ricardo, as well as from more heterodox economists like Malthus and Wakefield. Torrens' attempts, in the forties, to undermine the efforts of Russell and Peel to eliminate com-

---

[1] Mill, *Principles*, pp. 609–11.
[2] J. E. Cairnes, *Some Leading Principles of Political Economy* (London, 1884), pp. 300, 355–7, 359, 364, 369–72, 375–6, 386, 398, 406, 413–14, 417.
[3] Robert Giffen, *Essays in Finance* (London, 1880), pp. 137–41.
[4] Mill, *Principles*, p. 922.
[5] Letters included in Cobden Club Pamphlet, *John Stuart Mill on the Protection of Infant Industries* (London, 1911), pp. 11, 13–15, 17. Mill, *Principles*, pp. 922–5. Mill also discussed the view of the protectionists that free trade prevented the growth of cities and civilization in new countries, and suggested that 'Mr. Wakefield has pointed out a better way' than protection; Mill urged that the price of unoccupied land be raised, 'instead of lowering it, or giving away the land gratuitously, as is largely done since the passing of the Homestead Act'.

mercial restrictions were to earn the praise of Disraeli. In May 1846, Disraeli spoke of Torrens' 'series of very ingenious essays', the chief theme of which, 'that reciprocity should be the principle upon which an exchange should take place between nations', had been supported, Disraeli observed, by J. S. Mill.[1] There were immediate protests from the Radical side, and J. A. Roebuck, an old friend of Mill, asked Disraeli 'not to quote a work unless he had really read it'. In reply, Disraeli cited Mill's preface[2] in which Mill had described his views as 'identical in principle' with Torrens', though differing 'as to the extent of their practical application'; more particularly, in the matter of revenue duties on foreign goods which were neither 'necessaries of life' nor 'materials and instruments of production', Mill supported the principle of reciprocity.[3] Sidney Herbert, a younger son of the Earl of Pembroke who had recently served as the secretary to the admiralty in the Peel government, concluded the debate by a snide assertion that although Disraeli, 'with the ingenuity for which he was eminent, and with the degree of skill he showed on all subjects', might no doubt make 'an excellent case' that Mill was an advocate of reciprocity, yet he doubted if Disraeli could show Mill 'to be an advocate for hostilitics between countries as exemplified by restrictive tariffs'.[4] Herbert was, no doubt, safe in his challenge.

It is nonetheless clear that the principles of international trade which Mill had set forth in his essay of 1829 were capable of being extended, as Mill himself perceived, into an argument in favor of reciprocity. While loyal to Ricardian labor theory, modified into the cost of production, as a standard of domestic value, Mill turned, first in 1829, and then in his *Principles*, toward 'reciprocal demand' as the determiner of international value. There was a 'proportion' at which the demand of two countries for each other's products would 'exactly correspond' so that the value of exports to a country would be entirely paid for by the value of imports from that country. The country which drew the 'greatest share of the advantage of any trade' was that country for whose products there was in other countries a highly elastic demand. 'In so far as the productions of any country possess this property, the country obtains all foreign commodities at less cost', that is, 'it gets its imports cheaper, the greater the intensity of the demands in foreign countries for its exports', and 'the less the extent and intensity of its own demand' for the exports of foreign countries.[5] Mill

[1] *P.D.*, 3rd Series, LXXXVI (4 May 1846), 87–9.
[2] *P.D.*, 3rd Series, LXXXVI (8 May 1846), 275–81.
[3] Mill, *Some Unsettled Questions*, pp. v–vi.
[4] *P.D.*, 3rd Series, LXXXVI (8 May 1846), p. 282.
[5] Mill, *Principles*, pp. 590–3.

had further inquired, in 1829, as to whether a country, by its own legislative policy, could increase its share of the benefits of foreign trade. Arguing on the basis of this 'reciprocal demand' analysis, he asserted that a tax on exports might, under certain circumstances, be paid entirely by the foreigner, and sometimes even more than the amount taxed might be drawn from him; however, the exact determination as to how a country might gain or lose by such a tax was very uncertain. A tax on imports might, at times, also fall partly on the foreigner, but such a levy would only encourage retaliation, and, as a matter of policy, ought to be avoided. When the repeal of duties not designed to be protective was at issue, 'the only mode in which a country can save itself from being a loser by the duties imposed by other countries on its commodities', Mill declared, was 'to impose corresponding duties on theirs'.[1] On all such questions, Mill believed that the principle of reciprocity ought to prevail, since a country ought not to be expected to yield a trade advantage, without 'stipulating for an equivalent'.[2]

Torrens, as early as 1832, was to argue similarly. In March of that year, Torrens constructed resolutions which he intended, although he never did so, to present to the parliament. The resolutions warned that as a consequence of the indiscriminate cutting of tariffs, England was commanding 'a less quantity of the precious metals than that which was due to the superior efficacy of our labour'. Torrens urged the abolition of duties on raw materials used in manufactures, and the substitution of increased duties upon 'foreign fabrics and foreign luxuries', to be imposed so as to correlate with the action foreign governments might take concerning duties upon British goods.[3] In July 1832, in an address to the House of Commons, Torrens discussed the terms of trade in this same spirit. Since supply and demand, not 'the cost—the labour—of production', determined the value of a commodity in international trade, he declared, 'the advantages which the advocates of free trade had predicted could not be realized but on terms of perfect reciprocity'. Upon this occasion, George Robinson, an old opponent of Huskisson's tariff reforms, welcomed Torrens as an ally.[4]

---

[1] Mill, *Some Unsettled Questions*, pp. 21–9.

[2] *Ibid.* pp. 31–2. Mill, at this time, like Senior in his 1829 lectures, and Torrens in parliament, had also noted the injury that might be done to England's trading position by permitting the exportation of machinery, yet he found restrictions on such exportations unjustifiable 'either on the score of international morality or of sound policy', since it was the 'common interest of all nations' not to diminish the aggregate wealth of the world, even if it managed, by doing so, to secure a larger share of the smaller sum total.

[3] Printed in *Bolton Chronicle*, 31 March 1832, and quoted in Robbins, *Torrens*, p. 191. Robbins' work is the definitive treatment of Torrens' economic thought. Chapters VI and VII are most relevant to our subject.

[4] *P.D.*, 3rd Series, XIV (3 July 1832), 17–20.

In his *Letters on Commercial Policy*, also set forth in 1832, in the *Bolton Chronicle*, the arguments were repeated.[1]

Mountifort Longfield, who was named to the professorship of political economy at Trinity College, Dublin, when that chair was established in 1832, argued similarly. Longfield's *Lectures on Commerce*, published in 1835, though, on the whole, rather conventional exercises in Ricardian trade theory, supplemented by tedious sermons in praise of unrestricted trade, followed the lines of Mill's as yet unpublished essay, although, of course, Longfield would not have been aware of this, as well as of Senior's 1830 *Lectures*. Longfield argued that if Englishmen reduced their demand for foreign goods, leaving foreign demand for English goods the same, 'the price of our labour will rise, or that of theirs fall, until the relative alteration of prices induces us to purchase more of the goods of other countries, or compels them to demand less of ours'. Though surrounding his analysis with numerous liberal qualifications, Longfield suggested that such a state of affairs 'may show how, in some instances, judicious restrictions on our trade', by discouraging British purchases from abroad, 'may advance the prosperity of this kingdom'.[2] If, on the other hand, duties were remitted in the case of many goods manufactured abroad, Longfield continued, 'we shall find the effect to be a fall in the rate of wages here, and a rise in the price of wages abroad'. Furthermore, 'if this principle of letting in goods duty free, was carried far enough the nation might lose a great part of the advantages which its superior skill in some manufactures, might otherwise secure'.[3] Longfield sharply disagreed with McCulloch's contention that export duties fell entirely upon the foreigner, and import duties entirely upon the home consumer. More often than not, he declared, the greater part of import duties fell upon the producer of the goods.[4] 'The reduction of duties is frequently', therefore, 'the removal of a burthen which was wholly or practically borne by foreigners.'[5] Longfield, like Senior, reminded his readers that 'a competition exists between the producers of different commodities, as real, although not as obvious, as that which exists between those who manufacture the same article'.[6]

There was yet another, closely related, argument in favor of reciprocity, which Malthus had put forward in 1817. Without an increasing economic progress abroad, Malthus had argued, a manufacturing country would be obliged, 'as its skill and capital increased', to give 'a larger quantity of

---

[1] See discussion in Robbins, *Torrens*, pp. 194–5.
[2] Mountifort Longfield, *Three Lectures on Commerce* (Dublin, 1835), pp. 99–101.
[3] *Ibid*. p. 70.   [4] *Ibid*. p. 104.
[5] *Ibid*. p. 107.   [6] *Ibid*. p. 104.

manufactured produce for the raw produce which it received in return'.[1]
This was another reason, in Malthus' view, for England to resist the effort
to make her a predominantly manufacturing country. In 1833, G. Poulett
Scrope—following, though not explicitly, Malthus, and, of course, Wakefield
had expressed a similar view in *England and America*[2]—warned that unless
the efficiency of production in agricultural countries kept pace with the
growing efficiency of British industry, and this might be dependent upon a
considerable capital investment, the terms of trade must go against Great
Britain. Under such circumstances, Scrope observed, 'we carry on what may
be called a losing trade with them,—we are continually exchanging larger
quantities of the produce of our industry for lesser quantities of theirs'.
By relying upon foreign countries for food, consequently, England became
dependent for her supply 'upon the rate at which capital, population, and
the agricultural art may happen to advance among their inhabitants,—a
rate which we can do nothing to accelerate'. The solution lay in colonization.
Scrope suggested that England turn to her colonies, where, no longer
dependent 'on the slow increase of the productive capacities of foreigners',
England could 'employ our own capital and our own people, with all their
known and tried resources of skill, genius, enterprise, and perseverance',
in the provision of food. (Scrope urged, further, that food imported from
the colonies, particularly from Canada, be given preferential treatment,
indeed, be admitted entirely free of duty; this would not only mean the
'profitable employment of our surplus labour and capital' in agriculture
and manufactures, but 'let us add, *commerce* likewise—since our merchants,
shipping, and seamen, would be exclusively engaged in this trade'.)[3]

Torrens' *Colonization of South Australia*, in 1835, marking still another
phase of that versatile economist's unfolding views on empire, presented a
variation of this argument of Malthus, Wakefield, and Scrope. Torrens had,
by this time, become a disciple of Wakefield,[4] and this book was written as a

[1] Malthus, *Additions* (1817), pp. 114–15.
[2] Wakefield, *England and America*, pp. 220–31, 23–4.
[3] Scrope, *Principles*, pp. 381–3.
[4] Torrens entirely disassociated himself from the view of certain political economists 'that colonization, instead of being a source of opulence and power, tends to exhaust the resources of the parent
state'. These economists thought capital possessed an 'occult quality', which enabled it to
create the field in which it was employed and rendered 'demand co-extensive with supply'.
It was not the quantity of capital that was the factor of prime significance, but rather the extent
of land, in an agricultural country, and the 'extent of the foreign market', in a commercial
country, he declared, following Wakefield. The 'superstitious worshippers of capital'—the
Ricardians—did not regard economics as 'an inductive science' but rather took 'the "high
priori road"', Torrens complained. Their acceptance of Say's Law indicated a studious neglect
of the actual facts, he concluded. Robert Torrens, *Colonization of South Australia* (London,
1835), pp. 229, 239–40, 231–3.

reply to a *Westminster Review* article criticizing systematic colonization. In defending the Wakefield system, Torrens presented a new theory of glut: in a country 'exporting wrought goods in exchange for raw produce',[1] he wrote, there might be a 'general glut of capital', and a 'period of embarrassment and revulsion, of home competition, overtrading, and declining profits', when the quantity of capital employed in producing manufactured goods for the foreign market 'increases faster' than the quantity of capital employed in foreign countries 'in raising raw materials, and in exchanging them for finished goods'.[2] An inevitable effect of such a situation would be the turning of the terms of trade against the manufacturing nation.[3] Yet this was an unavoidable part of industrial development, Torrens observed, and it was necessary to retain those conditions which favored continued English accumulation—'that superior efficacy, in manufacturing industry, which causes the produce of a given quantity of English labour to command a greater proportion of the circulating medium of the world, than is commanded by the produce of the same quantity of foreign labour'.[4] What might be done? It was 'beyond our power' to extend the foreign market sufficiently to accommodate the increasing powers of production in England; even if English investors could increase the capital resources of foreign countries, there was no assurance that these countries would not erect tariffs and begin to manufacture for themselves. Like Scrope, Torrens was convinced that it was not to foreign countries that Britain had to look to absorb its redundant capital:[5] England had to employ this 'redundancy for the purpose of planting new nations';[6] the terms-of-trade disadvantages caused by industrial progress had to be countered by an extensive program of colonization. In the light of such a chronic trading problem, Torrens regarded the 'actual condition of the country' as so desperate that only an 'extensive, systematic, and self-supporting scheme of colonization' could 'save the country from a servile war'.[7]

Was such a pessimistic view of England's international trading position supported by the facts? The trade statistics give evidence of a progressively unfavorable net barter terms of trade (which describe the movement of export and import prices in relation to each other) for England during the first half of the nineteenth century. Because of the increasing investment in British industry, particularly the mechanization of cotton and woollen manufacture, and the resulting increased efficiency, the prices of British manufactured goods *were* declining in absolute terms and were, in relative

---

[1] Torrens, *Colonization of South Australia*, pp. 239–40.
[2] *Ibid.* pp. 245, 261–2.   [3] *Ibid.* pp. 236, 238, 246.
[4] *Ibid.* pp. 269, 292.   [5] *Ibid.* p. 247.
[6] *Ibid.* p. 261.   [7] *Ibid.* pp. 302–3.

terms, commanding fewer foreign raw materials in international exchange. But the prices of imports *also* fell during this period, and particularly the prices of staples for which there was a regular, steady demand, like cotton, dyestuffs, timber;[1] British investment in the construction of foreign railroads, as well as in other public utilities—and this constituted a major share of England's capital exports—by lowering the cost of the production and transport of primary products, did help to overcome certain of the terms-of-trade difficulties which had disturbed Malthus, Scrope, and Torrens. (The price of imported grain, the demand for which was irregular, did not decline so much.) Indeed, as Mill understood, although the net terms of trade were going against England, the gains from trade told a rather different story. 'On the whole,' Mill had written in 1829, 'England probably, of all the countries of Europe, draws to herself the largest share of the gains of international commerce: because her exportable articles are in universal demand, and are of such a kind that the demand increases rapidly as the price falls.'[2] Therefore, even during the period when the prices of manufactured cottons fell most severely, the rise in the volume of exports was sufficient to double the 'total gain from trade' (a modern category combining net barter terms of trade and gross barter terms of trade, i.e. the quantity relationships between imports and exports) between 1796 and 1830, to more than double them between 1842 and 1858, to double them again by 1866, and once again by 1871.[3] Yet, undoubtedly, if, unlike Mill, one were to fix one's attention upon the net barter terms of trade, as Malthus, Scrope, and Torrens did, there did seem cause for concern.

Torrens' Zollverein

The sum of Torrens' views—and Scrope's, and, in part, Wakefield's as well—on the need for colonial investment in order to rectify England's declining terms of trade, as well as the consummation of the views concerning reciprocity implicit in Senior's writings, and explicit in Mill's early essay, and in Longfield's lectures, were to be found in a collection of letters to the leading Whig and Tory statesmen of the early forties, which, along with a number of pamphlets, Torrens published, in 1844, as *The Budget*. In *The Budget*, Torrens moved several further steps along the path of

---

[1] Nassau Senior was able to write that 'not only do we obtain the bulk of the raw produce which we import in exchange for less than half the silver which they cost our grandfathers, but we also obtain that quantity of silver with about one-third of the labour which it cost them'. N. Senior, *Industrial Efficiency and Social Economy* (New York: Henry Holt, 1928), II, 152–3.

[2] Mill, *Some Unsettled Questions*, p. 45.

[3] Albert M. Imlah, *Economic Elements in the Pax Britannica* (Cambridge, Mass.: Harvard University Press, 1958), pp. 94–113.

imperial thinking. His early vision of trade empire, in his *Essay on the Corn Laws*, in 1815, had been powerfully supplemented, largely as a result of Wakefield's influence, by one of a vast colonial empire populated by persons of British stock—indeed, he had begun to speak in tribalistic terms of 'Anglo-Saxon race', a phrase still to have its vogue. Torrens, who began life as a colonel of marines, was not, by any means, the cosmopolitan economist of the stereotype presented by the landed interests in their battle against free trade. He may be thought of as the English counterpart of List and Carey—an English 'national' economist who was able to demonstrate that economic analysis could be fairly employed in arriving at very heterodox conclusions.[1] In *The Budget*, Torrens anticipated much of the program of the neo-mercantile 'imperialism' which Joseph Chamberlain was to offer the British public in 1903.

Though it had clearly been 'the intention of nature', Torrens declared semi-mystically in *The Budget*, that England 'should be the workshop of the world', it was only a question of time, under the conditions that prevailed, before England's rivals, particularly 'the robust and persevering German', drew up alongside of her. For a long period, the terms of trade had favored English efficiency, and 'the world became tributary to England'. This superiority had resulted from England's 'exclusive possession of the improvements in mechanical power', and from the 'monopoly of commerce' England had attained in the course of the wars with Napoleon. With the coming of peace, however, the difference between the 'efficacy' of British and foreign labor had diminished, and British merchants began to be faced with hostile tariffs. Consequently, there had been a decline in the British terms-of-trade advantages and a decline in wages. England's undoubted advantages—'the employment of superior machinery, greater energy and skill in the application of manual labour, and the possession of more accessible coal mines'—were being fast overcome,[2] despite the fact that, Torrens continued, 'the greater part of the world' had arrived at the 'precise state of improvement which, were her commercial policy founded upon correct principles, would enable England to obtain, in exchange for manufactured goods, unlimited supplies of raw materials at constantly decreasing prices'.[3]

What was a commercial policy based on 'correct principles'? Torrens continued to favor, as he had in 1815, a free trade in corn, but, in the early forties, he wished to restrict the application of free trade—and here was his

[1] See F. W. Fetter, 'Robert Torrens: Colonel of Marines and Political Economist', *Economica*, N.S., XXIX, no. 114 (May 1962), 152–65.

[2] Robert Torrens, *The Budget* (London, 1844), pp. 231–6, 73.   [3] *Ibid.* pp. 73–4.

heresy—exclusively to such 'elements of reproduction': he wished England to secure, without hinder, the cheapest raw cotton which America could offer, and desired the free admission of American or Polish corn so as to reduce the costs of feeding England's laboring force, but insisted that another rule had to be applied to other kinds of products. Noting that he was basing his analysis upon Ricardo and Senior,[1] Torrens contended that, in a trade confined to two countries and to two commodities, where neither of the commodities were 'elements of reproduction', the 'imposition of import duties by one country and not by the other, would cause the produce of a given quantity of the labour of the country imposing the duties, to exchange for the produce of a greater quantity of the labour' of the nation 'not imposing the duty'.[2] Consequently, he called for 'reciprocity' as 'the universal rule' where elements of capital were not involved, declaring that the one-sided abolition of restriction 'renders the country by which import duties are abandoned tributary to the country by which they are retained'. In the forties, in line with this reasoning, Torrens charged the free trade movement with partial responsibility for the economic distress which England was experiencing.[3]

Torrens joined these views on reciprocity to a call for a 'colonial Zoll-verein'. Long convinced that British 'productive power' had outgrown 'the field of employment', and that 'the most beneficial commerce' was 'that between a densely peopled country, possessed of manufacturing advantages, and a thinly peopled country, possessed of fertile wastes', Torrens, like Wakefield, might have accepted a free trade between England and a United States, in which, as he thought 'probable' under those circumstances, agricultural capital would increase 'in the same ratio as manufacturing capital in England', as a solution to the problem;[4] but such a 'perfectly free trade' with America was, in all likelihood, not possible. The permanent solution to England's difficulties, in Torrens' view, was colonization, along lines set down by Wakefield, and, most important, the formation of an imperial economic confederacy. The prosperity of England could not be 'arrested by the hostile tariffs of foreign rivals', if England would establish 'throughout her wide-spread empire a British commercial league—a colonial Zollverein'.[5] It was only in the 'colonial markets in which we could not be met by hostile tariffs', he noted.[6] Torrens carefully surveyed the

---

[1] Robert Torrens, *The Budget*, pp. v–vi, 19.
[2] *Ibid.* p. xliii.
[3] *Ibid.* pp. 62–5, 67, 69.
[4] *Ibid.* pp. 265, 267–8, 270.
[5] *Ibid.* p. 102; see also p. 317.
[6] *Ibid.* p. 21.

possibility of a system of 'differential duties in favour of the British Colonies',[1] or even of a perfectly free trade prevailing throughout an empire in which the 'British race, language, and institutions' would always prevail.[2]

Torrens proclaimed 'the mission of the Anglo-Saxon race to multiply and to replenish the earth';[3] through the erection of Anglo-Saxon colonies throughout the world, 'England might become a vast industrial metropolis, and the colonies agricultural provinces of unlimited extent'.[4] This was his alternative to 'a reckless and charlatan rush' into free trade without an attempt to obtain for England 'reciprocal advantages'. Such a swift 'death-bed conversion'[5] to free trade would probably give 'increased velocity' to the 'downward process' until 'wages touch the starvation level'.[6] By extending her colonial system, and combining this with 'the rigid enforce-ment of the principle of reciprocity', England might arm itself 'to break down hostile tariffs, and to establish free trade throughout the world'.[7] Torrens called for a statesman to carry forth this program: 'England's prosperity is not yet to pass away,' he declared; 'our sky may be overcast, but the bow is in the heavens.'[8] That 'statesman' was not to appear for over fifty years. Nine years later, in 1852, Torrens was to bemoan the fact that 'the power and the glory of England' found 'no place in the entries of the ledger' of 'the cosmopolites of the Manchester School'; 'for an additional million of exports,' he declared, 'they would yield up the trident without a struggle'.[9]

Nassau Senior, upon whose theories Torrens had claimed, accurately enough, to have based his call for reciprocity—although in private discussion, Senior, too, seems to have been troubled by the unfavorable shift in England's terms of trade[10]—disowned what he regarded as Torrens' lapse into mer-cantilist error. 'One of the great obstacles to the progress of the moral sciences is the tendency of doctrines, supposed to have been refuted, to reappear,' Senior observed. 'After a time new theorists arise, who are seduced or impelled by some moral or intellectual defect or error to reassert the exploded doctrine'; they have become 'entangled by some logical fallacy', or 'deceived' by inaccurate facts, 'or think that they see the means of acquiring reputation, or of promoting their interests, or of gratifying their political or their private resentments'—the last, most probably, a reference

[1] Robert Torrens, *The Budget*, p. 173. [2] *Ibid.* p. 138.
[3] *Ibid.* p. 300. [4] *Ibid.* p. 177.
[5] *Ibid.* p. 318. [6] *Ibid.* p. 417.
[7] *Ibid.* pp. 66–7. [8] *Ibid.* p. 319.
[9] Quoted in Fetter, 'Robert Torrens', p. 162.
[10] See *Political Economy Club, Centenary Volume* (London, 1921), pp. 256–7.

by Lord John Russell's economic advisor to that statesman's unexpected acceptance of Torrens' resignation from the South Australian Commission. In this class of revivers of 'exploded doctrine', Senior felt compelled to place Torrens' revival of 'mercantilism' at a time when 'the expediency of free trade' was admitted by the 'leaders of all the great political parties, by every writer above the rank of the mere daily or weekly journalists, and even by the merchants and manufacturers, whom Adam Smith stigmatized as its enemies'.[1] Senior's arguments were not telling, and Torrens made an able reply.[2] Herman Merivale also criticized *The Budget*, though in less extended fashion, in his lectures.[3] Torrens' ideas on reciprocity received some support among friends of free trade,[4] but the anti-corn law campaigners found it beneath consideration—Cobden, in a public meeting, compared Torrens' system to that of Japanese hari-kari.[5]

Torrens' proposals received strong, if private, support from a surprising source—J. R. McCulloch. In 1843 and 1844, the debate upon reciprocity, which Torrens had begun in his *Budget*, had repercussions within the Political Economy Club, described in the diaries of one of its leading members, Prevost, diaries written in French for the sake of privacy. McCulloch's initial defense of a system of colonial preference was made at the December 1843 meeting of the Club; McCulloch favored such a system, he declared, so that foreign governments might not have the power to halt the supply of necessary raw materials. It was Prevost's opinion, at that time, that McCulloch had presented such a heretical view 'doubtlessly for the sake of argument' ('pour faire causer sans doute'). Loyd, Tooke, and Merivale had opposed McCulloch. Two months later, however, at the meeting of February 1844, Prevost reported McCulloch's continuing insistence that there were circumstances in which both future national interests as well as the safeguarding of already acquired national wealth might justify protective duties—this while denying that he was in any way contradicting the accepted doctrines of political economy. McCulloch observed that free trade as an absolute principle was 'nonsense', and suggested a five-shilling tariff upon corn imports as an encouragement to English production; there was no mention of 'peculiar burdens'. In the course of the February meeting,

---

[1] Senior, *Industrial Efficiency*, pp. 154–9. See Senior's critique of Torrens' position, *ibid.* pp. 169–80.
[2] See Robbins, *Robert Torrens*, pp. 209–25, for a discussion of the entire controversy.
[3] See Merivale, *Lectures on Colonization*, pp. 240–7.
[4] Fairly sophisticated support came from the newly established *Foreign and Colonial Quarterly Review*; see articles on 'Reciprocal Free Trade', II, no. 2 (October 1843), 526, 530, 536, 550–1, and 'Causes of Distress—Systematic Colonization', III, no. 1 (January 1844), 217, 224.
[5] See 'Speech of R. Cobden, Esq., M.P., at a Meeting of the Anti-Corn Law League, held at the Hall of Commerce, London, May 29, 1843' (n.p., n.d.), p. 1.

Tooke, G. W. Norman—a former timber merchant who had made a reputation as a writer on currency and taxation, and a director of the Bank of England—and Merivale all argued against McCulloch's protectionism; and Prevost took the floor to decry McCulloch's having mixed politics with his political economy, an error of which, he declared, Adam Smith had also been guilty when he had defended the navigation laws. At the meeting of December 1844, Prevost reported McCulloch as having described Ricardo's chapter on foreign commerce as 'faulty'. From Prevost's diary entry of 5 February 1846, it would appear that even at this late date, after Peel had presented his proposal to repeal the corn laws to parliament, McCulloch was still advocating some protection for corn.[1] Was all this 'pour faire causer'? Or is it an additional confirmation of a 'mercantilist tendency', of which we have spoken, on the part of a number of the leading formulators of orthodox trade theory?

Less surprisingly, after the publication of *The Budget*, Torrens was frequently quoted by protectionist members of the House of Commons. His reputation as a political economist had been unimpeachable, and the protectionists delighted in having discovered division in the ranks of the enemy. In April 1843, Sir Robert Peel, though at the time engaged in wholesale, unilateral tariff cutting, taunted the 'hon. Gentlemen opposite' who 'turn away from Colonel Torrens now as a gentleman of no authority at all', and reminded the advocates of political economy that Torrens had relied upon Ricardo's chapter upon trade, and upon the views of Nassau Senior, as the bases for his analysis. If these were 'speculative doctrines upon which even free-traders are not agreed', Peel concluded, the House of Commons ought certainly not to endorse an abstract resolution in favor of free trade.[2] J. L. Ricardo, David's nephew, and a member for Stoke-on-Trent, naïvely told the House that, 'as far however as he recollected the opinions of Mr Ricardo, he did not think it possible that he would have advocated the principle of reciprocity'.[3] Inevitably, also, the limited character of Torrens' amendment to the principle of free trade was misunderstood, and R. A. Christopher of Lincolnshire, indulging in wishful thinking, rather inaccurately described Torrens, 'a gentleman of great talent', as having become convinced that the effect of the repeal of the corn laws would be 'ruinous to the agricultural interest of the country, and be productive of no good effect to the manufacturers'.[4]

---

[1] For the relevant sections of Prevost's diaries, see *Political Economy Club, Centenary Volume*, pp. 284–6, 294, 291; see also Mallet's diaries, pp. 233–4.
[2] *P.D.*, 3rd Series, LXVIII (25 April 1843), 967.
[3] *Ibid.* p. 970.
[4] *P.D.*, 3rd Series, LXIX (9 May 1843), 94.

However, it was not so much the idea of reciprocity, but that of an 'imperial Zollverein' which was to seize the imagination of protectionist members. In 1846, the year of defeat for the corn laws, many prominent Conservatives spoke in behalf of such a Zollverein, though perhaps only because they saw it as a useful weapon with which to combat free trade. The idea of such a customs union, moreover, gibed with the common protectionist view that a home market was, after all, best. Sir Howard Douglas, a protectionist M.P. from Liverpool, who had told the House in 1843 that 'England is England's best customer,'[1] would be found, in 1846, urging that England form, with her colonies, 'a commercial union such as might defy all rivalry', one based upon a 'free trade among ourselves' and 'under a reasonably moderate degree of protection from without'. When this commercial union had been formed, Douglas proclaimed, 'then might colonization proceed on a gigantic scale—then might British capital animate British labour, on British soil, for British objects, throughout the extended dominions of the British Empire'.[2] P. Miles, another protectionist M.P., made the same transition.[3] H. K. Seymer, a member for Dorsetshire, suggested that 'if the Colonies were properly attended to, we might be rendered independent of other countries', and he reminded Peel that at one time the prime minister had spoken of 'a sort of English Zollverein'.[4] Lord Stanley, a leader of the protectionists in the Lords, in May 1846, also subscribed to the concept of a 'great and imperial Zollverein', which would secure 'for our people certain employment and certainty of consumption, uninterfered with by foreign competition'.[5]

The navigation laws and Brougham

For nearly two centuries—ever since they had first been instituted by Oliver Cromwell to combat the supremacy of Dutch merchant shipping—the navigation laws had been the universally accepted basis of British commercial policy. Adam Smith, the apostle of free trade, had praised them upon the principle that 'defence was of more importance than opulence'. Ricardo and his followers were virtually alone in opposition, for a time, but as the years progressed, support for abolition of the Navigation Acts grew. Huskisson, in the twenties, although acknowledging that laws which were 'merely protective' would avail nothing, insisted upon the 'political

---

[1] *P.D.*, 3rd Series, LXIX (15 May 1843), 374.
[2] *P.D.*, 3rd Series, LXXXIII (13 February 1846), 850.
[3] *P.D.*, 3rd Series, LXXXIII (9 February 1846), 554, 556, 558.
[4] *P.D.*, 3rd Series, LXXXVI (12 May 1846), 460.
[5] *P.D.*, 3rd Series, LXXXVI (25 May 1846), 1165-7.

necessity' of the Navigation Acts upon which the paramount interests of 'safety and defence' were based.[1] Nevertheless, Huskisson did move to relax these laws, as Pitt had done in the eighties, on grounds that British manufacturers badly needed cheaper shipping. From the 1780s onward, restrictions on shipping engaged in the West India trade with the United States were lifted by stages. In the twenties, Robinson and Huskisson secured the passage of a number of acts to promote a direct trade between foreign states and British colonies; and, with the independence of Spanish colonies in South America, Huskisson, in 1825, secured legislation to permit the ships of these newly independent nations to carry their own products into British ports. By the thirties, indeed, only the carrying trade within the empire remained a monopoly of British shipping interests. The shipping interests, of course, protested. In a debate upon Huskisson's policy in 1827, the Hon. H. T. Liddell, M.P. for Northumberland, a poet and a translator of Horace and Virgil, and a spokesman for the shippers, sought theoretical support for the shipowners' position in a book upon colonial policy which the Radical leader Brougham had published in 1803.[2]

In 1845, the passage of a bill consolidating the Navigation Acts no doubt instilled a confidence that the special privileges of the shipping interests were not going to be further impaired. As a result, perhaps, in 1846, the shipping interests rejected the warnings and the advances of the agricultural protectionists; instead, the shippers joined the others of the mercantile community in voting for corn-law repeal, convinced that what remained of their own privileged position would not be attacked. The very next year saw the disappointment of their hope. The Navigation Acts were temporarily suspended in 1846 and 1847, and, in February 1847, J. L. Ricardo, who had published a work, the *Anatomy of the Navigation Laws*, calling for the abolition of the laws as the consummation of free trade—a move which, he declared, by lowering shipping costs, would best enable the British manufacturer to compete in the world market—proposed the constitution of a committee to investigate the possibility of their repeal.[3]

Liddell, now representing North Durham, who had defended the Navigation Acts against Huskisson two decades earlier, asked whether England was 'to be made merely the workshop of the world'; 'did we look for the recruiting of our army and the equipment of our navy from the stunted

[1] *P.D.*, N.S., xv (12 May 1826), 1145-6.
[2] *P.D.*, N.S., xvii (7 May 1827), 611.
[3] See Levi, *History of British Commerce*, pp. 299-301; see also *P.D.*, 3rd Series, LXXXIX (9 February 1847), 1007-20, 1035.

population of our manufacturing districts?'[1] When the debate was resumed the following year, George Hudson, the famous 'railway king', and the M.P. for Sunderland, berated the attempt 'to sacrifice the shipping interest to some fanciful principle of political economy',[2] and Disraeli warned that 'the empire of the seas' was in danger.[3] For another member of the House, the forces opposing the Acts were those of 'a Satanic school of politics', which 'could not form a conception how anything which was not good for cotton spinning could be good for anything else', and he quoted against Manchester, 'their darling, Adam Smith'.[4] Peel, now out of office, wondered, in reply to all this, how anyone could 'doubt that in this great seat of manufacturing industry—the greatest commercial country in the world—how can we doubt, I say, that upon all ordinary commercial principles, obstructions to the free interchange of products are injurious to prosperity?'[5]

In the House of Lords, in 1849, a rather surprising champion of the navigation laws emerged—Lord Brougham, whom we first encountered as the young Scotsman who had written the *Colonial Policy of European Nations*, in 1803. In that work, Brougham, while in general opposed to mercantile restrictions, nonetheless, unlike Smith whom he regarded as his master, argued for the maintenance of colonies, and, like Smith, favored the Navigation Acts. Henry Brougham's book of 1803 was a work of some insight and prescience, and Lord Brougham, in 1849, saw little reason to depart from his conclusions of nearly half a century earlier. Brougham had been growing more and more disenchanted with the Radical cause, having become displeased by the tactics employed by the Anti-Corn Law League and by Cobden, by whom he had been supplanted as a leader of the free trade forces.[6] It was, then, in the spirit which, in Senior's view, was most conducive to the revival of 'exploded' doctrine, that Brougham delivered his address, on 7 May 1849, in support of the navigation laws.

He had been 'taunted', Brougham told the peers, because 'I, the apostle

---

[1] Quoted in Levi, *History of British Commerce*, p. 1030; *The Times*, on the other hand, saw repeal as the means by which England might 'gain, and secure for herself that naval pre-eminence which Natur · undoubtedly intended'. *The Times*, 10 June 1848, 5d, e; see also 2 June 1848, 5a, b, and 3 June 1848, 5b, c.

[2] *P.D.*, 3rd Series, XCIX (2 June 1848), 279.

[3] *P.D.*, 3rd Series, XCIX (9 June 1848), 646; see also *ibid*. pp. 609, 613, 619; and *P.D.*, 3rd Series, XCIX (29 May 1848), 68–9.

[4] *P.D.*, 3rd Series, CIII (12 March 1849), 607–9.

[5] *P.D.*, 3rd Series, XCIX (9 June 1848), 651.

[6] See letter of Brougham to Peel of 24 June 1846, quoted in Parker, *Peel*, III, 372; the free traders returned Brougham's hostility, with good measure. See *The League* III, no. 122 (24 January 1846), 258. Brougham, in August 1845, went so far as to offer his help to Peel, in the interest of preserving the corn laws, suggesting that Adam Smith, whose life Brougham was then engaged in writing, would have approved of such a course. There was, Brougham wrote Peel, a 'broad ditch which separates me from Bright, Cobden, & Co.' Quoted in Parker, *Peel*, III, 193–4.

of free trade', who had 'signalized myself by joining in that great victory over the exploded policy of unenlightened times', should now oppose the repeal of the navigation laws. Brougham denied that the question of the navigation laws had 'the least connection with the free-trade controversy', and, calling upon the authority of Adam Smith, he spoke of the necessary bearing of the Navigation Acts 'on the best interests of the country, her defence, her very existence'. Brougham adverted 'to the opinions which I delivered very long—I grieve to think how long ago—prepared in 1801 and 1802, published in 1803', in which he had defended many aspects of the colonial system against Adam Smith, 'my illustrious master'. Brougham had no reason to change his opinion that England's greatness was substantially founded in 'colonial speculation': her colonies were 'invaluable, if only for the rich addition they make to our wealth—they are precious as a mercantile speculation—they are to be prized on the mere calculation of pounds, shillings, and pence—they are no less . . . our strength than our wealth—no less our glory and our profit in peace than our support in war'; 'the colonial monopoly', as represented by the Navigation Acts, Brougham observed, much as he had in 1803, was merely 'a return for the cost we incur in planting, and in ruling, and in defending' the colonies. Why should England permit foreign nations 'who never have paid one shilling, nor spilt one drop of blood to govern or keep' the empire to share in the benefits of the colonial trade?

'We have acquired an empire on which the sun never sets'; 'to abandon these magnificent establishments, to neglect these noble dominions, would be the very worst and basest policy which a British statesman could recommend to a British Parliament'. Yet, in insisting that the navigation laws be repealed, this was precisely what 'that sect' of 'ultra free-trade men' were advocating. Surely the Government must be aware that such a move, once made, could never be 'retraced'; 'the coasting trade, the manning clauses, will excite new agitation by other Ricardos and other Cobdens'. With revolution stalking the Continent, it was more important than ever that Britain remain strong. By the repeal of the Navigation Acts, Brougham concluded, 'the highest interests of the empire' were 'exposed to ruin'.[1]

The opinions of Lord Sheffield, in his defense of the old commercial system against Pitt and Shelburne in the 1780s, were little different from those of the self-proclaimed 'apostle of free trade', nearly three-quarters of a century later. With Robert Torrens advocating an Imperial Zollverein, and Lord Brougham defending the navigation laws, we have the illusion of having

[1] P.D., 3rd Series, CIV (7 May 1849), 1329–31, 1337–46, 1353–7.

come full circle. But the old colonial and the old commercial systems were dead, after both the corn laws, in 1846, and the Navigation Acts, in 1849, had been abolished. (We must remember, furthermore, that neither Torrens nor Brougham doubted the desirability of importing, free of tariff, the various raw materials necessary to manufacturing.) It had taken nearly a century of effort, since Dean Tucker had made the first attempt, to prove that a highly profitable trade, of a kind which formerly had been regarded as of a 'colonial' character, did not depend upon the maintenance of a formal imperial connection, and of a restrictive trading system, as the ever-increasing trade of the United States with Great Britain, in the years following independence, had amply proved. Supported by the principles of political economy, Great Britain was determined to set an example of free trade—unilaterally, if necessary—for all the world to follow, hoping that through such a system, England might maintain her leading position as the metropolis in an Empire of Free Trade, such as Torrens had described as early as 1815.

CHAPTER 9

Classical political economy, the Empire of Free Trade, and imperialism

I stand in the position of being senior member of this club [the Political Economy Club], and the only survivor of its original members . . . By being a member of this Club I became the companion of Mr Ricardo, of the two Mills, of Colonel Torrens, of Mr Malthus, and of Mr Tooke . . . And here I may say with respect to the doctrines of Political Economy as it was taught in those days, I think that the principles which I then learned are perfectly unattackable. I hear a great many objections made to the received doctrines of Political Economy. We are told by a distinguished gentleman . . . that the doctrines of Political Economy will only suit the exact conditions of England at a certain time, but I am not of that opinion. It seems to me that the real doctrines of Political Economy as they were first taught by Adam Smith and as they were subsequently explained by the persons whose names I have ventured to quote, remain unimpeached; that they have never been successfully attacked; that they are in fact unattackable; that they are true now and will be true to all time.

G. W. Norman, Speech at Banquet Commemorating
Centenary of *The Wealth of Nations*, 1876

IN 1948, J. B. Brebner wrote of *laissez-faire* as a 'myth', describing it as a battle-cry of the middle classes in their struggle with the landed aristocracy, and noting particularly that the philosophic Radicals—the Benthamites—were proponents not of *laissez-faire*, as they had been represented to be, but of a new bureaucratic collectivism.[1] It is becoming ever clearer that the reputed mid-Victorian policy of 'anti-imperialism' is likewise a myth.[2] It was the triumph of the Manchester School, and of Cobdenite cant, then, which was responsible for the usual view—one common to such diverse students of the period as Professors Schuyler and Langer, and Hobson, Lenin, and Schumpeter—of a mid-Victorian anti-imperialism.[3]

[1] J. B. Brebner, 'Laissez Faire and State Intervention in Nineteenth-Century Britain', *The Tasks of Economic History*, Supplement VIII of *Journal of Economic History* (1948), pp. 59–73.
[2] See J. S. Galbraith, 'Myths of the "Little England" Era', *American Historical Review* LXVII, no. 1 (October 1961), 34–48.
[3] For more recent defenses of mid-Victorian anti-imperialism, see O. Macdonagh, 'The Anti-Imperialism of Free Trade', *Economic History Review*, 2nd Series, XIV, no. 3 (April 1962), 489–501; and Platt, 'The Imperialism of Free Trade: Some Reservations', *passim*.

But even Manchester—even Cobden—set its sights upon England's maintenance of its industrial predominance, and its position as the Workshop of the World. In the thirties and forties, moreover, many Radicals united in seeking not only to erect a trading system in which Britain, content with its technological superiority and immense productive capacities, might preserve and extend this predominance, but also to establish formal colonies, which they regarded as a necessity if the unfortunate tendencies of the new industrialism were to be averted.

In the middle of the eighteenth century, Josiah Tucker, a free trade mercantilist, had argued that by means of a free trading system, a 'richer manufacturing Nation will maintain its Superiority over the poorer one, notwithstanding this latter may be likewise advancing towards Perfection'; indeed, Tucker continued, such a superiority might continue, and even grow, so far that 'no Man can positively define, *when* or *where* it must *necessarily* stop'. It was by means of Tucker's arguments, as we have shown, that Pitt had defended his trade policy during the eighties. It was by a variation of Tucker's arguments, supplemented by the trade theory of a later classical political economy, and bearing the mark of Torrens' early mercantilist vision of a Free Trade Empire, that a later generation of parliamentarians (Whig, Radical, and Peelite) were to demand a system of free trade as essential to Britain's maintaining her position as the Workshop of the World. David Hume had argued against Tucker in the 1750s, that despite all its apparent advantages, there would come a limit, a '*ne plus ultra*', at which point, 'by begetting disadvantages', the progress of the rich nation would be halted. With variations, this was to be the position of the agrarian economists, like Malthus, and of the parliamentary defenders of the corn laws, led by Disraeli. The fears of David Hume received more substantial shape in the arguments of the opponents of the export of machinery, and the defenders of the remaining Navigation Acts.

'Imperialism is above all a process—and, to some degree, a policy', Richard Pares wrote some years ago, a process and a policy which aimed 'at developing complementary relations between high industrial technique in one land and fertile soils in another'.[1] The new industrialism of the late eighteenth century created conditions which increased, substantially, the economic intercourse between regions at widely differing levels of social and economic development. The founders of the new economic science—constructed to describe the new industrial society—quite naturally directed themselves to an analysis of this new intercourse, which loomed large in the consciousness

[1] Pares, 'Economic Factors in the History of Empire', p. 144.

of the time, and which was closely associated in the minds of the first generations of political economists with the success of the new system. Both orthdoxy and the Wakefield school understood Britain's needs in the general terms set by Pares. Orthodoxy thought of transforming England into a commercial and industrial state, in conformance with the principle of comparative advantage, thus tying England's destiny to manufactures and to foreign trade, of creating an informal empire so that, as Ricardo had proclaimed, a vigorous foreign trade might avert the consequences of the law of diminishing returns in agriculture. To do this, it was necessary, by repealing the corn laws, to create a vast English market for foreign grain; in this way, the agricultural nations of the world might be given a stake in England's Empire of Free Trade. Wakefield, as we know, insisted even more forcefully upon the necessity of non-industrial areas to the new capitalism, upon the need for virgin land to extend 'the field of employment' for super-abundant capital and labor.

The Radical cry of 'anti-colonialism' was designed to bring down that vast network of patronage and privilege which was the 'old colonial system', and to replace it by a middle-class empire. For, although the group of Radicals led first by Hume and then by Cobden, relying upon the strength of an informal trading community, saw no need for 'formal' colonies, others, particularly the Colonial Reformers, far from being ideological opponents of colonialism, were advocates of positive programs of colonization. The Colonial Reformers were convinced that England needed a formal empire for investment and market conditions of special safety. They sought, through their programs of systematic colonization, to construct that empire upon middle-class foundations, and proposed a plan of colonization which would be undertaken by private companies, for profit, and in which free labor would take the place of the slave labor of eighteenth-century tropical plantations. They urged, moreover, that such colonies of settlement as Australia and New Zealand, founded largely under their auspices, and Canada, be given responsible government—thereby freeing them from the interference of the aristocratic 'lackeys' of the colonial office—since they saw them as tied so securely, by sentiment and economic necessity, to an imperial metropolis, which alone could provide manufactured goods for their agricultural exports, that it was no longer necessary to restrict colonial trade by legislation.

There was, of course, a less pleasant way of regarding their program. As we have seen, the parliamentary campaign of the Radical Colonial Reformers against the interference of the colonial office in the affairs of overseas colonies was largely inspired by their opposition to the efforts of

'Mr Mother-Country' Stephen and the humanitarian societies of Exeter Hall to halt the policy of land-grabbing which New Zealand colonists were pursuing at the expense of the Maori. (The Rhodesian government of Mr Ian Smith hoped for a similar freedom from the interference of the metropolis.) Nor can we forget that the Colonial Reformers had a distinct personal interest in such land-grabbing, and in promoting systematic colonization, generally.

The politics of the Empire of Free Trade had other unpleasant aspects as well. While a full-scale program of aggressive expansion was not required, during this period, the Radicals were not entirely free of the animus which contemporary opinion associates with an active imperialism. We have observed the Radical support for the Opium War, and their jingoistic demands, on other occasions, that force be employed to defend British merchants and to extend their markets. Along the Indian frontier, as in China, for instance, wars and annexations were the rule even in mid-century, and were applauded by such Radicals as Joseph Hume. Britain's keen interest in free trade was well understood in Europe, and powers who wished, for various reasons, to maintain English favor—Cavour's Piedmont, for example, or the France of Napoleon III—opted for trade freedom. In the last part of the century, in the eighties and nineties, during the time of the partition of Africa, the use of more informal techniques was seriously undermined by international competition for colonies, and as a result there had to be an even greater reliance upon a policy of war and annexation, whence came the view that imperialism had replaced anti-imperialism. What was actually happening was that the neo-mercantilist imperialism of certain continental nations, heralded by a revival of protection, was challenging a relatively 'cosmopolitan' British imperialism, a product of the earlier British industrial predominance; a policy which sought commercial monopoly was battling a policy whose objective had been the securing of free and safe access to markets for the manufactures of Britain's mid-century Workshop of the World.[1]

Political economy: science and 'ideology'

The question of the influence of the principles of political economy upon the formation of policy is a difficult one. It can be said that Tucker and Smith exercised a considerable, direct influence upon Pitt and Shelburne, and that Malthus and Ricardo were regarded as authorities by such statesmen as Wilmot-Horton and Huskisson. But the influence of the early

[1] See Gallagher and Robinson, 'The Imperialism of Free Trade', pp. 1–15.

theorists upon policy was most directly effective when substantial interests were not threatened thereby, and as soon as the writings of the political economists were directed against the corn laws, the houses of parliament dominated by landlords, offered resistance to abstract theory. It was at this point that other forces were enlisted, as Richard Cobden and John Bright aroused the bulk of the middle classes, and a good part of the working classes, to demand a free trade in corn. 'A cause seldom triumphs unless somebody's personal interest is bound up with it,' J. S. Mill wrote; 'it would have been long before the Corn Laws would have been abolished in Great Britain', if 'those laws had not been contrary to the private interests of nearly the whole of the manufacturing and mercantile classes'.[1] It was this public pressure, against a background of hard times and the fear of revolution, which persuaded the Peelites, as we have seen, to desert the corn laws—which, of course, does not diminish the role played by the science of political economy in helping to convince that generation of Englishmen that free trade was, indeed, the solution to the difficulties with which England was beset.

But what of the 'science' of political economy itself? How 'scientific' was, for example, its defence of free trade? List and Carey, and their followers, of course, charged that the devotion of the classical economists to an international free trade was grounded in their interest, as Englishmen, in keeping the rest of the world occupied in subordinate pursuits—mere hewers of wood and drawers of water for an industrial England. This is far from being a fair judgment.[2] All the leading economists, even quasi-protectionists like Malthus and Torrens, might agree, as scientists, concerning the desirability of universal free trade, even though they might have found in particular circumstances, and, no doubt, in class interests, reasons for advocating a ban on the export of machinery, reciprocity, or a bounty on corn exports. Indeed, we must remember that it was only after the phenomenal growth of English manufacturing and commerce during the Napoleonic Wars that the interests of the manufacturers began to correspond with the free trade conclusions already reached by the science of political economy. Yet, there is no doubt that the problems which political economy undertook to solve, and the solutions which it proposed, were substantially affected by the requirements of the new industrial classes. 'Observations are scarcely ever made or particulars noted for their own sake,' wrote McCulloch in 1824; 'it is,' he continued, 'in the peculiar phraseology of this science, the

---

[1] See Cobden Club, *Mill On the Protection of Infant Industries*, p. 16. Originally written in 1868.
[2] For a discussion of this subject, see Lionel Robbins, *The Theory of Economic Policy in English Classical Political Economy* (London: Macmillan, 1952), pp. 20-2, and *passim*.

effectual demand of the theorist that regulates the production of the facts or raw materials, which he is afterwards to work into a system'.[1]

Certainly, there are a number of important instances in which non-scientific factors played a distinct role in the development of political economy. There seems little doubt, for example, that it was because Say's Law—a proclamation of faith that the new industrialism was a harmonious, virtually automatic economic mechanism—boded so well for the new industrial order, that it received the accolade of 'correct doctrine', and that the 'orthodox' held to it with such intensity. Despite the arguments, supported by much contemporary evidence, of the 'heretical' agrarians, Ricardians continued to maintain Say's Law with determined steadfastness, seeing its invalidation as a weapon in the hands of obscurantist diehards, primarily agriculturists, who wished to stem the advance of industrialism.

It is even possible to argue that the most serious controversies which divided the political economists were—like that over Say's Law—more 'religious' than scientific in character. The schools of political economy had somewhat the aspect of the protestant denominations, and their conflicts might be said to have been grounded in much the same preconceptions about the character of the world, and the same psychological predispositions as once divided, say, Calvinist from Arminian, a matter to which we have already referred. Certainly, the adherents of political economy had their virtually unimpeachable, 'orthodox' theologians in Smith and Ricardo, and Malthus, at times, was honored in this number, even though certain of his opinions were tainted by an heretical, even a pagan, agrarian sin. Journals like the *Edinburgh* and the *Westminster* inquisitorially flushed out such heresy; penny-tracts were broadcast by the evangelicals of the Society for the Diffusion of Useful Knowledge, preaching the necessity of moral restraint and warning of the visitation of the four horsemen of the apocalypse. Classical political economy, in its most orthodox version, like all ennobling religions, preached salvation through suffering (despite the Pelagian optimism of Bastiat and Cobden); it had, however, its Antinomians in the Wakefield school who condemned frugality as sinful avarice, and preached the welcome doctrine of 'increase and multiply, and replenish the earth'. The development of political economy, it might be argued, would have proceeded quite differently in a nation less serious about religious questions, and with a substantially divergent religious history.

There were other great 'passions' at work in the formation of classical political economy. The foremost was probably 'nationalism'. Certainly,

[1] J. R. McCulloch, *A Discourse on the Rise, Progress, Peculiar Objects, and Importance, of Political Economy* (Edinburgh, 1824), p. 29.

the devotion to England as the Workshop of the World, which, in several forms, spanned the century from Tucker to Cobden, and from Pitt to Peel, offers some confirmation of this view. England—separated from the threats of hostile armies by the Channel, freed from the resentment of inferiority by her economic predominance, increasingly dependent upon a great world market for her food, for the sale of her products, for the profitable investment of her capital—was, indeed, the most cosmopolitan of European nations, and, cognizant of these advantages, the classical economists were among the most cosmopolitan of Englishmen; but it would be naïve to believe that there was no English nationalism, nor, as we have seen, were economists— even Bentham!—immune from its influence. (Some, indeed, like the Ricardian de Quincey, were fervent, even vulgar, nationalists and imperialists.[1]) Almost all the British economists, even Cobden, almost all Britons perhaps, indulged a certain national and religious snobbery which saw such qualities as energy, industry, and skill as almost inevitably protestant and British.[2] Virtually all the political economists hoped that England would not lose the predominance which she had acquired through the success of her industry and commerce, and that the foreign competition which they saw over the horizon would be successfully withstood. Radicals, as we have seen, were even prepared to cheer an aggressive, Palmerstonian policy where its purpose was to enlarge foreign markets. If the economists and the 'cosmopolitan' Radicals put first the interests of England and her empire, rather than those of the world at large, it was their good fortune that they lived at a time when they could readily persuade themselves that there was little disharmony between the two.

It might be said that the political economists were as much swayed by an irrational devotion to the principle of an unqualified free trade as by nationalism. This stubborn attachment to free trade was evident when Torrens' proposals for an 'imperial Zollverein' were roundly condemned by Mill, and Senior, and Merivale, among others, despite their general analytical soundness: free trade, for the political economists, was simply, in Mill's words, sound 'international morality', and 'sound policy'.

Similarly, there was a general view, widely shared by political economists, of European superiority, of the benefits that might be conferred by European, and, particularly, English rule. Jean Baptiste Say, the French economist, observed that English dominion in India had made accumulation possible, and that 'the situation of Hindostan was never happier'; since the people

---

[1] See Thomas de Quincey, *Works of Thomas de Quincey* (Boston, 1877), x, 436–8.
[2] See Cobden, *England, Ireland, and America*, pp. 14–15. In these pages, Cobden largely anticipated Weber's conclusions concerning protestantism and the capitalist ethic.

of Asia 'scarcely think it possible to live without a master', it was well, Say gallantly declared, that so satisfactory a master as England had been procured.[1] Karl Marx, a relatively orthodox economist of the school of Ricardo, had a similar opinion. It is interesting to see that, unlike some of his later followers who bemoaned the ruthless destruction of the Indian cotton industry, Marx saw it as inevitable that the dynamic economy of the West would dominate the backward, traditional economies of the East, and that he welcomed the extinction of the 'feudal' societies of Asia. In all this, England was acting as 'the unconscious tool of history', undermining 'the solid foundation of Oriental despotism', and promoting 'the only *social* revolution ever heard of in Asia'. 'The aristocracy wanted to conquer' India, Marx wrote, the 'moneyocracy to plunder it, and the millocracy to undersell it'. In the empire of the 'moneyocracy', the empire of an exploitative mercantile colonialism whose function was to promote the exchange of commodities, 'we find backward conditions'; indeed, 'merchants' capital in its supremacy everywhere', Marx declared, 'stands for a system of robbery'. Merchants' capital, i.e., commercial and financial capital, was allied to the landlord interest in opposition to progressive and 'productive' industrial capital, whose 'complete rule' had not been accepted by 'English merchants' capital and moneyed interests', Marx wrote, until after the abolition of the corn laws. It was the empire-building of industrial capital —Great Britain's new middle-class, free trade empire—which won Marx's praise. 'The millocracy', in order to transform India into 'a reproductive country' had not only destroyed feudalism, but it had also given India the means of irrigation and of internal communication; while industrial capital intended 'to endow India with railways with the exclusive view of extracting at diminished expenses the cotton and other raw materials for their manufactures', these railways would 'become the forerunner of modern industry'. Marx, like Say, indicated a firm preference for the British over other empires; the British alone could perform a 'regenerating' function, as well as a destructive one.[2] If foreign economists like Say and Marx could see the

---

[1] J. B. Say, *Historical Essay on the Rise, Progress, and Probable Results of the British Dominion in India* (London, 1824), pp. 5, 22–3, 26–7, 31–2, 35–6.

[2] Karl Marx, *British Rule in India* (Sydney: Modern Publishers, 193?), pp. 6, 8–9, 18, 19–21; and Karl Marx, *Capital; A Critique of Political Economy* (Chicago: Charles Kerr, 1915), III, 382, 385, 387–9, 392–3. Towards the end of his life, Marx came to view Western advances into Asia and Africa with less favor, and become exceedingly upset with instances of brutality in the colonies. He laid more and more stress upon the 'tribute' with which colonies were burdened: 'India alone', he observed, 'has to pay 5 millions in tribute for "good government", interest and dividends of British capital, etc., not counting the sums sent home annually by officials as savings of their salaries, or by English merchants as a part of their profit in order to be invested in England'; Englishmen owned foreign securities, European and American, upon which they drew similar 'tribute' in the form of interest and dividends. See *ibid.* pp. 693–4.

character of British dominion in these, on the whole, highly favorable terms, it would have been surprising if British economists had felt otherwise.

All these instances of the interweavings of science and ideology—as well as others we have yet to discuss—have a considerable importance in understanding the origins and development of the theory—or, more properly, theories—of capitalist imperialism.

The theories of capitalist imperialism

We have described a critique of the commercial-industrial system—one based upon the physiocratic critique of the mercantilism of the *ancien régime*, mounted primarily by Malthus, though subscribed to by other agrarian economists, such as Spence, Chalmers, and Dugald Stewart, and considerably extended by Wakefield—an agrarian critique which resembles nothing so much as the later Marxist critique of capitalism. These critics of the new commercial system—unlike other 'anticipators' of Marx—were not 'socialists' resting their arguments upon an extension of the labor theory of value. Yet in their view of the relationship between master and man under the new industrialism, in their description of a society faced with a growing polarization of wealth, in which competition was driving down the rate of profit and pushing smaller capitalists into the ranks of the working class, a society on the brink of revolution, these economists had pre-empted Marx. This seemingly 'Marxist' critique, moreover, was accepted by the leading Radical Colonial Reformers—by Buller, Molesworth, Ward, Rintoul, and others—who followed the major lines of Wakefield's analysis, almost two decades before Marx came to England. Furthermore, the Colonial Reformers, on the basis of this analysis and foreshadowing later theories of capitalist 'imperialism', had become convinced that the processes of the new industrialism had made it *essential* that Great Britain have ready access to undeveloped lands to which she could send her superfluous population, which would consume the excess capacity of her factories, and to which she could export the surplus capital which was driving down the domestic rate of profit. They maintained, in addition, that without a positive program to extend the 'field of production', England faced disastrous social revolution.[1] Thus, as early as the 1830s, the Colonial Reformers advocated a program of imperialism very similar to that which the Marxists were to accuse capitalism of following three-quarters of a century later, a

---

[1] The view of colonization as a cure for 'paltry, despicable, unnatural class-animosity' is frequently encountered. See, for example, *The Colonial Magazine and Commercial and Maritime Journal* VII (1842), no. 26, 134.

program, moreover, based upon a theory of imperialism which largely anticipated the neo-Marxist theory of capitalist imperialism. (These leading ideas, we might add, were also set forth, at least quasi-independently, by Poulett Scrope and Robert Torrens.)

There is a link, somewhat indirect, between the theory of capitalist imperialism set down by the Wakefield school, and the revival of a similar theory (that is, one similarly grounded on a view of the inadequacies of Say's Law), by J. A. Hobson in 1902. In the eighties and nineties, the Italian political economist, Achille Loria, published a number of works which Marx and Engels regarded, very much as they did the contemporary writings of the German *Katheder-Sozialisten*, as having derived from their own writings.[1] Though the influence of Marx was undeniable, Loria's 'socialism' was based, like that of Henry George with which it has been frequently compared, upon the view that the land was the primary factor of production, and that the way in which the land was owned, settled, and cultivated was the most important determinant of historical development. A recent scholar has found the sources of Frederick Jackson Turner's frontier thesis, in which a number of social and political characteristics of American society is attributed to the dispersion of population along the American frontier, in Turner's having read Loria, where all these matters had been set forth.[2] Curiously enough, thus far, no one has observed Loria's immense debt to Wakefield on all these matters.

In his earlier writings, Loria provided ample evidence of such a dependence, and it is probably more accurate to describe the Italian economist as a disciple of Wakefield, rather than, as is usually done, one of Marx or of George.[3] Not too surprisingly, under these circumstances, Loria wrote considerably on the 'capitalist theory of imperialism', very much along the lines which Wakefield had followed half a century earlier.[4] A work of Loria's which discussed imperialism in these terms had been translated into English

---

[1] See Karl Marx and Frederick Engels, *Werke* (Berlin: Dietz Verlag, 1967), XXXVI, 244; see also pp. 19–20, and XXXV, 444, 78.

[2] See Lee Benson, *Turner and Beard; American Historical Writing Reconsidered* (Glencoe, Ill.: Free Press, 1960), pp. 1–40.

[3] See, for example, Achille Loria, *The Economic Foundations of Society* (London: Swan Sonnenschein, 1899), pp. 1–9; Loria's *Analisi della Proprietà capitalista* (Torino: Fratelli Bocca, 1899) is, in the Wakefield manner, a view of the evolution of economic, particularly capitalist, institutions, as revealed by the history of colonization; for references to Wakefield, see II, 17, 24, 26, 42, 44, 56, 99, 109, 191, 357, 387, 419, 423, 466 and *passim*. There are many references as well to disciples of Wakefield, such as Merivale and Torrens. See also Achille Loria, *Corso Completo di Economica Politica* (Torino: Fratelli Bocca, 1910), pp. 19–30, on 'Il metodo comparativo coloniale'. The hints for such a view of capitalist development through Wakefield's colonial prism were, of course, also employed by Marx in the last chapter of *Capital*, I.

[4] See Loria, *Analisi, passim*. Also, for example, Loria, *Corso Completo*, pp. 665–71.

in time for it to be employed by Hobson in his work on *Imperialism*;[1] indeed, Hobson referred to this work on two occasions, and quoted from it at some length.[2] Hobson specifically noted no other authority, although an anonymous article in the *Contemporary Review*, which Hobson probably read, did make references to certain of the ideas of Torrens, Mill, and Ricardo on empire-building, in 1899.[3] Whether through this article, or, less directly, through Loria, more verifiably through the latter, Hobson, having as early as 1894 revealed himself a heretic on Say's Law,[4] may be regarded, then, as having taken up the theory of capitalist imperialism from the school of Wakefield, even though, it would seem, Hobson knew of Wakefield himself only as a champion of responsible government in the colonies.[5]

But there was an important difference between Hobson's and Wakefield's theories of imperialism. While Wakefield had insisted that the glut of capital made empire-building necessary to an industrial society, Hobson suggested that imperialism was not the only solution to the problem of glut—that a more equitable redistribution of the national income would provide a much more satisfactory alternative. Hobson, a liberal economist and journalist, writing in 1902, after the conclusion of the Boer War, denounced modern imperialism, as promoted by manufacturers of war materials, industrialists who required export markets for their surplus goods, and capitalists with idle funds; these business interests, and these interests alone, profited enormously by imperialism, Hobson insisted, while the remainder of the nation lost. Hobson placed the chief onus upon the holders of 'surplus capital', who wished more profitable investments than were available at home. 'The economic root of imperialism', Hobson declared, 'is the desire of strong organized industrial and financial interests to secure and develop at the public expense and by the public force private markets for their surplus goods and their surplus capital.' These surpluses, and consequently imperialism, were, he declared, the result of the maldistribution of the national product which left huge sums in the hands of the possessing classes. A more just distribution, Hobson urged, would remove this surplus income, and at the same time broaden the home market sufficiently to permit it to absorb the goods and capital which had heretofore

---

[1] Loria, *Economic Foundations*, pp. 262–77, and *passim*.
[2] Hobson, *Imperialism*, pp. 54–5, 73.
[3] Ritortus, 'The Imperialism of British Trade', *Contemporary Review* LXXVI, no. 403 (July 1899), 132–52; no. 404 (August 1899), 282–304.
[4] A. F. Mummery and J. A. Hobson, *The Physiology of Industry: being an exposure of certain fallacies in existing theories of economics* (New York: Kelley and Milman, 1956).
[5] Hobson, *Imperialism*, p. 118.

been shipped abroad. The success of the Trade Unions in procuring higher wages, and of the social reformers in improving the condition of the lower classes, would, consequently, in Hobson's view, work to make imperialism unnecessary.[1]

It was the neo-Marxists—particularly Hilferding, and, later, Lenin—who were to agree with the Wakefield school concerning the *inevitability* of capitalist imperialism, although their economic analysis of the process was quite different. Unlike Malthus, whose agrarian biases he continually denounced, and Wakefield (and, later, Hobson), Marx's attitude toward Say's Law had been ambiguous: he had specifically rejected the under-consumptionist argument when used by Rodbertus, and, as is well known, wrote, as a Ricardian, against Malthusian heresy.[2] Marx had his own theory of gluts and of the falling rate of profit to explain industrial crises: he saw the profits of the capitalist as originating entirely in the capital used to employ living labor; with sharply increased competition, the capitalist was compelled to invest more heavily in labor-saving machinery to reduce costs, and the greater weight given constant over variable (labor costs) capital within the total composition of capital proportionately reduced the rate of profit. There was, in consequence, a glut of capital, 'the overproduc-tion of capital always included the overproduction of commodities', and such gluts were accompanied by an 'over-population of laborers'.[3] Capital export and foreign trade were viewed by Marx as the means by which capitalism strove to ward off this inevitable fall of the rate of profit. Foreign trade, however, though it tended *initially* to raise the rate of profit by raising the rate of surplus value, and permitted 'an expansion of the scale of produc-tion', in the *long run* hastened the 'process of accumulation' and the 'reduction of the variable as compared to the constant capital', and thus occasioned a fall in the rate of profit.[4] Marx's theory of exploitation was

---

[1] Hobson, *Imperialism*, pp. 106, 81–4, 89–90, 140–5.

[2] See Meek, *Marx and Engels on Malthus*. It should be noted that a recent writer has taken great pains to disentangle Marx's 'complicated "position" on Say's Law', and has concluded that it was 'not one of inconsistency but the consequence of deliberate methodology'. See Bernice Shoul, 'Karl Marx and Say's Law', *Quarterly Journal of Economics* LXXI, no. 4 (November 1957), 611–29.

[3] Marx, *Capital*, III, 294–5, 300–1.

[4] *Ibid.* pp. 300, 302–3, 278. Marx attempted to answer the question concerning which Smith and Ricardo had differed: was the average rate of profit raised by the higher rate of profit which capital invested in foreign, and particularly in colonial trade, realised? Marx's answer, in support of Smith, was that he could see 'no reason' why higher rates of profit realized by such invest-ments 'should not enter as elements into the average rate of profit and tend to keep it up to that extent'. Yet, in the long run, Marx felt that Ricardo's more pessimistic view had been justified: for foreign trade developed capitalist production, and such development 'implies' the relative decrease of the variable as compared to the constant capital; in addition, it produced an over-production for the foreign market. *Ibid.* pp. 279–80.

also at the core of his conclusion that 'capitals invested in colonies, etc., may yield a higher rate of profit' not only 'on account of the backward development', but also because 'slaves, coolies, etc., permit a better exploitation of labor'.[1]

The neo-Marxists—Rosa Luxemburg, Rudolf Hilferding, and others—writing in the decade following Hobson's treatise, saw imperialism as the latest, and probably the last, stage of capitalist development, a stage in which free competition no longer existed, in which trusts, cartels, and monopolies were the rule, and financial capital had assumed control over industrial capital. Hilferding's analysis was substantially drawn from Marx; Luxemburg, while stressing the inadequacy of Say's Law in a monetary economy, thus coming to an under-consumptionist conclusion similar to Hobson's, saw, like Wakefield, the growth of capitalism as dependent upon the existence of undeveloped, non-industrial regions, upon which capitalism needed, parasitically, to feed. The arguments of Lenin's famous essay on imperialism, in 1917, were essentially those of Marx and Hilferding, though the writings of Hilferding, and of such other Marxists as Kautsky and Bauer, possessed an insight and a sophistication well beyond the somewhat crude assessment of Lenin's treatise.[2]

There has been a considerable controversy stemming from these theories of capitalist imperialism. Hobson and Wakefield differed from Marx and the neo-Marxists as to the causes of the phenomenon, but all agreed in seeing imperialism as a characteristic of capitalism—for Wakefield and the Marxists a necessary and ineradicable characteristic—whose most distinctive aspect was the export of capital. For Hobson, this export of capital, accompanied by the use of national force, at the instance of the capitalists, to safeguard investments, was 'imperialism'; the Marxists were ready to believe that capital export *per se* was imperialism, whether or not aggressive force accompanied the process. The rejoinder of Western social science has, increasingly, come to be a questioning of the reality of economic motives in modern imperialism. In this, they have taken their cue from Joseph Schumpeter, whose views, curiously, had been anticipated, in almost every detail, in the writings of Adam Ferguson, Charles Comte, Constant, and Saint-Simon,[3] over a century earlier.

---

[1] *Ibid.* pp. 279–80.

[2] R. Hilferding, *Das Finanzkapital* (1910); R. Luxemburg, *The Accumulation of Capital* (New Haven: Yale University Press, 1951)—originally published in 1913; Bauer, *Die Nationalitätenfräge* (1907); Lenin, *Imperialism* (1917).

[3] See Henri Saint-Simon, *L'Industrie*, in *œuvres* de Saint-Simon (Paris, 1868), XVIII, 53–5, 59, 109–13; Benjamin Constant, *L'esprit de conquête et de l'usurpation, dans le système mercantile* (Paris, 1918), pp. 11–15 (originally published in 1814); Charles Comte, *De l'impossibilité d'établir un gouvernement constitutionnel, sous un chef militaire, et particulièrement sous Napoléon* (Paris,

Schumpeter, an early opponent of the neo-Marxist view of a capitalist imperialism, as we know, insisted that capitalism was by its inner nature anti-imperialist. Were not nineteenth-century Liberals, he asked, the spokesmen of the rising British capitalism, the most vociferous opponents of militarism and colonialism? Modern imperialism, as well as protectionism, Schumpeter urged, were not products of rational, economic factors but of irrational sentiments which had managed to survive from feudal, pre-capitalist times. Schumpeter explained modern imperialism as an alliance between 'expansive interests' within capitalism, selfish interests constituting a minority of the capitalists, and the survivors of pre-capitalist classes—the feudal and military classes—in whose breasts the atavistic sentiments of imperialism still lodged.[1]

Our findings would suggest that there are deficiencies in all these interpretations. In the first half of the nineteenth century, for example, it might be said, contrary to Schumpeter, that there still existed a 'feudal' landed aristocracy, or, at any rate, a substantial part of this aristocracy, which opted for anti-imperialism because of its interest in agriculture. (In ancient Athens, after the Persian Wars, we may observe a similar situation of a conservative, anti-imperialist landed aristocracy opposing a bustling, imperialistic middle class, turning outward to further its trading interests.) We thus see an aristocracy, following the analysis of the agrarian economists, concerned, like Chalmers and Malthus, and as the French physiocrats had been earlier,[2] that mercantile legislators might urge war to find markets for surplus industrial production; this aristocracy, in supporting agricultural protection, found itself upholding the ideal of a self-sufficient Britain, of a British industry, in a balanced economy, turning to the home market for the vent of its products, rather than inviting a precarious dependence upon foreign markets by organizing its economy to become the Workshop of the World. (In this, we may see protection, again contrary to Schumpeter's and Hobson's view, as the basis for a system of anti-imperialism.[3])

Certainly the existence of an extensive body of analysis constructed by

---

1815), pp. 18–19. See also Adam Ferguson, *An Essay on the History of Civil Society* (Philadelphia, 1819), pp. 385–418 (originally published in 1767), for the similar views of this representative of the Scottish Historical School.

[1] Schumpeter, *Imperialism*, *passim*.

[2] Physiocracy, Schumpeter has assured us in another work, was a product of disgust for foreign adventures and colonialism which had brought France no advantage, and for the commercial and industrial undertakings of Colbert and his successors which had accompanied them, a turning inward, toward the land itself, as the only firm basis for advancing the wealth of the nation. Schumpeter, *History of Economic Analysis*, p. 236 f.n.

[3] Interestingly enough, Schumpeter seemed to suggest that this was at least *theoretically* possible. See *Imperialism*, p. 77.

the leading, contemporary political economists, both orthodox and hetero-dox, which insisted upon a chronic need, whether immediate or in the future, of the industrial system for empire, whether formal or informal, an analysis which, moreover, received forceful, practical application in Radical efforts, in parliament, in support of the preservation of Britain's industrial pre-dominance, and in behalf of the use of national power to extend and protect foreign and colonial commerce and investment, does argue, strongly, that Schumpeter's brilliant hypothesis that *fin-de-siècle* imperialism was an atavism, thoroughly out of line with the temper of capitalism in its classic period, is in error. Similarly, this evidence raises serious doubts concerning the neo-Marxist view that 'imperialism' was a product of a capitalism in its 'highest stage', a stage in which 'finance' not 'industry' was predominant. What probably put Schumpeter astray was that he—very much like Hobson, who agreed with him on this, and, as we shall see, on other matters as well—saw 'imperialism' as necessarily in a protectionist, neo-mercantile mould; for Schumpeter in 1919, as for Hobson in 1902, a free trade economy was, *ipso facto*, not imperialistic. (The defenders of England's Empire of Free Trade, between 1903 and 1914, against Chamberlain's neo-mercantilism, were, generally, regarded as anti-imperialists.) It no longer seems possible to accept such a view, as we have tried to demonstrate. But there is a good deal in both the Hobson and Schumpeter analyses which is very pertinent to our subject.

The idea of 'atavism', for example, seems a fruitful one, given our findings. Schumpeter, one of the great economists of our times, saw the issue as one between economic science, on the one hand, and irrational, atavistic sentiment, on the other, the first wielded by the defenders of free trade, and the latter to be found in selfish protectionist interests and in the aristocracy and the military classes. Our findings would suggest that such 'atavistic' sentiments were also to be found among the most stalwart defenders of free trade, in its heyday—e.g. in Radical jingoism, and in the Radical interest in preserving an industrial predominance. Moreover, analagous 'atavisms'—sometimes called 'exploded' theories by the men of the first half of the nineteenth century—were even to be found underlying certain of the leading principles of the new political economy, which the Radical defenders of free trade habitually invoked to defend their program. At a number of crucial points, the 'science' of political economy was riddled with assumptions, at times only barely explicit, which stemmed from the econo-mics of the 'pre-scientific' mercantilism of an overwhelmingly agrarian society.

Underlying many of these outmoded opinions was the persistence, especially among the orthodox political economists, of the view, realistic enough for the period in which it originated, which regarded the world as possessing a fixed quantity of severely limited resources, rather than, as was to become more realistically the case with the advance of the nineteenth century, a view which perceived a world in which an ever-growing supply of goods was being produced, a supply which, while hardly unlimited, yet made possible the vision of an age of plenty. There was joined to this view the assumption, also rooted in mercantilism, which we have traced from Tucker, through Mill, and Torrens, and the leading parliamentary advocates of free trade, that in a world where the supply of wealth was fixed, the national wealth might be increased only by the extraction of a profit from foreign trade. Pre-industrial society, relatively static, from the standpoint of population as well as production, was a world of seriously limited opportunities. It was from the economics of mercantilism, which had, with some accuracy, described that world, that the interest in industrial monopoly, which we have observed among the English free traders, had come. We have, intermittently, suggested that it was the pessimistic fatalism of the 'dismal' science of political economy, embodied in the laws of population and of wages, for example, also, perhaps, a remnant of millennia of scarcity, which was, in good part, at the bottom of the view that it was impossible for the working-man to enjoy, in the long run, more than a subsistence wage. The sum of all these preconceptions, when confirmed by other strong interests, as we shall soon see, was behind the rejection of the home market by free traders, in favor of markets overseas, and, ultimately, of imperialism. In the heyday of England's industrial and commercial predominance, only diehard, agrarian 'reactionaries', like Malthus and Spence, anxious to slow the rate of industrial advance, suggested that English factories might find a considerable or expanding market for their production among English factory hands or agricultural laborers, or in Ireland. The free traders, on the other hand, were convinced, with Perronet Thompson, that for every customer lost at home, by Britain's rapid transformation to an industrial state, 'ten twice as good would be acquired' abroad.

From an anti-mercantilist agrarianism, which received its most systematic expression in physiocracy, and whose leading English spokesman was Malthus, an agrarianism which, surveying a commercial and industrial system with a perception similarly formed in the age of scarcity, saw only the deficiencies of a system which aimed at turning men from the traditional, and godly tillage of the soil, came the view of Wakefield and his followers that only empire-building might conquer, if only for a time, the ever-increasing distress which must inevitably follow the 'sacrilegious' abandonment of agriculture. Of course, the Wakefield program of colonization was also based upon the survival of obvious mercantilist conceptions: the Colonial Reformers did not hesitate to embrace the slogan of the old colonial system which spoke of 'Ships, Commerce, Colonies', following a strain which received its most forceful, 'imperialist' expression in Torrens. But it was the agrarian economists who were the source of the socio-economic analysis of Wakefield's party, which saw an industrial society inevitably beset by inner contradictions, and facing the alternatives of revolution, on the one hand, and an intensive program of colonization, so as to overcome the glut of goods, capital, and population, on the other. Without such a view of the new industrialism as inevitably and necessarily requiring colonization to relieve itself of glut (and we must recall Rintoul's view, like Marx's, that free trade by itself would only increase capital accumulation), there would be no reason to go beyond the economic program of the party of Hume and Cobden. The party of Wakefield, proponents of the *necessity* of 'systematic colonization', therefore, was firmly committed to the view that an industrial society could not overcome glut by turning to the home market.

What made the Colonial Reformers so ready to accept the limitations of these assumptions? Viscount Palmerston, no protectionist and no Radical, but rather a conventional Liberal free trader, saw the great usefulness of turning to the home market. Palmerston granted that, 'no doubt a thriving Colony becomes a good Customer & gives Employment to Labour at Home', but nevertheless confessed that he had never been 'as sanguine & keen about emigration as many other people'; 'one would rather if it were possible,' he wrote in a letter to Lord John Russell, 'to lay out our money in improvements at home and keep our people at home, than spend our money in the comparatively unproductive process of dispeopling our country'. We must recall, at this point, Palmerston's cynical suggestion that 'Charles Buller & other Persons who have engaged in Land Speculations in our Colonies preach up Emigration upon a large Scale as a Cure for all our domestic Evils, because at all Events it would probably help them to turn their Lands to good account.'[1] It was no doubt easier for some of the Colonial Reformers to accept 'exploded' assumptions because many of them possessed a vested interest in colonial land speculation. Others, no doubt, were moved by a sentimental interest in colonies, and the expansion of England.

The bulk of the free traders with no such land interests, or sentimental

[1] Letter of Viscount Palmerston to Lord John Russell, 20 December 1844. Russell Papers, P.R.O. 30/22, 4D.

interests, were probably ready to ignore the possibility of extending the domestic market, because increasing the capacity of the home market would probably have been possible only at the cost of diminishing the rate at which Great Britain was being transformed into an industrial country. The persistence of such outmoded concepts, then, as the long-run inevitability of subsistence wages, or the possibility of extracting real additions to the national wealth only from foreigners, or the necessity of maintaining an industrial predominance, thus justified the industrial middle classes in their efforts to maintain, at the highest possible level, the rate of industrial growth which was putting them in control of the national economy, and would soon, they were confident, place them, similarly, at the head of the national polity. To accomplish this rapid transformation, a program of empire-building—if only that embodied in the conception of England as the Workshop of the World—was essential. Palmerston, a good Whig landowner, in defending the superiority of the home market, would, of course, be unmoved by such a consideration.

There is certainly no doubt that the classical economists were right in citing the advantages of foreign trade, as against the drawbacks and limitations of a 'closed commercial state', and we must reject the usefulness either to Great Britain or to the world at large, of the 'wall of brass' so dear to the agrarian and protectionist economists. For, despite Torrens' reservations, and even Torrens favored the free importation of corn and raw materials for industry, free trade *had* become an economic necessity for Great Britain by the middle of the nineteenth century. Imlah has held that even the limited protection of the twenties, thirties, and forties, had seriously limited British prosperity by intensifying the deflationary factors in the economy. Dear corn cut down severely the *home* demand for all other goods, of both foreign and domestic produce; and because protection did prevent the foreigner from selling goods and services at satisfactory prices in the English market, as was understood at the time, it seriously limited the amounts of British goods which foreign nations could purchase. The result of the adoption of free trade was, in Imlah's words, 'an escape from premature senescence', postponing 'for another generation' the 'transition towards a partly *rentier* status—the balancing of international accounts by drawing on the income of foreign investments'.[1] Still, even with free trade, as the bulk of the Chartist leadership dimly understood, greater attention to improving the capacities of the home market would have made the coming of industrialism considerably less painful, most especially to the working classes.

[1] Imlah, *Pax Britannica*, p. 61.

To sum up, the Empire of Free Trade, in its earliest days, was, like the neo-mercantile empires of the twentieth century, to a considerable extent erected upon assumptions which were derived, in Schumpeter's words, 'from the living conditions, not of the present, but of the past—or, put in terms of the economic interpretation of history, from past rather than present relations of production',[1] from the agrarian era of relative scarcity, which constituted the entire past of the race, and from the economic analysis of the age of mercantilism, which had immediately preceded. The persistence of such assumptions was undoubtedly more understandable at a time when the enormous powers of the new industrialism had not been fully displayed; that they did persist, and that they underlay the efforts for colonization, and those to make England the Workshop of the World, seems evident despite such *fin-de-siècle* liberals as Hobson and Schumpeter, who, seeing the more full-blooded atavism of a neo-mercantile imperialism, frequently blaring the tribal grunts of a primitive people's imperialism, could only view the preceding era as it had been depicted by a 'cosmopolitan' Cobdenite political economy. With free trade, which they saw as embodying the soundest international morality, under attack by a racist neo-mercantilism, and classical economics condemned by a new school of historical economists, almost all, typically, supporters of neo-mercantile programs, Hobson and Schumpeter may be pardoned for having ignored the distortions unavoidably present in the science of political economy in the time of its early development, and for having failed to see the possibility of a free trade imperialism.

While Marx, and later the neo-Marxists, and Wakefield, and his followers, agreed, then, on the basis of their apocalyptic and necessitarian critique that capitalist industrialism was so constructed as to admit of only two possible alternatives—imperialism or revolution—J. A. Hobson, having, like Palmerston, no vested interest, sentimental or practical, either in colonization, as did the party of Wakefield, or in a purifying revolution, as did the Marxists, was able to see capitalism, in a democratic society, as able to turn, under popular pressure, from frantic accumulation to a more equitable distribution of the national income. Nor could Hobson, who wrote at a time when England's industrial machine had been largely built, and was even growing a bit obsolescent, a time when England was beginning to experience the sharp pains of foreign competition, be persuaded to accept mercantilist assumptions because of their usefulness in promoting rapid industrial growth. Hobson wrote, indeed, after the depression of the seventies and eighties, which followed the prosperity of the third quarter of the

[1] Schumpeter, *Imperialism*, p. 65.

century, had once more displayed, to Hobson (and his associate, Mummery) at least, if not to economists, generally, the inadequacy of Say's Law. It was a time, moreover, when the effectiveness of trade unions in improving wages and the conditions of labor was being regularly demonstrated, and when, not only in England but on the Continent, a grand movement to redistribute the national income, by systems of old age pensions, and health and unemployment insurance had scored impressive initial successes. Alternatives to imperialism or revolution, which seemed inescapable to Marx and Wakefield and their followers, evidently existed. Hobson, like Malthus and Spence before him, recommended a policy of public works and governmental spending to compensate for the inadequacies of Say's Law in a monetary economy; a successor of Hobson's, who was to acknowledge both him and Malthus as the foremost of his own anticipators,[1] J. M. Keynes, was to offer a similar analysis and program a generation later.

The Hobson–Schumpeter theory

It is hard to understand why, in the light of considerable evidence to the contrary, it has become customary to speak of a Hobson–Lenin theory of imperialism, as if both men had proposed essentially the same theory. A more detailed examination of the Hobson thesis of 1902 seems useful—despite the fact that we have already alluded to most of its leading elements—so as to clear Hobson of the simplistic views so frequently attributed to him. Again and again, in his *Imperialism*, Hobson, unlike the Marxists, stressed that imperialism was not necessary to capitalist development. The home market was, for him, an ever-present, realistic alternative: 'The assumption, sometimes made,' he noted, 'that home demand is a fixed amount, and that any commodities made in excess of this amount must find a foreign market, or remain unsold, is quite unwarranted'; he insisted, rather, that 'there is no necessary limit to the quantity of capital and labour that can be employed in supplying the home markets, provided the effective demand for the goods that are produced is so distributed that every increase of production stimulates a corresponding increase of consumption'.[2] In his chapter concerning 'the economic taproot of imperialism', Hobson did, no doubt, speak of the belief, which he regarded as common among businessmen, 'that more goods can be produced than can be sold at a profit, and that more capital exists than can find remunerative investment', only to dismiss

---

[1] See J. M. Keynes, *The General Theory of Employment, Interest, and Money* (London: Macmillan, 1936), pp. 362–70.
[2] Hobson, *Imperialism*, p. 29.

such a view as fallacious. 'If the consuming public in this country raised its standard of consumption to keep pace with every rise of productive powers, there could be no excess of goods or capital clamorous to use Imperialism in order to find markets.'[1] It was 'not industrial progress' which made imperialism seem necessary to certain branches of trade, but 'mal-distribution of consuming power',[2] he concluded.

Not only was imperialism not necessary to capitalism, in Hobson's eyes, but, like Schumpeter, he did not think it was particularly useful, except to those he called the 'economic parasites of imperialism', groups virtually identical with Schumpeter's 'expansive interests'. J. A. Hobson had no illusions as to the rewards to the nation as a whole of the new imperialism which, he wrote, 'adds to our empire tropical and sub-tropical regions with which our trade is small, precarious, and unprogressive'; he further observed that 'no serious attempt to regard them as satisfactory business assets is possible', for both the quantity and quality of the export trade with Britain's new possessions were low.[3] 'The new Empire was even more barren for settlement than for profitable trade,' he observed.[4] Hobson even anticipated Schumpeter's view of an alliance between 'expansive interests' within capitalism, constituting a selfish minority of the capitalists, and the pre-capitalist feudal and military classes in whose hearts the atavistic sentiments of imperialism still prevailed. He identified these 'expansive', parasitic beneficiaries of imperialism as manufacturers for the export market, and foreign investors, as well as certain other groups: among these were 'the shipbuilding, boilermaking, and gun and ammunition making trades' ('a pushful policy is good for them'); the armed services were 'imperialist by conviction and by professional interest', and the 'direct professional influence of the services carries with it a less organized but powerful sympathetic support on the part of the aristocracy and the wealthy classes, who seek in the services careers for their sons'; the officials of the colonial service and of the Indian civil service. (Hobson repeated James Mill's view of Britain's empire as 'a vast system of outdoor relief for the upper classes', where the sons of the wealthy and titled might find careers as 'ranchers, planters, engineers, or missionaries', and 'in all the professions'.) The colonies offered an opportunity to the 'more reckless or adventurous', and 'for damaged characters and careers'. The 'business interests of the nation as a whole' had been 'subordinated' to those of 'certain classes and certain trades'; 'although the new Imperialism has been bad business for the

[1] Hobson, *Imperialism*, p. 81.
[2] *Ibid.* p. 85.
[3] *Ibid.* pp. 38–9.
[4] *Ibid.* p. 45.

nation, it has been good business' for these 'economic parasites of imperialism'.[1]

Hobson, no less than Schumpeter, was anxious to gain 'acceptance' for a theory of imperialism which 'dispels the delusion that expansion of foreign trade, and therefore of empire, is a necessity of national life'.[2] No less than Schumpeter, then, did Hobson suggest, dismissing the 'economic taproot' of imperialism as fallacious, the predominance of other than rational, economic motives. Much of Hobson's study of imperialism, indeed, discusses these non-economic motives.[3] For both Hobson and Schumpeter, the return to protectionism, an 'exploded' theory of mercantilist times, was the most characteristic aspect of the new imperialism.[4] Hobson particularly observed that the false protectionist 'assumption that there is only a given quantity of trade, and that if one nation gets any portion of it another nation loses so much, shows a blind ignorance of the elements of international trade'.[5] He did not see, however, that this, and similar assumptions, had also been at the bottom of the effort to establish the Empire of Free Trade, a half-century earlier.

[1] Hobson, *Imperialism*, pp. 46–51, 61. The *Spectator*, which, unexpectedly, was hostile to the Opium War, denouncing it as an '*unjust, unnecessary* and *dishonourable*' war ('The Opium War', *Spectator* XIII, no. 613 (28 March 1840), 297), saw the interests benefiting from the war in terms not unlike those in which Hobson (and Schumpeter) were to see the 'parasites of imperialism' (and the 'expansive interests') over two generations later. 'The Opium War party', the journal wrote, 'is strong', for 'note how numerous and influential are the chief gainers by war': 'The aristocracy—the predominant interest—the class which crowds the Church and the Bar with younger sons and needy cousins—find a vent for family hangers-on in the augmented Army and Navy. The veterans in both services rejoice in the recurrence of active employment; and many youngsters are eager to exchange dull parades and garrison-duty for the "rapture of the strife": their motives are not all sordid.' But there were others who supported the aristocracy: 'The dealers in clothing, arms, and provisions, who speculate upon profitable contracts—shipowners, who have transports ready to be hired—capitalists, who foresee the need of loans—all are ready to drive the country into war, by which they hope to gain at the public expense. And all these parties reckon, not without cause, on the easily-excited pugnacity of the multitude. The voice of the general mercantile community ought to be for peace: but it happens that in this quarrel with China a powerful diversion in favour of war is created by peculiar circumstances. Compensation for the opium delivered up to destruction "for her Majesty's service"—valued, without interest, at about two millions and a half sterling—can only be obtained by war: so the Government assures the opium-smugglers and their agents.' 'Of course,' the article continued, 'the influence of Government is used unsparingly to excite a hostile feeling against the Chinese'; 'it is of the utmost importance to appear at any rate to carry the popular feeling along with them'. The weekly concluded that the war 'is truly called THE OPIUM WAR; and never will it be known by any other name'. ('The Opium War, Its Supporters and Opponents', *Spectator* XIII, no. 618 (2 May 1840), 418.)

[2] Hobson, *Imperialism*, p. 91. Compare Schumpeter, *Imperialism*, p. 89; also f.n. 11 pp. 174–5, and *passim*.

[3] See, for example, Hobson, *Imperialism*, pp. 3–13, and almost all of part II (especially chapters I, II, III, IV).

[4] See *ibid*. pp. 64–70; also Schumpeter, *Imperialism*, pp. 75–92, and *passim*.

[5] Hobson, *Imperialism*, p. 66.

If we must dismiss the idea of a Hobson–Lenin theory, can we not, more appropriately, speak of a Hobson–Schumpeter theory? It was not the Hobson theory, but the neo-Marxist theory of capitalist imperialism which attempted to endow an imperialism, which saw England, France, and Germany frantically seizing and dividing deserts, jungles, and South Sea Islands among themselves in a scramble for prestige and power—a movement of twentieth-century irrationalism—with a 'rational' explanation derived from theorists of nearly a century earlier, theorists, curiously enough, who had, in a similar way, fashioned their own conceptions from the 'exploded', and the what ought to have been 'exploded', assumptions and objectives of the mercantile and agrarian economists of the seventeenth and eighteenth centuries. Hobson, indeed, may be said to have anticipated Schumpeter in displaying the new imperialism in the terms in which, increasingly, historians view it today.

It is a simplification of the Wakefield–Marx theory, as it perhaps ought properly to be described, as amended and extended by Hilferding and, in good part, vulgarized by Lenin, which has really been, and not unjustifiably, on the whole, the target of much recent criticism. A. J. P. Taylor has attributed the great hold of this theory (although he, in the usual manner, identifies it as that of a 'Hobsonian–Leninist analysis') to the fact that Hobson, and others who attempted to explain imperialism in economic terms, were 'rationalists', seeking 'a rational explanation for the behaviour of others', and that consequently, their theories were readily accepted by other rational, liberal intellectuals.[1] One might add that the theory was most strongly adhered to in the inter-war period, especially during the thirties, when the certainties of the apocalyptic 'religion' of a 'rational' Marxism gave special comfort to intellectuals, and when an increasing disillusionment with the War of 1914 and with the peace which followed, the economic depression, and increasing tension between classes, gave a particular relevance to such an interpretation. Why did not Hobson, who lived until 1940, clear up the misconception? In addition to the general 'climate of opinion' already noted, the wide acceptance of Lenin's statement of the theory, accompanied by Lenin's flattering acknowledgement of Hobson's priority,[2] would not be a particularly strong inducement for Hobson, whose ideas

---

[1] See A. J. P. Taylor, 'Hobson's Misapplication of the Theory', in Fieldhouse, *Theory of Capitalist Imperialism*, pp. 125–9.

[2] 'I made use of the principal English work, *Imperialism*, J. A. Hobson's book, with all the care that, in my opinion, that work deserves.' (Lenin, *Imperialism*, p. 7.) Subsequently, while noting that Hobson had adopted 'the point of view of bourgeois social reformism and pacifism', Lenin observed that Hobson's book 'gives an excellent and comprehensive description of the principal economic and political characteristics of imperialism' (*ibid.*, p. 15).

had been mocked at for so much of his lifetime, to disabuse his new-found admirers. Hobson may even have come to believe in the Leninist version of the theory of imperialism, but his own theory of 1902 was, nevertheless, a very different one from Lenin's.

Epilogue

During the decade after 1903, Joseph Chamberlain, Robert Torrens' heir, and the spokesman for the hard-pressed Midlands metals industries, calling for an 'Imperial Zollverein', made a determined effort to turn England from free trade to a neo-mercantile program of tariff protection and imperial preference, but he failed. The heirs of the Radicals of the first half of the century, and the defenders of the Empire of Free Trade, were the 'Liberal-Imperialists': Rosebery, Asquith, Haldane, Grey and their followers, who represented the views of finance and commerce, and of the still prosperous cotton manufacturers. These Liberals opposed the tariff 'imperialism' of men like Chamberlain and Milner, whose program threatened England's highly profitable 'informal' empire. But only in England, in the early twentieth century still the leading commercial and financial power, despite the loss of its industrial predominance, was there a struggle between the old empire-building of free trade and the neo-mercantile 'imperialism'. Supported by neo-classical economists—men such as Alfred Marshall, Bastable, Cannan, Edgeworth, and Pigou—the Liberals continued to look toward foreign investments, the profits of the carrying trade, and international financial transactions, as the means by which England's well-being might best be advanced. The historical economists, men such as Ashley, Cunningham, Mackinder, and Hewins, taking their inspiration from the German historical school of List and Schmoller, were, in neo-mercantilist fashion, suspicious of capital export, except within the empire, and sought by means of an Imperial Zollverein to reserve colonial markets for British manufactures, with Britain receiving in exchange, Canadian, Australian, or South African agricultural commodities.[1]

Neo-mercantilism was to carry the day on the European continent before 1914, and by the early thirties, protection and an imperial preferential system were adopted by Great Britain. In the twenties, thirties, and forties, the British economy suffered from what Hobson had earlier described as 'an overgrowth of certain manufacturing trades for the express purpose of effecting foreign sales';[2] this was a time when foreign, particularly Japanese,

---

[1] These questions have been discussed in Semmel, *Imperialism and Social Reform, passim.*
[2] Hobson, *Imperialism*, p. 88.

competition humbled a once powerful Lancashire. There was, furthermore, a more chronic imbalance against which the agrarian economists of the preceding century had warned, a lop-sidedness which compelled Great Britain to export a very considerable part of its production if she were to be able to purchase what she absolutely required from abroad. Not only the growth of foreign industry, but, ironically, the residues of her earlier imperial predominance, in particular the pressure of attempting to maintain some of the appearance of her former power, and the strain imposed upon her by her position as the master of one of the two great international currencies, the remnant of her former virtual commercial and financial hegemony, presented an intolerable burden for an economy which had for decades been paying the 'penalty of the lead', again a residue of her having, for a time, succeeded in her rule as the World's Workshop. Today, para-doxically, in an effort to correct a precariously disadvantageous balance of payments, so largely the fruit of her former predominance, a Labour government whose Labour predecessor had done so much to effect the redistribution of income, which Hobson and Keynes had urged to maintain an effective home demand, is attempting to cut back this demand so that, once again, British industry will be compelled to sell its products abroad.

The best noticed aspect of this neo-mercantile 'imperialism' was, of course, the struggle for colonies, and later mandates, concessions, and spheres of influence among the European powers in Africa, Asia, and Latin America. The international political situation, from, say, 1880, until 1945, was one in which there was little to inhibit struggles among great industrial European powers, the United States, and Japan, at the expense of economically back-ward continents. This classic 'imperialism', both free trade and neo-mercantile, during, approximately, the first half of our century, can be regarded as having brought peoples outside of the international economy—outside of history, in some cases—into the great world market, and the mainstream of world history. With the benefit of hindsight, and the passage of the years which somehow obscures almost all but the most blatant outrages associated with pre-1914 imperialism, at least to Western eyes, the 'imperialism' of the 1880s and onward takes on somewhat the appearance of a necessary stage for the dissemination of Western ideas and techniques, and for laying the foundations for what may become a universally beneficial international division of labor. This 'imperialism' has now been entirely altered by a new political situation, which, against a background of conflict between great power blocs, has seen the transformation of former colonies into independent nations.

Moreover, capital export, which was thought of as exploitative imperialism about a half-century ago, is now viewed, virtually, as benevolences extended to economically backward nations, starved for development capital. Today, the new governments of the undeveloped parts of the world fully recognize, as did Tucker in the eighteenth century, that economic growth, in its early stages, is difficult without capital advances from more advanced nations. It was Hobson, with the experience of the Boer War in mind, who was largely responsible for having changed the formerly favorable view of foreign investment which had prevailed in the nineteenth century, and even he, some ten years after writing his *Imperialism*, was to revert to the earlier opinion which regarded such investments as beneficial instruments of a cosmopolitan capitalism.[1] There is difficulty about supplying this capital at the present time with the widening of the domestic market through more equitable distribution of national income and the discovery of alternative uses for surplus capital and labor power in a new technological, electronic and cybernetic revolution. In addition, less advantageously, great hoards of capital are committed to the systematic waste of war production. All this has undermined the view that industrial societies must turn to a neo-mercantile, capital-export imperialism to avoid industrial crises.

While the old imperialism no doubt helped to maximize world production and income, there has not been anything like a proper or equitable distribution of this increasing income. Today, without the benefit of complex mercantile regulations, or the presence of imperial proconsuls or troops to ensure favorable trading arrangements, United Nations economists—most prominently, Gunnar Myrdal, the noted Swedish economist and the former director of the United Nations Economic Commission for Europe—assure us that the gap between the backward and the advanced nations of the globe continues to widen rather than to narrow, that the most essential characteristic of the usual trade between the two—between commodity and manufacture-exporting countries—is chronically disadvantageous to the former, this despite the fact that, occasionally, trade conditions do favor them.

Myrdal and others have thus revived the debate entered upon by Hume and Tucker, in the mid-eighteenth century, and then continued by the classical and national economists. Jacob Viner who is one of the foremost contemporary champions of the tradition of the classical economists, in opposing Myrdal, has acknowledged the 'almost exclusive orientation' of traditional economics to the 'interests, the needs, and the complacencies' of

---

[1] J. A. Hobson, *The Economic Interpretations of Investment* (London: Financial Review of Reviews, 1911), pp. 116 f., and *passim*.

industrially advanced countries.[1] Even so, classical economics, Myrdal has suggested, might still provide the lumber for a new theoretical edifice—a 'general theory of economic under-development and development' which was 'consistent' with the classical theory of international trade. When such a 'general theory' emerged, it would be found, Myrdal continued, to have 'salvaged many familiar arguments and theorems'; 'in economics, as in social theory generally, old thoughts are rarely discarded altogether, and no ideas are entirely new and original'.[2] Among the leading 'pioneers' of such a general theory, when it is finally constructed, will be, in all likelihood, Tucker, List, Hamilton, Senior, and Mill (for their appreciation of the qualitative differences which the immense productive powers of the new machinery made in the economies, and in the international trading positions, of the advanced countries of Europe), as well as Malthus, Ricardo, and Torrens. Such a general theory of economic development will probably be found to encompass a theory of 'imperialism'.

The problem of vast inequalities of development, and, consequently, of well-being, is capable of solution on the basis of immediate and immediately foreseeable technological resources. The problem, as we have seen, is not a new one; it has been a subject for economic analysis for almost two hundred years, and, on an intra-national basis—in efforts, for example, to protect the farmer, in the industrialized nations of the West, from an unpleasant exposure to free market competition—practical solutions have already been successfully explored.[3] The general direction of inter-national action is, comparatively, clear: a more equitable division of the benefits of trade, by continuing efforts, already begun, to regulate the production and marketing of raw materials, so vulnerable to the forces of the free market, and by a planned international program of the capital development of backward areas, to help, among other objectives, to sufficiently diversify undeveloped economies so as to enable them better to meet market fluctuations. Fairly immediate steps, on a global basis, must be taken if catastrophe is to be averted, and if the great goal of the political economists, a universally beneficial international division of labor, is to be more equitably achieved.

[1] See J. Viner, *International Trade and Economic Development* (Glencoe, Ill.: Free Press, 1952), pp. 24, 55–62, 142.
[2] G. Myrdal, *Economic Theory and Under-Developed Regions* (London: Duckworth, 1957), pp. 149–58.
[3] I have discussed many of these questions at some length in B. Semmel, 'On the Economics of "Imperialism"', in B. F. Hoselitz, ed., *Economics and the Idea of Mankind* (New York: Columbia University Press, 1965), pp. 192–232.

Selected Bibliography

The leading political economists wrote extensively for the quarterlies, but it did not seem useful to list these articles individually. I have noted the general categories of periodical, serial, and pamphlet materials investigated, and refer the reader to footnote references for specific items actually quoted. I have also declined to list any but the most useful of the biographies, general histories, and general discussions of the politics and ideas of the period. There are a number of more specialized books which proved useful for limited purposes, but did not seem sufficiently significant for inclusion, though many of them are cited in footnotes. Certain of the men whose ideas are discussed were prolific, but I have tried to confine bibliographical listings to only their most relevant writings, and I have employed this principle with the writings of the less prolific as well.

Newspapers

Manchester Guardian
The Times

Serials, periodicals, etc.

Annual Register
Annual Reports of the Aborigines Protection Society
Blackwood's Magazine
The Colonial Intelligencer; or Aborigines' Friend
The Colonial Journal
The Colonial Magazine and Commercial Maritime Journal
Corn Law Tracts (Edinburgh Anti-Corn Law Association)
Dictionary of National Biography
The Economist
Edinburgh Encyclopedia
Edinburgh Review
Extracts From the Papers and Proceedings of the Aborigines Protection Society
Foreign and Colonial Quarterly Review
Fraser's Magazine
The League
National Anti-Corn Law League Publications
New Quarterly Review
Punch
Quarterly Review
Sidney's Emigrant Journal
Simmonds's Colonial Magazine and Foreign Miscellany
Society for the Promotion of Colonization, Reports

Society for the Protection of Agriculture and British Industry, Publications
Spectator
The Struggle
Westminster Review

Parliamentary papers, debates, etc.

Parliamentary Debates

Parliamentary Papers:

Report from the Select Committee on Petitions Complaining of Agricultural Distress. 1820 (255) ii. 101.

Report from the Select Committee Appointed to Consider the Means of Maintaining and Improving the Foreign Trade of the Country. 1820 (300) ii. 365.

Report from the Committee on the Agriculture of the United Kingdom. 1821 (688) ix. 1.

Report from the Select Committee on the Agriculture of the United Kingdom. 1822 (165) v. 1.

Second Report from the Select Committee on the Agriculture of the United Kingdom. 1822 (346) v. 9.

Report from the Select Committee on Manufactures, Commerce, and Shipping. 1833 (690) vi. 1.

Report from the Select Committee on Aborigines (British Settlements). 1836 (538) vii. 1.

Report from the Select Committee on the Disposal of Lands in the British Colonies. 1836 (512) xi. 499.

Report from the Select Committee on Aborigines (British Settlements). 1837 (425) vii. 1.

Report from the Select Committee on New Zealand. 1840 (582) vii. 447.

Report from the Select Committee on Import Duties. 1840 (601) v. 99.

First Report from the Select Committee on South Australia. 1841 (119) iv. 1.

Second Report from the Select Committee on South Australia. 1841 (394) iv. 9.

Report from the Select Committee on New Zealand. 1844 (556) xiii. 1.

Manuscripts

Bentham Manuscripts. University College, London. Portfolio no. 8, Folders no. 1–8.

Gladstone Papers. British Museum, 44,355; 44,567.

Grey of Howick Papers. Prior's Kitchen, The College, Durham.

Francis Place Papers. British Museum, vol. I–XII. Add. MSS 27,798; 27,807; 27,857–8; 35,142–35,153; 35,251.

Minutes of General Meetings of the New Zealand Company, 1840–58. Public Record Office, C.O. 208/179.

Russell Papers. Public Record Office, 30/22.

E. G. Wakefield Papers. Letters, 1815–53. British Museum, 35,261.

Primary

Anon. *A Letter From a Manchester Manufacturer.* Manchester: Stockdale, 1787.

Anon. *A Letter to the Small Farmers and Peasantry of the United Kingdom on the Advantages of Emigration to South Australia.* London: Richardson, 1838.

Anon. *American Corn and British Manufacturers.* London: Clarke, 1845.

Anon. *Thoughts on the Policy of the Proposed Alteration of the Corn Laws.* London: Ridgway, 1827.

Alison, Archibald. *Free Trade and Protection.* Edinburgh: Blackwood, 1844.

Almack, John. *Character, Motives, and Proceedings of the Anti-Corn Law Leaguers.* London: Ollivier, 1843.

Anderson, James. *The Interest of Great Britain With Regard to her American Colonies Considered.* London, 1782.

Ashpitel, A. *A Few Facts on the Corn Laws.* London: Richardson, 1839.

Ashton, William. *A Lecture on the Evils of Emigration.* Sheffield, 1838.

Babbage, Charles. *On the Economy of Machinery and Manufactures.* London: Knight, 1832.

Barbon, Nicholas. *A Discourse of Trade.* London, 1690.

[Bartlett, J.S.]. *A Letter to the Right Honourable Baron Ashburton.* New York, 1842.

Barton, John. *An Inquiry into the Expediency of the Existing Restrictions on the Importation of Foreign Corn.* London: Ridgway, 1833.

—— *Observations on the Circumstances Which Influence the Condition of the Labouring Classes of Society.* London: Arch, 1817.

[Bentham, J.]. *Economic Writings of Jeremy Bentham.* (W. Stark, ed.) London: Allen & Unwin, 1952. 3 vols.

[——] *The Works of Jeremy Bentham.* (John Bowring, ed.) Edinburgh: Tait, 1843.

Bowring, Sir John. *The Political and Commercial Importance of Peace.* London: Peace Society, 1846.

Bowring, Lewin B., ed. *Autobiographical Recollection of Sir John Bowring.* London: King & Co., 1877.

Brougham, H. *An Inquiry into the Colonial Policy of the European Powers.* Edinburgh: Balfour, 1803. 2 vols.

Burke, E. *A Letter to a Noble Lord on the Attacks Made Upon Him and His Pension by the Duke of Bedford and the Earl of Lauderdale.* London: Owen, 1796.

—— *Speech on American Taxation, April 19, 1774.* London: J. Dodsley, 1775.

—— *Speech on Moving His Resolutions for Conciliation with the Colonies, March 22, 1775.* London: J. Dodsley, 1778. 3rd edition.

—— *Speeches at his Arrival at Bristol.* London: J. Dodsley, 1775.

—— *Thoughts and Details on Scarcity.* London: Rivington, 1800.

Cairnes, J. E. *Some Leading Principles of Political Economy.* London: Macmillan, 1884. (Originally published in 1874.)

[Carey, H. C.]. *American Civil War; Correspondence With Mr. H. C. Carey of Philadelphia.* Liverpool?, 1861.

—— *Commerce, Christianity, and Civilization, Versus British Free Trade: Letters in Reply to the London Times.* Philadelphia: Collins, 1876.

Carey, H. C. *The Harmony of Interests, Agricultural, Manufacturing, and Commercial.* Philadelphia: Skinner, 1851.
—— *Letters to the President on the Foreign and Domestic Policy of the Union, etc.* Philadelphia: Lippincott, 1858.
[——] *The North and the South.* New York: The Tribune, 1854.
—— *Principles of Social Science.* Philadelphia: Lippincott, 1858. 3 vols.
—— *Review of the Decade 1857–67.* Philadelphia: Collins, 1867.
—— *The Way to Outdo England Without Fighting Her.* Philadelphia: Baird, 1865.
Carpenter, William. *Emigration and Colonization Considered.* London: Strange, 1841.
Cayley, E. S., M.P. *Reasons for the Formation of the Agricultural Protection Society.* London: Ollivier, 1844.
Chalmers, Thomas. *An Enquiry into the Extent and Stability of National Resources.* Edinburgh: Oliphant & Brown, 1808.
—— *Political Economy in Connexion With the Moral State and Prospects of Society.* (1832) in *Select Works of Thomas Chalmers*, IX, 1–343. (W. Hanna, ed.) Edinburgh: Constable, 1856.
—— *The Supreme Importance of a Right Moral to a Right Economical State of the Community* (1832) in *Select Works*, IX, 345–411.
Coates, Dandeson. *The Principles, Objects, and Plan of the New Zealand Association Examined.* London: Hatchards, 1838.
[Cobden, Richard]. *The American Diaries of Richard Cobden.* (E. H. Cawley, ed.) Princeton: Princeton University Press, 1952.
—— *England, Ireland, and America.* Edinburgh: Tait, 1836.
—— *Extracts from the Works of Col. T. Perronet Thompson.* Anti-Corn Law League, 1841.
[——] *Russia.* Edinburgh: Tait, 1836.
[——] *Speeches on Questions of Public Policy by Richard Cobden, M.P.* (J. Bright and J. E. T. Rogers, eds.) London: Macmillan, 1870.
Crawford, John. *Letter on Emigration and Colonization.* Glasgow, 1842.
de Quincey, Thomas. *Politics and Political Economy.* Vol. x of *Works of Thomas de Quincey.* Boston: Houghton Mifflin, 1877?
Disraeli, Benjamin. *Lord George Bentinck.* London: Longmans, 1872. 8th edition.
Eden, William. *Four Letters to the Earl of Carlisle.* London, 1779.
Edinburgh Evening Post. *Ought the Corn Laws to be Repealed.* Edinburgh: Edinburgh Evening Post, 184?.
Fitzmaurice, Lord, ed. *Lettres de l'Abbé Morellet à Lord Shelburne.* Paris: Plon, 1898.
Giffen, Robert. *Essays in Finance.* London: Bell, 1880.
Graham, Sir James. *Corn and Currency; An Address to the Landowners.* London: Ridgway, 1826.
Grote, Mrs H. *The Philosophical Radicals of 1832; Comprising the Life of Sir William Molesworth and Some Incidents Connected With the Reform Movement from 1832 to 1842.* London: Savill & Edwards, 1866.
Hamilton, Alexander, *Papers on Public Credit, Commerce and Finance.* (Samuel McKee, Jr., ed.) New York: Columbia University Press, 1934.
Harwood, Philip. *Six Lectures on the Corn Law Monopoly and Free Trade.* London: Green, 1843.

233

Heale, Theophilus. *New Zealand and the New Zealand Company*. London: Sherwood *et al.*, 1842.

Holland, G. C. *The Millocrat*. London: Ollivier, 1841.

Hope, George. *Agriculture and the Corn Law. Prize Essay*. Manchester, 1842.

[Horner, Francis]. *Memoirs and Correspondence of Francis Horner, M.P.* (L. Horner, ed.) 2 vols. Boston: Little, Brown, 1853.

Hoy, J. B. *Manufacturers and Corn Growers*. London: Porter, 1839.

[Hume, David]. *David Hume; Writings on Economics*. (Eugene Rotwein, ed.) Edinburgh: Collins, 1955.

[——] *The Letters of David Hume*. (J. Y. T. Greig, ed.) Oxford, 1932.

Kell, E. *The Injurious Effects of the Corn Laws on All Classes of the Community*. London: Smallfield, 1840.

Kingston, H. G. *How the Unemployed May Better Their Condition*. London: Saunders, 1848.

Lauderdale, Earl. *An Inquiry into the Nature and Origin of Public Wealth*. Edinburgh: Constable, 1819.

—— *A Letter on the Corn Laws*. London: Constable; Longmans, 1814.

Longfield, Mountifort. *Lectures on Political Economy*. Dublin: Milliken & Son, 1834. (L.S.E. reprint, 1931).

—— *Three Lectures on Commerce, and one on Absenteeism*. Dublin: Milliken & Son, 1835.

McCulloch, J. R., ed. *Adam Smith's An Inquiry Into the Nature and Causes of the Wealth of Nations*. Edinburgh: Black & Tait, 1828. 4 vols.

—— *A Discourse on the Rise, Progress, Peculiar Objects, and Importance of Political Economy*. Edinburgh: Constable, 1824.

—— *The Literature of Political Economy*. London, 1845. (L.S.E. reprint, 1938.)

—— *Statements Illustrative of the Policy and Probable Consequences of the Proposed Repeal of the Existing Corn Laws*. London: Longmans, 1841.

Malthus, T. R. *An Inquiry into the Nature and Progress of Rent, and the Principles By Which It is Regulated*. London: J. Murray, 1815.

—— *An Investigation of the Cause of the Present High Price of Provisions*. London: Johnson, 1800.

—— *Essai sur le principe de population*. (P. Rossi and C. Comte, eds.) Paris: Guillaumine, 1845.

—— *An Essay on Population*. 1st edition. London: Johnson, 1798. 2nd edition, 1803. 3rd edition, 1806.

—— *Additions to the Fourth and Former Editions of An Essay on the Principle of Population*. London: J. Murray, 1817.

—— *The Grounds of an Opinion on the Policy of Restricting the Importation of Foreign Corn; Intended as An Appendix to 'Observations on the Corn Laws'*. London: J. Murray, 1815.

—— *Observations on the Effects of the Corn Laws, and of a Rise or Fall in the Price of Corn on the Agriculture and General Wealth of the Country*. London: J. Murray, 1815.

—— *Principes d'économie politique considérés sous le rapport de leur application practique*. (M. Maurice Monjean, ed.) Paris: Guillaumine, 1846.

Malthus, T. R. *Principles of Political Economy Considered With a View to Their Practical Application*. London: J. Murray, 1820.

Mann, William. *Letters on the Corn Laws*. London: Basil Stewart, 1828.

Martineau, Harriet. *A History of the Thirty Years' Peace, A.D. 1815–1846*. London: Bell, 1878. 4 vols.

Marx, Karl. *British Rule in India*. Sydney: Modern Publishers, 193?.

—— *Capital: A Critique of Political Economy*. Chicago: Kerr, 1915. 3 vols.

—— *Free Trade*. New York: Labor News Co., 1917.

—— *A History of Economic Theories From the Physiocrats to Adam Smith*. New York: Langland Press, 1952.

Merivale, Herman. *Lectures on Colonization and Colonies*. London: Longmans, Green, et al., 1861.

Mill, James. 'The Article "Colony", Reprinted From the Supplement to the *Encyclopaedia Britannica*.' London, 1821?

—— *Commerce Defended*. London: Baldwin, 1808.

—— *Elements of Political Economy*. London: Baldwin et al., 1821; also 3rd edition, 1826.

Mill, J. S. *Principles of Political Economy*. (W. J. Ashley, ed.) London: Longmans, Green, 1909.

—— *Essays on Some Unsettled Questions of Political Economy*. London, 1844.

[——] *The Letters of John Stuart Mill*. (H. S. R. Elliot, ed.) London: Longmans, Green, 1910. 2 vols.

[——] *The Earlier Letters of John Stuart Mill, 1812–1848*. (F. E. Mineka, ed.) (London: Routledge & Kegan Paul, 1963), in *The Collected Works of John Stuart Mill*, vols. XII and XIII.

[Molesworth, Sir William]. *Selected Speeches of Sir William Molesworth on Questions Relating to Colonial Policy*. (H. E. Egerton, ed.) London: J. Murray, 1903.

Morse, Arthur. *Agriculture and the Corn Law. Prize Essay*. Manchester, 1842.

Motte, Standish. *Outline of a System of Legislation, For Securing Protection to the Aboriginal Inhabitants of All Countries Colonized by Great Britain*. London: J. Murray, 1840.

[Mure, William]. *The Commercial Policy of Pitt and Peel, 1785–1846*. London, 1847.

[Porter, G. R.]. *The Many Sacrificed to the Few; Proved by the Effects of the Food Monopoly*. London: Hooper, 1841.

—— *The Progress of the Nation In Its Various Social and Economic Relations, from the beginning of the Nineteenth Century*. London: J. Murray, 1851.

de Pradt, Dominique Dufour. *The Colonies, and the Present American Revolutions*. London: Baldwin, 1817.

Raymond, Daniel. *The Elements of Political Economy*. Baltimore: Lucas & Coale, 1823.

Reid, William. *An Inquiry into the Causes of the Present Distress*. Edinburgh: Tait, 1833.

Ricardo, David. *On Protection to Agriculture*. London: Murray, 1822.

—— *The Works and Correspondence of David Ricardo*. (P. Sraffa, ed.) Cambridge University Press, 1950–66. 10 vols.

Robinson, John. *The Whole Scheme of the Corn Law Abolitionists Unmasked.* London: Ollivier, 1841.

Roebuck, J. A. *The Colonies of England.* London: Parker, 1849.

Russell, Earl. *Recollections and Suggestions, 1813–1873.* London: Longmans, 1875.

Say, J. B. *Historical Essay on the Rise, Progress, and Probable Results of the British Dominion in India.* London: Treuttel and Wurtz, 1824.

Scrope, G. P. *Political Economy for Plain People.* London: Longmans, Green, 1873.

—— *Principles of Political Economy.* London: Longmans, Rees *et al.*, 1833.

Senior, Nassau William. *Three Lectures on The Cost of Obtaining Money and on Some Effects of Private and Government Paper Money.* London: John Murray, 1830.

—— *Industrial Efficiency and Social Economy.* New York: Henry Holt, 1928.

Sheffield, Earl of. *Observations on the Commerce of the American States With Europe and the West Indies.* London, 1783.

Smith, Adam. *An Inquiry Into the Nature and Causes of The Wealth of Nations.* (Edwin Cannan, ed.) London: Methuen, 1930. 2 vols.

Spence, William. *Agriculture The Source of the Wealth of Britain.* London: Caddell and Davies, 1808.

—— *Britain Independent of Commerce.* London: Caddell and Davies, 1808.

—— *The Objections Against the Corn Bill Refuted; and the Necessity of This Measure to the Vital Interests of Every Class in the Community, Demonstrated.* London: Longmans, Hurst *et al.*, 1815.

Stanhope, Earl. *A Letter . . . on the Corn Laws.* London: Ridgway, 1826.

Stewart, Dugald. *The Collected Works of Dugald Stewart.* (Sir William Hamilton, ed.) Edinburgh, 1855.

Stourton, Lord. *Two Letters to the Right Honourable the Earl of Liverpool.* London: Mawman, 1821.

Tennant, Charles. *Letters Forming Part of a Correspondence With Nassau William Senior, Esq. Concerning Systematic Colonization etc.* London: Ridgway, 1831.

Thompson, T. P. *A Catechism on the Corn Laws.* London: Ridgway, 1827.

—— *Corn-Law Fallacies; With the Answers.* London: Wilson, 1839.

—— *Exercises, Political and Others.* London: Wilson, 1842. 6 vols.

—— *An Exposition of Fallacies on Rent, Tithes, &c.* London: Hatchard, 1826.

[Tod, Thomas]. A Merchant. *Consolatory Thoughts on American Independence; Showing the Great Advantages that Will Arise From It.* Edinburgh, 1782.

Torrens, Robert. *Address to the Farmers of the United Kingdom.* London: Longmans, 1831.

—— *The Budget.* London: Smith, Elder, 1844.

—— *Colonization of South Australia.* London: Longmans, Rees *et al.*, 1835.

—— *An Essay on the External Corn Trade.* London: Hatchard, 1815.

—— *An Essay on the Production of Wealth.* London: Longmans, Hurst *et al.*, 1821.

—— *The Economists Refuted; Or, An Inquiry into the Nature and Extent of the Advantages Derived From Trade.* London: Oddy, 1808. [Reprinted as Appendix to *The Principles and Practical Operation of Sir Robert Peel's Act of 1844, Explained and Defended.* London: Longmans, 1858.]

Torrens, Robert. *A Letter to the Right Honourable The Earl of Liverpool on the State of Agriculture of the United Kingdom.* London: Hatchard, 1816.

—— *Three Letters to the Marquis of Chandos on the Effects of the Corn Laws.* London: Longmans, 1839.

Tucker, Josiah. *A Brief Essay on the Advantages and Disadvantages Which Respectively Attend France and Great Britain With Regard to Trade.* (Reprint of 3rd edition of 1753.) London, 1787.

—— *A Letter to Edmund Burke.* Gloucester: R. Raikes, 1775.

—— *An Humble Address and Earnest Appeal.* London: T. Cadell, 1776.

—— *A Series of Answers to Certain Popular Objections Against Separating from the Rebellious Colonies.* Gloucester: R. Raikes, 1776.

—— *Cui Bono? Or, An Inquiry, What Benefits Can Arise Either to the English or the Americans, the French, Spaniards, or Dutch, from the Greatest Victories, or Successes, in the Present War.* London: T. Cadell, 1782.

—— *Four Letters on Important National Subjects Addressed to the Right Honourable the Earl of Shelburne.* Gloucester: R. Raikes, 1783.

—— *Four Tracts Together With Two Sermons, On Political and Commercial Subjects.* Gloucester: R. Raikes, 1774.

—— *Reflections on the Present Matters in Dispute Between Great Britain and Ireland.* London: T. Cadell, 1785.

—— *The Respective Pleas and Arguments of the Mother Country, and the Colonies, Distinctly Set Forth.* Gloucester: R. Raikes, 1776.

—— *Union or Separation.* London: J. Hatchard, 1799.

Wakefield, E. G., ed. *Adam Smith's An Inquiry into the Nature and Causes of the Wealth of Nations.* London, 1835.

—— *England and America; A Comparison of the Social and Political State of Both Nations.* New York: Harper & Bros., 1834.

—— *Householders in Danger from the Populace.* London: Effingham Wilson, 1831?

[——] *A Letter from Sydney.* London: Simpkin & Marshall *et al.*, 1829.

[——] *The New British Province of South Australia.* London: Knight, 1838.

[——] *Sketch for a Proposal For Colonizing Australasia, &c. &c. &c.* n.p., 1830?

—— *A View of the Art of Colonization.* London: Parker, 1849.

Western, Lord. *The Maintenance of the Corn Laws.* London, 1839.

Whitmore, W. W. *A Letter on the Corn Laws to the Manchester Chamber of Commerce.* London: Ridgway, 1839.

—— *A Letter to the Electors of Bridgenorth Upon the Corn Laws.* London: Cadell, 1826.

—— *A Second Letter on the Corn Laws.* London: Ridgway, 1839.

Wilcocks, J. B. *Emigration, Its Necessity and Advantages.* Exeter, 1849.

Wilmot-Horton, Sir R. J. *Letters on Colonial Policy.* London, 1832.

Secondary

Aydelotte, W. O. 'The Business Interests of the Gentry in the Parliament of 1841–47', appendix to Kitson Clark, *Making of Victorian England* (listed below), pp. 290–305.

Beer, G. L. *The Old Colonial System, 1660–1754.* New York: Macmillan, 1912. 2 vols.

Black, R. D. Collison. *Economic Thought and the Irish Question, 1817–1870.* Cambridge: Cambridge University Press, 1960.

Blaug, Mark. *Ricardian Economics, A Historical Study.* New Haven: Yale University Press, 1958.

Bloom, Solomon F. *The World of Nations; A Study of the National Implications in the Work of Karl Marx.* New York: Columbia University Press, 1941.

Bloomfield, Paul. *Edward Gibbon Wakefield, Builder of the British Commonwealth.* London: Longmans, 1961.

Bonar, James. *Malthus and His Work.* New York: Macmillan, 1924.

Bowley, Marian. *Nassau Senior and Classical Economics.* London: Allen & Unwin, 1937.

Brebner, J. B. 'Laissez-Faire and State Intervention in Nineteenth-Century Britain', *The Tasks of Economic History,* Supplement VIII, *Journal of Economic History,* 1948, pp. 59–73.

Buckley, J. K. *Joseph Parkes of Birmingham.* London: Methuen, 1926.

Burroughs, Peter. *Britain and Australia, 1831–1855; A Study in Imperial Relations and Crown Lands Administration.* Oxford: Clarendon Press, 1967.

Carrothers, W. A. *Emigration from the British Isles.* London: P. S. King, 1929.

Checkland, S. G. 'The Birmingham Economists, 1815–1850', *Economic History Review,* 2nd Series, I, no. 1 (1948), 1–19.

Clark, G. K. *The Making of Victorian England.* Cambridge, Mass.: Harvard University Press, 1962.

—— 'The Repeal of the Corn Laws and the Politics of the Forties', *Economic History Review,* 2nd Series, IV, no. 1 (1951), 1–13.

Clark, W. E. *Josiah Tucker, Economist.* New York: n.p., 1903.

Clarke, M. L. *George Grote, A Biography.* London: Athlone Press, 1962.

Clive, John. *Scotch Reviewers.* Cambridge, Mass.: Harvard University Press, 1957.

Cockburn, Lord. *Life of Lord Jeffrey.* Philadelphia, 1852. 2 vols.

Corry, B. *Money, Saving, and Investment in English Economics, 1800–1850.* London: Macmillan, 1962.

Davis, H. W. C. *The Age of Grey and Peel.* Oxford: Clarendon Press, 1929.

Dawson, W. H. *Richard Cobden and Foreign Policy.* London: Allen & Unwin, 1926.

Deane, P., and Cole, W. A. *British Economic Growth 1688–1959.* Cambridge: Cambridge University Press, 1967.

Dobb, Maurice. *Political Economy and Capitalism.* London: Routledge, 1937.

Egerton, H. E. 'The Colonial Reformers of 1830', in F. J. C. Hearnshaw, *King's College Lectures on Colonial Problems.* London: Bell, 1913.

—— *A Short History of British Colonial Policy, 1606–1909.* London: Methuen, 1932.

Ehrman, J. P. W. *The British Government and Commercial Negotiations With Europe, 1783–1793.* New York: Cambridge University Press, 1962.

Elton, Lord. *Imperial Commonwealth.* London: Collins, 1945.

Erickson, A. B. *The Public Career of Sir James Graham*. Oxford: Blackwell, 1952.

Fay, C. R. *Burke and Adam Smith*. Belfast: Boyd, 1956.

—— 'The Growth of the New Empire, 1783–1870', *Economic Journal*, LI (April 1941), 80–91.

—— *Huskisson and His Age*. London: Longmans, 1951.

—— *Imperial Economy and Its Place in the Formulation of Economic Doctrine, 1600–1932*. Oxford: Clarendon Press, 1934.

—— 'The Significance of the Corn Laws in English History', *Economic History Review* I, no. 2 (January 1928), 314–18.

Fetter, F. W. 'The Authorship of Economic Articles in the *Edinburgh Review*, 1802–47', *Journal of Political Economy* LXI, no. 3 (June 1953), 232–59.

—— 'The Economic Articles in the *Westminster Review* and Their Authors, 1824–51', *Journal of Political Economy* LXX, no. 6 (December 1962), 570–96.

—— 'The Economic Articles in The *Quarterly Review* and Their Authors, 1809–52', *Journal of Political Economy* LXVI, nos. 1–2 (February and April 1958), 47–64 and 154–70.

—— 'Robert Torrens; Colonel of Marines and Political Economist', *Economica*, N.S., XXIX, no. 114 (May 1962), 152–65.

Fieldhouse, D. K. '"Imperialism": An Historiographical Revision', *Economic History Review*, 2nd Series, XIV, no. 2 (December 1961), 187–209.

—— *The Theory of Capitalist Imperialism*. New York: Barnes & Noble, 1967.

Fitzmaurice, Lord. *Life of William Earl of Shelburne*. London: Macmillan, 1912.

Galbraith, J. S. 'Myths of the "Little England" Era', *American Historical Review* LXVII, no. 1 (October 1961), 34–48.

Gallagher, J., and Robinson, R. 'The Imperialism of Free Trade', *Economic History Review* VI, no. 1 (1953), 1–15.

Gammage, R. G. *History of the Chartist Movement* (1837–1854). Newcastle-on-Tyne: Browne & Browne, 1894.

Garnett, R. *Edward Gibbon Wakefield; The Colonization of South Australia and New Zealand*. London: Fisher Unwin, 1898.

Ghosh, R. N. 'Malthus on Emigration and Colonization: Letters to Wilmot-Horton', *Economica*, N.S., XXX, no. 117 (February 1963).

Gifford, John. *A History of the Political Life of the Rt. Hon. William Pitt*. London: Cadell, 1809. 6 vols.

Grampp, W. D. *The Manchester School of Economics*. Stanford: Stanford University Press, 1960.

Grossman, Henry K. 'W. Playfair, The Earliest Theorist of Capitalist Development', *Economic History Review* XVIII, nos. 1 and 2 (1948), 65–83.

Halévy, É. *The Growth of Philosophic Radicalism*. New York: Augustus Kelley, 1949.

—— *A History of the English People in the Nineteenth Century*. New York: Peter Smith, 1949–52. 7 vols.

Harlow, Vincent T. *The Founding of the Second British Empire (1763–1793)*. London: Longmans, Green, 1952, 1964. 2 vols.

Heckscher, E. *The Continental System: An Economic Interpretation*. Oxford: Clarendon Press, 1922.

—— *Mercantilism*. London: Allen & Unwin, 1935. 2 vols.

Henderson, W. O. 'The Anglo-French Commercial Treaty of 1786', *Economic History Review*, 2nd Series, x, no. 1 (1957), 104–12.

Hobson, J. A. *Imperialism: A Study*. London: Allen & Unwin, 1938.

—— *Richard Cobden, The International Man*. London: Fisher Unwin, 1919.

Hutchison, T. W. 'Bentham as an Economist', *Economic Journal*, LXVI (June 1956), 288–306.

Imlah, Albert H. *Economic Elements in the Pax Britannica*. Cambridge, Mass.: Harvard University Press, 1958.

Jenks, L. H. *The Migration of British Capital to 1875*. New York: Knopf, 1927.

Johnson, L. G. *General T. Perronet Thompson, 1783–1869*. London: Allen & Unwin, 1957.

Kaplan, A. D. H. *Henry Charles Carey; A Study in American Economic Thought*. Baltimore: Johns Hopkins Press, 1931.

Kayser, E. L. *The Grand Social Enterprise: A Study of Jeremy Bentham in his Relation to Liberal Nationalism*. New York: Columbia University Press, 1932.

Knaplund, P. *James Stephen and the British Colonial System, 1813–1847*. Madison: University of Wisconsin Press, 1953.

Knorr, Klaus E. *British Colonial Theories, 1570–1850*. Toronto: University of Toronto Press, 1944.

Koebner, R. *Empire*. Cambridge: Cambridge University Press, 1961.

Landes, David. 'Some Thoughts on the Nature of Economic Imperialism', *Journal of Economic History* XXI, no. 4 (December 1961), 496–512.

Leader, R. E. *Life and Letters of John Arthur Roebuck*. London: E. Arnold, 1897.

Levi, Leone. *The History of British Commerce and of the Economic Progress of the British Nation, 1763–1878*. London: John Murray, 1880.

Luxemburg, R. *The Accumulation of Capital*. New Haven: Yale University Press, 1951. Originally published 1913.

Maccoby, S. *English Radicalism*. London: Allen & Unwin, 1935–61.

Macdonagh, O. 'The Anti-Imperialism of Free Trade', *Economic History Review*, 2nd Series, XIV, no. 3 (April 1962), 489–501.

Mack, M. P. *Jeremy Bentham; An Odyssey of Ideas*. London: Heinemann, 1963.

Meek, R. L. *The Economics of Physiocracy*. London: Allen & Unwin, 1962.

—— ed. *Marx and Engels on Malthus*. London: Lawrence & Wishart, 1953.

Mills, R. C. *The Colonization of Australia (1829–42); The Wakefield Experiment in Empire Building*. London: Sidgwick & Jackson, 1915.

Monypenny, W. F. *Life of Benjamin Disraeli, Earl of Beaconsfield*. New York: Macmillan, 1911. 6 vols.

Morley, J. *Life of Richard Cobden*. London: T. Fisher Unwin, 1920.

Morrell, W. P. *British Colonial Policy in the Age of Peel and Russell*. Oxford: Oxford University Press, 1930.

Mosse, George L. 'The Anti-League: 1844–1846', *Economic History Review*, XVII, no. 2 (1947), 134–42.

Myint, H. 'The "Classical Theory" of International Trade and the Under-Developed Countries', *Economic Journal* LXVIII (June 1958), 317–37.

Myrdal, G. *Economic Theory and Under-Developed Regions*. London: Duckworth, 1957.

Neill, C. P. *Daniel Raymond; An Early Chapter in the History of Economic Theory in the United States.* Baltimore: Johns Hopkins University Press, 1897.

de Nemours, P. S. du Pont. *Examen du livre de M. Malthus sur le principe de population; auquel on a joint la traduction de quatre chapitres de ce livre supprimés dans l'édition française; et une lettre à M. Say.* Philadelphie: Lafourcade, 1817.

Nesbitt, G. L. *Benthamite Reviewing; The First Twelve Years of the Westminster Review.* New York: Columbia University Press, 1934.

New, C. W. *The Life of Henry Brougham to 1830.* Oxford: Clarendon Press, 1961.

—— *Lord Durham.* Oxford: Clarendon Press, 1929.

Newton, A. P. *A Hundred Years of the British Empire.* London: Duckworth, 1940.

Nicholson, J. S. 'The Economics of Imperialism', *Economic Journal* xx (March 1910), 155–71.

—— *A Project of Empire: A Critical Study of the Economics of Imperialism, With Special Reference to the Ideas of Adam Smith.* London: Macmillan, 1909.

Opie, Redwers. 'A Neglected English Economist: George Poulett Scrope', *Quarterly Journal of Economics* xliv, no. 1 (November 1929), 101–37.

Owen, D. E. *British Opium Policy in China and India.* New Haven: Yale University Press, 1934.

Paglin, M. *Malthus and Lauderdale: The Anti-Ricardian Tradition.* New York: Augustus Kelley, 1961.

Pappe, H. O. 'Wakefield and Marx', *Economic History Review*, 2nd Series, iv, no. 1 (1951), 88–97.

Pares, Richard. 'The Economic Factors in the History of the Empire', *Economic History Review* vii, no. 2 (May 1937), 119–44.

Parker, C. S. *Life and Letters of Sir James Graham, 1792–1861.* London: John Murray, 1907.

—— *Sir Robert Peel.* London, 1891–7. 3 vols.

Pearl, M. L. *William Cobbett.* Oxford: Oxford University Press, 1953.

Pike, Douglas. *Paradise of Dissent; South Australia, 1829–1857.* London: Longmans, Green, 1957.

—— 'Wilmot-Horton and the National Colonization Society', *Historical Studies; Australia and New Zealand* vii, May 1956.

Platt, D. C. M. 'The Imperialism of Free Trade: Some Reservations', *Economic History Review*, 2nd Series, xxi, no. 2 (August 1968), 296–306.

Political Economy Club, Founded in London, 1821. Centenary Volume, London: Macmillan, 1921.

Robbins, Lionel. *The Economic Causes of War.* London: Cape, 1939.

—— *Robert Torrens and the Evolution of Classical Economics.* London: Macmillan, 1958.

—— *The Theory of Economic Policy in English Classical Political Economy.* London: Macmillan, 1952.

Rose, J. H. *Life of William Pitt.* London: G. Bell, 1923.

Rostow, W. W. *British Economy of the Nineteenth Century.* Oxford: Oxford University Press, 1948.

Schumpeter, J. A. *History of Economic Analysis.* London: Allen & Unwin, 1955.

—— *Imperialism and Social Classes.* New York: Meridian Books, 1966.

Schuyler, R. L. *The Fall of the Old Colonial System; A Study in British Free Trade, 1770–1870.* New York: Oxford University Press, 1945.

Seligman, E. R. A., and Hollander, J. H. 'Ricardo and Torrens', *Economic Journal* XXI (September 1911), 448–68.

Semmel, Bernard. *Imperialism and Social Reform: English Social-Imperial Thought, 1895–1914.* Cambridge, Mass.: Harvard University Press, 1960.

—— *Jamaican Blood and Victorian Conscience; The Governor Eyre Controversy.* Boston: Houghton Mifflin, 1963.

—— 'On the Economics of "Imperialism", in B. F. Hoselitz, ed., *Economics and the Idea of Mankind.* New York: Columbia University Press, 1965.

Shoul, Bernice. 'Karl Marx and Say's Law', *Quarterly Journal of Economics* LXXI, no. 4 (November 1957), 611–29.

Siegfried, André. *Edward Gibbon Wakefield et sa doctrine de la colonisation systématique.* Paris, 1904.

Silberner, Edmund. *La Guerre dans la pensée économique du XVIᵉ au XVIIIᵉ siècle.* Paris: Librarie du Recueil Sirey, 1939.

—— *The Problem of War in Nineteenth Century Economic Thought.* Princeton: Princeton University Press, 1946.

Slosson, P. W. *The Decline of the Chartist Movement.* New York: Columbia University Press, 1916.

Sotiroff, G. 'John Barton (1789–1852)', *Economic Journal* LXII, no. 245 (March 1952), 87–102.

Stanhope, Earl. *Life of William Pitt.* London: J. Murray, 1867.

Stark, W. 'Jeremy Bentham as an Economist', *Economic Journal* LI, (I) (April 1941), 56–79; (II) (December 1946), 583–608.

Stephen, Sir Leslie. *The English Utilitarians.* London: Duckworth, 1900. 3 vols.

Stokes, E. *The English Utilitarians and India.* London: Oxford University Press, 1959.

Sutherland, George. *The South Australian Company; A Study in Colonization.* London: Longmans, Green, 1898.

Thompson, E. P. *The Making of the English Working Class.* New York: Pantheon Books, 1964.

Thomson, David, 'The United Kingdom and Its World-Wide Interests', in *The Zenith of European Power*, New Cambridge Modern History, vol. X.

Trevelyan, G. M. *The Life of John Bright.* Boston: Houghton Mifflin, 1925.

Tucker, G. S. L. *Progress and Profits in British Economic Thought, 1650–1850.* New York: Cambridge University Press, 1960.

Turnbull, Michael. *The New Zealand Bubble; the Wakefield Theory in Practice.* Wellington: Price, Milburn, 1959.

Viner, J. *International Trade and Economic Development.* Glencoe, Ill.: Free Press, 1952.

—— *Studies in the Theory of International Trade.* London: Allen & Unwin, 1955.

Wagner, Donald O. 'British Economists and the Empire', *Political Science Quarterly* XLVI, no. 2 (June 1931), 248–76; XLVII, no. 1 (March 1932), 57–74.

Wallas, Graham. *The Life of Francis Place, 1771–1854.* New York: Burt Franklin, 1951.

Webb, R. K. *The British Working Class Reader, 1790–1848: Literacy and Social Tension.* London: Allen & Unwin, 1955.

—— *Harriet Martineau; A Radical Victorian.* New York: Columbia University Press, 1960.

Weulersse, Georges. *Le Mouvement Physiocratique en France (de 1756 à 1770).* Paris: Alcan, 1910. 2 vols.

Wilberforce, R. I., and S. *The Life of William Wilberforce.* London: J. Murray, 1838. 5 vols.

Winch, D. N. 'Classical Economics and the Case for Colonization', *Economica*, N.S., xxx, no. 120 (November 1963), 387–99.

—— *Classical Political Economy and Colonies.* Cambridge, Mass.: Harvard University Press, 1965.

Winslow, E. M. *The Pattern of Imperialism.* New York: Columbia University Press, 1948.

Wright, Gordon. 'The Origins of Napoleon III's Free Trade', *Economic History Review* ix, no. 1 (November 1938), 47–64.

Index